38

THE CHURCH AND THE BOOK

THE CHURCH AND THE BOOK

PAPERS READ AT
THE 2000 SUMMER MEETING AND
THE 2001 WINTER MEETING OF
THE ECCLESIASTICAL HISTORY SOCIETY

EDITED BY

R. N. SWANSON

PUBLISHED FOR
THE ECCLESIASTICAL HISTORY SOCIETY
BY
THE BOYDELL PRESS
2004

First published 2004

A publication of the Ecclesiastical History Society
in association with The Boydell Press
an imprint of Boydell & Brewer Ltd
PO Box 9, Woodbridge, Suffolk IP12 3DF, UK
and of Boydell & Brewer Inc.
PO Box 41026, Rochester, NY 14604–4126, USA

ISBN 0 9529733 8 3

ISSN 0424–2084

A catalogue record for this book is available
from the British Library

Library of Congress Cataloging-in-Publication Data

Ecclesiastical History Society. Summer Meeting (2000 : University of
Wales, Lampeter)
    The church and the book : papers read at the 2000 Summer Meeting and
the 2001 Winter Meeting of the Ecclesiastical History Society / edited
by R.N. Swanson.
        p. cm. – (Studies in church history, ISSN 0424–2084 ; 38)
Includes bibliographical references.
    ISBN 0-9529733-8-3 (alk. paper)
    1. Books and reading – Religious
aspects – Christianity – History – Congresses.   2. Christian
literature – History and criticism – Congresses.   I. Swanson, R. N.
(Robert Norman)   II. Ecclesiastical History Society. Winter Meeting (2001
: University of London. Institute of Historical Research)   III. Title.
IV. Series.
    BR117.E34 2000
    261.5 – dc21   2003012829

Details of previous volumes are available from Boydell & Brewer Ltd

This book is printed on acid-free paper

Typeset by Joshua Associates Ltd, Oxford
Printed in Great Britain by
St Edmundsbury Press Ltd, Bury St Edmunds, Suffolk

CONTENTS

CONTENTS

CONTENTS

PREFACE

'The Church and the Book' has often been suggested in recent years as an appropriate theme for a volume of *Studies in Church History*. It was readily adopted by Dr Margaret Aston for the conferences of the Ecclesiastical History Society held under her presidency at the University of Wales, Lampeter, in July 2000, and at the Institute of Historical Research in London in January 2001. The contents of the resulting volume can reflect only some of the varied approaches to the theme which came to the fore at those sessions. The seven main papers delivered at the conferences are included, with a selection of the communications offered at the Lampeter gathering. As usual, the process of deciding which papers should be included proved extremely difficult; I am grateful to all those who commented on texts and so helped greatly in the process. I am also grateful to the authors for their tolerance of my editorial interventions.

The Society wishes to thank the University of Wales, Lampeter, for accommodating the summer conference, during a delightfully warm spell. Particular thanks are due to Janet Burton, Frances Knight, and William Marx for their labours as local liaisons, and for organising the excursions. Thanks are also due to the Institute of Historical Research in London and its staff for accommodating the January meeting and ensuring that the day ran smoothly.

Robert Swanson

LIST OF CONTRIBUTORS

Margaret ASTON (*President*)

James BETTLEY

Ruth CHAVASSE

Michael CLANCHY
Professor of History, Institute of Historical Research, University of London

Brian CUMMINGS
Reader in English, University of Sussex

James DAVIS
British Academy Postdoctoral Fellow, Wolfson College, Cambridge

Christoph EGGER
Assistent für mittelalterliche Geschichte, University of Vienna

Richard EMMS

Stuart G. HALL
Honorary Associate Research Professor, University of St Andrews

Sarah HAMILTON
Lecturer in History, University of Exeter

Elizabeth Morley INGRAM

W.M. JACOB
Archdeacon of Charing Cross

Geraint H. JENKINS
Director, University of Wales Centre for Advanced Welsh and Celtic Studies

Lars Peter LAAMANN
Research Assistant, Department of History, School of Oriental and African Studies, University of London

Oliver LOGAN
Lecturer in History, University of East Anglia

Rosamond McKITTERICK
Professor of Medieval History, University of Cambridge

Judith MALTBY
Chaplain and Fellow, Corpus Christi College, Oxford

Scott MANDELBROTE
Fellow of Peterhouse, Cambridge; Fellow of All Souls College,
Oxford

Susan MARTIN
Research Student, University of Birmingham

Jeremy MORRIS
Dean, Trinity Hall, Cambridge

Thomas O'LOUGHLIN
Reader in Historical Theology, University of Wales, Lampeter

M.A. OVERELL
Research Associate, The Open University

Graham W. SHAW
Head of Asia, Pacific and Africa Office Collections, The British
Library

Erik SIDENVALL
Research Student, Lund University

Norman TANNER
Professor of Church History, Gregorian University, Rome

Susan WABUDA
Associate Professor of History, Fordham University

Alexandra WALSHAM
Senior Lecturer in History, University of Exeter

ABBREVIATIONS

Abbreviated titles are adopted within each paper after the first full citation. Unless otherwise indicated, the place of publication for monographs is London. The following abbreviations are used for texts and periodicals cited frequently in the volume:

BAV   Biblioteca Apostolica Vaticana
BIHR   *Bulletin of the Institute of Historical Research* (London, 1923–86) [superseded by *HR*]
BL   London, British Library
BN   Paris, Bibliothèque Nationale
Bodley   Oxford, Bodleian Library
CChr   *Corpus Christianorum* (Turnhout, 1953–)
  CChr.CM *Corpus Christianorum, continuatio medievalis* (1966–)
  CChr.SL *Corpus Christianorum, series Latina* (1953–)
CathHR   *Catholic Historical Review* (Washington, DC, 1915–)
CIC   *Corpus iuris canonici*, ed. E. Richter and E. Friedberg, 2 vols (Leipzig, 1879–81)
CUL   Cambridge, University Library
EETS   Early English Text Society (London/Oxford, 1864–)
EHR   *English Historical Review* (London, 1886–)
es   extra series
JBS   *Journal of British Studies* (Hartford, CT, 1961–)
JEH   *Journal of Ecclesiastical History* (Cambridge, 1950–)
JThS   *Journal of Theological Studies* (London, 1899–)
MGH   *Monumenta Germaniae historica inde ab a. 500 usque ad a. 1500*, ed. G.H. Pertz *et al.* (Hanover, Berlin, etc., 1826–)
ns   new series
PG   *Patrologia Graeca*, ed. J.P. Migne, 161 vols (Paris, 1857–66)
PL   *Patrologia Latina*, ed. J.P. Migne, 217 vols + 4 index vols (Paris, 1841–61)
PS   Parker Society (Cambridge, 1841–55)
RS   Rerum Brittanicarum medii aevi scriptores, 99 vols (London, 1858–1911) = Rolls Series
sa   *sub anno*

SCH	*Studies in Church History* (London/Oxford/Woodbridge, 1964–)
SCH.S	*Studies in Church History: Subsidia* (Oxford/Woodbridge, 1978–)
Speculum	*Speculum: A Journal of Medieval Studies* (Cambridge, MA, 1925–)
STC	A.W. Pollard and G.R. Redgrave (rev. W.A. Jackson, F.S. Ferguson, and K.F. Pantzer), *A Short-Title Catalogue of Books Printed in England, Scotland, and Ireland, and of English Books Printed Abroad (1475–1640)* (2nd edn, 2 vols, London 1976–86).

*   *   *

Canon law citations are laid out according to the 'modern form' (see James A. Brundage, *Medieval Canon Law* [London and New York, 1995], app. 1), with quotations from *CIC*.

INTRODUCTION

I F books furnish minds as well as rooms, study of the Bible certainly
furnishes the history of the Church. The studies in this volume
reveal the many ways in which the Book and the Church have
interacted and, as cyber-space bears down on books and textuality on
reading, the sense that it was high time in 2000–1 to consider Church
and Book together has been amply justified.

Clearly the concepts of both Book and Church contain many
variables over the millennia and continents covered by these essays.
But a number of important themes emerged from the Society's sun-
drenched conference at Lampeter, a meeting that was not without
hazard, thanks to dissident attempts to disrupt a royal birthday that
severely dislocated travel, and inadvertent presidential proof that
neither lectern nor book is necessary to fell a speaker from a rostrum.
If the meeting began and ended without explicit confrontation of the
question of what we mean by a book, or when is a text not a book,
perusal of the following chapters may well prompt such queries. While
a book is essentially not a scroll and other than a newspaper, its quality
is related both to the format of its pages and the nature of its intended
use and duration. A broadsheet may readily turn into a paper kite (as
missionaries in India were dismayed to find happening to their texts of
the Ten Commandments), and a newspaper into wrapping paper or
worse, but conjoined pages of parchment or paper, written or printed,
contain an implicit intentionality of duration beyond the ephemera of
letter or poster. The chapters that follow show the problem of using
one word across so vast a range of time and space. 'Book' can mean
manuscript codex, *libellus*, and volume, as well as printed texts in
formats that include broadsheet converted into text with commentary,
tiny pocket and girdle books, and an influential Jesuit periodical whose
articles and serialized didactic novels appeared in book form. The
'book' of the ecumenical councils of the Church, like the book of
Scripture itself, was the product of prolonged discriminating appraisal
of discrete texts and manuscripts. The book of all periods may be
regarded as more of an *objet d'art* than a repository of reading matter,
and its relationship with the spoken word and oral communication
takes many forms.

Over the centuries the Christian community produced more kinds of books and readers than could be dreamt of by users of the uniform fleeting screens and continuous pages of our electronic age. Books (religious and ecclesiastical) promoted ends that were practical and visionary, legal and liturgical, official and unofficial, orthodox and heterodox. They could serve shared service and common worship or an individual's private meditation and prayer. Vast or minute, hand-written or printed, unadorned or lavishly illustrated, static or mobile, the relationship between text and user was infinitely variable. A treasured finely illuminated Book of Hours can be seen as 'the first step towards the purchase of paradise'.[1] It was also possible for book owners to have almost visionary reflective experiences with a text of this kind, through illustrative imagery that allowed them to imagine themselves (often women) as donors at prayer before the Virgin. Books could be worn as well as carried (as Books of Hours were observed being taken by English women to church about 1500). Girdle-books, sometimes with elaborately decorated bindings that made them objects of display, were also vade-mecums of personal devotion (like the New Testament hanging from Hugh Latimer's waist in 1555), the essential accompanying presence for *imitatio Christi*. Small books, tiny pocket books like the New Testaments of young men fighting on the Western Front in the First World War, conveyed the comfort of personal speech, immediate physical access to the spiritual presence. Erasmus's *Enchiridion* had something of that quality, and it was the new directness of apostolic encounter that in the early sixteenth century gave the newly translated New Testament the freshness of live confrontation. But owners and users of books were not necessarily readers in our sense of the word. A book might be treasured for text and image, even when its words had to be heard and followed through the articulation of other mouths than the owner's. Pages might be honoured without being construed. And books might themselves be the equivalent of images or relics, devotional objects more than texts, richly decorated with scriptural scenes. Book covers so embroidered or adorned are a reminder that after the Reformation, as before, scriptural imagery was visible in many places, including the bindings of Bibles and prayer books – perhaps with a freedom on the outside that was not deemed appropriate within the text itself.

The study of manuscripts and printed books has much to tell us

---

[1] Below, 106.

about the learning, institutions, and devotions of the Church. By this means we can learn about the transmission of new learning, as with the manuscripts that in the twelfth century took the teaching of Peter Abelard and Hugh of St Victor to monastic and cathedral libraries in Bavaria and Austria, while an early eleventh-century Vatican codex which amounted to a handbook reveals the teaching deemed essential for the pastoral care of the secular clergy. Italian incunables (often surviving only in single copies) reflect the affective power of penitential culture and the widespread interest (of monks as well as lay people) in a range of Marian miracle stories that spread across Europe. Texts, like vestments and relics, could be seen as links with the past, as well as conveying the miraculous possibilities of the present. Ancient liturgical books that formed part of the inherited possessions of a great monastic house might be appreciated not only because of their venerable association with a holy founding figure, but also because they represented an ancient historical tradition. In the fifteenth century Thomas Elmham called the eight heirloom liturgical books associated with St Augustine, which in his time were kept above the high altar in St Augustine's, Canterbury, the 'first fruits of the books of the whole English Church'.[2] The first fruits of a contemporary author of the following century might, contrariwise, be printed more out of Reformation respect for the experience of persecution and exile, than for their intrinsic merit – witness Bernadino Ochino's publishing history in England. And of course generations of reformers turned to their own advantage the first fruits of English heresy, calling on the precedent of Wycliffite Bible translations, as was notably done by Henry Wharton and John Lewis to defend the authority of the English Bibles against Catholics, non-jurors, and Dissenters.

Ecclesiastical historiography has long attributed an essential role to the printed text in the Reformation. Although Luther's Ninety-Five Theses started life as a broadsheet, they also circulated in book form, and the belief that this text marked the point of take-off for religious revolution was given vivid expression in a 1617 engraving celebrating the event of 1517. This image presents writing as an invincible medium, the pen a weapon, capable of accomplishing religious revolution through an unstoppable proliferation of texts. Just as in 1547 the book of the gospel could be shown descending with apocalyptic destructive force on the corrupt Catholic Church,

---

[2] Below, 33.

comparable to the millstone cast down by the angel at the fall of the great city of Babylon, so pens and texts were seen as aggressive instruments of divine intervention. Print continued and expanded scribal power by enhanced kinetic means. But in modern India the pen remained the respected instrument of professional scribal culture, imposing a barrier to the understanding and acceptance of print. As a result of missionary activity we have the interesting development of a hybrid form of print-script. Lithography, used for the multiplication of Christian tracts (though not the Bible), developed what amounted to the mass-produced manuscript. By this means written forms, with the acceptable appearance of calligraphy, could be reproduced in large numbers for a society deeply entrenched in its manuscript tradition.

Naturally the Book of Scripture is pivotal to this volume's theme. The interdependence of Church and Book is illuminated from different angles from the early Church to the nineteenth century. While the earliest surviving scriptural 'books' that we have indicate that from the start Christian writings were produced in a form that differentiated them from the literary texts of the pagan world, they also point towards a readership (or in today's parlance, a textual community) of a kind that remained at the core of subsequent Church history. Working individuals whose artisan labours involved famil- iarity with practical manuals were the likely owners of the *codices* or notepads which contained the earliest surviving New Testament texts. From the time of the early Church too, the dissemination of Scripture aided the growth of the Church. Constantine is recorded as having commissioned and circulated copies of the Greek New Testament and, centuries on, Charlemagne, the 'new Constantine', is associated with the huge enterprise of providing a corrected Vulgate text for leading monasteries and cathedrals of the whole Frankish realm. The Church's self-fashioning, its identity, was moulded around the scriptural canon. The awareness of this historical textuality, the sense of patristic continuity based on the books of Scripture, has been located here in Rufinus of Aquileia's restructuring of Eusebius' *Ecclesiastical History* and the *Historia Tripartita* of Cassiodorus-Epiphanius – works that may have been deliberately promoted in the Carolingian kingdom.

Eventually, fresh approaches to the study of the scriptural text themselves showed ways of transforming the relationship of Church and Book. In the 1840s the responses to Newman's *Essay on the Development of Human Doctrine* demonstrated the extent to which English anti-Catholic prejudice had become subsumed into assumptions about the integral relationship of Church and Book and Roman disregard for biblical authority. Yet in the same decade linguistic studies were beginning that made it seem possible to read the Bible not as 'a self-contained communication of the mind of God',[3] but as a work of literature alongside other great texts, applying the empirical study of language, philological criticism, to Scripture as a means to discovering the divine wisdom of the *logos* in history.

In the medieval Church, biblical knowledge had infused clerical learning at many levels. Canon law and theology were allied, and a short passage on the plenitude of papal power in Innocent IV's mid thirteenth-century *Commentaria* tellingly assumes a wide clerical understanding of Scripture and scriptural symbolism. But once sixteenth-century reformers had opened vernacular Scripture in print to the congregation at large, questions relating to the accessibility of the text, how it was placed, heard, circulated, and interpreted, multiplied to worry contemporary authorities and tease subsequent historians. The stratagems of evasion devised to circumvent proscription of scriptural circulation present parallels in different periods. The group of underground agents, whose organization for the funding and dissemination of vernacular Scripture earned them the name of 'Christian brethren' and the persecution of Thomas More in early sixteenth-century England, were working in ways that bear comparison with the experience of missionaries in eighteenth-century China and nineteenth-century India. Taking biblical texts to readers in their own language sometimes necessitated deceitful subterfuge. Missionaries in India saw the advantage of disguising Christian tracts under titles that would render them congenial to Hindus, just as misleading title-pages enabled Protestant books to end up in the hands of unsuspecting Catholic readers. An outstanding example of the latter is the extraordinary story told here of the Genevan Bible that (despite the retention of distinctive Reformist features) came to be accepted as the vernacular Bible of seventeenth-century French Catholics.

The holy text which in an older world belonged to trained clerks and was placed in church choirs and chancels, demanded new furniture as well as new assumptions in the changed world of Protestant evangelism. When vernacular Bibles finally arrived in English churches, their placing in naves called for chains and desks, while the elevation of the word raised pulpits as well as the voices of

---

[3] Below, 27.

preachers. Access to books, scriptural and confessional, became essential for pastoral care and the instruction of the laity. The Welsh translation of the Bible was first printed in Elizabeth I's reign (in London); it was only in 1718 that the first official printing press was set up on Welsh soil, and the availability of books (devotional works in Welsh) was then all-important for reviving religious life in Wales. The need to improve the pastoral care of the poorer clergy at large by means of parish libraries was an objective to which Thomas Bray directed his vision and huge energy, with the result that an astonishing number of such libraries were established between 1695 and 1720 in the British Isles and North American colonies.

Yet long after scriptural and liturgical texts became available in print, the exigencies of persecution provoked returns to oral transmission, enabling observances to continue when book ownership was hazardous or dangerous. The long century of missionary prohibition in China (1724–1840) resulted in the privy memorizing of writings hoarded from earlier days, enabling 'Christian sutras' to be recited and taught in domestic circles. Such means of confessional continuity, depending on old formulas and texts of earlier missionaries, resemble pre- and post-Reformation practices in England, where seventeenth-century bishops, committing Prayer-Book services to memory during the interregnum, were doing no less than proscribed Lollards had done five generations or so earlier. And in eighteenth-century China, as in sixteenth-century England, believers cherished writings of earlier teachers and sufferers for the faith, such as those of the Jesuit missionary Matteo Ricci. Books were the storehouse of credal continuity, but continuity of observance could be ensured by oral memory and tradition supplementing and reinforcing the longevity of the page.

'Who hath not heard it spoken/How deep you were within the books of God?' Unlike the Archbishop of York reproached in the second part of Shakespeare's *Henry IV*, the contributors to this volume may be applauded for illuminating the multifarious conjunctions of Church, churchmen, and 'exposition on the holy text'.[4]

Margaret Aston

---

[4] *The Second Part of King Henry IV*, 4.2, ll. 16–17, 7.

IN THE BEGINNING WAS THE CODEX: THE EARLY CHURCH AND ITS REVOLUTIONARY BOOKS

by STUART G. HALL

A revolution in book-production marked the beginning of the Church.[1] Almost all literary works were written on scrolls (or roll-books), and were read by unrolling from one hand to the other. It was and remains the obligatory form of the Jewish Torah-scroll. The revolution replaced the roll with the codex or leaf-book of papyrus or parchment: 'the most momentous development in the history of the book until the invention of printing'.[2] A quire or quires of papyrus or parchment, folded and bound at the back, produced the kind of book with pages familiar to us.

This revolution was intimately involved with the origins of the Church and the formation of its Bible. The papyrus evidence for this connection is overwhelming.[3] Only one non-Christian literary codex is certainly datable to the first century AD, against 253 surviving fragments of scrolls. Of all those fragments dated with certainty before AD 300 the ratio is 19:1313. There was a dramatic shift in the fourth century to approximate parity, and of the definitely fifth-century fragments eighty-eight out of ninety-nine are codices. With Christian works the situation is quite different. While the quantity of material is much smaller, it points clearly to the predominance of the codex. Colin Roberts and Theodore Skeat could count 172 biblical or near-biblical items from the first four centuries.[4] Of these at most

---

[1] This paper is heavily and gratefully dependent upon Colin H. Roberts and T.C. Skeat, *The Birth of the Codex* (2nd edn, 1987) [hereafter Roberts/Skeat], and Harry Y. Gamble, *Books and Readers in the Early Church* (New Haven, CT, and London, 1995) [hereafter Gamble], esp. ch. 2. Roberts/Skeat (updating C.H. Roberts, 'The codex', *Proceedings of the British Academy*, 40 (1954), 170–204) and Gamble give details of earlier research, and both use extensively material from E.G. Turner, *The Typology of the Early Codex* (Philadelphia, PA, 1977). H. Blanck, *Das Buch in der Antike* (Munich, 1992) is an excellent, amply illustrated, account of its subject; ch. 5 is directly relevant (75–101), and offers an alternative perspective. Since this paper was given, two further publications have come to my attention: Graham N. Stanton, 'The fourfold Gospel', *New Testament Studies*, 43 (1997), 317–46; Roger S. Bagnall, 'Jesus reads a book', *JThS*, ns 51 (2000), 577–88. Neither affects the basic argument here presented, but both add significant insights.

[2] Roberts/Skeat, 1.

[3] See full statistical table, ibid., 37.

[4] Ibid., 38–42.

I

fourteen are from scrolls; but even among those, five are opistho-graphs, that is, written on the back of existing scrolls, and therefore do not count, as their format was predetermined by the previous use; three are probably, two others possibly, Jewish rather than Christian; the remaining four all have unusual features like being written on the back of an unused scroll. From the point of view of date, there are eleven biblical fragments probably of the second century, and two from apocryphal gospels, all codices. Two more Christian fragments, from Hermas and Irenaeus, are on scrolls, but Hermas is on the reverse of a used roll. So even if the evidence is fragmentary, localized, and sometimes insecure in date, the picture is overwhelming: Christian texts are written in codices from the beginning, while the scroll remained the standard form of book.

Various explanations have been given for the Christian choice of the codex. A number of practical advantages have been suggested: economy, compactness, comprehensiveness, convenience of use, ease of reference.[5] These advantages are emphasised by Blanck, who adds that the compact bound book was easier to protect from damage than a roll.[6] Roberts and Skeat, however, judge them not decisive in accounting for the primitive Christian use. Writing on both sides of the page is a saving, but it is the labour of writing that is the main cost, and the binding of the codex is itself dearer. Compactness is a genuine advantage, which is mentioned by Martial the Roman poet (c.AD 40–101), who made an apparently unsuccessful attempt to market portable codex copies of his verse. Yet during the earlier centuries of the Church the biggest codex had only a hundred and fifty leaves, and most were much smaller. Comprehensiveness, whereby a single codex may hold together for example the four canonical Gospels and Acts (like the third-century Chester Beatty Codex), seems to have been only gradually observed, and the earliest fragments are not of comprehensive sets but of one or two Gospels. The convenience of the codex is obvious to us, since a roll needed two hands, and had to be rolled back to the beginning when finished with. But those expert in using rolls might have found this advantage negligible. As to ease of reference, whereby one might flip more easily through a codex to the desired passage, even that seems not to have concerned the makers of codex books, who leave no more signs in the text or margins to help the

5 Ibid., 45–51; cf. Gamble, 54–6.
6 Blanck, *Das Buch*, 100–1.

reader than do writers of scrolls. Furthermore, one may point out that rolls continued to be used in formal texts in the Middle Ages, and for some Byzantine liturgical texts, without apparent difficulty.[7] Why then did the early Christians defy the universal practice of writing classical literature and Jewish religious texts on scrolls, and go for the revolutionary codex? Gamble cites with approval Roberts's contention that, 'So striking an effect must have had a cause of comparable weight.'[8]

Looking for that cause has produced no agreement. In fact it divides two of our chief guides through the subject. Roberts first suggested that there is truth in the legend of Mark compiling his Gospel on the basis of notes taken from the Apostle Peter's preaching in Rome. This would naturally have been in a parchment codex, already in use for practical records in Rome. This format would make it easy to understand Mark's lost ending, since the authentic Gospel ends abruptly at 16.8, conceivably the effect of losing an end-leaf. Thereafter another legend carries Mark and his Gospel to Alexandria, where his format would be copied, albeit now on papyrus. So because Mark's was the first Gospel-book, the codex became the standard form for Christian literature.[9] This theory proved unconvincing, both because of the obscurity of Mark's Gospel, which is absent from the papyrus record until the fourth century, and because of the inappropriate use of legends.[10] Roberts and Skeat then together proposed that the codex and the characteristic Christian abbreviations of sacred names began together, probably in an influential centre like Jerusalem or Antioch, originating with note-taking of a kind mentioned in the Mishnah. It is claimed that, while the sacred text was always written on scrolls, the rabbis permitted the codex format for the supplementary oral law, albeit only on hard material, not on papyrus. Perhaps Jesus' teaching was so recorded in notes, and the practice led to papyrus gospel codices.[11] Once again the argument is ingenious, but unconvincing. The Mishnaic ruling cannot be earlier than about AD 150; there is no reason why a practice which gave lesser status to the Gospel than to the Torah should be found compelling; and there is no shred of evidence

[7] Roberts/Skeat, 50–3.
[8] Gamble, 56, citing Roberts, 'The codex', 187.
[9] Roberts/Skeat, 54–5, following Roberts, 'The codex', 187–9.
[10] Roberts/Skeat, 55–7, cf. Gamble, 56–7.
[11] Roberts/Skeat, 57–60.

for Jesus' message being written down at the time he spoke.[12] This theory may still have some relevance, as we shall see, if sayings of Jesus were collected later from the oral tradition in notebooks as practical manuals.

Undaunted, Theodore Skeat tried again in an article in 1994.[13] He begins with the unanimity of the papyrus Gospel fragments: twenty-two when Roberts first wrote, twenty more discovered since, and all from codices. He emphasises that the practical advantages are minimal, the cost advantage possibly nil. He then makes some space calculations based on the actual measurements and statistics of the Chester Beatty papyrus codex of the Gospels and Acts.[14] He reckons that a roll containing all four Gospels would have to be about thirty metres long. That is well beyond practical possibility. On a roll, which does not normally exceed ten metres, only one Gospel will go: Mark, the shortest, needs 576 cm, Matthew, the longest, needs 882 cm. A codex, however, could contain all four and Acts as well. The Bodmer Papyrus of Luke and John, probably dating from after AD 200 rather than before, Skeat suggests is one quire of a two-quire codex of the four gospels.[15] This points to his new theory, that the publication of the Gospel of John about AD 100 precipitated a crisis in the Church, which already had three Gospels, and the crisis was resolved by putting the canonical four in a single codex. So the use of the codex and the canon of New Testament Gospels were a momentous decision, which led to the general adoption of the codex for Christian sacred writing. Sadly, this theory must also fail. First, it goes against the trend of the papyrological evidence: the earlier codices, like the John Rylands fragment of John (about AD 125) contain one gospel only.[16] Secondly the canon of four and only four was fixed much later than the early second century, as the disputatious tone of Irenaeus and the activities of those nicknamed 'Alogi' indicate, not to mention Caius at Rome about AD 200.[17] Numerous gospels or collections of Jesus' sayings were

---

[12] Gamble, 57–8.

[13] T.C. Skeat, 'The origin of the Christian codex', *Zeitschrift für Papyrologie und Epigraphik*, 102 (1994), 263–70.

[14] Details in T.C. Skeat, 'A codicological analysis of the Chester Beatty papyrus codex of Gospels and Acts', *Hermathena*, 155 (1993), 27–43.

[15] Skeat, 'Origin', 264.

[16] C.H. Roberts, *An Unpublished Fragment of the Fourth Gospel in the John Rylands Library* (Manchester, 1935).

[17] H.Y. Gamble, *The New Testament Canon: its Making and Meaning* (Philadelphia, PA, 1985), 24–35; cf. S.G. Hall, 'Aloger', *Theologische Realenzyklopädie*, 2 (Berlin, 1978), 290–5,

in circulation before the four-fold canon was established, and continued in use past the year 200, and the canonical four apparently circulated in more than one form.[18] Churches will have begun with a single Gospel-book, and Mark, so little used in the early Church, probably survived because of the authority of a great original patron-church, such as Rome. Finally, if we postulate some general agreement on a four-Gospel canon early enough and of sufficient authority to establish the codex form before the second century, it is difficult to understand why at least three different orders of the four exist in the literary and manuscript evidence.[19]

A more promising line is pursued by Harry Y. Gamble. He accepts the premise of the theories we have outlined:

> Though the theories of Roberts and Skeat are unconvincing, the basic assumption behind them is sound: there must have a decisive, precedent-setting development in the publication and circulation of early Christian literature that rapidly established the codex in Christian use, and it is likely that this development had to do with the religious authority accorded to whatever Christian document[s] first came to be known in codex form.[20]

Gamble opts, instead of the Gospels, for an early edition of the letters of Paul. His theory is that the surviving early evidence, chiefly the Marcionite list of Pauline books commented upon by Tertullian, and the papyrus P^{46} of about AD 200, point to an unattested earlier collection in which the nine or ten letters of Paul (perhaps including Philemon, but not I-II Timothy and Titus) were presented as letters to seven churches.[21] The purpose of this grouping was by the mystic

---

and generally Bruce M. Metzger, *The Canon of the New Testament. Its Origin, Development, and Significance* (Oxford, 1987). T.C. Skeat's insights into Irenaeus are valuable, but he fails to appreciate the polemical context implied by what Irenaeus says: see his 'Irenaeus and the four-gospel canon', *Novum Testamentum*, 34 (1992), 194–9.

[18] A commonplace of New Testament scholarship; see for instance Heimut Koester, *Ancient Christian Gospels. Their History and Development* (London and Philadelphia, PA, 1990), and documentation there.

[19] Described by Skeat himself, 'Irenaeus', 196–8.

[20] Gamble, 58. He wrote before the publication of Skeat, 'Origin', but has privately informed me that his own position is unchanged. Professor Gamble's kindness in giving bibliographical advice is warmly appreciated.

[21] Gamble, 58–62. He first stated the theory in 'The Pauline corpus and the early Christian book', in William S. Babcock, ed., *Paul and the Legacies of Paul* (Dallas, TX, 1990), 265–80. The letters contained in P^{46} (Gamble, 59) also include Hebrews, following Romans, but Gamble regards this as irrelevant ('The Pauline corpus', 395 n.26).

number of perfection, seven, to turn the particular and local scraps of the Apostle's correspondence into a book of universal significance. This practice imitated in Revelation 2–3 and in Polycarp's collection of the seven Ignatian letters. The ordering would have gone with the editing of Paul's letters, some of which probably consist of compilations of genuine fragments (particularly II Corinthians and Philippians).[22] Such a collection, however, needed more than one roll of standard length, and hence a codex was used, and thus the codex became the norm for Christian sacred texts.

Gamble's proposal avoids some of the objections to the theories of Roberts and Skeat. The mini-canon of Paul was compiled in the first century, even if other documents (the Pastoral Letters and Hebrews) were added later. If we accept the idea of a single revolutionary event which stamped its authority on Christian book-production by the spiritual force of one great codex, his position is to be preferred. It is not, however, without difficulties. For one thing, it is not clear that the Pauline continuators, who undoubtedly existed to edit and extend the Pauline corpus, were universally highly regarded. The original church in Rome antedated Paul; that at Alexandria may have owed more to Barnabas and John Mark, with whom Paul quarrelled.[23] Paul's works are used more by those deemed Marcionite and gnostic heretics than by others in the second century.[24] So allowing Gamble's hypothetical seven-church collection of Paul's letters, it would struggle to win acceptance in a Church where diversity of traditions, gospels, and governance still prevailed.

Gamble's argument involves an important detail. In II Timothy 4.13 Paul writes, 'When you come, bring the cloak I left with Carpus at

[22] See for example A.H. McNeile, *An Introduction to the Study of the New Testament*, 2nd edn, rev. C.S.C. Williams (Oxford, 1953), 138–42, 179–80. More recent views and controversies are documents in Wolfgang Schenk, 'Korintherbriefe', *Theologische Realenzyklopädie*, 19 (Berlin, 1996), 620–40, esp. 628–32, and Horst Balz, 'Philipperbrief', ibid., 504–13, esp. 507.

[23] See the conclusions of J.J.F. Sangrador, *Los origenes de la comunidad cristiana de Alejandria*, Plenitudo Temporis, 1 (Salamanca, 1994).

[24] This formerly prevailing view was challenged, with thorough documentation, in Andreas Lindemann, *Paulus im ältesten Christentum: das Bild des Apostels und die Rezeption der paulinischen Theologie in der frühchristlichen Literatur bis Marcion*, Beiträge zur historischen Theologie, 58 (Tübingen, 1979). An American discussion is accessible in Andreas Lindemann, 'Paul in the writings of the Apostolic Fathers' and Martinus C. de Boer, 'Comment: which Paul?', both in Babcock, *Paul and the Legacies of Paul*, 25–45, 45–54. Lindemann holds that there was a considerable continuation of a Pauline school editing and enlarging his literary work.

Troas, and the books (τὰ βιβλία), particularly my notebooks (τὰς μεμβράνας)' (*Revised English Bible*). Though the word translated 'notebooks' means literally 'parchments', it is a Latin loan-word, apparently used as the Romans used *membranae*, to refer to a notebook of parchment sheets in codex form. If Paul (or his imitator giving verisimilitude) had merely meant 'books written on parchment', he could have used the Greek διφθέραι, in regular use for parchment or hide used as writing material.[25] It is a certain kind of book that he designates 'parchment sheets'; otherwise he has no cause to mention the writing material at all. The first uses of the word *caudex* or *codex* refer to collections of wood-and-wax tablets tied together and used for making notes or drafts of literary works. They had the advantage of being easily erased and reused. But so did parchment, that is, prepared animal-skin, which could easily be washed clean and reused. The literary evidence of Latin authors suggests that this was common practice, especially in the West, by the time of Julius Caesar. The word's transference to a papyrus book in the East was natural, where papyrus was the common writing material, and could apparently also be cleaned and reused.[26]

Here we have an important aspect of the codex in the first century AD. It is not regarded as a proper or normal way of writing and reading a book, but, whether in tablet form, on parchment, or on papyrus, is a practical notebook. Guilielmo Cavallo used this to account for the rise of the codex; to quote Roberts and Skeat:

> Admitting the priority of the Christian codex [Cavallo] argues that the early Christians came from the lower strata of society, among whom a book would have been a rarity, and that among such classes, whether Christian or not, the codex-form notebook would have been a familiar object used for memoranda, commercial transactions and the like. Such literature as these classes possessed would not have been the classics but either popular romances like the *Phoinikika* of Lollianus, itself a second-century codex, or, in the case of artisans, works of a technical or practical character. These classes would have been not merely indifferent to, but actually antagonistic to the roll, a form associated in their minds with an aristocratic élite. As the same circles developed into an increasingly powerful middle class, their preferences would have gradually

[25] Roberts/Skeat, 22; Gamble, 64–5.
[26] Roberts/Skeat, esp. 15–23.

dominated the book-production industry, and eventually even the aristocracy would have had to conform and accept the codex.[27]

This thought should be taken with the fact that the few early non-Christian codices include a disproportionate number of practical manuals and elementary school texts, perhaps most of the seventeen preserved from the second century.[28] Cavallo believes that the use by Christians merely represents a social development which would have taken place anyway, and rejects the view that they played a decisive role.[29]

An important more recent development is the astonishing archaeological evidence from Vindolanda on Hadrian's Wall.[30] We now know that the correspondence and military business of the northern legions in the first two Christian centuries was written mostly in ink on thin plates of wood, though more permanent records, such as legal bonds, were incised in wax on stouter tablets, which have more often survived. The day-to-day accounts, records, and letters written on thin wooden plates were the equivalent in the north-west of the empire to the papyrus codex in places nearer Egypt. Typically, Vindolanda produces only one literary line of Latin, an inaccurately copied verse of Vergil, probably a schoolboy's exercise. The records of supplies and pay are not codices. They are typically tied in concertina-fashion, with continuous writing on one side. We have here substantial evidence of a widespread literate but non-literary culture, in which books are not known or read, but records and letters are widely used.

This leads to a conclusion. The earliest Christians did not write or read literature. Poetry was poisoned with the demonic stories of the gods and their immoral doings, philosophy (including natural science and medicine) with the arrogant wisdom of this world, rhetoric with the models of gods and slaughter. The roll and its contents were

---

[27] Ibid., 67–8, describing the views of G. Cavallo, *Libri, editori e pubblico nel mondo antico: guida storica e critica* (Rome, 1975), xix–xxii, 83–6. I have not seen Cavallo's book; but see also Blanck, *Das Buch*, 100, and Cavallo's review of Roberts/Skeat: G. Cavallo, 'La nascita del codice', *Studi italiani di filologia classica*, 28/3rd ser., 3 (1985), 118–21.

[28] Roberts/Skeat, 71–3. The 17 examples balance against 857 non-Christian rolls from the same period, and 13 Christian texts, all of them codices.

[29] See his review, cited in n.27.

[30] A.K. Bowman and J.D. Thomas, *Vindolanda: the Latin Writing-Tablets*, Britannia Monographs Series, 4 (1983), esp. 32–45; Blanck, *Das Buch*, 48–50. For the excavations, Robin Birley, *Vindolanda: a Roman Frontier Post on Hadrian's Wall* (1977); further detail on the texts, with photographs, A.K. Bowman and J.D. Thomas, *The Vindolanda Writing-Tablets (Tabulae vindolandenses, II)* (1994).

anathema, as were the sexual mores, the acquisitiveness, the theatrical entertainment, the bloody sports, the machinery of conquest and military government, and the Roman gods. In the primitive Church we have a movement which in varying proportions repudiated religion, property, sexual intercourse, meat, and wine.[31] At the same time the largely lost documentation of primitive Christianity consisted of letters and practical notes.[32] Letters would be like Paul's, but chiefly no longer than Philemon or II-III John, needing a single tablet or papyrus leaf. Longer letters might be a once-folded papyrus, with two leaves and four sides, or a few more. Practical notes might be sayings, regarded as rulings, remembered from Jesus, gathered into collections like those in the compilation we know as 'The Sermon on the Mount', or the hypothetical Q. Prophetic sayings or rulings by past teachers or apostles would be there too, as in the *Didache*. Each of these has more the nature of a practical handbook than literature, science, or rhetoric. The sort of people who populate the New Testament Church are of the lower middle class: joiner and contractor, boat-owning fishermen, minor civil servants (*publicani* and *centuriones*), tent-makers, purple-dyer, tanner, garment-maker, prison governor, and physician.[33] Christians were the sort of people who needed practical reading and writing for accounts, designs, orders, business correspondence, instructions to subordinates, and tax returns, but who had no leisure for rolls of verse or rhetoric. To this may be added, but as a secondary point, that the Christians adopted the codex while the Jews used, and increasingly insisted upon, parchment scrolls for sacred texts. Early Christian congregations might possess only notes from the Law and the Prophets written on notebooks. By the time they were copying whole books, the differentiation from the Jews would be seen as an advantage of the codex: did not the unbelievers read Moses with a veil over their hearts? Was not the Law written on tablets of stone, while the Gospel was inscribed on believing hearts (II Corinthians 3.7–18)? So the early Church used for its letters and manuals practical notepads (that is, codices) and did not write literature, which came in books (that is, rolls). By the time they were collecting the sayings of Jesus and the acts

---

[31] This applied even to eucharistic wine: Andrew McGowan, *Ascetic Eucharists. Food and Drink in Early Christian Ritual Meals*, Oxford Early Christian Studies (Oxford, 1999).

[32] Gamble, 65–8, has useful comments on this, and the illustrations on p. 68 are particularly relevant to what follows here.

[33] Mark 1.16–20; 2.13–15; 6.3; Acts 9.36–9, 42; 10.1–48; 16.14–15, 25–34; 18.1–3; Colossians 4.14.

of apostles in continuous narratives, they were of course writing literature, and might do so self-consciously, as Luke does. But by then, following this argument, the standard of the codex for Christian records was already the habitual and principled norm, and its practical advantages had become apparent. By the middle of the second century, apologists like Justin and Clement of Alexandria were already trying to tame the philosophy and poetry of the classical world to Christian use; but we need look no further than Tatian or Athenagoras to see the bitter hostility to classical literature still remaining.[34] By then, however, no Christian was going back to the alien scroll as his medium of communication.

University of St Andrews

---

[34] Tatian, *Oratio ad Graecos*, 8–11: *Tatian,* Oratio ad Graecos *and Fragments*, ed. and tr. Molly Whittaker, Oxford Early Christian Texts (Oxford, 1982), 14–23; Athenagoras, *Legatio*, 18–122: *Athenagoras, Legatio pro Christianis*, ed. Miroslav Marcovich, Patristische Texte und Studien, 31 (Berlin, 1990), 55–74.

THE BOOK OF THE COUNCILS:
NICAEA I TO VATICAN II

by NORMAN TANNER

THE ecumenical and general councils[1] of the Church have produced arguably the most important documents of Christianity after the Bible. How this 'book' of the councils came to be composed is the subject of this paper. In the composition, Christians have had to confront three problems similar to those involved in establishing the book of the Bible. First, which councils are to be considered ecumenical or general, paralleling the question of which books are to be included in the Bible. Secondly, which decrees are to be considered the authentic decrees of a particular council, paralleling the question of which chapters and verses make up a particular book of the Bible. Thirdly, which manuscripts or editions form the best text of a given decree, paralleling the search for the best texts of Scripture. There are, too, the additional issues of establishing some hierarchy in the importance of the councils and their decrees – the great creeds and doctrinal statements outrank, surely, most decrees of a purely disciplinary nature, just as the Gospels have a certain priority within the New Testament or Romans and Galatians outrank in importance the Pastoral Epistles – and secondly the difficulties of translating the original texts into the vernacular languages, alike for the councils as for the Bible. Alongside these similarities between the book of the councils and that of the Bible was the tension between Scripture and Tradition. How far could Tradition, represented cumulatively and retrospectively by the councils, interpret or develop the teaching of Scripture? This tension was never far below the surface, and erupted especially in the Reformation controversies.

The limits of this paper are what are called, by Roman Catholics and in part by many other Christian churches, the twenty-one ecumenical and general councils from Nicaea I in 325 to Vatican II in 1962–5. The first seven of them, before the beginning of the schism between East and West in the eleventh century, from Nicaea I in 325 to Nicaea II in

---

[1] 'Council' and 'synod' are synonymous, 'council' will normally be used in this paper because it is more usual in English. The distinction between 'ecumenical' and 'general' councils should become apparent in due course.

787, are recognized as ecumenical councils – that is to say, councils of the whole Church – by the Orthodox and Catholic churches, sometimes by the Anglican Church,[2] and with varying emphases by many other Christian churches. Then follows the disputed eighth council, Constantinople IV in 869–70, which will be treated in its place later. This discussion might end with the seventh council, Nicaea II in 787; yet the Church's clock cannot be stopped even when a major schism occurs. In order to trace the story down to the present, to include the full sweep of Christian history, albeit from a more limited angle, or (to put the matter in another way) in order to include the full book of the ecumenical and general councils as recognized by one major church, the Roman Catholic Church, consideration will be given to the ten general councils of the Western Church in the Middle Ages, Lateran I in 1123 to Lateran V in 1512–17, and the three general councils of the Roman Catholic Church since the Reformation, Trent in 1545–63, Vatican I in 1869–70 and Vatican II in 1962–5.[3]

Given the great importance of these councils, due to their more or less binding authority for many Christians, as distinct from the lesser authority of other councils, it is not surprising that more labour on the part of Christians has gone into the composition of their decrees than into any other book of Christianity, the Bible again excepted: both the labour of the councils themselves and that of deciding what should go into the 'book'. With the Bible, the matter was largely solved early in the Christian era, with the establishment of the canon of Scripture between the second and fourth centuries; though the work of establishing the best texts of these books continued and some questions about the canon remained. With the book of the councils, on the other hand, major work has never stopped and has seen interesting variations in its focus through the centuries.

To begin with the first council of Nicaea in 325, the central difficulty is that no *acta* or minutes of the council survive. It is unclear whether records of some kind were kept but have been lost or whether they were never made. For our knowledge of the council, therefore, we depend on later accounts. For the creed, the council's most important document, the earliest texts come from the letters of two participants at the council: Athanasius, the young deacon and secretary of Bishop

[2] See *ODCC*, 3rd edn (1997), 'Oecumenical Councils', 1175.

[3] References below to the conciliar decrees are taken from *Decrees of the Ecumenical Councils*, ed. Norman P. Tanner, 2 vols (London and Washington DC, 1990) [hereafter *Decrees*].

Alexander of Alexandria, the leading opponent of Arius, who was soon to succeed Alexander as bishop; secondly, Eusebius of Caesarea, a supporter of Arius and opponent of Alexander and Athanasius, though in this case Eusebius' letter – which includes the text of the creed – survives only in Athanasius' citation of it. One might be suspicious of a text if Athanasius were the only source, but in fact there are only very small variations between the text of the creed in these two letters and in the other witnesses during the next century, including the first time the creed was quoted in full by another council, at Ephesus in 431.[4] The creed was too important for people to meddle with it.

The twenty disciplinary canons of Nicaea come down to us through various later collections of canons, most notably the sixth-century collections of John Scholasticus in the East and Dionysius Exiguus in the West, but the selection and formulation of the canons at the council itself remain obscure. Other decisions of the council are known to us through letters and various later sources: decisions about the date of Easter, the Meletian schism, and other matters. Indeed, it may be that this later evidence has refocused the purposes of the council. The formulation of the creed, which came to be considered as by far the most important achievement of the council, may not have been its overriding purpose at the time. Equally or more important may have been the other issues of Easter, the Meletian schism, and some disciplinary canons, or indeed the celebration of Constantine's twenty years as emperor.[5] In this respect it is noticeable that the creed is cited little in the years immediately after the council; even Athanasius appealed to it vigorously only much later in his life.[6] Still, there is the principle of reception: a council is constituted partly by how people later evaluated it, not only by how the members of the council saw it at the time, and according to this principle it is reasonable that the creed should have priority.

The situation regarding the second council, Constantinople I in 381, is even more obscure. The creed it promulgated, for which it is chiefly known, lay virtually unknown for seventy years until the council of Chalcedon in 451. At the latter council an impasse was reached when the creed of 325 was judged inadequate to the new situation. The creed

---

[4] Ibid., 1:3; G.L. Dossetti, *Il simbolo di Nicaea e di Costantinopoli* (Rome, 1967), passim.

[5] Cf. Henryk Pietras, 'Le ragioni della convocazione del Concilio Niceno da parte di Costantino il Grande. Un'investigazione storico-teologica', *Gregorianum*, 82 (2001), 5–35.

[6] J.N.D. Kelly, *Early Christian Creeds*, 3rd edn (1972), 254–62.

of Constantinople was suggested as a way forward, as a legitimate improvement upon the creed of Nicaea, better suited to the needs of the time, and after discussion it was accepted as such.[7] This creed has survived until today as the most widely accepted creed among the Christian churches; it is normally referred to simply as the Nicene creed (though many scholars prefer to call it more accurately the Nicene-Constantinopolitan creed). Its acceptance by the council of Chalcedon effectively promoted the first council of Constantinople into the book of ecumenical councils seventy years after it was held, the elevation of the creed carrying with it the elevation of the council. The council of Ephesus in 431 is well documented,[8] the difficulty is its inconclusive outcome. Those who supported Mary's title of θεοτόκος, Mother of God or God-bearer, led by Cyril of Alexandria, and those who supported Nestorius' dislike of the title, led by John of Antioch, held separate assemblies in Ephesus and refused to come together. They anathematized each other and eventually the emperor Theodosius dissolved the council without any agreed statement and imprisoned both Cyril and Nestorius. Cyril managed to escape from his arrest and returned back to Alexandria in triumph, but it was a further two years before some kind of settlement was reached between him and John of Antioch. Even then it was far from clear which decrees should be regarded as approved, and the boat was further rocked by the stormy council held in the same city of Ephesus eighteen years later in 449, Ephesus II or the so-called 'Robber' council.

Chalcedon is crucial not only for its 'Definition of Faith' but also because it effectively established the book of ecumenical councils up to that point, the canon of which councils should be regarded as ecumenical and which not. First, it endorsed the word 'ecumenical' as a more or less technical term in the Christian vocabulary to denote councils of the whole Church, councils that were therefore binding upon the whole Church, as distinct from diocesan or provincial or other councils of a more local authority. As Professor Henry Chadwick has shown, the earliest ecumenical councils were not church councils at all, rather 'ecumenical' gatherings – that is, gatherings of people

---

[7] Ibid., 296–301; R.P.C. Hanson, *The Search for the Christian Doctrine of God: The Arian Controversy 318–381* (Edinburgh, 1988), 812–13; W.-D. Hauschild, 'Nicäno-Konstantinopolitanisches Glaubensbekenntnis', *Theologische Realenzyklopädie*, 24 (Berlin, 1994), 444–56; S.G. Hall, 'Past creeds and present formula at the Council of Chalcedon', *SCH*, 33 (1997), 19–29.

[8] *Acta conciliorum oecumenicorum*, ed. E. Schwartz et al. (Berlin and Leipzig, 1914–), 1 (5 parts); *Éphèse et Chalcédoine: Actes des conciles*, ed. and tr. A.J. Festugière (Paris, 1982).

from all over the Roman Empire, which then regarded itself as practically co-terminous with the inhabited world (the meaning of οἰκουμενικὴ' 'where there are houses') – of actors, athletes and linen-workers, or their representatives.[9] Only gradually was the word baptized into the vocabulary of Christian ecclesiology. Nicaea I called itself the 'great' and/or 'holy' council, not 'ecumenical'.[10] Constantinople I was referred to as an ecumenical council on at least one occasion[11] but it is doubtful whether the word was being used in the full sense it later came to acquire: the council was clearly one of the Eastern Church rather than of the whole Church. The term develops at Ephesus I and Ephesus II, but the decisive step came at Chalcedon when, at the opening of the council's Definition of Faith, it described itself as the 'holy and great and ecumenical synod' – 'holy and great', following the language of Nicaea I, then the addition of 'ecumenical'.[12] After Chalcedon the meaning of the term was fairly clear and consistent.

Secondly, Chalcedon clarified which councils were to be regarded as ecumenical and which not. In its opening session it outlawed the disputed second council of Ephesus of 449 by reversing its decisions, then in its Definition of Faith it approved of three and only three previous councils: Nicaea I, Constantinople I, and Ephesus I.[13] It did not explicitly call them 'ecumenical', but the solemn approval accorded to them, alongside the authority of Chalcedon itself, meant that the list of ecumenical councils – four including Chalcedon – became established.

Thirdly, Chalcedon went some way towards sorting out the thorny question of which statements of these four councils were to be regarded as their authentic decrees, in doctrinal matters. For Nicaea I and Constantinople I this was straightforward enough: it mentioned and quoted in full the two creeds. In the case of Ephesus the matter was much more complex, but the council largely sided with Cyril of Alexandria, calling him, alongside Pope Celestine, the 'leader' of the council, and approving various of his letters. As for Chalcedon itself,

---

[9] Henry Chadwick, 'The origin of the title "Oecumenical council"', *Journal of Theological Studies*, 23 (1972), 132–5.

[10] *Decrees*, 1:7–16; though 'ecumenical' appears in one manuscript for canon 13 (ibid., 1:12).

[11] Ibid., 1:29.

[12] Ibid., 1:83.

[13] Ibid., 1:83–5.

the 'Definition' approved and quoted from the letter, or 'Tome', that Pope Leo had written to Flavian, patriarch of Constantinople, and thereby incorporated the letter into the Definition.[14]

For the next three councils – Constantinople II in 553, Constantinople III in 680–1, and Nicaea II in 787 – the story is comparatively straightforward. Each of them quoted with approval the preceding councils and only these councils, then added themselves to the list, making seven with Nicaea II.[15] Some other councils regarded themselves as ecumenical but were not received as such by the wider Church. The iconoclast council of Hieria in 753, for example, declared itself an ecumenical council and in terms of the large number of participants and the unanimity of its decisions it may have seemed to fulfil the conditions of ecumenicity; but its decisions were reversed by Nicaea II thirty-four years later. Two other councils are candidates for the book. In 692 the council of Trullo – or 'in Trullo' because it was held in the domed hall (ἐν τῷ τρούλλῳ) of the imperial palace in Constantinople – issued 102 disciplinary canons. It has always been regarded as an ecumenical council by the Eastern Church, though as an extension of the fifth and sixth councils (Constantinople II and III) rather than as a separate council, hence its other name of the Quini-Sext council. For various reasons, mainly the anti-Western tone of some of the canons, it has not maintained its place as ecumenical in the West. Conversely, Constantinople IV in 870–1, whose principal business was the deposition of Photius as patriarch of Constantinople, has been excluded from the list in the East but for long was included in the West – to the dismay of the Eastern Church on account of its veneration for Photius. Many Western scholars, including myself, are now ready to accept its exclusion, for reasons that are complex but mainly depend on accepting the authenticity of a letter allegedly written by Pope John VIII ten years after the council which annulled its decision to depose Photius.[16]

The situation after the beginning of the schism between East and West in the eleventh century changed dramatically. A conciliar tradition continued in both regions, but without communion between the two. Important councils in the East, for example, were those of

---

[14] Ibid., 1:85–6.

[15] Ibid., 1:108–9, 124–5, 134–5.

[16] Ibid., 1:157–8; V. Peri, 'C'è un concilio oecumenico ottavo?', *Annuarium historiae conciliorum*, 8 (1976), 52–79.

Constantinople in 1341 and 1351, which endorsed Hesychasm, and later those of Jassy in 1642 and Jerusalem in 1672, which taught concerning the Eucharist and the nature of the Church. This conciliar tradition would merit a separate discussion, but it is to the Western tradition that we should now turn, in accordance with the principles mentioned at the start of this paper.

The medieval general councils in the West differed in many ways from the ecumenical councils of the early Church. All of them were held in the West rather than in the East; the main language changed accordingly from Greek to Latin; most of them were presided over by the pope, the bishop of Rome, rather than by the emperor; and the main focus of attention moved from doctrine to church order. None of them is regarded as ecumenical by the Eastern Church, unsurprisingly since there was no Eastern representation at them, apart from small delegations at Lyons II in 1274 and Florence in 1439. Nor are they generally regarded as ecumenical councils by the churches of the Reformation, though mainly, it seems, on the slightly different grounds that the Church was seriously in error during this time and therefore was incapable of holding a valid ecumenical council. What about the attitude of the Western Church itself during this time to the ten councils of Lateran I to IV in 1123, 1139, 1179, and 1215 respectively, Lyons I and II in 1245 and 1274, Vienne in 1311–12, Constance in 1414–18, Basel-Florence in 1431–45 and Lateran V in 1512–17? There was little doubt that they were general councils of the Western Church and held a privileged position within it, though there were secondary questions about whether the representation at Lateran I and II had been large enough to make them into general councils, as well as debates about the legality of parts of Constance and Basel-Florence. But should they be considered ecumenical councils of the whole Church rather than general councils of the Western Church? On this crucial question medieval people who troubled to think about it seem to have been uncertain and to have preferred the view that they were only general councils of the Western Church, on the grounds that an ecumenical council was impossible without Eastern participation and in the belief that the schism would soon be healed and then a truly ecumenical council could be held again.

The evidence for this cautious approach to the medieval councils has been laid out by Professor Bermejo.[17] The council of Florence, for

---

[17] Luis M. Bermejo, *Church, Conciliarity and Communion* (Anand, 1990), 68–90.

example, was often referred to, even by popes and well into the sixteenth century, as the eighth or ninth (to include Constantinople IV) ecumenical council because the Eastern Church had been represented at it.[18] All the others were thus omitted from the list of ecumenical councils because they lacked Eastern representation. Strong evidence also comes from the council of Constance. After the three claimants to the papacy had been deposed or persuaded to resign, the council drew up a profession of faith that the man about to be elected as the new pope would be obliged to make. The profession contained this promise:

> I will firmly believe and hold the catholic faith according to the traditions of the apostles, of the general councils and of other holy fathers, especially of the eight holy ecumenical (Latin, *universalia*) councils – namely the first at Nicaea, the second at Constantinople, the third at Ephesus, the fourth at Chalcedon, the fifth and sixth at Constantinople, the seventh at Nicaea and the eighth at Constantinople – as well as of the general (Latin, *generalia*) councils at the Lateran, Lyons and Vienne.[19]

There is clearly a distinction in the profession between the eight ecumenical councils before the schism and the subsequent medieval councils, with priority being given to the former, even though the distinction is not expanded upon.

The drive to promote the medieval councils into the book of ecumenical councils, and to provide editions of all the decrees of all the ecumenical councils, indeed of other councils too, began in the sixteenth century. Two factors were decisive. First, the invention of printing, which made possible the printing of large collections of texts. Secondly, the Counter-Reformation, which encouraged Roman Catholics to justify the medieval Church. Part of the protest of the Reformation was to consider the medieval Church an aberration, as mentioned earlier, and legitimizing the medieval councils as truly ecumenical was a central plank in the Roman Catholic response to this protest. This legitimizing was part of the general heightening of historical awareness and justification in the early modern period, the Reformation for its part producing the Centuriators of Magdeburg and, in England, Foxe's *Book of Martyrs* and Wilkins's *Concilia*. A third

---

[18] Ibid., 77–8.
[19] *Decrees*, 1:442.

factor, within the Roman Catholic Church, was the interest in councils on the part of Gallican scholars in France.

The three milestones in this colossal work of scholarship were the so-called Roman edition of 1608–12, 'Mansi' (1759–1927) and 'Alberigo' (3rd edn, 1973).[20] The four volumes of the Roman edition, with its twofold title, *Τῶν ἁγίων οἰκουμενικῶν συνόδων τῆς καθολικῆς ἐκκλησίας ἅπαντα: Conciliorum generalia Ecclesiae catholicae Pauli V pontificis maximi auctoritate edita*, were produced by scholars in Rome working under the auspices of Pope Paul V. Its authority more or less established, at least for several centuries, the Roman Catholic Church's list of ecumenical councils: the ten medieval councils from Lateran I to Lateran V were included; some other candidates from the Middle Ages were excluded, for example some late eleventh-century Roman councils, the Council of Pisa in 1409, and the Basel part of Basel-Florence on account of its conflict with Pope Eugenius IV (though Basel later crept back into the list). The title of the work, by including both the words 'ecumenical' and 'general', cleverly blurred the distinction between the two, apparently equiparating them, but the result was that 'ecumenical' came to be the preferred term. The monumental *Sacrorum conciliorum nova et amplissima collectio*, 53 vols (Florence, Venice, Paris and Leipzig, 1759–1927), which was inaugurated by Giovanni Mansi and continued by many scholars, included local as well as ecumenical councils and much background material (minutes of debates, speeches, lists of participants, and so on), collectively known as *acta*, as well as the promulgated decrees. It is for councils what Migne's *Patrologia Graeca* and *Patrologia Latina* are for the Fathers of the Church: though strictly in terms of the decrees of the ecumenical councils, which is the concern of this paper, the improvements of 'Mansi' over earlier editions were relatively small except inasmuch as it made them more widely available. Finally in 1973 a team of scholars led by Giuseppe Alberigo produced a third edition of their *Conciliorum Oecumenicorum Decreta* (= *COD*). This volume provided, in addition to short introductions, notes, and so forth, the texts in the original Greek or Latin languages, according to the best versions then available, of all the decrees of all the ecumenical councils, numbering twenty-one according to the then tradition of the

---

[20] For a fuller review of the scholarship, including recent improved editions of the *acta* of the councils, see Norman P. Tanner, *The Councils of the Church: A Short History* (Crossroad, NY, 2001), 6–11.

Roman Catholic Church: eight before the East-West schism (including therefore Constantinople IV), the ten medieval councils from Lateran I to Lateran V, plus Trent, Vatican I and Vatican II.

In a sense *COD* closed the book of the ecumenical councils, at least until a new one assembles, but further refinements to the texts of particular decrees, by way of better critical editions, have already been made since 1973 and surely will continue. Considerable work, moreover, has been done since then in making the decrees more widely available to readers, chiefly through bilingual versions which reproduce the original texts of *COD* and provide a vernacular translation on each facing page.[21]

In another sense, however, the whole book has been reopened by a renewed questioning of which councils should be included in it. The list of ecumenical councils has never been defined by the Roman Catholic Church, notwithstanding the authority of the Roman edition of 1608–12 and later acceptance of its assumptions. The debate at the scholarly level was reopened in recent times mainly by the articles of V. Peri and Yves Congar, which questioned whether any councils after the East-West schism could be considered ecumenical.[22] Vatican II also contributed to the debate by extending the meaning of Church, for Roman Catholics, beyond the Roman Catholic community and therefore implicitly calling into question whether a council could be ecumenical without the participation of other Christian churches and communities. Significant, too, was the speech delivered by Pope Paul VI in 1974 on the seventh centenary of the second Council of Lyons (1274). In it he referred to Lyons II and the other medieval councils as 'general councils of the Western world' (*generales synodos in occidentali orbe*).[23] Pope Paul was normally very careful with his words and his preference for calling them general councils of the West, rather than ecumenical councils, was surely intentional.

The question of the status of the medieval councils, and, for similar reasons, of Trent, Vatican I, and Vatican II, is of huge importance in ecumenical relations since almost all the questions in debate between the Roman Catholic Church on the one hand, and the Orthodox Church and the Churches of the Reformation on the other, depend on

---

[21] *Decrees* is the original-English bilingual edition.

[22] V. Peri, 'Il Numero dei concili ecumenici nella tradizione cattolica moderna', *Aevum*, 37 (1963), 433–501; Yves Congar, 'Structures ecclésiales et conciles dans les relations entre Orient et Occident', *Revue des sciences philosophiques et théologiques*, 58 (1974), 355–90.

[23] *Acta Apostolicae Sedis*, 66 (1974), 620.

statements made by these later councils. The reopening of the question of their status within the Roman Catholic community, and the implication that Catholics may not be so absolutely bound to their statements as was previously thought, may prove to be a helpful way forward in the search for Christian unity. The book of the councils is full of surprises and it looks as though it may still have some in store.

Gregorian University, Rome

EARLY MEDIEVAL INTRODUCTIONS TO THE HOLY BOOK: ADJUNCTS OR HERMENEUTIC?

by THOMAS O'LOUGHLIN

IN a famous passage on the training of those who wished to become wise in sacred letters, in effect, learned readers of the Christian scriptures, Cassiodorus wrote:

> The first thing a student should do, having read [my] book is to go back and study carefully the works of those (*introductores*) who have written introductions to the sacred scriptures. We have found the following [useful]: Tyconius the Donatist; St Augustine's *De doctrina christiana*; Hadrian; Eucherius; and Junilius. I have carefully collected their works and bound them together into a collection so that through their various explanations and examples these men might make matters known who were previously unknown.[1]

Cassiodorus[2] assumes that these books will not only provide the student with facts about the scriptures and specimens of exegesis; but that when they have been mastered, the student will have a single apparatus to enable him to undertake exegesis within the tradition.[3] He therefore went to the trouble of setting up a practical method to ensure that their books survived and were disseminated.[4] These were writers he had found useful himself in the task of interpretation,[5] and, according to the conclusion in one manuscript of the *Institutiones*, it is to this collection (the *codex introductorium*) that the student should turn next for a noble and healthy start as an exegete.[6] This paper concerns

---

[1] *Institutiones* I.x.1–2, ed. R.A.B. Mynors (Oxford, 1937), 34; cf. T. O'Loughlin, *Teachers and Code-Breakers: The Latin Genesis Tradition* (Turnhout, 1999), 46–9, which examines the context in which Cassiodorus wrote. All translations are my own.

[2] See J.J. O'Donnell, *Cassiodorus* (Berkeley, CA, 1979) for the general background.

[3] I use masculine language as Cassiodorus wrote within a male monastic context and imagined only male students undertaking the training he envisaged.

[4] Alas, there is no extant copy of that collection.

[5] See O'Donnell, *Cassiodorus*, 210; A. Souter, 'An unrecorded reference to the Rules of Tyconius', *JThS*, 11 (1910), 562–3; idem, 'Cassiodorus's copy of Eucherius's *Instructiones*', *JThS*, 14 (1913), 69–72.

[6] *Institutiones*, II, conclusio 9 (p. 163 *in apparatu*).

the implications for later Latin theology of Cassiodorus' confidence in these, largely forgotten, writers and their works.

Only one of these five recommendations is still read: Augustine's *De doctrina christiana*.[7] Sometimes it is presented as a guide to hermeneutics, at other times it is viewed as a collection of exegetically useful tips. In fact, it is both, for it supplies a rationale for the exegesis as part of the human quest for a knowledge of reality through signs, as well as guidance on many topics in Scripture, such as how to explain apparent contradictions.[8] In it Augustine expounds his distinction between *signum* and *res*, and links a study of human understanding (book I) with the study of the problems specific to the scriptures (books II–III). Much later, he added a guide to speaking and communication (book IV). The work, central to studies of Augustine's semiotics, still generates interest.

What of the others? For Tyconius we have his *Liber regularum* which he produced partly to provide a fixed method for solving textual contradictions and doctrinal conundrums thrown up by the scriptures, and partly to show how beneath 'an immense wood of prophesy' lay a single, secret meaning.[9] Tyconius believed that his rules were 'keys' for use by human beings to gain access to this coherent and consistent message. Although it used the language of seven rules (*regulae*) for understanding Scripture, in actual operation they were stratagems so that particular passages or incidents could be reconciled to a general Christian teaching.[10] However, it did, as recent research has shown,[11] foster a general view of Scripture and read each passage from an apocalyptic perspective.[12] Given that perspective, and as Cassiodorus' text shows it was common knowledge that its author was a heretic, it may seem strange that Cassiodorus wished to put it into the hands of students. In this, however, he was following Augustine who, while

---

[7] I use the edition of J. Martin, *De doctrina christiana*, CChr.SL, 32 (Turnhout, 1962).

[8] For an example of how later writers put the techniques of *De doctrina christiana* to work, cf. T. O'Loughlin, '*Res, tempus, locus, persona*: Adomnán's exegetical method', *Innes Review*, 48 (1997), 95–111.

[9] F.C. Burkitt, ed., *The Book of Rules of Tyconius* (Cambridge, 1894); see the *prooemium* for Tyconius's intentions.

[10] In this regard it is interesting to note how he establishes a basic gospel story-line, and then reconciles other passages to it; cf. T. O'Loughlin, 'Tyconius' use of the canonical gospels', *Revue Bénédictine*, 106 (1996), 229–33.

[11] Cf. P. Bright, *The Book of Rules of Tyconius: Its Purpose and Inner Logic* (Notre Dame, IN, 1988).

[12] Cf. P. Fredriksen, 'Tyconius and Augustine on the Apocalypse', in R.K. Emmerson and B. McGinn, eds, *The Apocalypse in the Middle Ages* (1992), 20–37.

noting that Tyconius was a heretic, had nonetheless declared the book useful. Indeed, it was probably through Augustine's *De doctrina christiana* that Cassiodorus first made acquaintance with Tyconius, for Augustine had provided an epitome of his rules.[13] Therefore, it is likely that Cassiodorus was viewing the work (as had Augustine) as a toolbox for solving problems rather than as *Gestalt*. Tyconius' book exercised little direct influence on the Latin tradition. It survives in relatively few manuscripts;[14] but its method was enormously influential through the *De doctrina christiana*,[15] and for many centuries tricks such as 'recapitulation' developed by Tyconius were the preferred solution to such problems as inconsistencies of timing and sequences of events between the Gospels.[16] But that leaves another question unanswered: if one uses Tyconius as a set of tools for explaining individual problematic verses, does that activity create a particular view of Scripture among its operatives?

In the case of Hadrian's work, Εἰσαγωγη εἰς τας θειας γραφας (*Introduction to the Sacred Writings*), while undoubtedly available in Latin in Vivarium when Cassiodorus wrote, it did not survive and apparently played no subsequent role in Latin exegesis.[17] A text of this work, apparently an epitome, is extant;[18] but no Latin text survives.[19] Moreover, there are no records of this work from surviving medieval library catalogues. So while Cassiodorus was at pains to ensure its survival, his efforts did not meet with much success.

---

[13] *De doctrina christiana*, III.xxx.42–xxxvii.56.

[14] Burkitt's edition is based on only six medieval manuscripts. Gustave Becker's *Catalogi Bibliothecarum Antiqui* (Bonn, 1885) has only one reference to Tyconius: the catalogue from Corbie (*c*.1200) lists it among the contents of tome 172 of the library; the reference is problematic (see the appendix to this article) but refers to the whole work. Note also that Burkitt (xxviii) drew attention to another copy mentioned in a catalogue (*c*.1200) from Cluny.

[15] Burkitt edited an epitome – another means by which Tyconius in an abbreviated form influenced the tradition – along with the main text (89–98); and on p. xxiii gave a stemma showing the influence of Tyconius on later writers in Latin.

[16] See T. O'Loughlin, 'Julian of Toledo's *Antikeimenon* and the development of Latin exegesis', *Proceedings of the Irish Biblical Association*, 16 (1993), 80–98, on the problem of inconsistencies; and idem, '*Res, tempus, locus, persona*', for a series of applications of the notion of '*recapitulatio*'.

[17] What little we know of Hadrian is summarized by V. Nazzaro, 'Hadrian', *Encyclopedia of the Early Church*, 2 vols (Cambridge, 1992), 1:369.

[18] This can be found in *PG* 98, cols 1273–1312; cf. M. Geerard, *Clavis patrum graecorum*, 6 vols, *CChr* (Turnhout, 1974–98), 3:254, no. 6527.

[19] The Latin translation presented in *PG* is by an early modern editor (cf. *PG* 98, col. 1271).

Then we come to Eucherius[20] and Junilius.[21] While both authors are now forgotten, their manuals were amongst the most used works in Latin exegesis until the twelfth century. They were cited steadily in early medieval exegesis as the sources of motifs and comments, and such images as the 'threefold sense of Scripture' can be traced back to Eucherius[22] and that of the 'threefold nature of prophecy' back to Junilius.[23] For a period of more than five centuries they, and most especially Eucherius, were added to, excerpted, and incorporated into encyclopaedic works, until eventually their explanations became so commonplace that no authority had to be cited for them.

Eucherius had the greater impact on the tradition as his works were deliberately composed with the busy pastor in mind, and their structure enables them to be used as basic reference works which promised a solution to almost any exegetical difficulty. However, the cost of fulfilling this promise was very high. First, Eucherius was committed to a notion that every word in Scripture had a fixed meaning in interpretation, usually only one meaning (for example whenever one met the word 'field' - *ager* - one was to interpret this as referring to the material universe - *mundus* - based on Matthew 13.38), but sometimes a word could have a good meaning and diabolic meaning. The effect of this was to destroy any notion of the subtlety of language, awareness of context and culture (elements which Augustine had stressed in *De doctrina christiana*)[24] along with any awareness of the inherent problems of using such a heterogeneous collection of materials as the Christian canon. For such fixed meanings one has to imagine Scripture written as a single document, in one time, place, and language, and with a legal view of language where each word is a technical term with definition. Second, the surface meaning of the text has to be reduced to that of an illusion, for the real meaning

---

[20] Both of his exegetical manuals to which Cassiodorus must be referring, the *Formulae spiritalis intellegentiae* and the [*Liber*] *Instructionum*, were edited by Karl Wotke, *Sancti Eucherii Lugdunensis* [*Opera*], Corpus Scriptorum Ecclesiasticorum Latinorum, 31 (Vienna 1894).

[21] The sole work upon which his reputation rests is the *Instituta regularia diuinae legis*, in H. Kihn, ed., *Theodor von Mopsuestia und Junilius Africanus als Exegeten* (Freiburg, 1880), 465–528; but a satisfactory text can be found in *PL* 68, cols 15–42.

[22] For an analysis of Eucherius' distinctions of the 'senses of scripture', cf. O'Loughlin, *Teachers and Code-Breakers*, 172–80; and idem, 'The symbol gives life: Eucherius of Lyons' formula for exegesis', in T. Finan and V. Twomey, eds, *Scriptural Interpretation in the Fathers: Letter and Spirit* (Dublin, 1995), 221–52.

[23] For a introduction to the longstanding contribution of Junilius to Latin exegesis, cf. O'Loughlin, *Teachers and Code-Breakers*, 181–3.

[24] II.xi–xvi, but it is a theme found throughout book II of the work.

lies hidden beneath it. Eucherius was aware of this problem, and in the introduction to the *Formulae* pointed out that some texts were to be seen as wholly allegorical (like the Song of Songs), others to be read literally (such as the Gospels), while other texts fell between these extremes.[25] However, once the method was laid out for one part of Scripture, since it offered to give a more profound meaning to the text it was applied widely, and so the surface of the text was reduced to being simply the starting-point for the exegetical process whose main aim was to find the 'other', deeper, meanings.[26] This, in turn, meant that the reader in the early medieval period saw himself as the ideal reader for whom the text was intended, and the act of reading was essentially that of decoding an encryption perceived as a mystery.[27] Third, in stressing the distinction between the 'spirit' and the 'letter' of Scripture, Eucherius allowed on the one hand for a sacramental reading of the text which was to enhance spirituality, liturgy, and art,[28] while on the other hand contributing to a dualistic interpretation of religious symbols in terms of binary categories such as spirit/flesh, eternal/transient, and things 'of God' or 'of the Devil'.[29] Lastly, by assuming fixed meanings for words, the sentence became the basic vehicle for the message the reader was to take from the text: the text became a collection of sentences each of which carried not only a meaning, but a theological message, whether read in context or sundered into units. This was a process well under way by Eucherius' time,[30] but his method gave it free rein and facilitated the notion that any sentence could be read alongside any other. Thereby each text, and the whole canon, could be seen as a collection of propositions which must be harmonized with each other, for on no account could they contradict one another without threatening the whole edifice of interpretation.[31]

[25] See T. O'Loughlin, 'Seeking the medieval view of the Song of Songs', *Proceedings of the Irish Biblical Association*, 18 (1995), 94–116.

[26] On allegory as the act of despising the text, cf. M. Cahill, 'Reader-response criticism and the allegorizing reader', *Theological Studies*, 57 (1996), 89–96.

[27] See T. O'Loughlin, 'Christ and the Scriptures: the chasm between modern and pre-modern exegesis', *The Month*, 259 (1998), 475–85.

[28] See T. O'Loughlin, *Journeys on the Edges* (2000), 38–41.

[29] This is an aspect of his legacy within early medieval exegesis which has not received attention from scholars to date.

[30] See T. O'Loughlin, 'The controversy over Methuselah's death: proto-chronology and the origins of the western concept of inerrancy', *Recherches de théologie ancienne et médiévale*, 62 (1995), 182–225.

[31] Cf. O'Loughlin, 'Julian of Toledo's *Antikeimenon*'.

Now we face the question in the title of this paper: were these works simple introductory textbooks which provided an *organon* and a quarry of solutions to particular problems, or did such introductory texts combine to present a view of Scripture, its nature, and the human task in approaching it? If the former, then with the exception of *De doctrina christiana* they have settled into the obscurity that awaits all textbooks;[32] but if the latter, then they are key texts for understanding medieval theology, and remind us that the most potent works within a tradition may not be the great works which still command our attention, but the minor works which trained generations of teachers whose combined labours are responsible for the shape of the tradition.[33] So should we view these as early medieval student manuals or as keys to a hermeneutical universe?

It is the contention here that these widely differing works – or at least those which circulated in the early Middle Ages – shared some interesting common features in terms of their approach to exegesis, and are accordingly the keys to understanding much Latin theological writing from the period. Indeed, it may have been the recognition by Cassiodorus of these common theological traits that led him to assemble them and recommend them as a group.

Collectively they emphasised the notion that there was a sacred canon of writings which stood apart: the scriptures were in a unique category as books for they possessed a unique authority. They were the basic point of knowledge rather than a literary source of knowledge. All the authors of these introductions stress that the scriptural books had a privileged place because of their guarantee of truth, and a special excellence as vehicles of divine revelation. In fact, for both Eucherius and Junilius it is very hard to form a distinction between the notion of the book and the actual content of revelation. Moreover, the text of Scripture was the desired communication; other books, their own included, existed to help bring that communication to completion. In these works we see the beginnings of an approach to the scriptures as a self-contained communication of the mind of God, whose sacred value was independent both of the original events

---

[32] Textbooks, of their nature, operate within a paradigm, and they perish with that paradigm without being recalled in the way that the works which generate a paradigm are recalled as classics; moreover, since the textbook attempts to digest the current state of information within an area, they disappear through obsolescence.

[33] On the notion that a tradition is a continuity of teachers using the same basic textbooks, see O'Loughlin, *Teachers and Code-Breakers*, 12–17.

they recorded and of the interpreting community which valued them.

These introductory works were written at the time when the notion was gaining ground that, as a piece of writing, the scriptures were perfect in every respect.[34] These writers not only assumed this themselves, but did much to propagate it. Each little bit was true, valuable, and sacred since it was believed to show off its divine origin. Therefore each sentence, considered as a proposition, could be proven, and taken as a building block in any other argument. The scriptures as they possessed them were complete and sufficient, were expected to be internally consistent, and were believed to exhibit a fundamental rationale. Not only were they free from historical accidents, but all difficulties perceived within them – whether obscurities or contradictions – were to be located in the eye of the beholder and considered the result of weakness of the human intellect, never of weakness in the holy book.

Another feature uniting the writers of these introductory texts was their confidence in the ability of their methods to grasp the text, even if their authors were not confident of their own abilities as practitioners. Essentially, the problems of understanding Scripture were analogous to the solving of puzzles. Within this confidence lurked another belief: the text was written with them in mind and so its obscurities were, of their nature, transitory. As Christians they were 'the ideal readers', whose position in the final age of history enabled them to appreciate the text in the fullness of its message in a way that was not open to those who had first read the Old Testament, those who had first heard Christ's preaching, nor anyone who was not a believer.[35] Since the communication contained in the book was, from beginning to end, framed with them in mind, then their methods must be up to the task, and only their own weakness prevented their total comprehension of that message. Moreover, since the scriptures formed a class apart, the understanding of the nature of the list/rule (*canon*) that defined them began to change its meaning. When Augustine gave a list of the books that made up the scriptures in his church in the late fourth century his concern was that nothing be

---

[34] What would later be referred to as 'verbal inspiration'.

[35] Isidore of Seville, whose exegesis builds upon the work of the *introductores*, shows this tendency in its developed form; cf. T. O'Loughlin, 'Christ as the focus of Genesis exegesis in Isidore of Seville', in T. Finan and V. Twomey, eds, *Studies in Patristic Christology* (Dublin, 1998), 144–62.

left out,[36] and it was probably written to challenge the position of Jerome who argued for a shorter Old Testament canon restricted to books written in Hebrew.[37] However, within a short period of time the canon had assumed a far greater importance as that which segregated the word of God, whose depths pious study could reveal, from mere human writings. The *introductores* fostered the shift in the understanding of canon from being the list of inspired books (the position of one of their number: Augustine) to being the inspired list of those works with the divine guarantee of inerrancy.[38]

The manuals created an image of Scripture as sharing a common structure with that of the material creation and the pattern of history. Just as the material universe could point beyond itself to a spiritual realm, so the words of the book pointed beyond their immediate message to an more enduring and divine message. Equally, the events of history could be seen by those with faith as not simple strings of events in chronological order, but as the handiwork of providence. This common structure of the material creation, time, and the book was seen above all in their focus: Christ as the Word. This origin in the Word, pointing forward to the moment of the Incarnation, and then to the consummation at the Second Coming when they would cease and Christ 'be all in all' (cf. Colossians 3.11), meant that they mutually enlightened one another now in the period of the Church. To interpret, for example, passages from Genesis in terms of physics, to align its dates with all other human events, or to build an intellectual edifice from a mixture of these materials was not simply an act of rational naiveté, but flowed from the mutually consistent body of basic beliefs about creation and revelation reaching a conclusion in Christ. The authors of these early medieval manuals assumed that belief as a basic part of their own faith, but they gave it a new and concrete expression in the way they encouraged others to go about the task of exegesis.

Lastly, in stressing the perfection of Scripture as divine communication and its appropriateness to the situation in which the Christian

---

[36] *De doctrina christiana*, II.viii.13.

[37] Cf. H.H. Howorth, 'The influence of St Jerome on the canon of the western Church', *JThS*, 10 (1909), 481–96; 11 (1910), 321–47; 13 (1911), 1–18.

[38] See B.M. Metzger, *The Canon of the New Testament* (Oxford, 1987), 1: he distinguished between 'a collection of authoritative books' and 'an authoritative collection of books'. For the background to the question of a canon, cf. J. Barton, *The Spirit and the Letter: Studies in the Biblical Canon* (1997).

found him/herself, the human dimension of the text was reduced to an almost invisible minimum. The text was transformed in imagination from being an 'immense wood' (Tyconius) in which the investigator could become lost, to being an immense repository of hidden, divinely implanted, meanings which the skilled Christian reader was able to probe with the knowledge that he knew where he was at any point in his investigation. These textbooks, many of which looked to Augustine for inspiration, turned Augustine's semiotics on its head. Augustine imagined Scripture as a collection of *signa* standing in our world and pointing beyond this world; these textbooks imagined Scripture more in the manner of the medieval conception of a sacrament – a sign indeed, but one lowered into this world from above, a veritable taster of the divine fullness. As such, the hermeneutic they fostered was far more significant than the help they provided in the actual tasks of interpretation and preaching.

APPENDIX

The copy of Tyconius' *Liber regularum* at Corbie in the late twelfth century

Gustave Becker's *Catalogi Bibliothecarum Antiqui*, 281, gives this entry for the library of Corbie from the catalogue of *c.* 1200:

> *172. de remissione peccatorum. regula Ticonii. de promissis et lege. de specie et genere. de temporibus. de recapitulatione. de diabolo.*

It was the cataloguer's intention to list all the various works contained in the tomes in his library, and from the form of the entry, by comparison with other entries in the catalogue, it is clear that he thought that tome 172 contained seven distinct works: the *De remissione peccatorum*, the *Regula Ticonii*, and so forth.

However, the first entry apart, all these 'titles' belong to a single work: the *Liber regularum* of Tyconius. The cataloguer has confused five book titles from the *Liber* with those of distinct works. Thus:

De promissis et lege refers to Bk III [i.e. rule 3] of Tyconius;
De specie et genere refers to Bk IV [i.e. rule 4] of Tyconius;
De temporibus refers to Bk V [i.e. rule 5] of Tyconius;

De recapitulatione refers to Bk VI [i.e. rule 6] of Tyconius;

De diabolo [*et eius corpore*] refers to Bk VII [i.e. rule 7] of Tyconius.

The second entry, *regula Ticonii*, is inaccurate but accords with the form of the incipit to Bk I found in manuscripts used by Burkitt in his edition.[39] Probably what the compiler of the catalogue saw was '*regula Ticonii Ia*', he then missed the display incipit of Bk II, and on finding those of the remaining books of Tyconius' work he imagined them as indicators of separate texts. We can thus be sure that there was a complete copy of the *Liber regularum* in Corbie at that time.

University of Wales Lampeter

---

[39] See p. 1 *in apparatu.*

ST AUGUSTINE'S ABBEY, CANTERBURY, AND THE 'FIRST BOOKS OF THE WHOLE ENGLISH CHURCH'

by RICHARD EMMS

EARLY in the fifteenth century, Thomas of Elmham, who grew up in Norfolk and became a monk of St Augustine's abbey, Canterbury, began to write and illustrate an ambitious history of his monastery.[1] It may be that his interest in history arose from his early years at Elmham, site of the see of East Anglia in late Anglo-Saxon times. This could explain why he became a monk at the oldest monastic establishment in England instead of at the local Benedictine houses, such as Bury St Edmunds, Ely, or Norwich. Clearly he developed his historical interests at St Augustine's with its ancient books and relics, even though, apart from the chapel of St Pancras and St Martin's church nearby, pre-Conquest buildings were no longer to be seen.[2]

At St Augustine's abbey, Thomas became heir to a long and flourishing historical tradition.[3] The writings of Goscelin of St Bertin at the end of the eleventh century and at the beginning of the twelfth provided an essential base from which this tradition developed orally in the community. As they searched their archives and talked about the rights and privileges of their house they reacted strongly against archbishops of Canterbury who would not recognize their claims, and the monks of St Augustine's were almost continually at odds with their neighbours at the cathedral priory. The earliest surviving written expression of the St Augustine's historical tradition is found in the writings of Thomas Sprott in the thirteenth century. His

---

[1] Cambridge, Trinity Hall, MS 1. It was printed by Charles Hardwick with the invented title, *Historia monasterii S. Augustini Cantuariensis*, RS, 8 (1858) [hereafter *Historia*].

[2] An alternative possibility put forward by Rose Graham, *English Ecclesiastical Studies* (1929), 67, is that Elmham was first professed as a Cluniac who was later given papal licence to transfer to the important position of Treasurer of St Augustine's abbey, Canterbury. This would explain why he was collated as Prior of Lenton in 1414, shortly after that becoming Vicar-general of the English Province of the Order of Cluny. An earlier commitment to the Cluniac Order could explain why he left his *magnum opus*, the *Speculum Augustinianum* as he wished to call it, unfinished, moving on to take an active role in national affairs.

[3] For further details and references see my article, 'The historical traditions of St Augustine's Abbey, Canterbury', in Richard Eales and Richard Sharpe, eds, *Canterbury and the Norman Conquest* (1995), 159–68.

chronicle was followed closely, often word for word, by William Thorne writing late in the fourteenth century. It is likely that this tradition inspired Thomas of Elmham to further historical work and that its shortcomings prompted him to produce an improved chronology, the *Chronologia Augustiniensis*. He was, of course, promoting the interests of St Augustine's, even though Archbishop Arundel had, in 1406, finally granted the demands of the abbey for full exemption from episcopal control.[4] Defence of the lands of the abbey and its rights always demanded vigilance, especially as Lollard voices were being raised against church lands. A glance at the one surviving manuscript of the *Speculum Augustinianum*, likely to be Elmham's own work, shows his determination to produce the ultimate chronicle of the history and rights of St Augustine's. It is no surprise that the work remains incomplete, probably because of Elmham's promotion to become Prior of Lenton in Nottinghamshire.

In the second chapter of his work, Thomas of Elmham described the oldest books to be seen at St Augustine's, in the library, in the vestry, and above the altar.[5] These descriptions convey not only an awareness of the historical significance of the volumes as heirlooms of the abbey, but also bring out the sense that the history of the Church in England was encapsulated in books, specifically in books for liturgical use. He called them the 'first fruits of the books of the whole English Church'. First mentioned was what must have been the most magnificent of all: the two-volume *Biblia Gregoriana*. His description of the leaves, 'Some purple, some rose-coloured, which when held up to the light give a wonderful reflection', shows the quality of what must have been a luxury late antique Bible. He was moving on from valuing the book for its associations to appreciating its physical appearance for its own sake, as many bibliophiles do. It is an intriguing mystery whether this notable Bible still exists. According to Humphrey Wanley it was in the hands of English Roman Catholics in 1604, but he was unable to trace it a hundred years later.[6] If it was highly valued by recusants in the reign of King James I, it seems more likely that it was hidden away and lost, rather than destroyed.

It has been suggested that BL, MS Royal I.E.VI, a fragmentary Bible with some purple pages, is a surviving part of the *Biblia*

---

[4] *Historia*, 89, 209–10, and 1–73 for the *Chronologia Augustiniensis*.

[5] Ibid., 96–9; Montague Rhodes James, *The Ancient Libraries of Canterbury and Dover* (Cambridge, 1903), lxiv–lxix, provides an English translation with comments.

[6] *Antiquae literaturae septentrionalis liber alter seu Humphredi Wanleii* (Oxford, 1705), 172–3.

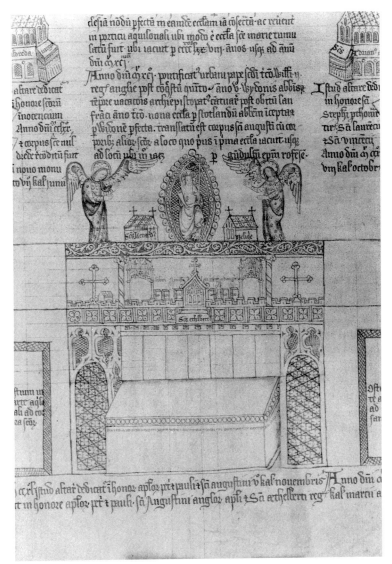

Fig. 1 Thomas of Elmham's drawing of the high altar of St Augustine's abbey, Canterbury, showing the books sent by Pope Gregory to Augustine. Cambridge, Trinity Hall, MS 1, fol. 77r. (Photo: Mildred Budny; by permission of the Master and Fellows of Trinity Hall.)

Gregoriana.[7] However, this is not possible as the Royal Bible became a fragment very early, having been partly dismembered in the thirteenth century. There are reasons to think that this early ninth-century luxury Bible was inspired by the *Biblia Gregoriana* and that its remaining leaves show something of the appearance and decoration of its exemplar. Perhaps too, as Mildred Budny has suggested, traces of the iconography of the *Biblia Gregoriana* can be detected in the illustrations of later Canterbury books such as the Old English Illustrated Hexateuch and the four detached leaves that were formerly in the Eadwine Psalter.[8]

Also in the library of St Augustine's and therefore no longer used for liturgical purposes was the *Psalterium Augustini*. This volume cannot be traced beyond Elmham's time and is not listed in the library catalogue of *c*.1491.[9] We can say little about this book, which may have been either late antique Italian or written at Canterbury in the seventh or eighth centuries. The list of hymns indicates that the manuscript (or its exemplar) was no later than the tenth century.[10] The 'facsimiles' of the forged charters included in Elmham's work show that he observed scripts closely and that he associated uncial with the time of St Augustine.[11] On this basis it is reasonable to conjecture that the *Psalterium Augustini* was written no later than the eighth century. It is interesting to note that this is the only one of the eight books described by Elmham as linked by name to St Augustine, a claim not specifically made for the remaining six on the list (excluding the *Biblia Gregoriana*). It is not impossible that this ancient tradition about the *Psalterium Augustini* was correct.[12]

Thirdly, Elmham mentioned a *Textus Evangeliorum* kept in the

---

[7] Mildred Budny, 'The *Biblia Gregoriana*', in R. Gameson, ed., *St Augustine and the Conversion of England* (Stroud, 1999), 237–84, esp. 237–48.

[8] The Old English Illustrated Hexateuch is now BL, MS Cotton Claudius B.iv; the Eadwine Psalter is now Cambridge, Trinity College, MS R.17.1; the four detached leaves now generally agreed to have belonged to it are New York, Pierpoint Morgan Library, MSS M 724 and M 521; BL, MS Add. 37472(1); and London, Victoria and Albert Museum, MS 661.

[9] The library catalogue is now Dublin, Trinity College, MS D.1.19. A new edition by Dr Bruce Barker-Benfield is eagerly awaited, as that by M.R. James (see n.5) suffers from some inaccurate transcription.

[10] Inge B. Milfull, *The Hymns of the Anglo Saxon Church* (Cambridge, 1996), 3–4.

[11] See Michael Hunter, 'The facsimiles in Thomas Elmham's History of St Augustine's, Canterbury', *The Library*, 5th ser, 28 (1973), 215–20.

[12] It is hoped that Dr Paul Remley's investigations into the prehistory of the Old English Gloss to the hymns of the Vespasian Psalter (BL, MS Cotton Vespasian A.1) will shed further light on the *Psalterium Augustini*.

Fig. 2 Evangelist symbol of St Luke. BL, MS Royal 1.E.VI, fol. 43r
(by permission of the British Library).

vestry. This gospel book was associated with St Mildreth, abbess of Minster-in-Thanet in the early eighth century, rather than with St Augustine himself. A possible candidate for this volume is (what is now called) the Gospels of St Augustine (Cambridge, Corpus Christi College, MS 286).[13] This manuscript, written in Italy in the later sixth century, was definitely at St Augustine's by the early tenth century, when a charter relating to a land-holding was copied into a space.[14] The book lacks the first twenty-two leaves, so it is not possible to check that it contained the ten Eusebian canon tables as described by Thomas of Elmham. Unfortunately, he did not give other details which would either confirm or deny this identification. There is no certainty about the early movements of the Gospels of St Augustine. It is generally assumed that this book did come to England at the time of Augustine, but it could have arrived later, perhaps at the time of Theodore and Hadrian. If so, it is likely that both the cathedral and the abbey had enough service books by 670, and this gospel book could have gone directly to one of the new Kentish foundations, such as Minster-in-Thanet. In the eighth century this double monastery became famous for its production of fine books, as demonstrated by the well-known request from Boniface for a copy of the Petrine Epistles written in gold.[15] This tradition makes plausible the possible association with Minster of the *Codex Aureus*, a luxury gospel book, particularly as its evangelist portrait of Luke has connections with the one in the Gospels of St Augustine.[16] In the ninth century the community at Minster moved to Canterbury in order to be less vulnerable to Viking incursions. In this way the gospel book could have passed to St Augustine's abbey, whilst retaining its Thanet title and the legend concerning a Thanet

---

[13] For details, see Francis Wormald, *The Miniatures in the Gospels of St Augustine* (Cambridge, 1954), reprinted in his *Collected Writings, 1: Studies in Medieval Art from the Sixth to the Twelfth Centuries* (1984), 13–35; Mildred Budny, ed., *Insular, Anglo-Saxon and Early Anglo-Norman Manuscript Art at Corpus Christi College, Cambridge: An Illustrated Catalogue*, 2 vols (Kalamazoo, MI, 1997), 1:1–50, for full description and bibliography; R.G. Gameson, *The Gospels of St Augustine of Canterbury* (forthcoming).

[14] For illustration and comment see my article, 'The early history of Saint Augustine's abbey, Canterbury', in Gameson, *St Augustine and the Conversion*, 417.

[15] *Die Briefe des Heiligen Bonifatius und Lullus*, ed. M. Tangl, *MGH, Epistolae selectae*, 1 (Berlin, 1916), no. 35.

[16] *Codex Aureus* is now Stockholm, Kungliga Bibliotek, MS A.135. The facsimile, *Codex Aureus*, ed. R.G. Gameson, 2 vols, Early English Manuscripts in Facsimile, 28–9 (Copenhagen, 2001–2), will be of great value for the study of this manuscript, but appeared too late for inclusion here.

Fig. 3 Evangelist symbol of St Luke and the beginning of his Gospel. Cambridge, Corpus Christi College, MS 286, fols 128v–9r. (Photo: Mildred Budny; by permission of the Master and Fellows of Corpus Christi College.)

countryman who swore falsely on the book and, as a consequence, lost the sight of his eyes.

The second psalter mentioned by Elmham, with a silver binding depicting the image of Christ and those of the four evangelists, was placed above the altar. There can be little doubt that this volume, without the magnificent covers, survives as the Vespasian Psalter.[17] The preliminary matter in this book coincides almost exactly with Elmham's description of the first eleven folios of his 'other' psalter. Written in the first half of the eighth century and no doubt modelled on a Gregorian book, perhaps in some details on the *Psalterium Augustini*, this psalter clearly displayed its antiquity. But Elmham did not associate it with Augustine himself in the way that he did his first psalter.

Elmham went on to mention a second gospel book, 'to which the ten canons are prefixed, with a prologue beginning "*Prologus canonum*"'. He provided no other details, so making it nearly impossible to identify this book among surviving gospel books or fragments from his description alone. However, a convincing identification of this book has been proposed: the so-called Cambridge-London Gospels (Cambridge, Corpus Christi College, MS 197B, + BL, MS Cotton Otto.C.V, with offsets of the canon tables in BL, MS Royal 7.C.XII).[18] The fact that the Royal volume, with the offsets, belonged to Cardinal Wolsey (d. 1530) suggests that the original gospel book was divided up and probably passed out of the keeping of St Augustine's abbey before its dissolution in 1538. It is significant that each part of the gospel book, Matthew and Mark which passed (eventually) into the hands of Sir Robert Cotton, and Luke and John which came into the keeping of Archbishop Matthew Parker, has an independent attribution to St Augustine himself. Cotton's description, 'Liber quondam Augustini Anglorum apostoli', contains the epithet 'apostolus anglorum' used exclusively at St Augustine's abbey to describe their founder.[19] Parker inscribed his portion, 'Hic liber olim missus a Gregorio papa ad Augustinum archepiscopum'.[20] It is most unlikely that both Cotton and Parker would have independently made up such an attribution;

---

[17] BL, MS Cotton Vespasian A.i. For facsimile and editorial discussion see *The Vespasian Psalter*, ed. D.H. Wright, Early English Manuscripts in Facsimile, 14 (Copenhagen, 1967).

[18] It is greatly to be hoped that the collaborative study of this gospel book and its component parts will be published. Meanwhile, some of the conclusions reached can be found in Budny, *Catalogue*, no. 3.

[19] See Thomas Smith, *Catalogue of the Manuscripts in the Cottonian Library, 1696*, ed. C.G.C. Tite (Woodbridge, 1984), 72.

[20] Cambridge, Corpus Christi College, MS 197B, fol. 1r.

Fig. 4   King David and his musicians. BL, MS Cotton Vespasian.A.I, fol. 30v (by permission of the British Library).

Fig. 5   Evangelist symbol of St John. Cambridge, Corpus Christi College, MS 197B, fol. 1r. (Photo: Mildred Budny; by permission of the Master and Fellows of Corpus Christi College.)

Fig. 6   Evangelist symbol of St Mark. BL, MS Cotton Otho.C.V
(by permission of the British Library).

therefore the tradition of Augustine's ownership must have grown up
in St Augustine's abbey and have been passed on with each part of the
gospel book to its new owner. Once again, we must note that Elmham
himself did not connect this book directly with St Augustine. He may
have seen that its Northumbrian style made it different in important
respects from the *Biblia Gregoriana* and the *Psalterium Augustini*. It is

likely that popular tradition at the abbey made the association which Elmham took for granted.

Elmham mentioned three other books in magnificent bindings kept above the high altar: the Passions of the Apostles, the Passions of the Saints, and Expositions of the Epistles and Gospels from Easter 3 through to Pentecost 4. It is not to be expected that these display volumes would have been entered in the later library catalogue. No doubt they were despoiled when their valuable bindings were removed. There seems to be no evidence of the fate of these books or of successful attempts to identify them with surviving manuscripts.

We may wonder why other ancient books, known to have been in the library of St Augustine's abbey in Elmham's time, were not included in his list. Perhaps the most obvious candidate is the early eighth-century Acts of the Apostles (Oxford, Bodlian Library, MS Selden Supra 30) written in uncial and generally connected with the double monastery at Minster-in-Thanet because of a prayer added by a nun, in which she refers to herself as 'me indignam famulam tuam'. In addition, in another place, 'EADB' has been scratched in dry point below the text; this could refer to Abbess Eadburh.[21] The book is a working copy with minimal illumination and in spite of its ancient script may not have seemed worthy of St Augustine. There is also another possibility. The entry for this book in the library catalogue was added later than the main entries. Perhaps this thin quarto volume, probably at that time disbound, to judge from the darkened front and back pages, had been hidden from view and was added to the catalogue when it came to light after 1500.[22]

How did the perception that these eight books had once belonged to Augustine of Canterbury arise? It is notable that Elmham specifically associated only the *Biblia Gregoriana* and the *Psalterium Augustini* with Augustine himself. One gospel book was associated with St Mildreth; the other five books are not linked with individuals. Was Elmham by using the phrase 'Primitiae librorum totius ecclesiae anglicanae' trying to imply that all eight books should be associated with Augustine? Commentators from Humphrey Wanley onwards have taken this to be the case and indeed Elmham must have been willing to imply this association, even if he did not state it explicitly. It is very likely to have been the accepted view in the community at the time that he was

[21] Bodleian Library, Oxford, MS Selden Supra 30, pp. 47, 70.
[22] James, *Ancient Libraries*, 210.

writing, which he would not have wished to counter. No doubt he approved the labelling of the books above the altar as 'Libri missi a Gregorio ad Augustinum', even if he did not attempt to attach Augustine's name to each of them individually.

There seem to have been two main factors leading to the association of this group of early books with Augustine himself. The first was the cult of St Augustine. The evidence for this cult in the pre-Conquest period is distinctly thin. There can be no doubt that the cult of its sainted founder was always important to the abbey, but before the 1090s was marked neither by translation of his remains nor by a written life of the saint.[23] This situation changed with the magnificent ceremonies of the translation of the remains of Augustine and other early saints into the new Romanesque church in September 1091, and with the production of suitable *vitae* by Goscelin of St Bertin.[24] The cult of St Augustine continued to be important through the Middle Ages even if, in contrast to the cult of St Thomas Becket at the cathedral, it did not gain a large popular following. It ensured that any objects that could, rightly or wrongly, be connected with Augustine acquired special value; as well as books, Elmham mentioned vestments and sacred vessels (the latter had disappeared by the time that he was writing).[25] Even if the cult of St Augustine did not draw the crowds it remained of fundamental importance to the abbey that he founded. This helps to explain why books that could be associated with him were particularly valued and in some cases given magnificent bindings, with a place above the altar.

The second factor associating the books with the saint must be historical tradition at St Augustine's. This tradition was not primarily academic, being fuelled by repeated conflicts with successive archbishops and long-lasting competition with the cathedral priory. It was concerned to protect the rights and lands of the abbey and it is no surprise that in closed communities, which medieval monasteries largely were, such feelings became particularly intense. However, this involvement could lead into something approaching historical investigation for its own sake as the more academic monks, in the later Middle Ages with university training, studied old charters, read in their

---

[23] For discussion see Alan Thacker, 'In Gregory's shadow? The pre-Conquest cult of St Augustine', in Gameson, *St Augustine and the Conversion*, 374–90.

[24] See Richard Sharpe, 'The setting of St Augustine's translation (1091)', in Eales and Sharpe, *Canterbury and the Norman Conquest*, 1–13.

[25] *Historia*, 99–102.

extensive library, and themselves wrote in various ways about their abbey. In some cases, notably that of Thomas of Elmham, the interest of the materials and the questions they raised began to overshadow the original polemical intentions. Thomas moved on from defending the rights of his house to admiring the *Biblia Gregoriana* as a beautiful object in its own right. Similarly he became concerned with details of history in the early Anglo-Saxon period that did not affect the rights of his abbey. He has been described as a fifteenth-century antiquary, in some respects anticipating the better-known antiquaries of Tudor and Stuart England and, of course, Jean Mabillon, the Maurists, and the Bollandists.[26] A consciousness of the antiquity of the Gregorian and Augustinian books evolved in this community with its long historical traditions. Elmham wrote in a monastery which had existed for more than eight hundred years and provided the right conditions for the development of heightened historical consciousness. The appreciation of ancient books for their association with past saints was leading on to appreciation of these books for their antiquity and beauty. If this interpretation is correct, something comparatively unusual was taking place on this venerable site. Elmham may, quite unintentionally, have been breaking new ground in regarding some books as objects to be admired in their own right, even if many of his fellow monks regarded books as objects to be used, taken apart, and recycled, as happened in the case of the Royal Bible, the Cambridge-London Gospels, and even the Gospels of St Augustine.[27] We owe to Elmham the modern idea of attaching particular importance to the Gospels of St Augustine by presenting them ceremonially to each archbishop of Canterbury on his enthronement. This practice, which began with the enthronement of Archbishop Fisher in 1945, shows how we still value the one surviving book that can convincingly be connected with St Augustine of Canterbury.[28]

[26] For the wider background see Antonia Gransden, 'Antiquarian studies in fifteenth-century England', *Antiquaries Journal*, 60 (1980), 75–97; David Knowles, *Great Historical Enterprises* (Edinburgh, 1963), 3–62.

[27] For further discussion, see Mildred Budny, 'The tip of the iceberg: reconstructing lost manuscripts from fragments' (forthcoming).

[28] I am grateful to Mrs Catherine Hall, Archivist of Corpus Christi College, Cambridge, for providing this information and describing how the idea of presenting the Gospels of St Augustine came to be adopted. I should like to thank Dr Michelle Brown and Dr Mildred Budny for reading preliminary drafts of this paper and making helpful comments and suggestions. The final version has also benefited from the discussion following delivery at Lampeter. I wish to thank librarians and staff at the British Library, at Corpus Christi College, Cambridge, and the Bodleian Library, Oxford, for allowing me to see manuscripts discussed here.

THE CAROLINGIAN CHURCH AND THE BOOK

by ROSAMOND McKITTERICK

IN 849, Gottschalk of Orbais was summoned to the Synod of Quierzy. From his own studies of the patristic theologians he had formed views on predestination that had found little favour with the established Church of his day. No text of the proceedings at Quierzy survives but we do have reports from eye-witnesses in the contemporary Annals of St Bertin – interpolated by Archbishop Hincmar of Rheims to Gottschalk's disadvantage – and by Florus the Deacon of Lyons. Hincmar is very scathing on how much Gottschalk's learning had led him astray; he was too erudite for his own good. Hincmar tells us that at the synod, Gottschalk was accused of errant views, condemned, flogged, and compelled to burn the books containing his teachings (*librosque suarum adsertionum*).[1] Florus the Deacon, however, provides crucial extra information. While Hincmar gives the impression that Gottschalk went to Quierzy more or less to be publicly punished, Florus' account suggests that Gottschalk, at least as far as he, Gottschalk, was concerned, went to engage in dispute. He may even have been buoyed up with the hope of convincing his audience of bishops and abbots from the ecclesiastical province of Rheims, including Paschasius Radbertus of Corbie and Gottschalk's own abbot from Orbais (in the diocese of Soissons), that he was justified in his views. Florus tells us that what Gottschalk had to burn were the sections from the Bible and patristic writings that vindicated his opinions and that he had brought with him to the synod.[2] Gottschalk's reference collection

---

[1] *Annales Bertiniani, sa* 849, ed. R. Rau, *Quellen zur karolingischen Reichsgeschichte*, 3 vols, Ausgewählte Quellen zur deutschen Geschichte des Mittelalters, 5–7 (Darmstadt, 1955–60), 2:72–7; tr. J.L. Nelson, *The Annals of St Bertin* (Manchester, 1991), 66–8, and see her argument concerning Hincmar's interpolation into Prudentius of Troyes' text, ibid., 14, supporting, as she points out, views already put forward by scholars in the eighteenth century. Hincmar claims that Gottschalk had gone to Italy, Dalmatia, Noricum, and Pannonia. Compare the *Annals of Fulda*'s account of the earlier decision by bishops in Louis the German's kingdom (also recorded in the *Annals of St Bertin*) (Mainz 848) who sent him to Hincmar, in Rau, *Quellen*, 3:36. On the synods see W. Hartmann, *Die Synoden der Karolingerzeit im Frankenreich und in Italien* (Paderborn, 1989), 226–8.

[2] W. Hartmann, ed., *Die Konzilien der karolingische Teilreiche 843–859*, MGH Concilia III: Concilia aevi Karolini 843–859 (Hanover, 1984), 197: 'Quia inaudito irreligiositatis et crudelitatis exemplo, tandiu ille miserabilis flagris et caedibus trucidatus est, donec (sicut narraverunt nobis, qui praesentes aderant) accenso coram se igni libellum, in quo sententias

---

sounds very much like the dossiers assembled at other councils (not least Nicaea II in 787) compiled from authoritative writings to support views maintained in discussion.[3]

Gottschalk himself was flogged almost to death and condemned to silence. Thus Gottschalk's interpretation, the writings of authority, and his oral expression of his views, were all done away with. More crucially the treatment of Gottschalk's sources by the Frankish bishops and abbots at Quierzy indicates also an attempt to control their meaning, to exert power over those particular texts from the Bible and Church fathers, and to assert the right to exclusive understanding of them. Although the burning of books at Quierzy was a symbolic destruction, for these were only Gottschalk's copies of texts readily available elsewhere, such ritual burning was a grand and violent act of official disavowal of particular texts. Death was inflicted by proxy with destruction and purification by fire. The context, moreover, is obviously one in which knowledge is gained from books. Acts against particular writers to achieve silence and prevent the dissemination of their ideas witness to the notion that the act of writing invoked a power and authority beyond that of the author himself. The Carolingian clergy who sought to destroy Gottschalk's writings and his sources out of fear of their power, therefore, clearly appreciated the potency of the written word.

The Carolingian destruction of Gottschalk's books needs to be set within the context of other instances of this violent activity from Antiquity and the early Middle Ages. Quite apart from the burning of the prophecies of Jeremiah recorded in the Old Testament,[4] and the establishment of book burning as a form of legal punishment towards the end of the reign of the Emperor Augustus,[5] the most dramatic

scripturarum sive sanctorum patrum sibi collegerat quas in concilio offeret, coactus est iam pene emoriens suis manibus in flammam proicire atque incendio concremare; cum omnes retro haeretici verbis et disputationibus victi atque convicti sunt.'

[3] On Nicaea II see Marie-France Auzépy, 'Francfort et Nicée II', in R. Berndt, ed., *Das Frankfurter Konzil von 794*, 2 vols (Mainz, 1997), 1:279–300, at 291. On predestination see J. Marenbon, 'Carolingian thought' in R. McKitterick, ed., *Carolingian Culture: Emulation and Innovation* (Cambridge, 1994), 171–92, esp. 181–3; D. Ganz, 'Theology and the organization of thought', in R. McKitterick, ed., *The New Cambridge Medieval History, II, 700–900* (Cambridge, 1995), 758–85, esp. 767–73; D. Nineham, 'Gottschalk of Orbais: reactionary or precursor of the Reformation?', *JEH*, 40 (1989), 1–18.

[4] Jer. 36.23.

[5] F.H. Cramer, 'Book burning and censorship in ancient Rome. A chapter from the history of freedom of speech', *Journal of the History of Ideas*, 6 (1945), 157–96, and see also Acts 19.19 for the account of the burning of magical texts at Ephesus (incidentally the value of the books there burnt was estimated at 50,000 pieces of silver).

incidents in the early Church are linked with the Donatists,[6] the conflicts between the Arians and the Catholics, and the first recorded proscription of texts in the interests of the Catholic Church. Constantine proscribed the works of Porphyry and Arius in a letter to 'the bishops and people', stating that if any treatise composed by Arius should be discovered it should be consigned to the flames in order not only that his depraved doctrine might be suppressed but also that no memorial of him might by any means be left.[7]

Implicit in such condemnation of texts, whether by pagans of political or Christian works or by Christians of heretical works, is the reaction to a set of texts defined by each group as of central importance to their identity and group self-consciousness. To destroy such a text or set of texts was to attack a community, whether spiritual or actual.[8] Conversely, the creation of a text and its dissemination in book form, owned by, or accessible to, members of a group, reinforced the sense of belonging to that group. By adopting his unorthodox reading of Scripture and the fathers, therefore, Gottschalk put himself on the margin of his own textual community. He undermined not only ecclesiastical authority but also the Frankish clergy's understanding of their place as guarantors of orthodoxy and upholders of the learning and interpretations of the fathers within the Carolingian world. He challenged their own reading of books as familiar to them as they were to him. Like many original theological thinkers before him, he attempted to insert difference into an intellectual history that had been received as a solid interpretative scholarly tradition and which most of his contemporaries wished to preserve.

The reception and content of that tradition is a crucial aspect of any

---

[6] Compare Diocletian's Edict of 297 (or 302) against the Manichees, 'Comparison of the laws of Moses and the Romans', ed. P.E. Huschke, E. Seckel, and B. Kuebler, *Iurisprudentia Anteiustiniana*, 2 vols in 3 (Leipzig, 1908–27), 2:381–3; see A.D. Lee, *Pagans and Christians in Late Antiquity: A Sourcebook* (London, 2000), 66–7, for a succinct placing of the Diocletian decree in context and an English translation. For Diocletian against the Christians in 303, ordering the churches to be razed and the Scriptures destroyed by fire see Eusebius (ed. E. Schwartz and T. Mommsen), *Eusebius Werke 2: Die Kirchengeschichte und die lateinische Übersetzung des Rufinus*, Die griechischen christlichen Schriftsteller des ersten drei Jahrhunderte, 9 (Leipzig, 1903) [hereafter Schwartz and Mommsen], 8.2 (742–3). For general discussion see W. Speyer, *Büchervernichtung und Zensur des Geistes bei Heiden, Juden und Christen* (Stuttgart, 1981), and H. Gamble, *Books and Readers in the Early Church. A History of Early Christian Texts* (New Haven, CT, 1995).

[7] See W. Jacob and R. Hanslik, *Cassiodori-Epiphanii Historia ecclesiastica tripartita*, Corpus Scriptorum Ecclesiasticorum Latinorum, 71 (Vienna, 1952), II.15 (109).

[8] See the stimulating discussions in P. Biller and A. Hudson, eds, *Heresy and literacy, 1000–1530* (Cambridge, 1994).

collective study of the Church and the book. This paper aims to demonstrate that the relationship of the Carolingian Franks to the books in their libraries was not simply that of scholars to a repository of learning. The books in Frankish libraries, as part of a past which the Franks had assimilated to themselves, formed part of the Frankish sense of identity. In other words, the Franks were indeed a textual community in relation to the Bible, as has long been recognized,[9] but they were also a textual community in terms of their intellectual and textual inheritance. The formation and ramifications of this very particular understanding of books and place in history within the Carolingian world and the Carolingian Church, therefore, are explored in what follows.

* * *

Notker Balbulus of St Gallen (*c.* 840–912) is one of many Carolingian writers who gives us a cue. In 885 he sent his *Notatio de viris illustribus*, a guide to the study of the Bible, to Salamo, a newly-made deacon who became in due course Bishop of Constance.[10] Notker's *Notatio* provides the basic essentials and is cast in the form of 'if you would know or understand a certain thing (fact, knowledge of a topic), you should read the following text'. The bibliographical recommendations and comments are organized more by subject than by author. It is not a comprehensive indication of what Notker might have had at his disposal. That is available in the famous ninth-century library catalogue from St Gallen which includes many of his annotations and additions.[11] For the young Salamo, however, Notker provided a concise programme of study, concentrating on Scripture and Christian

---

[9] See, for example, M. de Jong, ed., *The Power of the Word. The Influence of the Bible on Early Medieval Politics*, special issue of *Early Medieval Europe*, 7 (1998); J.J. Contreni, 'Carolingian Biblical Studies', in U.-R. Blumenthal, ed., *Carolingian Essays* (Washington, 1983), 71–98, reprinted in J.J. Contreni, *Carolingian Learning, Masters and Manuscripts* (Aldershot, 1992), ch. V; M.C. Ferrari, *Il 'Liber sanctae crucis' di Rabano Mauro. Testo-immagine-contesto* (Bern, 1999). The fruitful notion of 'textual community' is of course from B. Stock, *The Implications of Literacy; Written Language and Models of Interpretation in the Eleventh and Twelfth Centuries* (Princeton, NJ, 1983). For a recent assessment see also C.F. Briggs, 'Historiographical essay. Literacy, reading, and writing in the medieval West', *Journal of Medieval History*, 26 (2000), 397–420.

[10] E. Rauner, 'Notker des Stammlers "Notatio de illustribus viris"', *Mittellateinisches Jahrbuch*, 21 (1986), 34–69; also E. Dümmler, ed., *Das Formelbuch des Bischofs Salomo III von Konstanz* (Leipzig, 1857, repr. Osnabrück, 1974).

[11] See Susan Rankin, '"Ego itaque Notker scripsi"', *Revue Bénédictine*, 101 (1991), 268–98, and W. von den Steinen, *Notker und seine geistige Welt* (Bern, 1948), 58–63.

learning. He offered many brusque and very personal evaluations of particular works of the fathers and more recent authors such as Bede, Alcuin, and Hraban Maur. His range of examples of types of work and author could be paralleled in most monastic and cathedral schools and libraries throughout the Carolingian empire.[12]

Thus Notker recommended Jerome's works for understanding the Old and New Testaments, and Jerome on Hebrew names. He suggested that Augustine should be consulted for a refutation of the Manichees' views on creation. Ambrose's *Hexameron*, Origen on Leviticus and Exodus, and Augustine's *Quaestiones* on the Heptateuch are also recommended as exegetes of the first books of the Bible. Notker proposed Eugippius on Augustine as a handy collection of extracts and indicated how many people have written about the Psalter. He tells Salamo that Gregory the Great had explained the difficult Book of Job, Jerome the Proverbs of Solomon, and Bede had written on Tobit, Esdras, and Maccabees. On the New Testament Notker said it would be enough if Salamo were to read Jerome and Bede on Matthew and Mark, and Augustine on John. Augustine should be consulted on the Sermon on the Mount. Eugippius' *collectaneum* of the works of Augustine was also recommended. For further reading after these basic essentials, Notker recommended Origen on the Epistle to the Romans; Ambrose on Luke's Gospel and on Paul's Epistles and the Letter to the Hebrews; Jerome on the Epistles to the Galatians, Ephesians, Titus, and Philemon; and Bede on the seven canonical epistles. Then there were the homilies of John Chrysostom, Origen, Augustine, Gregory, Maximin, Leo, and Bede to be read. On Revelation Notker commended the works of Augustine, Jerome, Gregory, Bede, Tychonius, and Primasius. If Saloman wanted glosses, Hraban Maur (the ninth-century archbishop of Mainz) had them on the whole of Scripture.

Study should not be confined to Scripture and biblical exegesis. There were other things Salomon needed to read, such as Augustine's *Confessions* and his other works; Cassian on the monastic life; Isidore of Seville's *Etymologiae*, *Sententiae*, and the *De officiis*. On pastoral care and the ministry Gregory the Great's *Regula pastoralis* was the principal guide. As for letters, Notker recommended the letters of Jerome, for they touched on a huge range of topics Salamo should know about, rather than the many letters of Alcuin (who is described as the *magister*

---

[12] See R. McKitterick, *The Carolingians and the Written Word* (Cambridge, 1989), ch. 5: 'The organization of knowledge', 164–210.

of Charlemagne) to his friends, despite their abundance, *quia tibi puerulo cum supercilio scriptae videntur.* The grammars of Donatus, Nichomachus, Dositheus, and Priscian were worth reading. For poetry there were plenty of Christian works on martyrs and in praise of God, such as Alcimus Avitus, Iuvencus, Sedulius, and the hymns of Ambrose. Salamo should also read the passions of the saints, especially those of the time of Diocletian and the Caesars and the persecution of the Church.[13] Most crucially, Notker recommended the accounts of the fathers in the desert and particular histories of the Church, namely that of Eusebius and the *Historia tripartita* of Cassiodorus compiled from Socrates, Sozomen, and Theodoret. For guidance on the *ecclesiastici scriptores*, Salamo should turn to the work of Jerome and Gennadius.

These allusions to Jerome–Gennadius' *De viris illustribus*, Eusebius–Rufinus' *Historia ecclesiastica*, and Cassiodorus-Epiphanius' *Historia tripartita* need to be investigated further in order to account for their inclusion in Notker's guide. Of these works the first, Jerome's *De viris illustribus*, offers a very particular and original perspective on the early Church, for he constructs what is in effect a history of the Church[14] in terms of the authors who contributed the narratives and theological debates perceived as central to the establishment of the Christian faith and to the Church's development. The work was compiled *c.*392. It contains entries on 135 authors from Peter to Jerome himself. They are largely from the Mediterranean littoral and Asia Minor. Gennadius' continuation was made *c.*480. It comprises ninety-nine authors, including notes on a little group of Gallo-Roman authors and Gennadius himself, probably made shortly thereafter.[15] Gennadius added many Gallic authors, thus incorporating his own region into Christian history and the construction of authority. He appears, moreover, to have had semi-Pelagian leanings as far as his selection of authors and

---

[13] See F. Brunhölzl, *Histoire de la litterature latine du moyen âge. II: De l'époque carolingienne au milieu du onzième siècle* (Turnhout, 1996, rev. edn tr. H. Rochais from German edn of 1992), 39–41, and E. Curtius, *Europäische Literatur und lateinisches Mittelalter* (Bern, 1948), Excursus VI.6, 457–8 (Eng. tr. W. Trask, *European Literature and the Latin Middle Ages* (London, 1953), 463–4).

[14] Brunhölzl, *Histoire*, 41.

[15] Jerome–Gennadius, *De viris illustribus*, ed. E.C. Richardson, *Hieronymus De viris inlustribus*, Texte und Untersuchungen zur Geschichte der altchristlichen Literatur (Leipzig, 1896). See also C.A. Bernouilli, ed., *Hieronymus-Gennadius De viris illustribus* (Freiburg im Breisgau and Leipzig, 1895), who supplies fuller details on some of the manuscripts, though Richardson's text has been agreed by subsequent scholars to be the best.

emphasis is concerned.[16] Isidore of Seville provided a further continuation, with thirty-three authors. Spanish writers predominate but notable Gallo-Roman, African, Greek, and Italian theologians of the sixth century, most obviously Gregory the Great, are included. Indeed, given the very laconic account of Gregory's works in the *Liber pontificalis*, the stress on Gregory's wisdom and relatively detailed note on the *Pastoral Care* and the *Moralia in Iob* are striking.[17]

Jerome stated in his preface, addressed to his friend Dexter, that he wished to provide a Christian and ecclesiastical equivalent for Tranquillus' *De illustribus grammaticis* and *De claris rhetoribus*, and

> do for our writers what Tranquillus did for the illustrious men of letters among the gentiles, namely to set briefly before you all those who have published any memorable writing on the Holy Scriptures from the time of our Lord's passion until the fourteenth year of the Emperor Theodosius. . . . Let those who think the church has no philosophers or orators or men of learning, learn how many and what sort of men founded, built and adorned it, and cease to accuse our faith of such rustic simplicity and recognize their own ignorance.[18]

Jerome uses words such as 'founded', 'built', 'adorned' (*fundare, struxere, adornare*), usual in contexts of discussion of art and architecture, and applies them to the provision of texts.[19] The entries take the form of 'X living in Y in the time of Z (or who died during the reign of Z emperor) wrote the following works'. Sometimes there are additional comments about the quality of the work, aspects of an individual's

---

[16] Bruno Czapla, *Gennadius als Litterarhistoriker. Ein Quellenkritische Untersuchung der Schrift des Gennadius von Marseille. De viris illustribus*, Kirchengeschichtliche Studien 4.1 (Münster, 1898).

[17] C.C. Merino, *El 'De viris illustribus' de Isidoro de Sevilla. Estudio y edicion critica*, Theses et studia philologica Salamanticensia, 12 (Salamanca, 1964). See also Gustav von Dziatowski, *Isidor und Ildefons als Litterarhistoriker. Eine Quellenkritische Untersuchung der Schriften De viris illustribus des Isidor von Sevilla und des Ildefons von Toledo*, Kirchengeschichtliche Studien 4.2 (Münster, 1898); W. Smidt, 'Ein altes Handschriftenfragment der "Viri illustres" Isidors von Sevilla', *Neues Archiv*, 44 (1922), 122–35; H. Knoeppler, 'De viris illustribus and Isidore of Seville', *JThS*, 37 (1936), 16–34. Compare the *Liber Pontificalis*, Life 66, in L. Duchesne, ed., *Le Liber Pontificalis* (Paris, 1886), 312.

[18] Richardson, *De viris inlustribus*, 2; Eng. tr. E.C. Richardson, 'Jerome and Gennadius. Lives of Illustrious Men', in H. Wace and P. Schaff, eds, *A Select Library of Nicene and post-Nicene Fathers of the Christian Church*, 2nd ser., 3 (Oxford and New York, 1892), 359. A new translation is in preparation by Mark Vessey for the Liverpool Translated Texts for Historians series.

[19] Richardson, *De viris inlustribus*, 2.

career, the degree to which a work attributed to a particular author is really by him, or whether the work is strictly orthodox.

On St Peter, for example, he notes that he wrote two Epistles, that some ascribed Mark's Gospel to him, and books called the Acts, Gospel, Preaching, Revelation, and the Judgement of Peter, are rejected as apocryphal. On Mark himself he explains that he was a disciple and interpreter of Peter and wrote a short Gospel at the request of the people of Rome embodying what he had heard Peter tell him. Jerome states that the text was approved by Peter and published to the churches. In the entry for Hegesippus he adds detail about a history in which Hegesippus writes concerning the monuments of the pagans, notably the games celebrated and city built in honour of Antinous, of whom it was said that the Emperor Hadrian was enamoured. On the other hand, Jerome does not go into detail about the works of Tertullian because 'they are well known to most'. He records that Pantaenus was sent to India by Demetrius, Bishop of Alexandria. He found there that Bartholomew, one of the twelve apostles, was preaching according to the Gospel of Matthew and on his return to Alexandria Pantaenus brought the Gospel with him, written in Hebrew characters. He tells us that Pamphilus was so inflamed with the love of sacred literature that he transcribed the works of Origen with his own hand and that these are still in the library at Caesarea. On Ambrose he withholds judgement as he is still alive; Jerome does not wish to appear to praise or blame Ambrose, lest in the former case he be criticized for adulation and in the latter for speaking the truth.[20]

Gennadius follows Jerome's format faithfully, saying of Rufinus, for example, that he had a fine talent for translation and opened up to the Latin-speaking Church the greater part of Greek literature. Of Pelagius Jerome concedes that before he was proclaimed a heretic he wrote books of practical value for students. He does not mention Pelagius' British origins though he does refer, in a later entry, to Bishop Fastidius of the Britons (*episcopus Britannorum*) who wrote books on the Christian life and on virginity. Gennadius devotes a long entry to Orosius, who 'wrote seven books against those enemies of the Christians who say that the decay of the Roman state was caused by the Christian religion'. On the contrary, 'the Roman empire owed to the Christian religion its undeserved continuance and the state of peace which it enjoyed for the

---

[20] Ibid., Jerome, nos I, VIII, XXII, XXXVI, LXXV, CXXIV (6–7, 12, 20–1, 26, 41, 53).

worship of God'. It was, moreover, Orosius who brought the relics of the martyr Stephen to the West.[21]

The *De viris illustribus* of Jerome–Gennadius, therefore, is an apologetic text, but it is also a polemic against paganism with an arsenal of Christian texts hurled at its rivals. It is a new kind of history in its emphasis on Christian men of learning; it insists on their fame and importance because of what they have thought and what they have written rather than on what they have done. The perception of fame and orthodoxy is formed by their writing and their contributions to theological debates. Texts are defined in relation to the orthodox standard. It is essential to register, moreover, that Jerome and Gennadius also provide a clear and progressive chronology and that Jerome is punctilious, even if Gennadius and Isidore are less so, in supplying the geographical details of each author as well. Readers and hearers of *De viris illustribus*, therefore, would form a cumulative Christian geography in their mind's eye, in which the Christian landscape spanned the world from Britain to India, and in which certain places, such as Rome, Antioch, Caesarea, and Alexandria, assumed prominence because of what had been written there and by whom.

Yet such readers and hearers would also have had their imagination and knowledge shaped by the text to which Jerome himself was most indebted in the construction of the *De viris illustribus*, as he acknowledged in his preface, namely Eusebius' *Historia ecclesiastica*. Not the least of Jerome's debts was that Eusebius had enabled him to construct the *De viris illustribus* in chronological order. A greater legacy of Eusebius' *Historia ecclesiastica*, however, was the way it constructed the Christian past in terms of books and authors. It is not necessary here to reiterate at length the enormous influence and importance of Eusebius' account of the development of the Christian Church, and the dramatic transformation in historiographical method he effected in his recourse to letters, edicts, and reports of the events he narrated.[22] He pioneered a new kind of written history, 'Christian historiography' (as against

[21] Ibid., Gennadius, nos XLIII, LVII, XL (77, 81, 76); tr. Richardson, 'Jerome and Gennadius', 393.

[22] See the fine analysis in R.A. Markus, 'Church history and early church historians', *SCH*, 11 (1975), 1–17, and the useful survey in H.W. Attridge and G. Hata, eds, *Eusebius, Christianity and Judaism* (Detroit, 1992), esp. G.F. Chesnut, 'Eusebius, Augustine, Orosius and the later patristic and medieval Christian historians', 687–713. See also G.F. Chesnut, *The First Christian Histories. Eusebius, Socrates, Sozomen, Theodoret and Evagrius* (Paris, 1977/Macon, GA, 1986).

'pagan historiography'),[23] in his concentration on the many important events in the history of the Church; the leaders, heroes and heroines, and martyrs of the earliest Christian communities; on heretics; on the fate of the Jews; and the eventual peace and recovery of the Church.[24] We have all been taught how much Eusebius was used in the early Middle Ages, by Gregory of Tours, by Bede, and by many other writers. That use, however, has not been adequately defined and appears in fact to have been rather limited; the *Historia ecclesiastica* does not seem to have acted as a powerful model for a narrative, even if its particular emphases, overall theme, and methods were influential.[25] The *Chronicle* of Eusebius–Jerome was a far more obvious model for many historical writers of the early Middle Ages.

What needs emphasis, however, is that Eusebius was transmitted to the Latin West in the translation made by Rufinus of Aquileia, the translator of Greek texts so highly praised by Gennadius and thus a preserver of a significant number of patristic texts.[26] He had been educated in Rome and Alexandria, spent time in Jerusalem, and was such a staunch defender of Origen's orthodoxy that he became involved in bitter dispute with Jerome. Rufinus changed the shape of the ecclesiastical history of Eusebius, and thus its emphasis. Eusebius' ten books were extended to eleven. As Rufinus explains in his preface, addressed to Chromatius, Bishop of Aquileia, in 401, and after protesting at his lack of skill in translating:

> I must point out the course I have taken in reference to the tenth book of this work. As it stands in the Greek it has little to do with the process of events. All but a small part of it is taken up with discussions tending to the praise of particular bishops and adds nothing to our knowledge of the facts.[27] I have therefore left out this superfluous matter and whatever in it belonged to genuine

[23] A. Momigliano, 'Pagan and Christian historiography', in idem, *The Conflict between Paganism and Christianity in the Fourth Century* (Oxford, 1963), 79–99.

[24] Schwartz and Mommsen.

[25] See the useful (and qualifying) comments by W. Goffart, *The Narrators of Barbarian History* (Princeton, NJ, 1988), esp. 157, 226, 299.

[26] C. Hammond, 'A product of a fifth-century scriptorium preserving conventions used by Rufinus of Aquileia', *JThS*, ns 29 (1978), 366–91; C. Hammond-Bammell, 'Products of fifth-century scriptoria preserving conventions used by Rufinus of Aquileia', *JThS*, ns 30 (1979), 430–61; eadem, 'Products of fifth-century scriptoria preserving conventions used by Rufinus of Aquileia', *JThS*, ns 35 (1984), 347–93.

[27] This appears to be a reference to the very lengthy panegyric on the rebuilding of the church at Tyre.

history I have added to the ninth book, with which I have made his history close. The tenth and eleventh books I have myself compiled, partly from the traditions of the former generation, partly from facts within my own memory; and these I have added to our previous books, like the two fishes to the loaves. If you bestow your approval and benediction upon them I shall have a sure confidence that they will suffice for the multitude. The work as now completed contains the events from the Ascension of the Saviour to the present time; my own two books those from the days of Constantine when the persecution came to an end, on to the death of the emperor Theodosius.[28]

At the end of the ninth book Rufinus added a note:

Thus far Eusebius has given us the record of the history. As to subsequent events as they have followed up to the present time, as I have found them recorded in the writings of the last generation, or so far as they are covered by my own knowledge, I will add them, obeying as best I may in this point also the commands of our father in God.[29]

The two new books added by Rufinus provide an account of the synod of Nicaea with a version of the creed and a summary of the decrees. Rufinus is eloquent on the subject of the Arian schism. He tells us of the conversion of India and Ethiopia, and of the setback for Christianity under Julian. He provides a remarkably detailed and dramatic description of the temple of Serapis in Alexandria and the downfall of the ancient wooden image of the god. It is Rufinus who relates the story of the finding of the True Cross by Helena, mother of the Emperor Constantine. Rufinus adds also many apparently first-hand details about Egypt, including a fascinating little aside about the flood gauge of the Nile. He gives a brief, somewhat matter of fact, account of the penance of Theodosius. His emphasis is consistently on the precariousness of Christianity, too easily jeopardized by contention among Christians and the impiety of emperors. Chromatius had wished this translation of Eusebius to distract the citizens of Aquileia

---

[28] Schwartz and Mommsen, 952; Eng. tr. W.H. Freemantle, 'Life and Works of Rufinus with Jerome's Apology against Rufinus', in Wace and Schaff, *Select Library of Nicene and Post-Nicene Fathers*, 3:565, and see also P.R. Amidon, *The Church History of Rufinus of Aquileia, Books 10 and 11* (New York and Oxford, 1997).

[29] Schwartz and Mommsen, 957; Eng. tr., Freemantle, 'Life and works', 565.

from the activities of Alaric and his Goths in Italy. Rufinus comments that the purpose of the history was 'that the mind of those who heard it read to them might be held so fast by it that in its eager desire for the knowledge of past events it might to some extent become oblivious of their actual sufferings'. The citizens' 'distraction' took the form of an expansive view of a constantly beleaguered, if nevertheless triumphant, Church. Doubt was cast many years ago on the extent to which these two new books were Rufinus' own work, as distinct from more translating of unacknowledged sources. Certainly one of the prime candidates, Gelasius of Caesarea, produced a Greek continuation of Eusebius.[30] Thelamon, however, has vindicated Rufinus and shown that he was writing according to a clear plan of his own;[31] though he is less assiduous in naming his sources than Eusebius had been. The history of the Church is presented here as a progressive account.

Adding two books and cutting most of Eusebius' tenth book was not, however, all that Rufinus did to Eusebius' text. Rufinus was the very opposite of a literal translator of Books I–X (= I–IX in Rufinus). In the words of Oulton, indeed, Rufinus 'was not a satisfactory or faithful translator. He is continually taking unjustifiable liberties with his original. He omits, abbreviates, expands according to taste; and perhaps his favourite method is to produce a kind of paraphrase which gives the general sense.'[32] The modern attitude to Rufinus has been, indeed, somewhat condemnatory when it has been acknowledged at all, for it has focused on the faithfulness and accuracy of the translation rather than on the nature of the new text thereby created. Even Oulton conceded, however, that many passages of Rufinus' version, such as those on Rome, Jerusalem, Philippi, Egypt, or the Life of Origen and the martyrdom of Paul and Peter, contained additional matter, new facts, or corrected Eusebius. In those places where Rufinus can also be checked against a third source, he is shown to be reliable. Where he is the only authority for a statement, therefore, Oulton concluded that Rufinus was 'not lightly to be set aside'. Where Rufinus introduces material from other sources to augment Eusebius'

---

[30] F. Winkelman, 'Das Problem der Rekonstruktion der Historia ecclesiastica des Gelasius von Caesarea', *Forschungen und Fortschritte*, 38 (1964), 311–14, and idem, *Untersuchung zur Kirchengeschichte des Gelasios von Kaisareia*, Sitzungsberichte der deutschen Akademie der Wissenschaften zu Berlin (Berlin, 1966).

[31] F. Thelamon, *Païens et chrétiens au IVe siècle: l'apport de l'histoire ecclésiastique de Rufin d'Aquilée* (Paris, 1981).

[32] J.E.L. Oulton, 'Rufinus's translation of the church history of Eusebius', *JThS*, 30 (1929), 150–174 at 150.

account, such as on the passions of the martyrs, he supplies additional vivid details. It is in Rufinus, as noted above, that we find the earliest account of the finding of the True Cross by Helena, Constantine's mother, as well as the independent note about the penance of the Emperor Theodosius.

Thorben Christensen took up this more positive assessment in his definitive and posthumously-published study of Rufinus' translation of Eusebius' Books VIII and IX, especially as far as Rufinus' style in comparison with that of Eusebius was concerned.[33] He criticized Eusebius's untidy, repetitious, verbose, long-winded, contradictory, and very varied account. Many of Rufinus' changes analysed by Christensen were in the interests of providing a clear Latin translation. Others were corrections and amplifications from his own knowledge (such as on Origen) All were to spell out the religious and moral teachings of the Christian *historia rerum gestarum*.[34] Christensen regarded Eusebius's Books VIII and IX as a mess, both from a compositional and literary point of view; he considered Rufinus' version to be a distinct improvement. Further, Rufinus merits attention precisely because he offers an independent presentation of the development of the Christian Church for Latin readers. Rufinus, in short, should be regarded as an interpreter and editor of Eusebius.

If we focus for the moment on changes, these are most striking in Rufinus' theological adjustments to make any theologically dubious portions of Eusebius more orthodox. Oulton suggested that this is what motivated Rufinus to omit the panegyric on the rebuilding of the church at Tyre in the original Book X. Oulton suggested that the panegyric could be read as indicating that Eusebius was inclined towards Arianism. Further, when Eusebius discussed the canon of Scripture, Rufinus slightly adjusted the definition of what is accepted in the New Testament, apparently in order to take account of the situation in his own day.[35] Thus he modified Eusebius' rejection of James and expanded the degree to which other texts, such as Jude or II Peter, are accepted. He rescued Revelation from the contradictory comments Eusebius had made about it as both accepted and spurious,

---

[33] T. Christensen, *Rufinus of Aquileia and the Historia Ecclesiastica Lib. VIII–IX, of Eusebius*, Historisk-filosofiske Meddelelser, 58 (Copenhagen, 1989). See also the summary of his conclusions in idem, 'Rufinus of Aquileia and the Historia Ecclesiastica, lib. VIII–IX, of Eusebius', *Studia Theologica*, 34 (1980), 129–52.

[34] Christensen, *Rufinus of Aquileia*, 334.

[35] Schwartz and Mommsen, II.23 (174–3); see Oulton, 'Rufinus's translation', 156–9.

and classed it simply as disputed.[36] Of the Epistle to the Hebrews Eusebius wrote 'some authorities have rejected the Epistle to the Hebrews pointing out that the Roman church denies it is the work of Paul'. Rufinus is more emphatic: 'Hebrews even now among the Latins is not thought to be the Apostle Paul's.'[37]

What Oulton, Thelamon, and Christensen have all emphasised, therefore, is that Rufinus' extended eleven books, together with his treatment of the original, mean that the Latin version of Eusebius known and exerting an influence in the West was very different from the Greek Eusebius. Quite apart from its extension of the story to include much of the fourth century, it was doctrinally more orthodox, its definition of the New Testament canon is more precise, and the emperors (especially in Books X and XI), play a more prominent role.

In another fundamental respect, however, Rufinus faithfully transmits the emphasis of his original.[38] This is particularly the case in his translation of the early Books, I–VII. In Books VIII and IX, as already mentioned, Eusebius had stressed his own contemporary knowledge and memory as well as his recourse to records. Rufinus preserves this and follows suit in Books X and XI. What both Eusebius and Rufinus highlight in Books I–VII, however, is the accretion of Christian writings and authoritative texts, and the definition of the scriptural canon. This can be illustrated with some examples, coupled with the further observation that Rufinus appears to transmit Eusebius without any major paraphrasing or omissions in these sections, apart from the adjustments already mentioned.

The scriptural canon of both the Old and New Testaments is defined with deference to Irenaeus.[39] There is discussion of the twenty-two books of the Hebrew Old Testament canon. In Book III, as already mentioned, Rufinus retains Eusebius' discussion of the Apostolic letters and whether they can be accepted or are still disputed, albeit somewhat modified. Rufinus also provides, incidentally, a far fuller and clearer account of the *Hexapla* of Origen; he had

---

[36] Schwartz and Mommsen, III.25 (250–1).

[37] Ibid., III.3 (190–1); and see Oulton, 'Rufinus's translation', 157.

[38] The attitude towards the Jews of both Eusebius and Rufinus, moreover, would merit further study. Compare Bede's commentary on the Canticle of Habakkuk and the observations on the salvation history of Jew and Gentile in S. Connolly, *Bede on Tobit and on the Canticle of Habakkuk* (Dublin, 1997), 18–37.

[39] Schwartz and Mommsen, V.8 (443–4).

obviously seen a manuscript, for he describes its layout in detail.[40] When sources are quoted, an account is given of that particular author and his works. Protagonists are characterized in terms of their contribution to the patristic corpus. There are lengthy lists provided in Books I–VII of many authors and their works, such as Philo in Book II, Clement of Rome, Josephus, Ignatius, Papias, Polycarp, Irenaeus and his contemporaries, Justin Martyr, Ambrose, Hegesippus, Dionysus of Corinth, Philip, Apollinaris, Melito, Musanus, Modestus, Tatian, Tertullian, Origen, and many more. For his part Rufinus adds, in Books X and XI, accounts of the writings of Basil the Great and Gregory Nazianzus.

Authors, therefore, are cited as support for the information offered. More crucially these sections set up yet another writer and thinker as a pillar of the Church. In all cases, moreover, there is precise attention to time and place so that, as in Jerome–Gennadius, a Christian intellectual geography is created alongside an emphasis on sacred places and delineation of the Holy Land.[41] Eusebius' aim was faithfully preserved and extended by Rufinus. Like Eusebius, who said he would discuss the men of each generation who 'by preaching or writing were ambassadors of the divine word', Rufinus' aim was to write about those men 'seu scribendo seu docendo verbum dei nobiliter adstruxere'.[42]

This extraordinary attention to authors has been feebly characterized in the past as 'Eusebius' synthesis of intellectual currents existing in the church',[43] as Eusebius giving us a 'handy definition of the Old and New Testament canons',[44] or Eusebius' intention 'to create a church history that was a literary history at the same time'.[45] Certainly Eusebius and Rufinus do all these things, but such comments reflect a failure to read Eusebius–Rufinus' history in its contemporary, let alone its early medieval, context, and thereby seriously underestimate this crucial aspect of the work. To concentrate only on the information Eusebius and Rufinus provide for modern historians making inventories of early Christian texts is to miss the point. What the

---

[40] Ibid., VI.16 (555).

[41] R. Wilken, 'Eusebius and the Christian holy land', in Attridge and Hata, *Eusebius, Christianity and Judaism*, 736–60. See also R.L. Wilken, *The Land called Holy: Palestine in Christian History and Thought* (New Haven, CT, and London, 1992).

[42] Schwartz and Mommsen, 7.

[43] M.E. Hardwick, *Josephus as an Historical Source in Patristic Literature* (Atlanta, GA, 1989), esp. 114.

[44] R.M. Grant, *Eusebius as Church Historian* (Oxford, 1980), 126–41.

[45] Ibid., 66.

ecclesiastical history of Eusebius–Rufinus does is offer a very particular presentation of the past and of the history of the Church. The history of Christianity is presented as the history of written authority, of the formation of the scriptural canon and of its essential continuation by the fathers of the Church in their writings. The sequence of Christian writers, teachers, and preachers, and the scriptural canon, as Robert Markus observed twenty-five years ago, are 'part of the church's self-identity'.[46] The whole method of exposition within their narrative framework is designed to reinforce the perception that individuals and texts form the past and that it is only with reference to these texts that the Church can be understood. It is in this respect that Eusebius and Rufinus alike are truly revolutionary. It is this aspect of Eusebius–Rufinus' work that is of far more importance for the Christians of the early Middle Ages even than the work's philosophy of history as continuous progress.

Eusebius–Rufinus, furthermore, is substantially reinforced, not only by Jerome–Gennadius, but also by another immensely popular and influential ecclesiastical history of the early Church, namely the Latin *Historia tripartita* of Epiphanius translated from three Greek ecclesiastical histories by Socrates, Sozomen, and Theodoret[47] (and also making use of a Greek compilation of the same three texts that had been made by 'Theodorus Lector').[48] Despite the text's importance and interest, modern study of it has been almost solely confined to analyses of the translation methods, and particularly the errors, of Epiphanius in rendering the original Greek into Latin from the syntactical and lexical point of view.[49] The work of Epiphanius was initiated and encouraged by Cassiodorus and described by Cassiodorus himself in his *Institutiones* as part of a more general enterprise at sixth-century

---

[46] Markus, 'Church history', 5.

[47] Jacob and Hanslik, *Cassiodori-Epiphanii*.

[48] J. Bidez, *La Tradition manuscrite de Sozomène et la Tripartite de Théodore le lecteur*, Texte und Untersuchungen zur Geschichte der altchristlichen Literatur, 32 (Leipzig, 1908); and see also Theodoret, *Kirchengeschichte*, ed. Léon Parmentier, rev. F. Scheidweiler, Die griechischen christlichen Schriftsteller, 44 (Berlin, 1954), and J. Bidez, B. Grillet, G. Sabbah, and A.-J. Festugière, *Sozomène Histoire ecclésiastique*, Sources Chrétiennes, 306 (Paris, 1983).

[49] F. Weisengruber, *Epiphanius Scholasticus als Übersetzer zu Cassiodorus-Epiphanius Historia ecclesiastica tripartita*, Österreichische Akademie der Wissenschaften, phil.-hist. Klasse, Sitzungsberichte, 283, = Veröffentlichungen der Kommission zur Herausgabe des Corpus der lateinischen Kirchenväter, ed. R. Hanslik, Heft 5 (Vienna, 1972), and Sven Lundström, *Übersetzungs technische Untersuchungen auf dem Gebiete der christlichen Latinität* (Lund, 1955).

Vivarium in central Italy to translate essential texts from Greek into Latin.[50] Theodoret, Socrates, and Sozomen had each certainly regarded himself as a continuator of Eusebius. In some respects the *Historia tripartita* covers the same ground as the additional Books X and XI of Rufinus, though for the most part it provides complementary material for the overlapping years of the fourth century, and of course new material up to the middle of the fifth century. Certainly the *Historia tripartita* provides a dramatic presentation of the Arian conflict, much of which is particularly indebted to Theodoret's impassioned account of Constantine and Constantine's successors' conflicts with the Arians. It is in the *Historia tripartita*, moreover, that we find the account of the burning of the works of Arius recorded by Socrates,[51] of the distribution of copies of Scripture by Constantine,[52] of the concern of the Roman emperor for the Christians of Persia,[53] of the discussions and attendance at the Council of Serdica,[54] and of the dispute between the Emperor Constantius and Liberius, Bishop of Rome, about the condemnation of Athanasius which is presented in dialogue form with interjections by Eusebius the eunuch.[55] The dispute ended with Liberius going into exile after having refused all offers of money to pay his travelling expenses from the Emperor, the Empress, and the eunuch Eusebius. In the *Historia tripartita* is also to be found the account of how Julian emulated Christian practices in promoting his new paganism,[56] a description of Gothic movements in Thrace,[57] the story of the sack of Rome by Alaric,[58] and details of the stoning to death of Hypatia.[59]

The vividness of the narrative, however, does not detract from the maintenance of the emphasis of Eusebius–Rufinus, namely, on the writers who were the pillars of the Church, on the definition of authority, and on the great controversies and discussion about the faith and the Trinity. That these concerns became a particular focus of writers and thinkers in the fifth century is also reflected in Gennadius'

---

[50] Cassiodorus, *Institutiones*, ed. R.A.R. Mynors (Oxford, 1937), XVII.1 (56).
[51] Jacob and Hanslik, *Cassiodori-Epiphani*, II.15 (108–9).
[52] Ibid., I.16 (109–10).
[53] Ibid., III.3 (138–9).
[54] Ibid., IV.24 (179–91); compare V.45 (294–5).
[55] Ibid. V.17 (237–41).
[56] Ibid. VI.29 (345–8).
[57] Ibid., VIII.13 (485–91).
[58] Ibid., XI.9 (638–9).
[59] Ibid., XI.12 (643–5).

greater preoccupation with the documenting of contributors to christological debates. Arianism remained a major issue.[60]

Jerome–Gennadius, Eusebius–Rufinus, and the *Historia tripartita*, therefore, together comprise a distinctive presentation of the history of the Christian Church. Symbolic resonance and historical detail go hand in hand. The close association and essential continuation of Scripture within the chronological framework of the history of the Church presented the development of the Church as a textual history. The histories of the Church written from the fourth century onwards provided both framework and context for a past and an identity built on texts.

*   *   *

That the Carolingian church understood the significance of these histories and the texts and authors so closely interwoven into their narratives is amply indicated by the evidence of the library catalogues and the production and the dissemination of manuscripts in the Frankish realms in the later eighth and the ninth century. This is more than a matter of the reception of particular texts and the evidence that they were read, though these are also of great importance. A striking instance of the way both Eusebius–Rufinus and the *Historia tripartita* could be drawn on by readers, scribes, and artists, is the context they provided for the understanding of the development of canon law. In the Vercelli canon law collection of the second quarter of the ninth century, for example (Vercelli, Biblioteca capitolare, Cod. CLXV),[61] an artist in northern Italy provided a vivid portrayal on fol. 2v of the burning of the Arian books under Constantine. This, as noted earlier, was also recorded by the Greek church historian Socrates in his ecclesiastical history, and was excerpted and translated in the Latin *Historia tripartita* of Cassiodorus-Epiphanius. Fol. 2r of the same canon law collection illustrates the finding of the True Cross.[62] The only

---

[60] Ibid. VIII.13 (488–9) gives the hostile account of the account of the conversion of the Goths by Ulfilas.

[61] See the discussion by K. Bierbrauer, 'Konzilsdarstellungen der Karolingerzeit', in Berndt, *Das Frankfurter Konzil von 794*, 2:751–65, at 759–65, who cites J. Straubinger, *Die Kreuzauffindungslegende* (Paderborn, 1912), 66–76, as her source for the information that the story derives solely from a fifth-century Syriac source. I have been unable to consult Straubinger. See also C. Walter, 'Les Dessins carolingiens dans un manuscrit de Verceil', *Cahiers archéologiques*, 18 (1968), 99–107.

[62] Both illustrations are reproduced in J. Hubert, J. Porcher, and W. Vollbach, *Europe in the Dark Ages* (1969), 142–3.

older representation of the scene known to Bierbrauer is in the
Sacramentary of Gellone (BN, MS lat. 12048, fol. 76v), written in the
diocese of Meaux at the end of the eighth century, while there is a full
picture cycle of the legend in Munich, Bayerische Staatsbibliothek
22053, produced c.814.[63] All these would suggest that it is the
Carolingian artists responding to a written story of the discovery of
the Cross who created these pictures, though there are significant
differences between Rufinus' version and that illustrated in these
pictures.[64]

There is more at stake, however, than documenting whether or not
the Franks in the Carolingian period knew Jerome–Gennadius,
Eusebius–Rufinus, and the *Historia tripartita*. In order to demonstrate
this we must turn to the evidence of library catalogues and manuscript
dissemination and its implications for our understanding of the
Carolingian Church and the book.

Most of the extant library catalogues and book lists from the
Carolingian period record the presence in their libraries of Jerome–
Gennadius, Eusebius–Rufinus, or Epiphanius-Cassiodorus. In the principal ninth-century catalogue of the library of the Rhineland monastery
of Lorsch (BAV, MS pal. lat. 1877, fol. 3r-v), for example, there is a small
group of books listed after the notes of various volumes of Maccabees,
Acts, the seven canonical epistles, and letters of St Paul.[65] The list
includes the *Historia ecclesiastica* of Eusebius, eleven books of the *Historia*
of Josephus (that is, the *Antiquities*, a Greek text also translated into
Latin in the enterprise at Vivarium initiated by Cassiodorus),[66] the
history by 'Isyppi' in five books (which is presumably a reference to the
Latin version of Josephus' *Jewish War* made by Hegesippus and notable
for its account of the fall of Jerusalem), the *historia* of Orosius (namely

[63] This is the famous *Wessobrunner Gebet* manuscript: see K. Bierbrauer, *Die vorkar-
olingischen und karolingischen Handschriften der Bayerischen Staatsbibliothek. Katalog der
illuminierten Handschriften der Bayerischen Staatsbibliothek*, 2 vols (Wiesbaden, 1990), 1, no.
155 (83–4) and 2, pl. 319–36.
[64] For a fuller discussion of these manuscripts and their implications see my 'Perceptions
of the history of the church in the early middle ages: the role of texts', in M. Mostert and
M. Hagemann, eds, *Reading Images and Texts. Medieval Images and Texts as Forms of
Communication*, Utrecht Studies in Medieval Literacy, forthcoming.
[65] B. Bischoff, *Lorsch im Spiegel seiner Handschriften*, Münchener Beiträge zur Mediävistik
und Renaissance-Forschung, Beiheft (Munich, 1974), Tafel 3 and pp. 13–15.
[66] Mynors, *Institutiones*, c.XVII.1 (55). Eusebius also made copious use of Josephus, but the
reading of Josephus in the early Middle Ages must await another occasion: see, for example,
Hardwick, *Josephus*, and H. Schreckenberg, ed., *Jewish Historiography and Iconography in Early
and Medieval Christianity* (Assen and Minneapolis, MN, 1992).

Orosius' *Seven Books of History against the Pagans*, written *c.*417), and the *Chronicle* of Eusebius–Jerome and Bede. The *Chronicle* of Eusebius in Jerome's Latin translation ran from Abraham to 325 and was continued by Jerome and adapted by others subsequently, not least Bede who drew on it for the world chronicle in chapter 66 of his *De temporum ratione*.[67] This *Chronicle* of Eusebius–Jerome was the major source for the chronology of the early Church and particularly important for the events of the third and fourth centuries.

The Lorsch list continues on the top of the next page with the *Tripartita historia* in twelve books by Socrates, Sozomen, and Theodoret in one volume, the *Liber pontificalis*, the pseudo-Clementine *Recognitiones*, Gregory of Tours' *Histories*, Jordanes' *Historia Romana*, Daretus Phyrgius on the history of Troy, Aethicus Ister's *Cosmography*, an epitome of Livy, Quintus Julius Hilarion on the origins of the world up to the resurrection of Christ, Hydatius' chronicle from Theodosius to the reign of Justinian, Solinus, and Josephus' *Antiquities*, books 12–19. Lorsch also owned Jerome–Gennadius, *De viris illustribus*.[68]

The juxtaposition of the history books immediately after portions of the New Testament in the Lorsch catalogue is suggestive. In other catalogues the history books are sometimes listed together in groups, most commonly after the section on Jerome, or more rarely listed separately under different authors. They are certainly, therefore, seen for the most part as a genre of texts which belong together regardless of author. The Lorsch catalogue, however, makes explicit the essential continuation of Scripture and New Testament authors into the writings of the early fathers of the Church as documented in the early histories of the Church, especially Eusebius–Rufinus and the *Historia tripartita*.

No other Carolingian library can quite match Lorsch's recorded wealth in history books, but Eusebius and the *Historia tripartita* and often Jerome–Gennadius as well were also, to cite only a few instances, at St Germer-de-Fly,[69] Würzburg (where Eusebius is attributed to

---

[67] See C.W. Jones, ed., *Bedae Opera didascalica*, 2, CChr.SL, 123B (Turnhout, 1977), with ch. 66 supplied from T. Mommsen, *Chronica minora*, 3, *MGH Auctores Antiquissimorum*, 13 (Berlin, 1898), 247–321, and the excellent translation and commentary provided by F. Wallis, *Bede: The Reckoning of Time* (Liverpool, 1999), 157–237, 353–66.

[68] In the muddled edition of G. Becker, *Catalogi biblothecarum antiqui* (Bonn, 1886), 83–4. Jerome–Gennadius is listed at 95. [See also n.111 below.]

[69] *Gesta Fontanellensis coenobii*, 13.6, ed. P. Pradié, *Chronique des Abbés de Fontenelle (Saint-Wandrille)* (Paris, 1999), 172. I wrongly located Flaviacum (St Germer) at Flavigny in my *Carolingians and the Written Word*, 175.

Jerome and which also owned Jerome–Gennadius),[70] Bobbio,[71] St Riquier,[72] Murbach (which also owned Jerome–Gennadius and many of the other history books recorded at Lorsch listed together under the heading *De historiis*),[73] St Gallen (which attributed the Latin *Historia tripartita* to Cassiodorus and also owned Jerome–Gennadius),[74] and Reichenau (which also had Jerome–Gennadius).[75] The *Historia tripartita* is listed in Wulfad of Bourges's personal collection of books.[76]

The manuscript evidence allows us to extend the range of centres holding these texts still further. Of the 114 surviving manuscripts of Jerome–Gennadius collated by Richardson, nineteen date from the ninth and tenth centuries or earlier and are distributed among a sufficient number of different types defined according to variants to indicate a wide dissemination.[77] The two oldest manuscripts of Jerome–Gennadius, for example, are from the seventh century and are the top scripts of palimpsests. BAV, MS reg. lat. 2077, is Italian, possibly from Rome (the underlying text is Cicero's *In Verrem*), and BN, MS lat 12161, is from Corbie (the underlying texts include the Visigothic ruler Euric's law code).[78] There are three later eighth-century manuscripts from northern Italy and Francia, and in the ninth century the text was often incorporated by Frankish scholars into what I have classified as bibliographical handbooks,[79] and was

---

[70] E.A. Lowe, 'An eighth-century list of books in a Bodleian manuscript from Würzburg and its probable relation to the Laudian Acts', *Speculum*, 3 (1928), 3–15, reprinted in E.A. Lowe (ed. L. Bieler), *Palaeographical Papers 1907–1965*, 2 vols (Oxford, 1972), 1:239–50 and pl. 27–30. See B. Bischoff and J. Hofmann, *Libri sancti Kyliani. Die Würzburger Schreibschule und die Dombibliothek im VIII. und IX. Jahrhundert* (Würzburg, 1952), 143, 146.

[71] Becker, *Catalogi bibliothecarum antiqui*, 65, but see the discussion by P. Collura, *La precarolina e la carolina a Bobbio*, Fontes Ambrosiani, 22 (Milan, 1943).

[72] Hariulf (ed. F. Lot), *Chronique de l'abbaye de Saint-Riquier Ve siècle-1104* (Paris, 1894), 89, 93.

[73] W. Milde, *Der Bibliothekskatalog des Klosters Murbach aus dem 9. Jht. Ausgabe und Untersuchung von Beziehung zu Cassiodors Institutiones*, Beihefte zum Euphorion, Zeitschrift für Literaturgeschichte, 4 (1968), 37, 43, 44, and the section *De historiis*, 47.

[74] P. Lehmann, *Mittelalterliche Bibliothekskataloge Deutschlands und der Schweiz. 1: Die Bistümer Konstanz und Chur* (Munich, 1918), 73, 76.

[75] Ibid., 246, 265. For a fuller list of early medieval library catalogues containing these works see A. Siegmund, *Die Überlieferung der griechischen christlichen Literatur*, Abhandlungen der Bayerischen Benediktiner Akademie, 5 (Munich, 1949), 56–7, 73–6.

[76] M. Cappuyns, 'Les *bibli Wulfadi* et Jean Scot Erigène', *Recherches de théologie ancienne et médiévale*, 33 (1966), 137–9.

[77] Richardson, *De viris inlustribus*, IX–XXXV.

[78] E.A. Lowe, *Codices Latini Antiquiores*, 11 vols (Oxford, 1934–66) [hereafter *CLA*], 1, no. 114; 5, no. 624.

[79] McKitterick, *Carolingians and the Written Word*, 206–9.

used as a guide for acquisitions for libraries: Frankish copies come from such centres as Weissenburg, Rheims, and St Gallen. I have commented elsewhere on the historical ordering of the *De viris illustribus* and how it provided a definition of a canon of knowledge which was of fundamental importance for the construction of libraries and the production of books in the Carolingian period,[80] quite apart from its distinctive perception of history as stressed in this paper. The production of Jerome–Gennadius and the clear evidence of its guidance being followed are indicative of the influence it had.

The earliest manuscripts containing the additional sections by Isidore of Seville survive in manuscripts from both Francia and the Christian kingdoms of northern Spain. Merino postulates an Irish episode in the transmission of Isidore's section, on the basis of a handful of 'Irish' symptoms (the doubled consonants in orthography and scribal confusion of 'r' and 'n') in the earliest surviving manuscript of Isidore's text, Montpellier, École de Médécine, H406. This is a manuscript of the early ninth century but is possibly based on a late eighth-century exemplar.[81] In this codex, as in Hereford Cathedral Library, O.3.ii, a late ninth-century codex from Rheims, Isidore is included with Jerome–Gennadius as part of a bibliographical hand-book. Other Frankish copies, such as Bern, Burgerbibliothek 289, which is now part of a composite manuscript that may have originated in a different context;[82] the late ninth- or early tenth-century fragments from Werden in Wetzlar, Staatsarchiv 46;[83] BN, MS lat. 1791, a composite manuscript of which the Isidore text comprises the tenth-century Frankish portion; or the now-lost copy from St Gallen mentioned in the ninth-century St Gallen library catalogue, may have been free standing. What the complex *stemma codicum* suggested by Merino establishes is a very wide distribution of Jerome–Gennadius–Isidore in Francia and northern Spain in the ninth and tenth centuries.[84]

---

[80] Ibid., 165–209, esp. 200–5.

[81] The colophon added at the end of the Isidore section suggests this exemplar was written between 768 and 771, as it refers to the joint rule of Charles and Carloman after the death of Pippin: Merino, *El 'De viris illustribus'*, 126, and see McKitterick, *Carolingians and the Written Word*, 201–3.

[82] B. Bischoff, *Katalog der festländischen Handschriften des neunten Jahrhunderts (mit Ausnahme der wisigotischen), I: Aachen-Lambach* (Wiesbaden, 1998), no. 570 (121).

[83] Smidt, 'Ein altes Handschriftenfragment', 125–35.

[84] Merino, *El 'De viris illustribus'*, 87–128.

The manuscript survival of Eusebius–Rufinus and the *Historia tripartita* is similarly significant. Among approximately forty-three extant manuscripts from before the eleventh century of the former is a copy from Chelles.[85] Chelles was the convent presided over by Charlemagne's sister Gisela, and this book is one of a group that Bischoff associated with texts copied for the archbishop of Cologne by the nuns of Chelles.[86] Other copies come from Alemannia (later Freising), north-east France, the Loire region, Constance, northern Italy, Franconia, Rhaetia, and St Amand, as well as Lorsch itself.[87] The Lorsch manuscript (BAV, MS lat. 822), no doubt to be identified with the volume listed in the Lorsch catalogue, is to be dated to the late eighth or early ninth century, and is written in an early Caroline minuscule.[88] None of these books is illustrated, though many have markedly elaborate layouts of capitals, uncials, headings, chapter titles, incipits, and the like. The opening of the Copenhagen Eusebius written at St Amand in the first quarter of the ninth century is a case in point.[89] It should be noted, moreover, that no early medieval history books of any kind are illustrated, apart from the Bible itself and the historical illustrations added to the Vercelli canon law manuscript mentioned above.

The manuscripts of the *Historia tripartita* are striking in their layout, but also lack illustrations. The earliest witness to the *Historia tripartita* is St Petersburg, Saltykov-Schedrin Public Library, MS F.v.I, no. 11.[90] It is written in the curious script known as 'a–b' once located to Corbie, still associated with Corbie, but usually now attributed to a group of nuns,

[85] BN, MS lat. 18282 (*CLA*, 5, no. 674), but compare BN, MS lat. 10399 fol. 4,5 + BN, MS lat. 10400, fol. 27 (*CLA*, 5, no. 594, a different redaction of Eusebius–Rufinus), and R. McKitterick, 'Nuns' scriptoria in England and Francia in the eighth century', *Francia*, 19/i (1992), 1–36, at 6–11, reprinted in eadem, *Scribes and Learning in the Frankish Kingdoms, 6th-9th Centuries* (Aldershot, 1994), ch. VII.

[86] See B. Bischoff, 'Die Kölner Nonnenhandschriften und das Skriptorium von Chelles', in idem, *Mittelalterliche Studien*, 3 (Stuttgart, 1966), 16–34.

[87] Siegmund, *Überlieferung*, 78–80, greatly augments the list of four manuscripts provided by Schwartz and Mommsen in their edition.

[88] Bischoff, *Lorsch*, 23 and pl. VI.

[89] Copenhagen, Kongelige Bibliotek, MS Gl. Kgl. S.163, illustrated in K. van der Horst, W. Noel, and W.C.M. Wüstefeld, *The Utrecht Psalter in Medieval Art* (Utrecht, 1996), 11. *Pace* Bischoff, *Katalog der festländischen Handschriften*, no. 1981 (411), I consider this manuscript to have been written at St Amand rather than Saint-Germain-des-Prés, but possibly used at the latter.

[90] O.A. Dobias-Rozdestvenskaja and W.W. Bakhtine, *Les anciens manuscrits latins de la Bibliothèque publique Saltykov-Scedrin de Leningrad, VIIIe-début IX siècle* (Paris, 1991), no. 39 (98–101) and pl. VII.

perhaps at Soissons.[91] This particular copy is said, by an eleventh-century annotator, to have been made for Adalhard of Corbie, Charlemagne's cousin. Some years ago, however, I suggested that the 'a-b' script should be seen as a continuation of the 'b-minuscule' type developed in the eighth century at Jouarre and Chelles, the Carolingian royal convent par excellence.[92] Other ninth-century copies of the *Historia tripartita* are from Orleans, Constance, Regensburg, and Tours. There are distinct families of the *Historia tripartita* text associated with northern France, northern Italy, and southern Germany, and in a later distribution pattern southern France and Catalonia and western Germany.[93] This is a sure indication of an early and exceptionally wide dissemination of this text.

There are two points that need to be stressed about the distribution and survival patterns of both Eusebius–Rufinus and the *Historia tripartita*. The first is that the earliest witnesses to these texts, apart from some sixth-century fragments in half-uncial script of a copy of Eusebius–Rufinus,[94] are from the late eighth and early ninth centuries. Secondly, again with the probable exception of the sixth-century fragments of Eusebius–Rufinus, they are Frankish and more particularly from centres that can be closely associated with the royal court. Given that Lorsch, Corbie, and Chelles had close links with the court, and that some of the books of Chelles can be linked with production of books for the archbishops of Cologne,[95] it is possible that this astonishing concentration of early Church history manuscripts and their remarkably wide dissemination could reflect the deliberate provision of this book at an early stage in the Carolingian reform movement. They are part, moreover, of a wider provision of history books more generally

---

[91] See D. Ganz, *Corbie in the Carolingian Renaissance*, Beihefte der Francia, 20 (Sigmaringen, 1990), 48–56.

[92] McKitterick, 'Nuns' scriptoria', 18–20.

[93] See W. Jacob, *Die Handschriftliche Überlieferung der sogenannten Historia tripartita des Epiphanius Cassiodor*, Texte und Untersuchungen, 59 (Berlin, 1954). Jacob was reported as missing, presumed dead, on 1 Feb. 1942, though the proofs of his edition had been ready in 1939. His work was therefore apparently done in ignorance of Siegmund, *Überlieferung*, also completed in 1939 under the supervision of Paul Lehmann. Siegmund was able to offer more precise indications of the date and origin of some of the manuscripts; on Cassiodorus, for example, see 56–8.

[94] *CLA*, 3, no. **38. These fragments – Turin, Biblioteca Nazionale F.IV.29 (binding), BAV, MS lat. 5760, fols i–ii, and Milan, Biblioteca Ambrosiana, C.91 inf., fols 128, 129 – were used at Bobbio for binding purposes in the fifteenth century; see also Siegmund, *Überlieferung*, 79.

[95] Bischoff, 'Die Kölner Nonnenhandschriften'.

within the Carolingian realm, though the demonstration of this would require another paper. Thus the St Amand copy, for example, now in Copenhagen, was, like the history books at Lorsch, part of a comprehensive collection of history books produced and read at St Amand and still in the library in the twelfth century.[96]

Such a deliberate dissemination of particular history books would be entirely in keeping with what we know about one of the main thrusts of the reforms initiated by Charlemagne. Carolingian royal patronage was inextricably bound up with the themes of *correctio* and *emendatio*, which are a fundamental part of the cultural and religious achievement scholars have described as the Carolingian Renaissance.[97] Corrected texts, or texts copied from exemplars regarded as authoritative, were prepared under the auspices of Charlemagne and Louis the Pious, of Sacramentaries and canon law, the homiliary, the Gospels, the Bible, and the Rule of Benedict, as well as the secular laws of the peoples under Frankish rule. The commissioning of a correct text of the Bible has a parallel with Constantine's commissioning and circulation of codices of the Greek New Testament recorded by Theodoret in his *Ecclesiastical History* and translated by Epiphanius in his *Historia tripartita* (II.16). When Charlemagne is hailed as a new Constantine by Pope Hadrian, therefore,[98] it may be as much for this specific promotion of the Bible as for his more general championing of the Christian Church. A new edition of the Gospels was prepared under the auspices of a Frankish ruler, initiated either by Pippin III or Charlemagne.[99] Charlemagne, Louis the Pious, Lothar, and possibly Charles the Bald as well, extended and developed what may have begun as the provision of a clear text for use in the palace chapel into the provision of a Carolingian Bible text for the entire Frankish kingdom. The Christian ruler ensured that the word of God in a proper and corrected form was

[96] R. McKitterick, 'The reading of history at St Amand', *Sewanee Medieval Studies*, 11 (2001), 27–46.

[97] I discussed some aspects of this in 'Unity and diversity in the Carolingian church', *SCH*, 32 (1996), 59–82.

[98] *Codex Carolinus*, ed. W. Gundlach, *MGH Epp.* III (Berlin, 1892), no. 60 (587), ll. 16–18 (the letter is usually dated 778); and see M. Garrison, 'The Franks as the New Israel?', in Y. Hen and M. Innes, eds, *The Uses of the Past in the Early Middle Ages* (Cambridge, 2000), 114–61.

[99] B. Fischer, 'Bibeltext und Bibelreform unter Karl dem Großen', in B. Bischoff, ed., *Karl der Grosse. Lebenswerk und Nachleben, 2: Das Geistige Leben* (Düsseldorf, 1965), 156–216; W. Koehler and F. Mütthelich, *Karolingische Miniaturen*, in progress (Berlin, 1930–), 2 (*Die Hofschule Karls des Grossen*), 3 (*Die Gruppe des Wiener Krönungsevangeliar. Metzer Handschriften*).

disseminated to all his leading monasteries and cathedrals. Charlemagne is particularly associated with the massive Frankish enterprise for the correction of the Vulgate Bible text, of which the editions produced at Tours and Orleans were the most famous and successful and the most widely disseminated.[100] Such dedications as the Vivian Bible to Charles the Bald reflect a continuing and Constantinian association of the ruler with the dissemination of Scripture.[101]

The Carolingians wished to exert power over texts and to control both their use and their meaning. They were able to exert power through texts by using the written word to organize, control and challenge the world. For them the written word was sacred; it represented cumulative wisdom encoded. Thus for the Franks in the early Middle Ages the written word and the book were not only symbols of power and authority but also the practical means of exercising power and authority in the Carolingian world.

Although perhaps originally conceived in terms of the relation to the word of God and the secular legislation of rulers, moreover, the degree to which written transmission lent special authority to the status of the ideas they contained can be observed in every category of written text extant from the Carolingian period. Author portraits of evangelists and of Gregory, such as the portrayal of Gregory's inspiration by the Holy Spirit in the form of a dove in the Sacramentary fragment from Charles the Bald's palace school,[102] emphasise the divine source of inspiration for writers.

The act of writing in itself created authoritative knowledge. The methods of working of Carolingian authors show them to have worked through the medium of authority. The more their wisdom rested on the wisdom of others, the greater its power. Hraban Maur's compilatory method of exegesis, for example, created a bulwark of authority against ignorance and doubt.[103] Representations of books

---

[100] Fischer, 'Bibeltext'; Koehler, *Karolingische Miniaturen*, 1 (*Die Schule von Tours*); E. Dahlhaus-Berg, *Nova antiquitas et antiqua novitas. Typologische Exegese und isidorianisches Geschichtsbild bei Theodulf von Orléans* (Cologne, 1975), esp. 39–76; and R. Gameson, ed., *The Early Medieval Bible: its Production, Decoration and Use* (Cambridge, 1994).

[101] BN, MS lat. 1: see P. E. Dutton and H. L. Kessler, *The Poetry and Paintings of the First Bible of Charles the Bald* (Ann Arbor, MI, 1997).

[102] BN, MS lat. 1141, fol. 3r, illustrated in F. Mütherich and J. Ghaede, *Carolingian Painting* (1976), 32.

[103] See M. de Jong, 'Old law and new-found power: Hrabanus Maurus and the Old Testament', in J.M. Drijvers and A.A. MacDonald, eds, *Centres of Learning: Learning and Location in Pre-Modern Europe and the Near East* (Leiden, 1995), 161–76.

in Carolingian book illuminations, moreover, stress the power of the written word and by implication those who controlled and produced books.[104] The scenes from the life of Jerome in the Vivian Bible (BN, MS lat. 1), produced at Tours, and the Bible of San Paulo fuori le mura, produced at Rheims, for example, present such incidents as his departure from Rome, his intellectual activities in Palestine, and the dissemination of the completed Vulgate translation of the Bible.[105] Jerome's work formed an apt parallel, as Kessler has suggested, for the enterprise at Tours in the ninth century for the production of a revised and corrected Vulgate text.[106]

* * *

Charlemagne in Alcuin's *De rhetorica* had asked, 'How can our speech attain the authority which that of the ancients had?' Alcuin had responded: 'Their books ought to be read and their words well impressed upon our memory.'[107] In commenting on the importance of biblical *historia* in the Carolingian period, Mayke de Jong has elucidated how the Frankish present was enveloped in the authoritative past outlined by Scripture.[108] For guidance in spoken and written expression as well as for understanding and knowledge, the Franks resorted to books. The Franks in the Carolingian period identified themselves in relation to particular texts and recognized them above all as symbols of the authority of the Church and of God. I have documented elsewhere the definition of a canon of writings regarded as authoritative and of those that were perceived as a threat. The library catalogue evidence, extant manuscripts, and citations in the

[104] A. Bowman and G. Woolf, eds, *Literacy and Power in the Ancient World* (Cambridge, 1994), and R. McKitterick, 'Essai sur les représentations de l'écrit dans les manuscrits carolingiens', in F. Dupuigrenet Desroussilles, ed., *La Symbolique du livre dans l'art occidental du haut moyen âge à Rembrandt*, Revue française d'histoire du livre, 86–7 (Bordeaux, 1997), 37–64.

[105] BN, MS lat. 1, fol. 3v, illustrated in Mütherich and Ghaede, *Carolingian Painting*, 21, and San Paolo fuori le mura, fol. 3v, illustrated in H.L. Kessler, *The Illustrated Bibles from Tours*, Studies in Manuscript Illumination, 7 (Princeton, NJ, 1977), pl. 131.

[106] H.L. Kessler, 'A lay abbot as patron: Count Vivian and the First Bible of Charles the Bald', in *Committenti e produzione artistico-letteraria nell'alto medioevo occidentale*, Settimane de Studio del centro Italiano di studi sull'alto medioevo, 39 (Spoleto, 1992), 647–76.

[107] Alcuin, *Disputatio de rhetorica et de virtutibus sapientissimi regis Karli et Albini magistri. The Rhetoric of Alcuin and Charlemagne*, ed. with Eng. tr. W.S. Howell (Princeton, NJ, 1941), 132–3.

[108] M. de Jong, 'The empire as *ecclesia*: Hrabanus Maurus and "biblical *historia* for rulers"', in Hen and Innes, *Uses of the Past*, 191–226.

writings of Frankish scholars, together indicate the degree to which such major early medieval authors as Bede, Alcuin, Hraban Maur, and many other Carolingian authors were incorporated alongside all those mentioned in Eusebius–Rufinus, Jerome–Gennadius, and the *Historia tripartita* into the canon of required knowledge.[109] Notker's *Notatio de viris illustribus* and the later *Liber de scriptoribus ecclesiasticis* of Sigebert of Gembloux, or Honorius Augustodunensis' *De luminaribus ecclesiae*, not only catalogue the Frankish authors of the eighth and ninth centuries along with the patristic authors as part of their intellectual foundations;[110] they also preserve the essential perception of Jerome-Gennadius and Eusebius–Rufinus of the history of the Church being one that is built on texts.

What this paper has explored is one further aspect of the process by which books and writing became both symbols of authority and knowledge in the Carolingian world and essential elements of Frankish identity and their sense of the past. Reading the histories of the Church was then, and remains for us, not only a matter of gaining knowledge of the events and protagonists described, but also of being aware of how those histories are constructed, on what authorities they are based, and how they are being used. Thus what we observe is the consolidation of the Frankish textual community centred on the Bible in the context of the Franks' place in the entire textual history of the Church.[111]

Newnham College, Cambridge

---

[109] I discuss the role of Cassiodorus' *Institutiones* in this respect as well in my *Carolingians and the Written Word*, 200–5.

[110] Sigebert of Gembloux, *De viris illustribus*, ed. R. Witte, *Catalogus Sigeberti Gemblacensis monachi de viris illustribus*, Lateinische Sprache und Literatur des Mittelalters 1 (Bern, 1974) – and also in *PL* 160, cols 547–88; Honorius Augustodunensis, *De luminaribus ecclesiae* (*PL* 172, cols 197–234), see V.I.J. Flint, 'The place and purpose of the works of Honorius Augustodunensis', *Revue Bénédictine*, 87 (1977), 97–127.

[111] Addendum to n.68: In the new edition by A. Hase, *Mittelalterliche Bücherverzeichnisse aus Kloster Lorsch: Einleitung, Edition und Kommentar*, Beiträge zum Buch- und Bibliothekwesen, 42 (Weisbaden, 2002), 137, Jerome–Gennadius is listed at 151.

THE *RITUALE*: THE EVOLUTION OF A NEW LITURGICAL BOOK

by SARAH HAMILTON

ODO of Sully, Bishop of Paris (1200–8), decreed in his statutes that each parish priest within his diocese should have a book called a *manuale*, which should contain the *ordo* of service for extreme unction, the catechism, baptism, and everyday things.[1] His prescription is the earliest mention in the episcopal legislation that a parish priest should have one particular book dedicated to the liturgy for all the services associated with pastoral care.[2] But codices concerned with the sacerdotal rites for the *cura animarum* have a history which goes back to the late ninth and tenth centuries.[3] These early *ritualia* were often combined with the monastic collectar, as in the mid-tenth-century *Durham Collectar*.[4] There are also some examples from the late tenth and eleventh centuries of *ritualia* made for the secular clergy.[5]

---

[1] 'Librum qui dicitur Manualis habeant singuli sacerdotes parochiales, ubi continetur ordo servitii extreme unctionis, cathechismi, baptismi et hujusmodi': *Les Statuts synodaux français du XIIIe siècle: les statuts de Paris et le synodal de l'ouest*, ed. Odette Pontal (Paris, 1971), 70.

[2] P.-M. Gy, 'Collectaire, rituel, processional', *Revue des sciences philosophiques et théologiques*, 44 (1960), 441–69 at 459–61. *Rituale* is a late medieval Italian term which was popularized by the Council of Trent (1545–63), which defined the *rituale* as one of the seven main liturgical books of the Roman rite: P.-M. Gy, 'Typologie et ecclésiologie des livres liturgiques médiévaux', *La Maison-Dieu*, 121 (1975), 7–21.

[3] E.g. the collection of liturgical texts, which include rites for the anointing of the sick, death and burial, penitentials, episcopal capitularies, and canon law, compiled at Lorsch for use as a pastoral text by the secular clergy in s. ix$^{3/4}$: F. Paxton, '*Bonus liber*: a late Carolingian clerical manual from Lorsch (Biblioteca Vaticana MS Pal. lat. 485)', in L. Mayali and S.A.J. Tibbetts, eds, *The Two Laws. Studies in Medieval Legal History Dedicated to Stephan Kuttner* (Washington DC, 1990), 1–30; the *libellus* containing rites for penance and the anointing of the sick added to a sacramentary from Saint-Amand *c*.900: Éric Palazzo, 'Les Deux rituels d'un libellus de Saint-Amand (Paris, Bibliothèque nationale lat. 13764)', in P. de Clerck and É. Palazzo, eds, *Rituels. Mélanges offerts au Père Gy OP* (Paris, 1990), 423–36; the *rituale* element of the Fulda Sacramentary (*c*.980): *Sacramentarium Fuldense Saeculi X*, Gregor Richter and Albert Schönfelder, eds (Fulda, 1912); repr. Henry Bradshaw Society [hereafter HBS], 101 (Farnborough, 1977), 279–356.

[4] *The Durham Collectar (Durham, Cathedral Library, MS A.IV.19)*, ed. Alicia Corrêa, HBS, 107 (Woodbridge, 1992).

[5] E.g., Paris, Bibliothèque Mazarine, Codex 525 (Asti, s. x); Milan, Biblioteca Ambrosiana, Codex T. 27, Sup. (N. Italy, s. xi), ed. C. Lambot, *North Italian Services of the Eleventh Century*, HBS, 67 (1931).

Odo of Sully was thus providing his powerful support to an existing practice rather than instituting a new form of service book.[6] This paper investigates further the context in which these early examples of 'parish' rituals were compiled, beginning with the Carolingian background.

The significant contribution made to the liturgy by the Carolingians is well known, but recent research is beginning to highlight the importance of the post-Carolingian period, the late ninth and tenth centuries, for significant changes in how the liturgy was recorded.[7] For it is from the late ninth century that various new genres of liturgical book first survive: *missals*,[8] pontificals,[9] benedictionals,[10] collectars,[11] and *ritualia*. The overall question of why this period saw this diversification in types of service book requires further research on the early history of each of these new books before it can be answered. Whilst a start has been made on the early history of pontificals and missals, the *ritualia* remain little studied.[12]

When he defined the books which a presbyter should own, Odo of Sully was following a tradition which began in the ninth century with the Carolingian episcopal *capitula*. Conscientious bishops were always anxious to ensure that their clergy performed the duties of the *cura animarum*, and that they did so correctly.[13] One of the obvious methods

---

[6] *Contra* Gy, 'Collectaire', 460: 'Le rituel paroissial est un fruit de l'effort des statuts synodaux du XIIIe s. en matière de pastorale sacramentaire.'

[7] On the Carolingian contribution see Roger E. Reynolds, 'The organization, law and liturgy of the western Church, 700–900', in Rosamond McKitterick, ed., *The New Cambridge Medieval History II: c.700–c.900* (Cambridge, 1995), 587–621.

[8] Eric Palazzo, *A History of Liturgical Books from the Beginning to the Thirteenth Century*, tr. Madelaine Beaumont (Collegeville, MN, 1998), 107–10; first published as *Le Moyen Age: Des origines au XIIIème siècle* (Paris, 1993).

[9] Niels Krogh Rasmussen, *Les Pontificaux du haut moyen âge. Genèse du livre de l'évêque*, Spicilegium sacrum Lovaniense: Études et documents, 49 (Louvain, 1998).

[10] E.E. Moeller, *Corpus benedictionum episcopalium*, 4 vols, CChr.SL, 162 (Turnhout, 1971–3).

[11] Gy, 'Collectaire'; Corrêa, *Durham Collectar*; Palazzo, *History*, 145–8.

[12] Gy, 'Collectaire'; idem, 'Ritual', in J.R. Strayer, ed., *Dictionary of the Middle Ages*, 10 (New York, 1988), 407–9. See also Walter von Arx, 'Zur Entstehungsgeschichte des Rituale', *Zeitschrift für schweizerische Kirchengeschichte/Revue d'histoire ecclésiastique suisse*, 63 (1969), 39–57; Cyrille Vogel, *Medieval Liturgy: an Introduction to the Sources*, rev. and tr. William G. Storey and Niels Krogh Rasmussen (Washington DC, 1986), 257–65; Palazzo, *History*, 187–94. The work of J.B. Molin is mostly confined to the later Middle Ages: 'Un type d'ouvrage mal connu, le Rituel. Son intérêt et ses caractéristiques bibliographiques', *Ephemerides Liturgicae*, 63 (1959), 218–24.

[13] For example, Bede's letter to Egbert, Archbishop of York (734), *English Historical Documents I*, ed. Dorothy Whitelock, 2nd edn (1977), 799–810, esp. at 801–2.

for ensuring liturgical uniformity was through books. Theodulf, Bishop of Orléans (d. 821), wanted to inspect the books of his diocesan clergy; he ordered his priests to bring their books with them to the synod, 'in order that it may be proved how carefully, how zealously, you perform God's service'.[14] What the 'necessary and correct books' which a presbyter should own should be was first spelt out in the early ninth-century *capitula* of Bishop Ghaerbald of Liège (d. 809).[15] Priests should own a missal, a lectionary, a martyrology, a penitential, a psalter and other books.[16] Similar lists can be found in episcopal *capitula* from the later ninth and tenth centuries.[17] Such an extensive library must have been beyond the means of many of the poorer clergy who, as Janet Nelson notes, had difficulty making ends meets.[18] But there is evidence in the polyptych of Saint Rémi, Rheims and the ninth-century charters from the diocese of Freising that several rural churches in these two areas were well equipped, and owned several of these books.[19] As Rob Meens has suggested, these ambitious lists need not have always been represented in separate codices, but rather different works could be, and were, bound within the same codex in the sort of manuscripts which are often now characterized as handbooks.[20] There has been a tendency to view such handbooks as episcopal manuals, made for owners whose office necessarily made

[14] c.4, *MGH Capitula Episcoporum*, I, ed. P. Brommer (Hanover, 1984) [hereafter Brommer].

[15] The phrase is taken from Ruotger of Trier's *capitula* (927x928), c.5: 'Ut sacerdotes libros sine necessarios correctos habeant': Brommer, 63. It is found earlier in Radulf of Bourges' *capitula* (c.853x866), c.5: 'missalem et lectionarium, psalterium sive alios libellos sibi necessarios bene correctos habeant': Brommer, 237.

[16] 'Ut unusquisque secundum possibilitatem suam certare faciat de ornatu ecclesiae, scilicet in patenam et calicem, planetam et albam, missalem, lectionarium, martyrologium, paenitentialem, psalterium, vel alios libros, quos potuerit, crucem, capsam, velut diximus iusta possibilitatem suam': Ghaerbald of Liège, *Capitula III*, c.9, Brommer, 39–40.

[17] E.g. Bishop Haito of Basel (before 813), c.6, Brommer, 211; Radulf of Bourges (c.853x866), c.5, ibid., 237; Ruotger of Trier (915–31), c.5, ibid., 63.

[18] Janet L. Nelson, 'Making ends meet: wealth and poverty in the Carolingian Church', *SCH*, 24 (1987), 25–36.

[19] *Polyptyque de Saint-Rémi de Reims*, ed. B. Guérard (Paris, 1857), 38, 56, 61–2, 78. On the Freising charters see Carl I. Hammer Jr, 'Country churches, clerical inventories and the Carolingian Renaissance in Bavaria', *Church History*, 49 (1980), 5–17.

[20] Rob Meens, 'Priests and books in the Carolingian era' (unpublished paper delivered at the Leeds International Medieval Congress, July 1998). See also his identification of thirty-two early medieval manuscripts containing penitentials for use in a pastoral setting: 'The frequency and nature of early medieval penance', in Peter Biller and A. J. Minnis, eds, *Handling Sin: Confession in the Middle Ages*, York Studies in Medieval Theology, 2 (Woodbridge, 1998), 42–3, 56–8.

them itinerant, touring their dioceses, inspecting their clergy, consulting the penitential canons in difficult cases of law, and so forth.[21] Such episcopal attributions are, no doubt, often correct; but recent research has argued that such codices would also have been within the means of the secular rural clergy.[22]

Although there is no explicit reference in any of the early medieval *capitula* to one codex which included all the rites for pastoral care, they make it clear that priests were expected to administer the rites for the *cura animarum* correctly. They should provide baptism, penance, and burial services freely.[23] Hincmar, Archbishop of Rheims (845–82) required that priests should know the prayers for baptism in both the male and female forms, plural and singular.[24] This insistence on correct grammar explains a feature of many liturgical books in which the prayer texts contain alternate female and plural readings above the line of the main text.[25]

Carolingian episcopal concerns about how priests delivered pastoral care were repeated by conscientious tenth-century bishops like Ruotger, Archbishop of Trier (915–31) and Atto, Bishop of Vercelli (924–60).[26] Similar sentiments crop up in the sermons in the tenth- and eleventh-century synodal *ordines*, the most famous of which being the so-called *Admonitio synodalis*.[27] The widespread copying of these didactic texts, targeted at the secular clergy, suggests a continuing concern amongst conscientious bishops in the post-Carolingian period to ensure that their clergy could do their job, one of whose most

---

[21] On episcopal handbooks see Rosamond McKitterick, *The Frankish Church and the Carolingian Reforms, 789–895* (1977), 35–44. Also F. Kerff, 'Libri paenitentiales und kirchliche Strafgerichsbarkeit bis zum Decretum Gratiani. Ein Diskussionsvorschlag', *Zeitschrift der Savigny-Stiftung für Rechtsgeschichte, Kanonistische Abteilung* [hereafter *ZRG Kan. Abt.*], 75 (1989), 23–57.

[22] Meens, 'Priests and books'; idem, 'Frequency'; Yitzhak Hen, 'Knowledge of canon law among rural priests: the evidence of two Carolingian manuscripts from around 800', *JThS*, 50 (1999), 117–34. The Carolingian experience is surveyed by Donald Bullough, 'The Carolingian liturgical experience', *SCH*, 35 (1999), 29–64, esp. 43–9.

[23] Radulf of Bourges (*c.*853x866), c.18: Brommer, 246–7.

[24] Hincmar, *Capitula* I, c.3, *MGH Capitula Episcoporum*, II, Rudolf Pokorny and Martina Stratmann, eds (Hanover, 1995), 35. A sentiment repeated by Riculf of Soissons (post 889) in his third *capitula*: c.7, ibid., 103.

[25] E.g. BAV, MS Chigi C.V.134, a tenth-century *rituale*.

[26] Ruotger: Brommer, 61–70. Atto: *MGH Capitula Episcoporum*, III, ed. Rudolf Pokorny (Hanover, 1995), 262–304; Suzanne Fonay Wemple, *Atto of Vercelli. Church, State and Christian Society in Tenth-Century Italy* (Rome, 1979), 109–44.

[27] R. Amiet, 'Une "Admonitio synodalis" de l'époque carolingienne. Étude critique et édition', *Mediaeval Studies*, 26 (1964), 12–82.

important aspects was correct delivery of the *cura animarum*.[28] Evidence in the legislation for widespread awareness of the significance of this issue therefore provides a possible context for the emergence of these 'parish' service books in this period.

Research to date has turned up several early monastic *ritualia*, some of which may have been used in a secular context, but no definitively secular rituals from before the late tenth century.[29] The reasons for this bias probably owe much to the benefits of institutional inertia; monastic libraries have the space to preserve redundant books, whilst the small libraries of rural churches were more vulnerable to loss and damage over time. Historians of *ritualia* to date have concentrated their research efforts on French and German manuscripts;[30] but Italy provides one of the earliest known secular *rituale*, a tenth-century manuscript from northern Italy,[31] and research amongst the Italian manuscript catalogues suggests there may be several others of a similar date, including one Vatican codex, MS Archivio S. Pietro H. 58, which contains a variety of liturgical and legal texts, and a section on the rites for the *cura animarum*.[32] A closer study of this codex demonstrates how such a handbook can provide evidence for the context in which the *ritualia* made their first appearance.

* * *

The Vatican manuscript[33] is a complex codex of some hundred and fifty folios which belongs to the category of ecclesiastical manuscript known as a handbook. It includes a *rituale* element, covering the rites for the *cura animarum*; an *ordo missae*; the service for Palm Sunday; the

---

[28] Carolingian *capitula* continued to be copied in significant numbers in the tenth and eleventh centuries: Brommer, 76–99, 145–7.

[29] E.g. Paxton, 'Bonus liber'; Palazzo, 'Deux rituels'.

[30] For the French collections, Gy, 'Collectaire'; for the German collections, von Arx, 'Entstehungsgeschichte'.

[31] Paris, Bibliothèque Mazarine, MS 525 (s. x, Asti).

[32] Other rituals worth further investigation include Monza, Biblioteca capitolare, Cod. B-15/128 (on which see Ferdinando dell'Oro, 'Un rituale del secolo X proveniente dall'Italia settentrionale (Monza, Bibl. Capitolare, cod. B-15/128)', in De Clerck and Palazzo, *Rituels*, 215–49; Paris, Bibliothèque Mazarine, MS 525; Rome, Biblioteca Vallicelliana, Cod. B.63; BAV, MSS Vat. lat. 576, Chigi C.V.134.

[33] Briefly described by Pierre Salmon, *Les Manuscrits liturgiques latins de la bibliothèque vaticane*, 5 vols, Studi e testi, 251, 253, 261, 267, 270 (1968–72), 2:106. He has also made two short studies of this codex: 'Un "libellus officialis" du XIe siècle', *Revue Bénédictine*, 87 (1977), 257–88; 'Un témoin de la vie chrétienne dans une église de Rome au XIe siècle: le liber officialis de la basilique des Saint-Apôtres,', *Rivista di storia della chiesa in Italia*, 33 (1979), 65–73.

blessing of water on Holy Saturday and a nuptial mass; a martyrology; two passions; some canon law on liturgical questions; a computus and a paschal table; a homily; two penitentials; and some liturgical commentary (see Appendix I for further details).[34]

The rites in the *rituale* element suggest it was compiled for use by the secular clergy. The baptismal rite was intended for infant baptism.[35] The presence of two *ordines* for the visitation of the sick requires investigation: the first is the longer and more elaborate.[36] It was to be administered by the 'sacerdotes et ministri ecclesie', who should, after anointing the sick person, say the office of vespers and matins with reverence for that person every day until his death. This *ordo* therefore appears to have been written for a church with a relatively large clerical community, for use within that community. The second rite for the visitation of the sick is much shorter and is presented in the form of an exchange between the priest and the dying man: it consists of confession, a profession of faith, unction, and a mass at which the sick person is given communion in both kinds.[37] This second rite therefore seems more appropriate for an itinerant priest, visiting the homes of the dying.

Although the codex contains a rite seemingly intended for an itinerant priest, the book itself is not very portable: it measures *c*.28.5 × 20 cm.[38] The text is written in two main hands in an undecorated, functional script: hand A wrote fols 1–80, 135–50, hand B fols 81–122. (The manuscript was rebound in the early modern period, accounting for the confusion in the current arrangement of the quires). Both hands have been attributed on palaeographical grounds to early eleventh-century Rome.[39] Pierre Salmon has convincingly suggested that the codex should be attributed to the basilica of SS Apostoli in Rome; unfortunately we lack records to

[34] Certain of the canonical aspects of this codex are considered in articles by Roger E. Reynolds: 'Excerpta from the Collectio Hibernensis in three Vatican manuscripts', *Bulletin of Medieval Canon Law*, ns 5 (1975), 1–9; 'A South Italian liturgico-canonical mass commentary', *Mediaeval Studies*, 50 (1988), 626–70; 'The South-Italian canon law Collection in Five Books and its derivatives: new evidence on its origins, diffusion and use', *Mediaeval Studies*, 52 (1990), 278–95.

[35] Thus the *ordo* begins: 'Cum ductus fuerit infans ad ecclesiam': fol. 34rb.

[36] Fols 29–34.

[37] Fols 41–2.

[38] If we take a height of 20 cm. as the boundary between portable and non-portable as suggested by S.J.P. Van Dijk and J. Hazelden Walker, *The Origins of the Modern Roman Liturgy* (Westminster, MD, 1960), 32.

[39] Paola Supino Martini, *Roma e l'area grafica romanesca (secoli X–XII)* (Rome, 1987), 72–5.

determine who was in charge of the church in the early eleventh century, although we know that by 1127 it was run by a house of canons.[40]

Despite their seemingly disparate nature, the contents of this codex bear a strong resemblance to the checklist for the standards expected of the secular clergy given in the popular synodal sermon, the *Admonitio Synodalis* (for a comparison see Appendix 2). The order of items in the codex closely follows those in the *Admonitio*, which has been called a 'handbook of canon law on the official duties of the parish clergy'.[41] Its precise date of composition is still debated, but it circulated widely in the tenth and eleventh centuries.[42] Certainly known in Italy by the time the Vatican codex was composed in the early eleventh century, the *Admonitio* was cited in full by Rather, Bishop of Verona, in a letter addressed to his diocesan clergy in 966,[43] and was attached to the *ordo synodalis* in the Romano-German pontifical which was known in central Italy by the late tenth century.[44] It is not therefore inherently improbable that the Vatican codex was compiled to conform to the precepts in the *Admonitio Synodalis* or some other similar guidelines on the sort of books a priest should own.

Who was this codex made for? It was written by Roman scribes but the absence of references to, or rites for, a bishop suggest that it is not a papal or episcopal book. The inclusion of pastoral rites for baptism and a nuptial mass, as well as those for the more clerical rites of visitation of the sick and burial, suggest that the book was made to aid the secular clergy in the delivery of pastoral services to the laity. However, the elaborate first rite for the visitation of the sick suggests it was composed for a clerical community. The book's pastoral concerns are confirmed by the inclusion of a didactic poem attributed to Sedulius

---

[40] Salmon, '"Libellus officialis"'.

[41] F. Lotter, 'Ein kanonistiches Handbuch über die Amtspflichten des Pfarrklerus als gemeinsame Vorlage für den Sermo Synodalis "Fratres presbyteri" und Reginos Werk "De synodalibus causis"', *ZRG Kan. Abt.*, 62 (1976), 1–57.

[42] It also circulated in two versions, the short and the long; the canons cited in the Appendix belong to the longer version.

[43] *Die Briefe des Bischofs Rather von Verona*, ed. F. Weigle, *MGH Die Briefe der deutschen Kaiserzeit*, I (Weimar, 1949), no. 25 (124–37).

[44] *Ordo* LXXX.51: *Le Pontifical Romano-Germanique du dixième siècle*, ed. Cyrille Vogel and Reinhard Elze, 3 vols (Vatican City, 1963–72), 1:286–9. On the evidence that the Romano-German Pontifical was known in late tenth-century Rome, see ibid., 3:46–50. For a revision of the optimistic picture put forward by Vogel and Elze (taking their lead from Michel Andrieu) for the early diffusion of the Romano-German pontifical see Sarah Hamilton, *The Practice of Penance c.900–c.1050* (2001), App. 1.

on the *Vita pastoralis*.[45] The pseudo-Sedulian verses, which survive in only one other Italian manuscript, of the ninth or tenth centuries, provide a brief guide to the duties and behaviour of a priest: he should guard his sheep carefully; read and study; know the seven canonical hours and when they should be observed; remember the importance of attending the synod; know the significance of baptism and of the mass and how it is celebrated; refrain from accepting money for his services, carrying arms, and marrying; and know the importance and significance of penance and the rites for the dying.

This Vatican compilation therefore shows the clergy of SS Apostoli *c.* 1000 trying to meet the standards set for them. Because it is not portable, it is probable that it was a teaching or reference book. But its distinct *rituale* element suggests that these folios may have been the model for portable *libelli* taken out by the church's clerics when visiting members of their flock.[46]

The codex suggests that this new genre of service books for use by the secular clergy, the *ritualia*, emerged out of a post-Carolingian episcopal context which continued to think that the delivery of pastoral care was important. There is certainly considerable evidence for local concern for reform in various regions of Italy throughout the first half of the eleventh century. A regional bias in both the evidence and historiography makes it impossible to draw up a universally accurate picture of local church reform. But the general pattern, be it in the diocese of Lazio or those of Lucca or Verona, seems to be for a move in the eleventh century away from the early medieval system of *pievi* with dependent *oratoria*, in which the *pievi* had a stranglehold on baptismal and burial rites, to one where parish churches controlled burial rites, although the *pievi* usually retained the baptismal rites.[47] This change occurred at the same time as a physical increase in the number of churches: in the diocese of Verona in 1150 there were twice as many ecclesiastical institutions (churches and monasteries) as in 1000, with most of the growth occurring in

---

[45] Edited by Bernhard Bischoff, 'Ein karolingische "Vita pastoralis": "Sedulius, Carmen alpha"', *Deutsches Archiv für Erforschung des Mittelalters*, 37 (1981), 559–75.

[46] Henry Mayr-Harting has suggested a similar model of use for the Fulda Sacramentary (*c.*980): *Ottonian Book Illumination: An Historical Study*, 2 vols (1991), 2:133–4.

[47] On Lazio see Pierre Toubert, *Les Structures du Latium médiévale. Le Latium méridional et la Sabine du IXe siècle à la fin du XIIe siècle* (Turin and Paris, 1973), 789–933; on Lucca see Luigi Nanni, *La Parrochia studiata nei documenti lucchesi dei secoli VIII–XIII*, Analecta Gregoriana, 47 (Rome, 1948); on Verona see Maureen C. Miller, *The Formation of a Medieval Church. Ecclesiastical Change in Verona, 950–1150* (Ithaca, NY, and London, 1993).

the countryside.[48] Architectural historians confirm that the eleventh century saw frenzied building activity as new churches were built in both the town and countryside.[49] This change at a local level in the churches from which pastoral services were delivered demonstrates a concern amongst church patrons – both lay and ecclesiastical – for the delivery of pastoral care. The increase in the number of churches was accompanied by increased concern about the lives led by the clergy, and about how they should be educated and how they should live.

Historians are most familiar with the criticisms of the lives of the secular clergy made by the mid-eleventh-century papal reformers. Peter Damian and Hildebrand (later Pope Gregory VII, 1073–85), exercised by what they portrayed as the widespread ignorance, avarice, and sexual immorality of the contemporary secular clergy, recommended that they should live in reformed canonical communities.[50] In reviving the idea of the canonical life, the papal reformers were merely developing a trend which had begun, at least in Italy, around the year 1000.[51] The most famous sponsor was Romuald, founder of the Camaldolese, who persuaded the clergy at Val Castro to adopt the communal life.[52] The urban and rural churches in the diocese of Verona also saw a number of *scole*, that is communities of clerics, being set up in the first half of the eleventh century. Maureen Miller has suggested that this phenomenon was a consequence of the increase in the number of new parishes: a need for priests encouraged the formation of institutions at which they might be trained.[53] Alongside the increase in *scole* in Verona there was also an increase in communities of clergy based at rural *plebes*.[54] Both types of community received generous lay donations. The Verona experience predates the

---

[48] Ibid., 22–40.

[49] Many of the central and northern Italian *plebes baptismales*, formerly dated to the eighth and ninth centuries, have been re-dated to the eleventh century: L. Moretti and R. Stopani, *Chiese Romaniche in Val di Pesa e Val di Greve* (Florence, 1972).

[50] G. Morin, 'Reglements inédits du pape Saint Grégoire pour les chanoines reguliers', *Révue Bénédictine*, 18 (1901), 177–83; Gustave Bardy, 'Saint Grégoire VII et la reforme canoniale au XIe siècle', *Studi Gregoriani*, 1 (1947), 47–64; Jean LeClercq, *Saint Pierre Damien, ermite et homme de l'église* (Rome, 1960).

[51] In addition to the references cited below, see John Howe, *Church Reform and Social Change in Eleventh-Century Italy: Dominic of Sora and his Patrons* (Philadelphia, PA, 1997).

[52] *Petri Damiani Vita Beati Romualdi*, ed. Giovanni Tabacco, Fonti per la storia d'Italia, 94 (Rome, 1957), c.35.

[53] Miller, *Formation*, 48–54.

[54] Ibid., 51–2.

Roman papal reform movement of the mid-eleventh century, but is contemporaneous with the Vatican codex. That codex suggests that within the city of Rome herself there was a similar movement for secular clerical reform going on in the early eleventh century. These changes at a local level in the provision of what, for want of a better word, we can call 'parish' church services provide a possible context for the emergence of what became one of the most important liturgical books of the late medieval and early modern periods.

University of Exeter

APPENDIX 1

The contents of Vatican, Biblioteca Apostolica Vaticana, Archivio S. Pietro, H. 58 (folios indicated in brackets)

I Rituale (1–45)
   a) *Ordo missae* (1–4)
   b) *Missa in dominica ad palmas* (4–9v)
   c) Litany and blessing of holy water and salt on Holy Saturday (10v–12r)
   d) *Ordo in agenda mortuorum (quando anima egreditur de corpore)* (12–29)
   e) *Ordo ad visitandum infirmum* I (29–34)
   f) *Ordo ad cattecumenum faciendum* (34–40)
   g) Blessings (40)
   h) *Ordo ad visitandum infirmum* II (41–2)
   i) *Ordo poenitentiae* (42rb–5ra)
   j) Ebo, Archbishop of Rheims' letter to Halitgar, Bishop of Cambrai, requesting a penitential (45ra–va)
   k) Halitgar's response (45va–vb)
II Collection of canons on liturgical questions (45–59)
   a) Extracts similar to those in *Collectio canonum in V libris,* III (45vb–8vb)
   b) Extracts from the *Collectio Hibernensis,* II–XI (49ra–53vb)
   c) Extracts from Isidore, *De ecclesiastica officia* and *Collectio Hibernensis,* X (53vb–6vb)
   d) *Sedulius carmen alpha cecinit ita* (57r–8ra)
   e) Extracts similar to *Collectio canonum in V libris,* III (58ra–9ra)

III   Bede's Martyrology (59rb–79ra)
      Ed. 'Martyrlogium e codice basilicae vaticanae nunc primum
      editum', *Analecta Bollandiana*, 49 (1931), 51–97
IV   Paschal table and *computus* (79–80v)
V   Passions
      a) *Passio sanctae Luciae* (81–4v)
      *Bibliotheca hagiographica latina antiquae et mediae aetatis novum
      supplementum*, ed. Henricus Fos (Brussels, 1986), no. 4992 (545).
      b) *Festivitas ss. Eustrati et sociorum eius, lectiones I–IX* (84v–102v)
      Fos, *Bibliotheca hagiographica*, no. 2778 (317).
VI   *Homilia in natali sanctarum virginum*, Haymo of Auxerre, no. 84
      (102v–8)
      See H. Barré, *Les Homéliares carolingiens de l'école d'Auxerre*, Studi
      et testi, 225 (Rome, 1962), 118.
VII   *Missa sponsaricia* (108–9v)
VIII Penitential
      a) Penitential ordo (109–12v): *Quotiescumque christiani . . .*
      Ed. H.J. Schmitz, *Die Bussbücher und die Bussdisciplin der Kirche, II:
      Die Bussbücher und das kanonische Bussverfahren* (Düsseldorf,
      1898), 199–203.
      b) Penitential canons (112v–21v)
      Ed. L. Körntgen, 'Ein italienisches Bußbuch und seine frän-
      kischen Quellen: das anonyme Paenitentiale der Handschrift
      Vatikan, Arch. S. Pietro H 58', in H. Mordek, ed., *Aus Archiven
      und Bibliotheken: Festschrift für Raymund Kottje zum 65. Geburtstag*
      (Frankfurt am Main, 1992), 189–205.
[NB fols 123–7 omitted from the foliation]
IX   Canonical texts on the liturgy (128va–38ra)
      Includes a group of short text on the divine offices (128va–9ra);
      Hrabanus Maurus, *De institutione clericorum libri tres*, I.31 (129v);
      Walahfrid Strabo, *De exordiis et incrementis . . .* (131r); Amalarius
      of Metz, *Liber officialis*, I.37, I.29, III.44 (131r); material drawn
      from the *Collectio Hibernensis*, I, and Isidore of Seville's *Origines*
      (135r–8ra)
X   Halitgar's Penitential, III–V.16 (138r–43ra)
XI   Miscellaneous canons from Greek councils, popes, and the
      Collectio Herovalliana (143ra–9ra)
XII   Canonical texts on the liturgy (149rb–50vb)

APPENDIX 2

The provisions of the *Admonitio Synodalis* (ed. R. Amiet, 'Une *Admonitio synodalis* de l'époque carolingienne. Étude critique et édition', *Mediaeval Studies*, 26 (1964), 12–82) and the contents of BAV, Archivio S. Pietro H. 58.

Admonitio synodalis	BAV, Archivio S. Pietro H. 58 (folios in brackets)
c. 87: 'Let him understand well the prayers of the Mass and the canon, and if not, let him be able to quote them from memory clearly.'	I a) *Ordo missae* (1–4) I b) *Missa in dominica ad palmas* (4–9v)
c. 90: 'Let him be able to utter distinctly and individually the exorcisms and prayers for making catechumens, for blessing the water also, and the rest of the prayers over the male and female, plural and singular.'	I c) Litany and blessing of holy water and salt on Holy Saturday (10v–12r) I f) *Ordo ad cattecumenum faciendum* (34–40)
c. 91: 'Likewise he must at least know how to say the order for the baptism and visitation of the sick and according to the manner canonically reserved for it the order of reconciling and anointing of the sick, and the prayers also relating to that necessity.'	I f) I e) *Ordo ad visitandum infirmum vel ingendum (vel communicandum)* I (29–34) I h) *Ordo ad visitandum infirmum* II (41–2)
c. 92: 'that he should visit the sick and reconcile them spontaneously and not for money but through charity, and say the prayers and seven special psalms over them.'	I e) I h)

Admonitio synodalis	BAV, Archivio S. Pietro H. 58 (folios in brackets)
c. 93: 'Likewise that he know the orders and prayers for making the obsequies of the dead.'	I d) *Ordo in agenda mortuorum (quando anima egreditur de corpore)* (12–29)
c. 94: 'Likewise the exorcisms and benedictions of salt and water he should know by heart.'	I c) I g) Blessings various (40)
c. 95: 'He should know the lesser compute, that is the epacts, and the Easter chronology and the rest, if possible.'	IV Paschal table (79) *Computus* (80v)
c. 96: That he should have a martyrology and a penitential.	III Bede's martyrology (59–79) VIII Penitential (109v–21v) X Halitgar's Penitential, III–V (138r–43r) (see also I j)
c. 98: That everyone should have this little book and frequently read it and observe what is in it.	

THE SCHOLAR'S SUITCASE: BOOKS AND THE TRANSFER OF KNOWLEDGE IN TWELFTH-CENTURY EUROPE[1]

by CHRISTOPH EGGER

O NE day early in the thirteenth century a wandering scholar broke his journey at the Benedictine monastery of Prüfening near Regensburg in Bavaria. Of the books this scholar was carrying, one Liebhard, a monk of the monastery, was especially fascinated by a copy of Peter the Chanter's *Distinctiones Abel*, a dictionary of the Bible for the preacher's use and a prominent example of the recently developed literary genre of biblical *distinctiones*.[2] Unfortunately, soon afterwards the scholar resumed his interrupted journey, and was not willing to leave the book behind at Prüfening, so Liebhard was unable to copy the full text but could only take down excerpts, which he later completed with texts from other sources. The result, which he called *Horreum formicae* (the ant's harvest),[3] still extant in at least two manuscripts,[4] combines the approach of the masters of the Parisian schools with that of monastic theology. It is, therefore, an excellent example of a process ongoing throughout the whole twelfth century: the transfer of knowledge from the centres of learning in the north of France (Laon, Chartres, Paris) and of Italy (Bologna) towards the periphery of medieval Europe, resulting in the reception and critical discussion of new concepts and ideas, a process most readily visible in the distribution of books. This paper offers a preliminary

[1] Research for this paper was funded by a grant from the Austrian Academy of Sciences, APART (Austrian programme for advanced research and technology). I am grateful to Brenda Bolton and Julia Wannenmacher, who read earlier versions.
    [2] Richard H. and Mary G. Rouse, 'Biblical *Distinctiones* in the thirteenth century', *Archives d'Histoire doctrinale et littéraire du moyen âge*, 41 (1974), 27–37; Nikolaus M. Häring, 'Commentary and hermeneutics', in Robert L. Benson, Giles Constable, and Carol D. Lanham, eds, *Renaissance and Renewal in the Twelfth Century* (Cambridge, MA, 1982), 173–200.
    [3] The title is an allusion to Prov. 6.6–8.
    [4] Munich, Bayerische Staatsbibliothek, Clm 13107 (probably the author's own manuscript); Salzburg, Erzabtei St Peter, MS a.VII.21. For the *Horreum* see Martin Grabmann, *Die Geschichte der scholastischen Methode*, 2 vols (Freiburg im Breisgau, 1909–11), 2:485–7; Ludwig Hödl, 'Liebhard von Prüfening', *Die deutsche Literatur des Mittelalters: Verfasserlexikon*, 2nd edn, 5 (Berlin and New York, 1985), cols 808–11.

sketch of this process with special emphasis on medieval Bavaria and Austria.

Present-day Austria and Bavaria seem to be especially appropriate areas for this kind of research. It is well known that the libraries of this part of Europe are still the custodians of a rich tradition of twelfth-century scholarly texts, mostly in contemporary manuscripts. That some of these texts have only come to our attention by means of these manuscript survivals has already been pointed out by such scholars as Heinrich Weisweiler, Heinrich Fichtenau, Nikolaus Häring, Peter Classen, and Winfried Stelzer,[5] but many questions remain. Who brought these texts to medieval Austria? To what uses have they been put? Was there a 'clash of cultures', between the new scholastic and the old monastic cultures? Finally, which methodological rules should be observed when dealing with these questions?

In this paper, the focus will be on the years from c.1080 to 1215, a period often considered coterminous with the 'renaissance of the twelfth century'.[6] Geographically it centres on the medieval ecclesiastical province of Salzburg, which covered most of present-day Austria, with special emphasis on the Austrian segment of the diocese of Passau. The monasteries of southern Bavaria also have to be included,

---

[5] Heinrich Weisweiler, *Das Schrifttum der Schule Anselms von Laon und Wilhelms von Champeaux in deutschen Bibliotheken*, Beiträge zur Geschichte der Philosophie und Theologie des Mittelalters, 33/i-ii (Münster, 1936); Heinrich Fichtenau, 'Ein französischer Frühscholastiker in Wien', *Jahrbuch für Landeskunde von Niederösterreich und Wien*, NF 29 (1944-8), 118-30; idem, 'Magister Petrus von Wien', in idem, *Beiträge zur Mediävistik*, 1 (Stuttgart, 1975), 218-38 (first in *Mitteilungen des Instituts für Österreichische Geschichtsforschung*, 63 [1955], 238-97); Peter Classen, 'Zur Geschichte der Frühscholastik in Österreich und Bayern', in idem, *Ausgewählte Aufsätze*, ed. Josef Fleckenstein, Vorträge und Forschungen, 28 (Sigmaringen, 1983), 279-306 (first in *Mitteilungen des Instituts für Österreichische Geschichtsforschung*, 67 [1959], 249-77); idem, *Gerhoch von Reichersberg. Eine Biographie. Mit einem Anhang über die Quellen, ihre handschriftliche Überlieferung und ihre Chronologie* (Wiesbaden, 1960); Nikolaus M. Häring, *Die Zwettler Summe. Einleitung und Text*, Beiträge zur Geschichte der Philosophie und Theologie des Mittelalters, NF 15 (Münster, 1977); Winfried Stelzer, *Gelehrtes Recht in Österreich. Von den Anfängen bis zum frühen 14. Jahrhundert*, Mitteilungen des Instituts für Österreichische Geschichtsforschung, Ergänzungsband, 26 (Vienna, Cologne, and Graz, 1982).

[6] Charles Homer Haskins, *The Renaissance of the Twelfth Century*, 5th edn (Cambridge, MA, 1971); Richard W. Southern, 'The place of England in the Twelfth-Century Renaissance', *History*, 45 (1960), 201-16, at 201, revised in idem, *Medieval Humanism and Other Studies* (Oxford, 1970), 158-80; Peter Classen, 'Die geistesgeschichtliche Lage im 12. Jahrhundert. Anstöße und Möglichkeiten', in idem, *Ausgewählte Aufsätze*, 327-46; Bernhard Schimmelpfennig, 'Renaissance/Proto-Renaissance, Renovatio/Renewal, Rezeption. Bericht über eine Begriffsdiskussion', *Kontinuität und Transformation der Antike im Mittelalter*, ed. Willi Erzgräber (Sigmaringen, 1989), 383-90; Robert N. Swanson, *The Twelfth-Century Renaissance* (Manchester and New York, 1999), esp. 1-11.

because of their often close relations to the Austrian part of the diocese.

'Early scholastic theology', which emerged from the schools of the twelfth century, is characterized by the use of logic and dialectics in discussing theological problems. Among its most characteristic literary genres are collections of sentences, glosses, commentaries, *quaestiones*, and *summae*. Some texts do not fit into the traditional categories of literary genres. Because these texts are highly significant for the medieval transmission of knowledge, they will be treated in detail later on.

According to modern historiography, the scholastic way of thought is opposed to monastic theology. The latter is characterized by a rather meditative approach to the divine mysteries, resistance to logic and dialectics, and intensive use of allegory and typology. Its authors – including prominent figures such as Bernard of Clairvaux or Rupert of Deutz – were in general attached to a monastic milieu.[7] In Austria, for instance, the names of the Benedictines Gottfried and Irimbert of Admont or the regular canon Gerhoch of Reichersberg suggest themselves. Nevertheless, it is important not to impose too strict a distinction between scholastic and monastic theology. Both were often linked, whether in peaceful co-existence or in conflict. For instance, Bernard of Clairvaux was a well-known author among scholastic theologians; Hugh of St Victor was attached to both milieux; and Peter the Lombard was quoted by the Austrian Cistercian author, Hermann of Rein. As for conflict, there are Bernard's attacks on Peter Abelard and Gilbert of Poitiers, or Gerhoch of Reichersberg's heated assaults on Peter the Lombard and Peter of Vienna – but even in the latter case an exchange of ideas and knowledge was taking place.

A reasonable starting point is the medieval library catalogues. These are available in critical editions both for Austria[8] and

---

[7] Jean Leclercq, *L'Amour des lettres et le désir de Dieu. Initiation aux auteurs monastiques du moyen age*, 3rd edn (Paris, 1990); idem, 'Naming the theologies of the early twelfth century', *Mediaeval Studies*, 53 (1991), 327–36; Feruccio Gastaldelli, 'Teologia monastica, teologia scolastica e lectio divina', *La dottrina della vita spirituale nelle opere di san Bernardo di Clairvaux. Atti del convegno internazionale, Roma, 11–15 settembre 1990*, Analecta Cisterciensia, 46 (1990), 25–63; Thomas Head, ' "Monastic" and "scholastic" theology: a change of paradigm?', in Nancy van Deusen and Alvin E. Ford, eds, *Paradigms in Medieval Thought: Applications in Medieval Disciplines. A Symposium*, Mediaeval Studies, 3 (Lewiston, NY, 1990), 127–41.

[8] *Mittelalterliche Bibliothekskataloge Österreichs* [hereafter *MBKÖ*]. Five volumes have so far been published: 1: *Niederösterreich*, ed. Theodor Gottlieb (Vienna, 1915, repr. Vienna, 1974); 2: index for vol. 1, ed. Artur Goldmann (Vienna, 1929); 3: *Steiermark*, ed. Gerlinde Möser-Mersky (Graz, Cologne, and Vienna, 1961), 4: *Salzburg*, ed. Gerlinde Möser-Mersky and

Bavaria.[9] If the Austrian monasteries alone are taken into account, twelfth- and early thirteenth-century booklists are available for the Benedictines in Göttweig (Lower Austria), Kremsmünster and Lambach (Upper Austria), Mondsee and St Peter (Salzburg), and St Lambrecht (Styria); the Cistercians in Heiligenkreuz and Zwettl (Lower Austria) and Baumgartenberg (Upper Austria); the regular canons in Klosterneuburg (Lower Austria), St Florian (Upper Austria), and Vorau (Styria); and the library of the cathedral chapter of Salzburg. Though this number seems to be rather large, a closer look at the individual lists is quite disappointing. In many cases, it is obvious that the extant lists do not give an exhaustive index of all the library's holdings, but of just some of its parts, and it is only too often impossible to find the criteria according to which the list was compiled.[10] Moreover, items were sometimes added to a list later, and by different scribes. Such additions mirror the development of a library, but they could also mislead the reader whose interest lies in the state of the library, or in the presence of a certain title there at a certain time. Therefore, a very careful reading of the catalogue, preferably of the original manuscript, is necessary, because superficial interpretation of medieval library catalogues could lead to false conclusions.

Another problem is that it is not always possible to identify the titles given in a list. The catalogue of St Peter in Salzburg, for instance, mentions a glossed copy of the Book of Revelation.[11] If only we knew the author of these glosses, in order to establish whether the manuscript comes from the scholastic milieu; but from the scanty description in the catalogue we are not even able to tell whether this is a

Melanie Mihaliuk (Graz, Cologne, and Vienna, 1966); 5: *Oberösterreich*, ed. Herbert Paulhart (Vienna, Cologne and Graz, 1971). Additions to vol. 1: *Niederösterreich. Bücherverzeichnisse in Korneuburger, Tullner und Wiener Neustädter Testamenten*, ed. Paul Uiblein (Vienna, Cologne, and Graz, 1969).

[9] *Mittelalterliche Bibliothekskataloge Deutschlands und der Schweiz.* For the Bavarian dioceses 6 vols have been published so far, covering the dioceses of Augsburg (vol. 3/i, ed. Paul Ruf, Munich, 1932), Eichstätt (vol. 3/ii, ed. Paul Ruf, Munich, 1933), Bamberg (vol. 3/iii, ed. Paul Ruf, Munich, 1939), Passau and Regensburg (vol. 4/i, ed. Christine Elisabeth Ineichen-Eder, Munich, 1977), and Freising und Würzburg (vol. 4/ii, ed. Günter Glauche and Hermann Knaus, Munich, 1979).

[10] For example the list from the Benedictine monastery of Göttweig (*MBKÖ*, 1:11–12) is not a catalogue of the library, but a list of books given to the monastery by a certain brother Henry, whose identity is unknown. The relationship of the books mentioned in this list to the library of the monastery is a difficult problem.

[11] *MBKÖ*, 4:71 l.17: *Apokalipsis Iohannis glosatus*(!). The catalogue can be roughly dated to the last quarter of the twelfth century; some of the entries might have been added slightly later.

manuscript containing the *Glossa ordinaria*. The *Sententie Petri Bailardi* in the same catalogue[12] clearly point to a work of Peter Abelard or his school. It would be highly interesting to learn more about it, but once again, neither the text nor a surviving manuscript can be identified.[13] In short, although medieval booklists are indispensable tools for researching the holdings of a library and the intellectual background of the owning body, we have to be thoroughly aware of the inherent limitations so characteristic for this type of source.

In some cases entries in medieval booklists can be identified and associated with still extant manuscripts. This identification is extremely helpful with respect to another difficult issue, namely the question of provenance and *Bibliotheksheimat*. A manuscript's provenance is, of course, where it was written; the *Bibliotheksheimat* is the library (or the libraries) where it was kept. Both can be, but by no means have to be, the same.[14] The methodological importance of this distinction can hardly be over-emphasised. For only if a manuscript's presence in a twelfth-century Austrian library can be proved with certainty can it be used as evidence for the process of knowledge transfer. Establishing the provenance and the *Bibliotheksheimat* of a manuscript is not easy. In fact there are deplorably few Austrian manuscripts bearing twelfth-century ownership marks. One example is Oxford, Bodleian Library, MS Lyell 49, which until 1936 belonged to the Benedictine monastery of Admont in Styria.[15] It is a composite manuscript bound early in the

---

[12]   Ibid., 71 l.1.

[13]   For the transmission of Abelardian texts see Julia Barrow, Charles Burnett, and David Luscombe, 'A Checklist of the manuscripts containing the writings of Peter Abelard and Heloïse and other works closely associated with Abelard and his school', *Revue d'histoire des textes*, 14–15 (1984–5), 183–302: for Salzburg see 221, 238–9; for Munich, where some manuscripts from St Peter are kept, 205–6; for the *Sententiae Petri Abaelardi* cf. 260–1. According to Constant J. Mews, 'The Sententie of Peter Abelard', *Recherches de théologie ancienne et médiévale*, 53 (1986), 137, the St Peter manuscript contained a copy of the so-called *Sententie Hermanni*.

[14]   Even a scholar as experienced as Peter Classen sometimes missed this distinction: in his article 'Zur Geschichte der Frühscholastik', 286–7, he mentioned Carpentras, Bibliothèque Inguimbertine, MS 110, as of French origin. In fact the manuscript, which contains the so-called *Sententiae Herimanni* of the school of Peter Abelard and theological *Quaestiones*, was probably written in Austria or Bavaria. See John R. Williams, 'The twelfth century theological "Questiones" of Carpentras Ms. 110', *Mediaeval Studies*, 28 (1966), 300–27. However, the manuscript requires a more thorough study.

[15]   Oxford, Bodleian Library, MS Lyell 49. The manuscript, which was sold in 1936, was formerly no. 382 in the library of Admont. See Albinia de la Mare, *Catalogue of the Collection of Medieval Manuscripts Bequeathed to the Bodleian Library Oxford by James P. R. Lyell* (Oxford, 1971), 131–3.

fourteenth century, but each of its parts was written in the second half of the twelfth century. The manuscript contains commentaries on Boethius' *Opuscula sacra*, among them texts attributed to Thierry of Chartres and his school,[16] and Peter Abelard's *Theologia Summi Boni*.[17] For the second half of the twelfth century, its presence in Admont can, for one part at least, be proved by a contemporary possession mark: 'Hic claustri sancti Blasii liber est Ademunt' (fol. 80v). Whether the other parts of the manuscript were in Admont at that time remains a matter for investigation, but on palaeographic grounds it seems highly probable. As Häring has pointed out, the Admont manuscript is closely related to a manuscript written in the Cistercian monastery of Heilsbronn in the diocese of Eichstätt (Bavaria). Neither of the manuscripts could have been directly copied from the other.[18] Perhaps both were copied from a now lost manuscript from the monastery of Michelsberg in Bamberg. Close contacts existed between Bamberg and Heilsbronn as well as Admont. Indeed, for Admont a possible personal link could be cited: Irimbert, monk of Admont, became abbot of Michelsberg in 1160; in 1172 he returned as abbot to his former monastery.[19]

One of the leading intellectual figures in twelfth-century Austria was Gerhoch of Reichersberg. The manuscript Vienna, Österreichische Nationalbibliothek, MS 1562, a copy of Gilbert of Poitiers' commentary on the epistles of St Paul, can be proved to have been in Gerhoch's hands, for it contains glosses in his handwriting; but it is not known to which library the manuscript belonged.[20] Though it is likely that the manuscript was owned by the canons of Reichersberg, this is difficult to prove, as in the late seventeenth century the major part of the library was destroyed by fire.[21]

---

[16] Nikolaus M. Häring, *Commentaries on Boethius by Thierry of Chartres and His School*, Pontifical Institute of Mediaeval Studies: Studies and Texts, 20 (Toronto, 1971), 25–7.

[17] Nikolaus M. Häring, 'A third manuscript of Peter Abelard's Theologia summi boni (MS Oxford, Bodl. Lyell 49)', *Mediaeval Studies*, 18 (1956), 215–24; Petrus Abaelardus, *Theologia Summi Boni*, ed. Eligius Buytaert and Constant Mews, CChr.CM, 13 (Turnhout, 1987), 60–3.

[18] Erlangen, Universitätsbibliothek, Cod. 182. Häring, 'Third manuscript', 216; Buytaert and Mews, *Theologia Summi Boni*, 57–60.

[19] Ibid., 62–3; Volker Honemann, 'Irimbert von Admont', *Die deutsche Literatur des Mittelalters: Verfasserlexikon*, 2nd edn, 4 (Berlin and New York, 1983), cols 417–19.

[20] Vienna, Österreichische Nationalbibliothek, Cod. 1562. The manuscript was already in the library in 1576. Classen, *Gerhoch*, 435–8, prints some of the glosses.

[21] Julian G. Plante, 'The Library of Stift Reichersberg' (Fordham University, Ph.D. thesis, New York, 1972); idem, *Catalogue of the Manuscripts in the Library of Stift Reichersberg* (Paris,

Vatican Library, MS Vat. lat. 254 provides further evidence of the theological discussions in twelfth-century Austria. Its exact provenance is not known,[22] but it was certainly written in Austria or Bavaria. It contains the *Liber de synodis* of Hilary, Bishop of Poitiers, together with excerpts from his *De Trinitate*. There are a few glosses in the margins, which make clear that the manuscript was used by one of the numerous critics of Gilbert of Poitiers: 'Error hic tercius Gisilbertinis uicinus est dicentibus unam singularem substantiam a tribus commun-icatam qua quisque trium sit deus et que non sit deus.'[23] Hilary of Poitiers was, in fact, the favourite author of Gilbert and his followers. Therefore, their Austrian opponents, Gerhoch of Reichersberg and his partisans, did their best to become well acquainted with the writings of Hilary. The Vatican manuscript is related to a group of manuscripts in Klosterneuburg and Zwettl, containing collections of texts and excerpts of Hilary's works,[24] which demonstrate medieval endeavours to find support for one's own opinion in the writings of the enemy's favourite author. Careful study of the handwriting, illumination, and codicology, and comparison with other manuscripts, can help to establish a manuscript's provenance and *Bibliotheksheimat*, but too often it happens that all efforts prove vain.

Not only the study of the manuscripts but also a thorough examination of the texts and their literary genres can provide interesting insights. The only manuscript of the so-called *Sententiae Florianenses* from the school of Peter Abelard is today in the library of the regular canons at St Florian in Upper Austria. The manuscript is composite, with parts from the twelfth, thirteenth and fourteenth centuries bound together.[25] The *Sententiae Florianenses*[26] are written by

1973); idem, 'The medieval library of the Augustinerchorherrenstift Reichersberg, Austria: towards its reconstruction from two surviving catalogues (Munich, Staatsbibliothek Cod. Bav. 2)', in Kurt Treu, Jörg Dummer, Johannes Irmscher, and Franz Paschke, eds, *Studia Codicologica*, Texte und Untersuchungen zur Geschichte der altchristlichen Literatur, 124 (Berlin, 1977), 363–73.

[22] BAV, Cod. Vat. lat. 254. The upper part of fol. 40, which perhaps bore an ownership mark, is cut off. Cf. Marcus Vatasso and Pius Franchi de' Cavalieri, *Codices Vaticani latini*, 1: *Codices 1–678* (Rome, 1902), 185.

[23] Fol. 15r, right margin. The glossed text is Hilarius of Poitiers, *Liber de synodis*, c.68, ad v. *error hic tercius* (*PL* 10, col. 525).

[24] Klosterneuburg, Stiftsbibliothek, MSS 206, 777; Zwettl, Stiftsbibliothek, MSS 33, 261. Classen, 'Zur Geschichte der Frühscholastik', 297–8.

[25] St Florian, Stiftsbibliothek, Cod. XI, 264. Fols 1, 119–163, twelfth century; fols 2–118, thirteenth century; fols 164–213, fourteenth century.

[26] Fols 147r–163v; the text is incomplete towards the end.

a twelfth-century scribe, probably Austrian or Bavarian. David Luscombe has characterized the text as wholly Abelardian, but remarkably rough in style and elaboration. Abelard's teachings are summarized to such an extent that for a less well informed reader they are likely to cause misunderstandings: 'one has the impression of a private compilation made primarily for personal use'.[27] Another text in the same part of the St Florian manuscript is a treatise on several theological matters (fols 119r–46v). Part of the text (fols 127v–35v) is closely related to the so-called *Sententiae divinitatis* from the school of Gilbert of Poitiers,[28] extant in two manuscripts from the Bavarian monasteries of Tegernsee and St Nikola at Passau.[29] The *Sententiae* and the notes were certainly not copied from each other, but they do have a common source. Is it possible that this common source was not another written text, but the oral teaching of a master of the schools, and that the extant texts are the notes taken by students, elaborated not for publication but for private use? Given the codicological evidence, one might well suspect that the manuscript was originally kept in loose quires, which were later united with other material to form one manuscript. It could be that the texts represent a student's notebook, or a copy of it, brought to medieval Austria by a former student of the Parisian schools.[30] At present these are just conjectures, but it is obvious that the notebook as a literary genre is highly significant for describing the process of transmission of knowledge, and justifies a strong emphasis.

One manuscript still preserving its notebook character is Vienna, Österreichische Nationalbibliothek, MS 2486. Although the texts contained in it have been frequently studied, it seems that until recently nobody has considered its codicology and history.[31] The

[27] David Luscombe, *The School of Peter Abelard. The Influence of Abelard's Thought in the Early Scholastic Period*, Cambridge Studies in Medieval Life and Thought, ns 14 (Cambridge, 1969), 153–8, at 154; *Sententiae Florianenses*, ed. Heinrich Ostlender, Florilegium Patristicum, 19 (Bonn, 1929); Artur M. Landgraf, *Introduction à l'histoire de la littérature théologique de la scolastique naissante*, Université de Montréal: Publications de l'Institut d'études médiévales, 22 (Montréal and Paris 1973), 85.

[28] *Sententiae divinitatis*, ed. Bernhard Geyer, Beiträge zur Geschichte der Philosophie und Theologie des Mittelalters, 7/ii–iii, 2nd edn (Münster, 1967), 52 l.4–97 l.27; Bernhard Geyer, 'Neues und Altes zu den Sententiae divinitatis', in *Mélanges Joseph de Ghellinck S.J.*, 2 vols, Museum Lessianum, Section historique, 13–14 (Gembloux, 1951), 2:617–30; Landgraf, *Introduction*, 112–13.

[29] Munich, Bayerische Staatsbibliothek, Clm 18918, 16063, both twelfth century.

[30] For the *Sententie Florianenses* this was first suggested by Mews, 'The Sententie', 156–74.

[31] The manuscript is especially well known among historians of logic: Martin

manuscript is a small octavo volume consisting of ten quires (all of four leaves except for two, which are of three), each of which is cut in a slightly different size. The cover is made of two reused parchment leaves from an eleventh-century manuscript with texts of Cicero,[32] which were formerly sewn together with thin strips of parchment. The back is strengthened with three small leather ribbons, through which the quires are sewn together. The manuscript contains a large number of texts, written by several twelfth-century scribes. Most of these texts deal with logic and grammar, but also with theological matters. Every empty space is covered with notes. The provenance and original owner of the manuscript are as yet unknown, but a *probatio penne* perhaps provides a clue for further research. This says 'probatio penne gallus nupsit suum (!) henne',[33] *henne* being the German word for 'hen' – it can be assumed, therefore, that the writer was of German tongue. Interestingly enough, there is a similiar *probatio penne* in a manuscript from Indersdorf, a community of regular canons, in the Bavarian diocese of Freising, also written by a certain Gallus.[34] Of course Gallus is not necessarily a proper name, but could perhaps indicate someone coming from France. Nevertheless the *probationes penne* in these two manuscripts might provide a clue not only to the *Bibliotheksheimat* but also to a previous owner of the manuscript, possibly even to the person who brought it to Bavaria.

The question of ownership leads to the problem of prosopography. With respect to the process of transmission of knowledge this is a key issue. Who went to France and Italy to study, and why? Did foreign masters come to Austria? The first question is easier to answer in the general context of the intellectual movement of the twelfth century. A scholar trained in the schools was eligible for an ecclesiastical career, so in addition to intellectual curiosity a strong motive might have been the expectation of receiving a prestigious ecclesiastical

Grabmann, 'Ein Tractatus de Universalibus und andere logische Inedita aus dem 12. Jahrhundert im Cod. lat. 2486 der Nationalbibliothek in Wien', *Mediaeval Studies*, 9 (1947), 56–70; Lambert M. de Rijk, *Logica Modernorum. A Contribution to the History of Early Terminist Logic*, 2 vols in 3, Wijsgerige Teksten en Studies, 6, 16/i–ii (Assen, 1967), 2/i:89–91; idem, 'Some new evidence on twelfth century logic: Alberic and the School of Mont Ste Geneviève (Montani)', *Vivarium*, 4 (1966), 1–57.

[32] Birger Munk Olsen, *L'Étude des auteurs classiques latins aux XIe et XIIe siècles*, 1: *Catalogue des manuscrits classiques latins copiés du IXe aux XIIe siècle. Apicius – Juvenal* (Paris, 1982), 314 no. C.570.

[33] Fols 60vb, 76v.

[34] Munich, Bayerische Staatsbibliothek, Clm 7809, fol. 61v: *Probacio penne Gallus*. Cf. Munk Olsen, *L'Étude*, 1:231, no. C.301.

appointment.[35] Many twelfth-century bishops are known to have spent some time studying in the schools. Otto of Freising, for instance, fifth son of the Austrian margrave Leopold III, went to Paris *c*.1130 and perhaps also to Chartres. His teachers are not known, but it is probable that Hugh of St Victor, Peter Abelard, and Gilbert of Poitiers were among them. In his *Gesta Friderici* Otto gave a thorough description of the conflicts of Abelard and Gilbert of Poitiers with Bernard of Clairvaux, showing his great sympathy towards Gilbert.[36] On his way back from Paris, Otto entered the Cistercian order, and in 1138 he became bishop of the Bavarian diocese of Freising. He died in 1158. It was perhaps through his intervention that, early in the 1150s, master Peter, a French theologian and follower of Gilbert of Poitiers, came to Austria. Very probably Peter lived at the court of the Austrian dukes (margraves until 1156). He became famous not only because of his sometimes heated debates with Gerhoch of Reichersberg, but also for a theological *summa* which he wrote before he left France, still extant in two manuscripts in the monasteries of Zwettl and Admont.[37] It might well be that the remarkable holdings of texts connected with Gilbert of Poitiers and his school in Austrian libraries are associated with Peter's presence.[38]

Eberhard, from 1147 until his death in 1164 archbishop of Salzburg, was another former student in France.[39] As monk of the Benedictine monastery of Prüfening and co-founder and abbot of the abbey of Biburg he was firmly rooted in the monastic tradition. Therefore it is not surprising that he composed an abridged version of Gregory the Great's *Moralia in Iob*, a copy of which he gave to the monastery of St Peter in Salzburg.[40] But other manuscripts in his possession show that

---

[35] Peter Classen, 'Die hohen Schulen und die Gesellschaft im 12. Jahrhundert', in idem, *Studium und Gesellschaft im Mittelalter*, ed. Johannes Fried, *MGH, Schriften*, 29 (Stuttgart, 1983), 1–26.

[36] Otto of Freising, *Gesta Friderici Imperatoris*, I.48–61, ed. G. Waitz, 3rd edn, *MGH, Scriptores rerum Germanicarum in usum scholarum*, [46] (Hanover and Leipzig, 1912), 67–88.

[37] Zwettl, Stiftsbibliothek, MS 109; Admont, Stiftsbibliothek, MS 593. See Häring, *Zwettler Summe*, and the articles of Fichtenau and Classen cited above, nn.5 and 6, and Loris Sturlese, *Die deutsche Philosophie im Mittelalter. Von Bonifatius bis zu Albert dem Großen 748–1280* (Munich, 1993), 145–56.

[38] Häring, *Zwettler Summe*, 8.

[39] 'Quia igitur chorum clericalem monastice tonsus non decuit, sumptibus datis in Franciam discendi causa cum magistro suo directus est. Ubi in tantum profecit, quod sibi seniores suos sensu crescente subegit': *Vita et miracula beati Eberhardi archiepiscopi*, c.2, ed. Wilhelm Wattenbach, *MGH, Scriptores*, 11 (Hanover, 1854), 98 ll.15–17.

[40] *MBKÖ* 4:71 ll.7–8: *De moralibus excerptus, liber beate memorie Eberhardi archiepiscopi*. He also gave a four-volume edition of the *Moralia* and some writings of St Augustine and

his interests ranged further. The cathedral library of Salzburg received a copy of Hugh of St Victor's Commentary on the *Hierarchia caelestis* of (pseudo-)Dionysius the Areopagite.[41] To the library of Admont Eberhard gave Peter the Lombard's commentaries on the Psalms and the Pauline epistles.[42] These texts were part of the scholastic tradition. Like Liebhard of Prüfening, mentioned at the beginning of this paper, Eberhard was educated and interested in both of the twelfth-century theological traditions. As in the case of Liebhard, Eberhard's interest in books shows the concern to keep abreast of contemporary developments in theology, and so integrate the Austrian dioceses and religious houses into the emerging mainstream of scholastic ideas. To achieve this, books were the ideal medium.

University of Vienna

Rupert of Deutz to the Salzburg cathedral library. These manuscripts are now Vienna, Österreichische Nationalbibliothek, MSS 673–6, 727, 1015; Munich, Bayerische Staatsbibliothek, MS 15812.

[41] Vienna, Österreichische Nationalbibliothek, MS 1041. The gift is recorded in a note on fol. 1v: 'Eberhardus archiepiscopus dedit hunc librum ad ecclesiam sancti Ruodberti.'

[42] Admont, Stiftsbibliothek, MSS 36, 52.

BIBLICAL AUTHORITY IN THE WRITING OF POPE INNOCENT IV (1243–54)

by SUSAN MARTIN

WHEN discussing the thirteenth-century concept of Christian unity, Jack Watt asserted, 'Too little is as yet known of the interaction of theological and canonical thought to be able to say with precision just what the canonists contributed to this development among more abstract thinkers and what they received from it.'[1] Thirty-five years on this comment largely remains true for our knowledge of the inter-relation of theology and canon law in the thirteenth century. Little attention has been paid to the impact of theology on canon law, and even less to canon law on theological thinking. G.R. Evans claimed, 'Canon law glosses tend to be conservative and less theologically sophisticated than contemporary theological work.'[2] That comment could be seen as an explanation for how little attention has been paid to the theological content of canonical writing. However, canon law glosses were written principally to investigate law. The area of 'sophistication' was different. Yet, this is not to say that there was no interest in theological questions and their possible solutions on the part of the canonists. All canon lawyers had a theological education, and they cited biblical references to support their arguments extensively. This paper aims to show that the use and understanding of contemporary medieval theology had an important impact on the writing of thirteenth-century canon lawyers, which should not be readily overlooked by modern scholars.

To investigate this idea, the relationship between two books, the Bible and a legal commentary, will be discussed through one extract. The passage has been taken from the *Commentaria* of Pope Innocent IV

---

[1] John A. Watt, *The Theory of Papal Monarchy in the Thirteenth Century: the Contribution of the Canonists* (1965), 105.

[2] G.R. Evans, 'Exegesis and authority in the thirteenth century', in M.D. Jordan and K. Emery, Jr, eds, *Ad Litteram: Authoritative Texts and their Medieval Readers* (Notre Dame, IN, 1992), 98. Evans's article makes a compelling case for a change in the approach to authorities in the thirteenth century. However, as with much of the secondary material on biblical exegesis, its focus is the consideration of specifically theological writings.

(1243–54).[3] The *Commentaria* provides historians with a synthesis of Innocent's legal thinking throughout his career, based upon his understanding of the body of canon law held within the *Liber Extra*. The text is presented as a collection of theoretical comments on legal technicalities. Innocent's discussion of the competency of courts and the appropriate choice of courts for particular cases highlights a number of aspects of Innocent's use of biblical texts within legal commentary.[4] This one short passage from 'De foro competenti' embodies the interdependence of theology and canon law in the medieval Church.

The overall concern of the chapter from which the passage is taken is the consideration of papal plenitude of power.[5] Innocent starts by looking at the relationship of the pope to the emperor, particularly in an imperial vacancy. He claims that when there is a failing (*defectum*) with imperial power, the pope should take control, as imperial power is derived from papal power.[6] However, Innocent is careful to point out that this only happens in the given situation because of the special relationship between pope and emperor, and that the pope does not have recourse to power normally when there is a secular vacancy.[7] The text continues with examples of when the pope could intervene in secular affairs. However, Innocent was aware that any papal interference was open to criticism. He comments that some people did not think that the pope should be ascribed so much trust. To counter this criticism, he produces a lengthy pedigree for the papacy, claiming that the accusers are committing sacrilege by making such accusations.[8] The evidence for this pedigree is a 'history

---

[3] Innocent IV, *Commentaria in quinque libros apparatus* (Venice, 1610). Various editions of the commentary exist; although there are textual problems and inaccuracies, these are not substantial in the extract being used here.

[4] Ibid., Ad X 2.2.10 (238–9), 'De foro competenti'.

[5] Watt discussed the political significance of this passage: *Theory of Papal Monarchy*, 65–70.

[6] *Commentaria*, 238b: 'Vacante – hoc est propter defectum imperii, in iure enim tantum imperii papa succedit.'

[7] Ibid., 238b: 'unde si alius rector alii superiori quam imperatori subditus negligens esset in reddenda ratione, vel non esset rector in aliqua terra, tunc non devolvetur iurisdictio ad papam, sed ad proximum superiorem, nam specialis coniunctio est inter papam et imperatorem, quia papa eum consecrat et examinat, et est imperator eius advocatus, et iurat ei, et ab eo imperium tenet.'

[8] Ibid., 239a: 'Sed dicet aliquis, hoc summos pontifices statuere pro se, unde cum non sine culpa sacreligii loquatur, non est sibi tanta fides adhibenda . . . sed hi si diligenter attendunt quod dicunt, veri sacreligii culpam incurrunt.'

of the world', to show the bases upon which the pope holds his power.[9]

The 'history' gives a synopsis of the first nine chapters from Genesis in one paragraph, then, in the following paragraph, there is a brief explanation of the designation of Peter as Christ's successor, which had given the pope his role as ultimate judge. In total the extract runs to little more than three hundred words. The particular areas Innocent highlights are the creation of heaven and earth; the giving and breaking of God's law by Adam and Eve; the punishments of Adam, Eve, Lamech, Ham, and others; government and law of the world being given to Noah; and, finally, the priestly activities of Noah. He ends the first paragraph by saying the vicariate ultimately went to Christ, 'qui fuit naturalis dominus et rex noster'. The second paragraph concentrates upon the influence of Christ. Innocent points out that Christ conferred the vicariate on Peter and his successors by giving Peter the keys to the kingdom of heaven, and by the instruction, 'Feed my sheep'. This vicariate conferred on the pope the role of ultimate judge. He comments that 'licet in multis distincta sint officia et regimina mundi', even so papal justice can, and should, still be sought in the given circumstances.

Innocent's analysis works on a number of levels, representing something of the complexity of the claim for papal power. The text is a chronological list of the steps by which St Peter, the predecessor of the popes, received the keys to the kingdom of heaven from Christ. The position of pope is legitimized within the Bible itself, especially on the basis of the New Testament. Matthew 16.18–19 tells of Peter's establishment as head of the Church as an institution, whilst John 21.17 has him being made substitute shepherd for the community of believers. There is not just one tenuous claim for the importance of papal power. Peter's designation by Christ is clear and irrefutable. Yet this proof is not to be found only in the New Testament: Old Testament evidence prophesying Christ's ministry can be traced all the way back to the first chapter of Genesis. Innocent begins his 'history' with the earliest of the Genesis stories, the Creation: 'deus creavit in principio coelum et terram.' God is the creator of each and every thing, and so also of the pontiff. So, firstly, origins are important; but the length of the pedigree is also worth noting. The long lineage described here gives gravity to the role of

---

[9] See appendix for text.

pope. The forebears of the pope include the patriarchs, judges, priests, and kings, representing the four eras of succession used in analysis of biblical chronology in the Middle Ages.[10] There is an inevitability that the lineage described in the Old Testament preordained the vicariate of St Peter. The history then ends with Christ and St Peter from the New Testament, confirming beyond doubt that the pope has a solid claim to his role as leader of Christian men. The chronology spans the six ages, from the creation of Adam, to the coming of Christ,[11] emphasising the magnitude of the pontiff's office. The first paragraph acts as an explanation and justification for the second. There is biblical authority to prove that the pope holds his position as ultimate judge from God, and that this is part of the natural order, predestined since Creation.

How this argument is presented merits close attention. The Genesis stories were so well known and frequently interpreted that Innocent did not need to use any more than the bare bones of their structure. His intended audience, university-educated canonists, would have had a common background, and the study of Genesis would have been an integral part of that education. Yet his choice of highlighted sections is revealing. He says little about the creation of the world, but a lot about the origins of the Christian community, a community which was firmly united by the Flood and entry into the Ark, 'per quam ecclesia significatur'. B.B. Price argues that the Old Testament provided the justification for a clergy that is distinct from the laity – that God gave the government of his creation to a special group.[12] She further argues that the clergy were perceived as being descended from the Apostles, and therefore not from the community at large, that they were, in fact, specially nominated by God, which manifested itself in the central role of bishops in the medieval Church. Innocent supports this idea by identifying Noah and his line as having been given the governance and law of the Church to administer, 'Dominus Noe et filiis rectoriam et legem sibi dedit.' God had chosen Noah as a leader, to be responsible for the creation of the Church through the building of the Ark. Noah was the first priest, from whom all others are descended.

James H. Morey observed in 1993 that 'Genesis is not so much the

---

[10] M.-D. Chenu, *Nature, Man, and Society in the Twelfth Century: Essays on New Theological Perspectives in the Latin West* (Chicago, 1968), 180.

[11] Ibid., 180.

[12] B.B. Price, *Medieval Thought: an Introduction* (Oxford, 1992), 19.

story of Creation as the story of the Fall.'[13] This comment seems to be upheld by Innocent's commentary. The elements of Genesis that Innocent picks out focus on the personalities involved, and so on the need for Christ to save the world, and then elect Peter to continue his ministry. Beyond 'in the beginning God created heaven and earth', which is to establish a timeframe before which there is nothing, Innocent's selected highlights only concern people: Adam, Eve, Cain, Abel, Noah, Lamech, and Ham. The Old Testament was viewed as full of prophecies which were fulfilled by the New. The prophecy of Christ's coming started right back with the creation of Adam, who caused the fall of man, and so the need for Christ to come and give man salvation. God then needed to create a priesthood by which he could govern man.

The use of signs and symbols is a further element of biblical interpretation that needs attention here.[14] Signs are an important feature of a religion because they provide an instant point of recognition. They also obviate the need for a common language, or literacy.[15] In Christianity, the most prominent of these signs is the cross. In this passage, we have two signs that require a greater biblical knowledge, the keys and the Ark. Arguably this particular choice reflects a more 'intellectual' or 'taught' approach to the Bible. The high Middle Ages saw an increased elevation of the reliance on textual authority, whether that be in the form of legal collections or 'historia'. Innocent's *Commentaria* was written by an intellectual for an educated audience who would have been strongly conscious of the symbolic nature of these two items. The symbolism is necessary to explain the world properly.[16] If one were oblivious to the fact that the Ark signified the Church, then the understanding of Genesis would not be complete, and the lengthy pedigree of the Church dating back to Genesis would not be fully recognized. Innocent did not expect that

[13] James H. Morey, 'Peter Comestor, biblical paraphrase and the medieval popular Bible', *Speculum*, 68 (1993), 16.

[14] Although a number of writers distinguish between them, I have used the terms 'sign' and 'symbol' interchangeably.

[15] Price, *Medieval Thought*, 16.

[16] From the other point of view, note Gerhart Ladner, 'Medieval and modern understanding of symbolism: a comparison', *Speculum*, 54, (1979), 230–1: 'Moreover, the symbolic world view of the Middle Ages cannot be understood without reference to a sacred history which was conceived as a coherent sequence of divinely planned happenings, from creation through the events of the Old and New Testaments and the salvation-oriented progression of mankind.'

any of the above required explanation, rather he anticipated a readership with a common background: 'Nota quod' connotes 'remember that' rather than 'listen carefully to what I am explaining to you'. This accounts for the cursory nature of the passage. He is running through the obvious, rather than providing any new interpretation.

Signs function in a number of ways in a text. Firstly, there is the need to identify them. In Ad X 2.2.10 we have the two signs, the Ark and the keys. The Ark is the more explicit of the two. Innocent flags its presence by saying, 'sibi Dominus gubernationem arche per quam ecclesia significatur'. After identification comes interpretation. Very simplistically, the Ark is a symbol for the Church. However, there are slightly more subtle implications in what Innocent actually writes. He says, 'God committed to him [Noah] the governance of the Ark, by which the Church is signified.' *'Ecclesia'* originally meant a meeting of people, and so Noah's governance of this group also symbolizes the beginning of an organized Church and Church hierarchy. The Ark, as a vessel, survived a flood which destroyed the rest of the world, providing an effective vehicle to safety for those on board, and so a step, symbolically, towards salvation. The keys were given to St Peter to symbolize the granting of the guardianship of the Church. Along with the keys, Christ gave Peter the ability to bind and loose members of the Christian community, thus assigning him the authority to judge and hand out judgements.[17] Finally, there is the expectation that consideration of the above will lead to the extrication of meaning. Innocent's meaning in this context becomes more apparent when the second paragraph is reconsidered.

The second paragraph of the extract extends the history up to the thirteenth-century present. Innocent discusses the significance of 'claves regni coelorum'. When Christ gave these keys to St Peter and his successors, he was assigning them authority over all peoples. Numerous different 'officia et regimina' are allowed in the world; however, there are circumstances under which the pope needs to become involved. Innocent gives four instances of when this intervention would be necessary.[18] Each of these refers to an occasion when the implementation of ecclesiastical justice would be put in jeopardy if the pope did not step in. The first situation was if a judge was in doubt

[17] Matt. 16.19.
[18] *Commentaria*, Ad X 2.2.10.

as to which sentence to give. The second was when a superior judge was needed, with the pope as the only candidate, being the supreme judge in canon law. The third case required the assistance of the pope if lesser judges could not execute their sentences, or, as in the fourth case, if these lesser judges did not want to exercise justice. These four cases contribute to an impression of Innocent's view of the extent of papal monarchy. The text considers the basis for the authority of the pope in order to show that the ultimate source to justice lies in that office. The psalm quoted (72, or 71 in the Vulgate) identifies Christ as the administrator of God's justice. Through St Peter, Christ's designated vicar, the pope wields this power in the medieval Church. Even the Old Testament elements cited relate to justice and law. First, God enforced order and dispensed punishment. He then gave the law and responsibility for its enforcement to Noah and his sons. This office was passed on through the four successions, 'et sic duravit usque ad Christum, qui fuit naturalis dominus et rex noster'. This responsibility for justice now rested in the hands of the pope, because Christ chose St Peter as his vicar. The pope, as lawgiver and dispenser of punishment, assumed these duties on behalf of God.

This assessment of a passage from Innocent IV's *Commentaria* shows clearly that biblical exegesis could play a fundamental part in medieval legal commentary. Innocent made complex, and subtle, use of Old and New Testament references. He associated papal history firmly with biblical history, thus producing a solid and indisputable heritage, which it would be sacrilegious to dispute. His views on legal practice in the thirteenth century were supported, again, by using the powerful weapon of biblical authority. However, this should not be viewed as unusual. Innocent was writing in a format familiar to his contemporaries, which is not fully acknowledged by historians. The 'interaction' between medieval theology and canon law is still a rich seam to be mined.

University of Birmingham

APPENDIX

[Innocent IV, *Commentaria in quinque libros apparatus* (Venice, 1610), p. 239]

Quod ut melius intelligas praenominata, nota quod deus creavit in principio coelum et terram et omnia quae in eis sunt, angelicam et humanam naturam, spiritualia et temporalia, ipsaque per seipsum rexit, sicut factor suam rem gubernat, et homini quem fecit praecepta dedit, et transgrediendi poenam imposuit, ut Gen. 2[.16], 'ex omni ligno', et c., ipsis etiam peccantibus poenam imposuit per seipsum, scilicet Adae et Evae, Gen. 3[.16–17]: 'mulieri quoque dixit' et c., et ibi 'Ade vero dixit' et c. Qualiter autem Chain per seipsum puniverit, et Lamech, et Cham, et quosdam alios, in eodem librum Gen. 4 et 5 legitur. Et sic recto mundo per ipsum Deum usque ad Noe. Ex tempore Noe coepit Deus creaturas suas regere per ministros duos. Primus fuit Noe, de quo quod fuerit rector populi ex eo apparet quia sibi dominus gubernationem archae, per quam ecclesia significatur, commisit, Gen. 5 et 6. Item, quia etiam dominus Noe et filiis rectoriam et legem sibi dedit, Gen. 9. De Noe etiam, licet non legatur sacerdos fuisse, officium tamen exercuit sacerdotis statim post ingressum *[sic]* archae antequam leges populo daret, Gen. 8[.20]:, 'aedificavit autem Noe'. Quod officium sacerdotis simul Abel et Chain primo fecerant. In hac autem vicaria successerunt patriarchae, iudices, reges, sacerdotes, et alii qui pro tempore fuerunt in regimine populi iudaeorum, et sic duravit usque ad Christum qui fuit naturalis dominus et rex noster, de quo dicitur in psalmo [71.2]: 'Deus iudicium tuum regi da' et c.

Et ipse Iesus Christus vicarium suum constituit Petrum et successores suos quando ei dedit claves regni coelorum, et quando dixit ei [John 21.17]: 'pasce oves meas'. Licet in multo distincta sint officia et regimina mundi, tamen quandocunque necesse est, ad papam recurrendum est, sive sit necessitas iuris quia iudex dubius est quam sententiam de iure proferre debeat; vel necessitas facti, quia alius non sit iudex superior; sive facti puta, quia de facto minores iudices non possunt suas sententias exequi vel nolunt ut debent iusticiam exercere.

IMAGES OF LADIES WITH PRAYER BOOKS:
WHAT DO THEY SIGNIFY?

by MICHAEL CLANCHY

Monastic illumination of manuscripts gave to writings a force and prestige which was unprecedented. Throughout the millennium of western monasticism (500–1500 A.D.), the rich founded monasteries so that monks might pray and worship on their behalf. The monks displayed the fruit of their labours to their patrons in their churches and other works of art, particularly in their books. When with growing prosperity from about 1250 onwards the demand for individual prayer reached down to the middle class of knights and burgesses, they began to want wonder-working books of their own. They could not afford to buy a chantry chapel or a jewelled reliquary, but a small illuminated manuscript came within their means as the first step towards the purchase of paradise. Ladies in particular took to reciting the Latin Psalter and treasuring illuminated Books of Hours. In fifteenth-century depictions of the Annunciation, Mary is often shown seated in a sunlit bower with an open Book of Hours on her lap or displayed on a lectern. Likewise she is sometimes depicted with the Child Jesus on her knee, showing him a Book of Hours. The habit of possessing books might never have reached the laity if writing had not been so luxurious and so covetable. Illumination introduced the laity to script through images which could not fail to attract the eye. The children of the prosperous were introduced to the Psalter by their mothers or a priest for the purpose both of learning to read and of beginning formal prayer. To own a Psalter was therefore an act of familial as well as public piety.[1]

THESE words were written twenty years ago, for a conference at the Library of Congress in 1980 on 'Literacy in historical perspective'. Since then, these themes have been addressed in several lectures and research papers at conferences, and I would stand by the main ideas expressed in that passage. Monks had indeed given

---

[1] M.T. Clanchy, 'Looking back from the invention of printing', in Daniel P. Resnick, ed., *Literacy in Historical Perspective* (Washington DC, 1983), 14.

extraordinary prestige to books and in particular to the illuminated liturgical book, which is a medieval invention.[2] By the thirteenth century such books were being adapted for lay use and ownership, typically in Books of Hours.[3] However, it is mistaken to say that lay use 'began' then, as the aristocracy – particularly in Germany – had been familiar with prayer books for centuries. In the twelfth century, Hildegard of Bingen was said to have learned only the Psalter 'as is the custom of noble girls'.[4] A Psalter for lay use dating from *c*.1150, which belonged to Clementia von Zähringen, has been preserved.[5] It contains a full-page portrait of a lady – presumably Clementia herself – at folio 6v between the end of the Calendar and the Beatus page beginning the Psalms. This book has 126 folios in its present state (possibly one folio is missing at the end) and it measures 11 cm × 7 cm, no larger than a woman's hand. The biography of Marianus Scotus, the eleventh-century Irish hermit who settled at Regensburg, describes how he wrote for poor widows and clerics 'many little books and many Psalter manuals' ('multos libellos multaque manualia psalteria').[6] The diminutive form 'libellos' and the adjective 'manualia' emphasise that these manuscripts were small enough to hold in the hand, like Clementia von Zähringen's book.

The demand for personal prayer books had 'reached down to the middle class of knights and burgesses' by the fifteenth century, but not as early as 1250 (as suggested in 1980). The ownership of books is often difficult to establish. Where the ownership of private prayer books is known, the earliest ones tend to belong to aristocratic women, like Clementia von Zähringen, or the great ladies (starting with Eleanor of Aquitaine) whose images are discussed later in this paper. A notable

---

[2] In general see Jonathan J.G. Alexander, *Medieval Illuminators and Their Methods of Work* (New Haven, CT, 1992) and Christopher de Hamel, *A History of Illuminated Manuscripts*, 2nd edn (1994).

[3] The difference between Psalters and Books of Hours, and the evolution for lay use of the latter from the former, is succinctly explained by John Harthan, *Books of Hours and their Owners* (1977), 12–19.

[4] 'More nobilium puellarum': James Westfall Thompson, *The Literacy of the Laity in the Middle Ages* (Berkeley, CA, 1939), 100, 115, n.154. Michelle P. Brown, 'Female book ownership and production in Anglo-Saxon England: the evidence of ninth-century prayer books', in Christian J. Kay and Louise M. Sylvester, eds, *Lexis and Texts in Early English: Studies Presented to Jane M. Roberts*, Costerus, ns 133 (Amsterdam and Atlanta, GA, 2001), 45–67, appeared after this paper had been completed.

[5] Baltimore MD, Walters Art Gallery, MS W.10. There is no published description of this book.

[6] Thompson, *Literacy of the Laity*, 92–3.

exception to the rule that such books belonged to women is the Luttrell Psalter dating from c.1330, as it declares: 'Sir Geoffrey Luttrell had me made.'[7] Grand books like this 'must, in effect, have belonged to the household rather than to individuals', as Peter Coss points out.[8] The generalization that the earliest private prayer books belonged principally to aristocrats may be skewed by the circumstances of their survival. Families tended to keep, and collectors have particularly valued, the most precious illuminated manuscripts. The cheaper and plainer books, which Marianus Scotus for example was writing for poor widows in Regensburg, would not have survived daily use over many decades, nor would they have been attractive to collectors in the first place. Generally in medieval culture it is the commonplace that is hardest to find out about, because things in day-to-day use were not deliberately preserved.

My generalization of 1980 that 'ladies in particular took to reciting the Latin Psalter and treasuring illuminated Books of Hours' is confirmed by publications of the last two decades. The path-breaking article of 1982 by Susan Bell on 'Medieval women book owners: arbiters of lay piety and ambassadors of culture' is reinforced by the work (still in progress) of Adelaide Bennett of the Princeton Institute of Christian Art.[9] In 1991 Claire Donovan published her monograph on the exceptionally early and fine Book of Hours which was made in Oxford in c.1240 by the illuminator and scribe William de Brailes. The unidentified female owner (possibly named Susanna) is portrayed at prayer in some of its initials and Donovan points out that 'before the end of the thirteenth century, ordinary laywomen were portrayed in five more of the eight surviving Books of Hours made in England'.[10] She comments that 'from her portrait it appears that she [Susanna] was no aristocrat'.[11] The ordinariness of these women is questionable, however, as only the upper class commanded the wealth to commis-

---

[7] 'Dominus Galfridus louterell' me fieri fecit': Michael Camille, *Mirror in Parchment: the Luttrell Psalter and the Making of Medieval England* (1998), 49 and pl. 29.

[8] *The Lady in Medieval England, 1000–1500* (Stroud, 1998), 169.

[9] Bell's article was first published in *Signs*, 7 (1982), 742–68. It has been reprinted twice: in Mary Erler and Mariane Kowaleski, eds, *Women and Power in the Middle Ages* (Athens, GA, 1988), 149–87, and in Judith M. Bennett, ed., *Sisters and Workers in the Middle Ages* (Chicago, 1988), 135–61. See also Adelaide Bennett, 'A thirteenth-century French Book of Hours for Marie', *The Journal of the Walters Art Gallery*, 54 (1996), 21–50.

[10] *The de Brailes Hours: Shaping the Book of Hours in Thirteenth-Century Oxford* (1991), 152. 'Susanna' is shown at colour plates 2, 15 and 16a.

[11] Ibid., 24.

sion manuscripts as richly illuminated as these are. Nevertheless, Donovan is surely right to conclude that 'while the Book of Hours was by no means used only by women, it is certainly in these manuscripts that literate women emerge most visibly during the thirteenth century; and it is in these books that the life of the laity, in relation to the life of the Church, also emerges'.[12]

Private prayer books belonged to the domestic sphere of the household, like bed linen, jewellery, and clothing. In 1438 a Spanish priest, Martinez de Toledo, remonstrated that women should value sacred books and not secular songs and love letters: in their coffers should be found 'Hours of Holy Mary, the Seven [Penitential] Psalms, lives of the saints, and the Psalter in the vernacular'.[13] The *Sachsenspiegel*, along with other German lawbooks dating from the 1220s and 1230s, mentions among household things 'the Psalter and all books pertaining to the service of God which women usually read'.[14] What is meant by 'read' ('lesen' in the *Sachsenspiegel*) in the context of women's prayer books? Even among the aristocracy, women's knowledge of Latin was declining from the thirteenth century onwards, as the gulf widened between boys educated in grammar schools and girls brought up at home. At the same time writing in vernaculars was on the increase, and upper-class women might master this rather than Latin. In order to compete with the secular tone of much of this new literature, all sorts of religious material was translated from Latin, like the version of the 'Psalter in the vernacular' ('salterio de romance') mentioned by Martinez de Toledo. Nevertheless, the texts of prayer books continued to be written predominantly in Latin because the principal purpose of a Book of Hours was to provide in the home a programme of authentic devotions which matched those of the regular clergy in church.

The comment by Bishop John Fisher, who had been Lady Margaret Beaufort's confessor earlier in his career, is sometimes cited to show that women had little comprehension of the Latin in their prayer books. In a sermon of 1509 he said that her knowledge consisted of 'a

---

[12] Ibid., 156. On the closeness of male and female lay piety, cutting across gender lines, see Coss, *The Lady*, 169–73.

[13] A. Martinez de Toledo, *Arciprestre de Talavera o Corbacho*, ed. J.G. Muela (Madrid, 1970), 135. I owe this reference to Dr Jane Whetnall.

[14] *Sachsenspiegel*, Lxxiv.3, ed. K.A. Eckhart, *MGH, Fontes Iuris* (Gottingen, 1955), 91. D.H. Green, *Medieval Listening and Reading: the Primary Reception of German Literature, 800–1300* (Cambridge, 1994), 290, 414 n.246.

little perceiving specially of the rubric of the ordinal for the saying of her service which she did well understand'.[15] In other words, she could work out the day and order of service by identifying the correct rubricated initial in her book. As Lady Margaret, the mother of Henry VII of England, translated portions of *The Imitation of Christ* and other devotional works into English, her linguistic competence was probably greater than Fisher was willing to allow.[16] But these translations were done from French, and Margaret was typical of fifteenth-century ladies in receiving no formal schooling in Latin. This being so, how could she have made sense of the texts in her prayer book? Throughout the Middle Ages 'reading' (*legere*) and 'understanding' (*intellegere*) were recognized as distinct and progressive stages of attainment. The essential element in reading was correct pronunciation. This is best illustrated by the incident in Chaucer's Prioress's Tale where the boy beginning school asks an older pupil to explain the words of the Latin Antiphon which he knows by heart. He receives the answer: 'I can expound no more in this matter; I learn song, I know but little grammar.'[17] Abelard complained that many monasteries only taught chant, which is 'merely a way of forming words without understanding them' like the bleating of sheep.[18] But elsewhere he had commended to Heloise and her nuns St Jerome's advice that 'one reaches the sense of the words from their sound, and someone who learns to pronounce them will already want to understand them.'[19] The fifteenth-century friar Osbern Bokenham in his life of St Elizabeth of Hungary explained that she had no knowledge of Latin, but she would often have a Psalter open before her, which she mused on 'as though she had read even by and by'.[20]

Clerics believed that Latin could only be understood by experts like themselves who had been painfully instructed in it over many years. But repeated recitation of the same texts, articulated into short accessible passages, might itself be a process of learning which could

[15] Margaret Aston, *Lollards and Reformers: Images and Literacy in Late Medieval Religion* (1984), 124 n.72; Nicholas Orme, *From Childhood to Chivalry: the Education of the English Kings and Aristocracy, 1066–1530* (1984), 161.

[16] Alexandra Barrett, ed., *Women's Writing in Middle English* (London, 1992), 301–10. For Margaret Beaufort see also the references in Coss, *The Lady*, 171, 201 n.60.

[17] *The Complete Works of Geoffrey Chaucer*, ed. F.N. Robinson, 2nd edn (Boston, MA, 1957), 162 ll.535–6 (my modernization).

[18] M.T. Clanchy, *Abelard – a Medieval Life* (Oxford, 1997), 61; PL 178, cols 307–8.

[19] Clanchy, *Abelard*, 62; PL 178, col. 328a.

[20] Orme, *From Childhood*, 161 (my modernization).

lead the user of a prayer book to 'read even by and by'. Adelaide Bennett argues that the Book of Hours 'provided the chief means of instructing a laywoman to read in Latin. It was a primer. Through pronunciation, recitation, and familiarity of Latin texts in her constant practice of devotions, she learned to read.'[21] There will never be general agreement among modern scholars about medieval women's understanding of their prayer books, as opinions about this differed at the time. A snapshot of a lady at prayer is provided in Matthew Paris's account of an attempt to assassinate Henry III of England in 1238. A man had broken into the palace at night; but Margaret Biset, one of the queen's ladies, raised the alarm. She was still awake because she was reciting (literally 'chanting', 'psaltebat') her Psalter by candlelight.[22]

The archetypal image of the lady at prayer, vigilantly awaiting her hour of destiny, is that of the Virgin Mary kneeling or sitting with her book open at the moment of the Annunciation. This image had developed in parallel with women using Books of Hours in their homes. In the thirteenth century and earlier, Mary was generally shown at the Annunciation occupied in meditating while she spins yarn or clasps a closed book, which originally signified the prophecy in Isaiah 7.14, 'Behold, a virgin shall conceive'.[23] From the fourteenth century onwards, by contrast, Mary's book is nearly always shown open and it is often represented as a small illuminated manuscript, like the prayer books which women used. This is why in 1980 I described Mary as having a 'Book of Hours on her lap'.[24] There is a difficulty here, however, as the Hours of the Virgin (which is the commonest liturgy in a Book of Hours) includes prayers to Mary herself. It would be nonsensical, for example, for her to have been reciting the 'Hail Mary' from her book at the moment of the Annunciation. Nevertheless, there are numerous prayers in a Book of Hours which would be appropriate for Mary herself to say, especially the extracts from the Psalms.

[21] 'A thirteenth-century French Book of Hours', 29. See also Marjorie Curry Woods, 'Shared books: Primers, Psalters and the adult acquisition of literacy among devout laywomen and women in orders in late medieval England', in Juliette Dor, Lesley Johnson, and Jocelyn Wogan-Browne, eds, *New Trends in Feminine Spirituality: the Holy Women of Liege and their Impact* (Turnhout, 1999), 181–8.

[22] *Matthei Parisiensis Chronica Majora*, ed. H.R. Luard, 7 vols, RS (1872–83), 2:497, 4:200; Margaret Howell, *Eleanor of Provence: Queenship in Thirteenth-Century England* (Oxford, 1998), 22–3.

[23] M.T. Clanchy, *From Memory to Written Record: England 1066–1307*, 2nd edn (Oxford, 1993), 192. In general see K. Schreiner, 'Marienverehrung, Lesekultur, Schriftlichkeit', *Frühmittelalterliche Studien*, 24 (1990), 314–68.

[24] See n.1 above.

Moreover, the supernatural scenes depicted in Books of Hours stand outside time. As Queen of Heaven and Mother of God, Mary commands knowledge of the past, present, and future. The prayers prescribed in a Book of Hours allow her, together with the earthly user of the book, to weep for her son at the crucifixion or rejoice at the moment of his conception.

Roger Wieck has published a pair of pictures, on facing pages in a French Book of Hours from the 1450s, which demonstrate how the image of the Virgin with her book open functioned as a role model for the anonymous woman owner of this book.[25] She is depicted on the left-hand page, kneeling at prayer with her book open on a prie-dieu, facing on the right-hand page an image of the Virgin with her book open on an altar in front of a closed tabernacle flanked by candles, which presumably contains the consecrated host of the Eucharist. (The reference to the Eucharist and the portrait of the book owner emphasise how such scenes stand outside historical time.) This is in fact an Annunciation scene spread over two pages. On the left the Angel Gabriel stands behind the owner of the book and puts his hand on her shoulder, as if encouraging her in her prayer or introducing her to the Virgin on the page opposite. Mary on her side is shown being miraculously impregnated by the Holy Spirit, in the conventional form of a dove, while she looks directly out of the picture, as if she might at any moment make eye contact with the book owner. A Latin text is placed on each page, immediately beneath each picture: on the left is the 'Hail Mary', which is appropriate as the book owner's prayer; on the right is verse 17 of Psalm 50 in the Vulgate text (Psalm 51.15 in the Authorized Version), which is the beginning of Matins in the Little Office of the Virgin. This would be an appropriate prayer for the Virgin herself to say at the moment of the Annunciation, as it reads: 'O Lord, open thou my lips; and my mouth shall shew forth [annunciabit] thy praise.' Commenting on this pair of pictures, Sandra Penketh points out that the figure of the book owner and that of the Virgin are on the same scale and juxtaposed in the same space: 'this equality of composition helps to promote the sense of intimacy, the feeling of actually being present at the event'.[26]

<hr>

[25] *The Book of Hours in Medieval Art and Life* (1988), 44 and fig. 12, see also colour plate 14.

[26] 'Women and Books of Hours', in Jane H.M. Taylor and Lesley Smith, eds, *Women and the Book: Assessing the Visual Evidence* (1997), 272.

This book owner is depicted as if she were herself present at the moment of the Annunciation, the crucial event in the Christian dispensation. How could a lay person be so privileged, when she was neither a saint, nor a priest, nor even a man? This image, together with the many others which show female book owners experiencing intimate visions of God, suggests that the significance of personal prayer books goes far beyond the question of whether their owners were literate or not. Certainly 'illumination introduced the laity to script through images which could not fail to attract the eye';[27] but beyond that these images themselves provide evidence of lay women's spirituality through the ambitious models they present of personal prayer.[28] This issue, however, must be addressed circumspectly, to avoid the pitfalls which Michael Camille has characterized as 'art as text' and 'art as mirror'.[29] Images of ladies with their prayer books are not descriptions ('texts') of how reading was done and neither are they depictions ('mirrors') of reading taking place. The images are not evidence of literacy in a modern functional sense because the reading ability of these ladies is itself enigmatic.

Images of ladies with their prayer books indicate something more personal and profound than an ability to read. 'It is through the image that we construct the imaginary,' Michael Camille argues, 'and in psychoanalytic terms, the subject.'[30] The anonymous lady, who is depicted kneeling at her prie-dieu between the Angel Gabriel and the Virgin Mary, is entering into – and engaging with – the imagined experience of the Mother of God. The Latin texts of Books of Hours, like liturgical texts in general, are standardized and limited in scope. In reciting them, lay prayer book users imitated their priests and chaplains in ways which look passive and derivative. There must have been 'a considerable amount of what might be labelled "passive literacy"', as Robert Swanson has suggested.[31] As distinct from the uniformity of liturgical texts and of collective worship in church services, however, the images in prayer books allowed their users an active and individual role in religion in the privacy of their own homes. 'Books of Hours with female owner portraits provide us with

---

[27] See n.1 above.
[28] *From Memory*, 2nd edn, 13, 19, 111–12, 135, 188–96, 251–2, 290.
[29] 'Art history in the past and future of medieval studies', in J. van Engen, ed., *The Past and Future of Medieval Studies* (Notre Dame, IL, 1994), 367.
[30] Ibid., 366.
[31] *Religion and Devotion in Europe, c.1215–c.1515* (Cambridge, 1995), 79.

evidence not only of a strong female patronage but also of an active participation in personal worship on the part of their owners.'[32] Through the skill of the artist, a picture can represent the imaginary as readily as it records what is actually seen. This is why images can play such a powerful role in religion. In her prayer book the anonymous lady owner can be placed, in her modest but fashionable fifteenth-century dress, in the presence of the Angel Gabriel and the Virgin Annunciate.

In her discussion of 'Devotional literacy', Margaret Aston cites the remarkable statement of Bishop William Durandus that *pictura* (meaning 'painting' or 'picturing' in all its senses) is more potent than *scriptura* (meaning 'writing' in all its senses, including Holy Scripture).[33] Durandus was writing in the latter half of the thirteenth century and his context was the classic statement of Pope Gregory the Great that painting was done in churches so that 'those who do not know letters may at least read by seeing on the walls what they are unable to read in books'.[34] In Gregory's argument pictures were an ancillary aid for the illiterate, whereas Durandus went further by suggesting that 'picturing [*pictura*] seems to move the mind more than writing [*scriptura*] does'.[35] He exploited all the ambiguities in the Latin words he deployed in order to make this statement look at one and the same time like a small development from Gregory's thought and a radical reinterpretation of it. Durandus' statement can just as well be translated: 'A picture is seen to move the feelings [*animum*] more than a writing does.' The Latin *animus* is a word rich in meanings, including mind, spirit, heart, soul, feeling, and passion. Durandus gave a psychological explanation for the power of *pictura*: it places an action or event directly before the eyes, whereas a description in writing moves the feelings less because the action is recalled to the memory as it were by hearing. (This contrast depends on the assumption, which was commonplace in medieval culture, that reading involves the laborious process of listening as each word on the page is pronounced.) He was consequently able to conclude that

32 Penketh, 'Women and Books of Hours', 280.

33 Aston, *Lollards and Reformers*, 116.

34 This passage is cited and discussed by Celia M. Chazelle, 'Pictures, books and the illiterate: Pope Gregory I's letters to Serenus of Marseilles', *Word and Image*, 6 (1990), 139.

35 'Pictura namque plus videtur movere animum quam scriptura': *Guillelmi Duranti Rationale divinorum officiorum*, ed. A. Davril and T.M. Thibodeau, CChr.CM, 140 (1995), I.iii.4 (36). The translation of this passage cited by Elizabeth G. Holt, *A Documentary History of Art: The Middle Ages and Renaissance* (Princeton, NJ, 1947), 123, is misleading.

this is why 'in church we do not show as much reverence for books as we do for images and pictures'.[36]

Durandus' argument is tendentious and one-sided, as writing too can stimulate the imagination. Nevertheless, his emphasis on the power of images to affect the feelings helps explain how pictures functioned in prayer books. Images were even more amenable than texts to a variety of interpretations because they left their meaning unsaid and perhaps unsayable. Up until the Reformation the imaginary scenes which religious images constructed were not subjected to the same degree of standardization and scholastic control as texts were. This is why the images in women's prayer books, like later medieval images in general, contain such potential for feeling and imagination. Some of this is very difficult to interpret and it can look unorthodox or even blasphemous. Like the Scripture itself, some images might have been understood to function at different levels of meaning; interpreting them is further complicated by their ostensible meanings not being spelled out. In the paired images already discussed, for example, of the lady book owner interposed between the Angel Gabriel and the Virgin Annunciate, we have no explicit knowledge of what was intended. The scene was apparently not thought presumptuous or even daring, and yet it places this lady uniquely at the centre of the divine dispensation for the world. But this is precisely where every worshipper should be when he or she is at prayer. Seen in this way, the image is simply a practical aid to prayer and meditation. The kneeling book owner humbly aspires to reach the heights of the divine presence through her devotion to the Virgin. Her prayer book shows her uniquely, but also universally, blessed within the structure of Christian belief and expectations. The novelty of the scene lies in the visualization of devotional practice, rather than in the religious aspiration itself. Through the skill of the artist, a lay person and a woman has literally been incorporated into the promise of the Annunciation.

* * *

The rest of this paper will discuss a few well-known images of ladies with their prayer books and speculate on how they 'move the mind' or feelings in Durandus' terms and 'construct the imaginary' in Camille's terms.[37] The earliest representation I know of a lay woman holding a

---

[36] Davril and Thibodeau, *Guillelmi Duranti Rationale*, 36; Aston, *Lollards and Reformers*, 116.

[37] See nn.35 and 30 above.

prayer book open is the life-size effigy of Eleanor of Aquitaine at Fontevraud.[38] There are earlier images of nuns holding closed books. Thus the Swabian abbess Uta of Niedermunster (985-1025) is shown clasping a large volume in the manuscript containing the rule she gave to her nuns; this book is probably intended to represent the text of her rule rather than being a prayer book.[39] The effigy of Eleanor of Aquitaine presents the idea of the lady with the book in grand style, but there is no contemporary documentation for it and no inscription. It is closely associated with the similar painted stone effigies at Fontevraud of her husband, Henry II, and her son, Richard I. All three effigies are life-size and represent the dead person on a draped bier as if lying in state. The effigies differ in detail and they are not necessarily by the same artist, though they date stylistically from much the same time around 1200. They could have been commissioned all together, or each one separately at the time of death. There are no obvious precedents for them. They are so magnificent and unusual that they may have been commissioned by Eleanor herself, though there would have been as strong reasons for an abbess of Fontevraud to commission them in order to gain endowments for the convent as a Plantagenet mausoleum.

The two kings, Henry II and Richard I, are shown crowned with their hands resting on sceptres as symbols of their authority. Eleanor too is crowned, but in place of a sceptre she holds up an open book. When she was buried at Fontevraud in 1204, she was no longer a reigning queen. She had been accepted by the convent as a holy widow and its necrology describes her as 'renowned for her unmatched goodness'.[40] Her resting place is with the nuns, even though the effigy shows her crowned as a queen and not vested as a nun. There is no text visible on the sculpted pages of the book she holds to prove that it is indeed a prayer book. In Chrétien de Troyes's romance *Yvain*, which dates from Eleanor's time, the lady Landine remains alone and grieving after the funeral of her husband 'as she reads her psalms in her gilt-lettered Psalter'.[41] The book which Eleanor holds is not much

---

[38] Illustrated in Bonnie Wheeler and John Carmi Parsons, eds, *Eleanor of Aquitaine: Lord and Lady* (New York and Basingstoke, 2002), 379–83.

[39] Adam S. Cohen, 'The art of reform in a Bavarian nunnery around 1000', *Speculum*, 74 (1999), 1003.

[40] Owen, *Eleanor of Aquitaine*, 102.

[41] 'Et list an un sautier ses saumes, anlumine a letres d'or,' *Yvain*, Wendelin Foerster's edn, ll. 1414-15, ed. T.B.W. Reid (Manchester, 1942), 40.

larger than her hands and it could be a Psalter manual, like Clementia von Zähringen's book or the little books which Marianus Scotus wrote for widows.[42] The effigy at L'Epau dating from *c.*1240 of Richard I's queen, Berengaria, shows her holding a closed book. It is almost twice as big as Eleanor's, and Berengaria displays its outer cover, on which is depicted a mirror image of a queen lying on a bier holding a book and flanked by a pair of tall candles.[43] The closed book in this instance may symbolize the invocation of funeral prayers for the dead. (From later in the thirteenth century there is also the strange effigy at Jouarre of a queen holding a book open, which she is displaying to the viewer.)[44] Unlike Berengaria, Eleanor holds her book as if she were reading it and yet she is looking upwards rather than directly at it.

The angle of the book and of Eleanor's hands may have been altered, as book and hands are missing entirely in Charles Stothard's drawing of the damaged effigy in 1816.[45] But the book is shown in place, at a similar angle, in earlier engravings of the Fontevraud effigies.[46] Eleanor's book and hands are more likely to be a repair done after 1816 than a complete nineteenth-century replacement of the original. The book is depicted realistically in its binding and leafed folios and this realism accords with the way other features of the effigy are presented, notably the cushion on which Eleanor's head rests and the drapery spreading in soft folds over the carrying poles of the bier. Is the book intended to represent Eleanor's own prayer book? Possibly so, as it might have been placed between her hands on her bier to symbolize her holy death. Perhaps she does not look directly at the book because the effigy is showing her at the very point of crossing from life to death and from death to eternal life. The ambiguity as to whether Eleanor is alive or dead contributes to the power of the effigy.

Even if an actual prayer book of Eleanor's is depicted on her effigy, its function is primarily symbolic. Nuns and abbesses – and by extension holy widows and great ladies who endowed religious houses – were differentiated from ordinary women by their possession

---

[42] See n.6 above.

[43] Illustrated in John Gillingham, *Richard I* (1999), pl. 8, 9.

[44] Otto von Simson, ed., *Propylaen – Kuntsgeschichte: Das hohe Mittelalter*, 6 (Berlin, 1972), pl. 81, comment at 120 (effigy of St Osanna).

[45] T.S.R. Boase, 'Fontevrault and the Plantagenets', *Journal of the British Archaeological Association*, 3rd ser., 34 (1971), 8 and pl. II, 2.

[46] Ibid., pl. II, 1, and Francis Sandford and Samuel Stebbing, *A Genealogical History of the Kings and Queens of England* (1707), pl. 64.

of books. Earlier in the twelfth century Abelard had assured Heloise that in becoming a nun she had 'turned the curse of Eve into the blessing of Mary'.[47] 'How unseemly', he explained, 'that those holy hands which now turn the pages of sacred books [*divina revolvunt volumina*] should be degraded by the obscenities of women's cares.'[48] Labour and foulness are the curse of women's sexuality. God has deigned, Abelard added, to raise us up above this contagious filth and 'perhaps by our example to deter from such presumption others who are expert in letters'.[49] Like Heloise, Eleanor has been 'degraded' by women's cares and sexual intercourse. She may not have been as 'expert in letters' (meaning as good at Latin) as Heloise, but she too might be raised up and convert 'the curse of Eve into the blessing of Mary' by turning over the pages of her book. The sacred page signals and encapsulates her prayer and the promised word of God in Scripture. Whereas formerly she had embraced men in her nuptial bed, she now grasps the divine Word on her death bed. The good book will guard her more surely than the kings of this world have done: her husbands, Louis VII and Henry II, and her sons, Richard I and King John.

To be with a book was to be at peace, the peace of the cloister. The quiet concentration of meditation contrasts with the bustling life of the rich and powerful (the restlessness in Eleanor's case of Henry II, Richard I and John) and the desperately overworked life of the poor. Images in Books of Hours depict the aristocratic lady in her private chamber or oratory enjoying the peace and ordered leisure of prayer. The ideal of the Virgin Annunciate in her immaculate and sunlit bedchamber contrasted strongly with the realities of housework, even if a great lady like Eleanor only had to supervise such work. With its white pages, ruled lines, and bright illuminations, a prayer book epitomized cleanliness, order, and light. In the long hours of darkness it was no less attractive, as candlelight enriched the colours and made the parchment shimmer. A prayer book was also an object of luxury in itself, with its gold lettering, ornamented binding, and embroidered bag to protect it. It was not necessarily more expensive than other items in a lady's coffers, like jewellery and silk, but it fitted in with

---

[47] Clanchy, *Abelard*, 43; *PL* 178, col. 208b.
[48] Ibid., col. 208c (my translation). Cf. *The Letters of Abelard and Heloise*, tr. B. Radice (Harmondsworth, 1974), 150.
[49] Ibid.

them most appropriately.[50] In the history of literacy the special physical characteristics of medieval books need to be taken into account. The habit of keeping books in the home 'might never have reached the laity if writing had not been so luxurious and so covetable'.[51]

These features are illustrated in the full-page owner portrait, identified as Yolande countess of Soissons, in a late thirteenth-century Book of Hours now in New York.[52] Accompanied by her pet dog and with her prayer book open, she kneels in her golden heraldic gown before a statue of the Virgin and Child. The statue has come to life and the Child blesses Yolande. This was a special effect which the painter could achieve as readily as depicting the statue as an inanimate object. In the Lambeth Apocalypse (which was made for Yolande's contemporary, Eleanor de Quincy) a monk is shown who miraculously brings a statue of the Virgin and Child to life as he paints it.[53] This idea originated in a rather different miracle story, in which a monk pictured the Virgin in his imagination so fervently that she appeared to him in a vision.[54] By combining the artist's visualization with her own imaginative fervour, Yolande can feel herself in the presence of the Virgin and Child. Her portrait shows her in a state of transformation, somewhere between home and church (the picture includes features of both) and between worldliness and spirituality. She has been transported outside time; she has not yet perhaps experienced the vision in her prayer book, but her portrait shows her how she might achieve it. Similar considerations apply to the owner portraits from the fifteenth century which show ladies invoking their patron saints, as they kneel with their prayer books open. Exceptionally luxurious examples are the portraits of Anne, Duchess of Bedford, in the 1420s, and of Anne of Brittany in the 1500s, each in the presence of their namesake, St Anne.[55]

---

[50] In general see Jonathan Alexander and Paul Binski, eds, *Age of Chivalry: Art in Plantagenet England, 1200–1400* (1987), 26–179.

[51] See n.1 above.

[52] New York, Morgan Library, MS M. 729, fol. 232v, illustrated in Roger S. Wieck, *Painted Prayers: the Book of Hours in Medieval and Renaissance Art* (New York, 1997), pl. 1 (colour), and in Karen Gould, *The Psalter and Hours of Yolande of Soissons* (Cambridge MA, 1978), pl. 19 (black and white).

[53] Suzanne Lewis, 'The English Gothic illuminated Apocalypse, lectio divina, and the art of memory', *Word and Image*, 7 (1991), 8 and fig. 5.

[54] Ibid., 7–8.

[55] Colour illustrations in Coss, *The Lady*, pl. 10; Harthan, *Books of Hours*, 127; and Janet Backhouse, *The Bedford Hours* (1990), pl. 47.

The imaginative power of prayer is visualized most elegantly in the Book of Hours from *c.*1470 identified with Mary of Burgundy.[56] She is depicted seated in comfort in her chamber or oratory with a pet dog on her lap and jewellery on the window sill. Her gaze is directed downwards, to the prayer book which she holds open. But the windows of the chamber are likewise wide open and they reveal a large church, where the Virgin and Child sit before an altar being adored by angels and an aristocratic lady with attendants. A convincing explanation for this double picture is that it shows Mary of Burgundy's visualization of her prayer to her patron, the Virgin. 'Through prayer Mary imagines herself in the Madonna's presence. Mary of Burgundy's closeness to the Virgin grows out of absorbed contemplation. Her Book of Hours creates a physical and psychic space for solitude and contemplation.'[57] The ideal of contemplative concentration which miniatures in prayer books can create so effectively is frequently undermined, if not destroyed, by the disturbing images on the margins of the page. For example, on the page facing that where Mary of Burgundy contemplates herself in the presence of the Virgin and Child, a monkey is visible wielding a club among the foliage at the foot of the page. The individual's imagination and the artist's skill could just as readily create scenes from dreams or nightmares as construct sublime visions of Christ and the Virgin. An extreme example of a lady's prayer book full of grotesque imagery, including misbehaving monkeys, is the St-Omer Hours dating from *c.*1350 which may have been made for Marguerite de Beaujeu.[58] Various explanations have been suggested for the prevalence of such imagery, which occurs not only in prayer books but more generally in illuminated manuscripts from northern Europe, particularly in the fourteenth century.[59] Whatever explanations are offered – and no single one will fit all cases – we have to acknowledge that grotesque imagery is an integral part of the design of many prayer books. It must have been considered appropriate by patrons, clerics, and artists, and it certainly makes these books more fascinating and enticing.

[56] Colour illustration in Harthan, *Books of Hours*, 110. Facsimile, with commentary and bibliography by Eric Inglis, *The Hours of Mary of Burgundy* (1995).

[57] Wieck, *Books of Hours*, 44. See also Penketh, 'Women and Books of Hours', 266–8.

[58] Colour illustrations in Harthan, *Books of Hours*, 50–2, and in Michael Camille, *Image on the Edge: the Margins of Medieval Art* (1992), pl. 14.

[59] Lucy Freeman Sandler, 'The study of marginal imagery: past, present and future', *Studies in Iconography*, 18 (1997), 1–49.

In this paper only a few prayer books belonging to aristocratic women have been discussed. Very few people ever saw the images in them, as they were enclosed in books designed for private use. Their significance might therefore be thought to have been very limited. Colour photography has made these books accessible today in a way they never were in the Middle Ages. The finest books, which are the most frequently reproduced, are not typical of surviving Books of Hours as a whole. Estimates of how many families possessed prayer books are impossible to make, though there is no doubt that they were much more common in 1500 than in 1300. Elsewhere I have argued that in the fourteenth and fifteenth centuries there was a 'shift in the focus of literacy from monastic church to noble household'.[60] Books of Hours gave their owners an active role in contemplating the Word of God and likewise in understanding the actual words on the page. The changing iconography of the Virgin Mary, the greatest lady of all, is the best indicator of the growing importance of prayer books. The Virgin was a role model for all women through the numerous public representations of her in sculpture, stained glass, and wall paintings. The ideal she presents, particularly in scenes of the Annunciation and of the Virgin and Child, is of the lady in her place of private prayer meditating on her Book of Hours. The majority of the population, who could not afford books of their own, might nevertheless have aspired to this ideal because the Word of God was imagined and visualized as a lady's prayer book. This symbol may have been as influential as the growing reality of increasing numbers of books for private prayer.

The image of St Anne teaching the Virgin to read, which developed in northern Europe and in England in particular in the fourteenth century, is the most explicit indicator of the new status given to ladies with their prayer books.[61] St Anne is often depicted in an explicitly didactic pose, instructing the Virgin as a young girl from the text of a Book of Hours. The purpose of the image is to show instruction in the Word of God, but the means of doing this is through instruction in reading. This is most explicit in the primer of Princess Claude of France dating from *c.*1510; this is a short book of fourteen pages

[60] *From Memory*, 2nd edn, 252.

[61] Independently of each other, Wendy Scase and Pamela Sheingorn published articles on this in 1993: Scase, 'St Anne and the education of the Virgin', in Nicholas Rogers, ed., *England in the Fourteenth Century: Proceedings of the 1991 Harlaxton Symposium* (Stamford, 1993), 81–96; Sheingorn, 'The wise mother: the image of St Anne teaching the Virgin Mary', *Gesta*, 32 (1993), 69–80. See also Gilia Slocock, ed., *St Anne in History and Art* (Oxford, 1999).

beginning with the ABC.[62] On the first page Claude is portrayed kneeling with her own book closed and on the last page she is shown again, this time with her book open: she has learned to read – and learned to pray – just as the Virgin as a girl learned from St Anne. To conclude with Claude's primer is to conclude with a prayer book made for another lady of very high rank, albeit a girl. This is the dilemma of using the most spectacular evidence from existing books, as these tend to be collector's pieces from aristocratic households. How much importance should be attached to images of ladies with their prayer books in the development of the Church as a whole in the later Middle Ages remains debatable. Did the practice of aristocratic households and the idealization through images of the Virgin Mary with a prayer book promote religious devotion and literacy generally in society? Or did such images really only make an impression on a few very privileged and unusually discriminating owners of Books of Hours? Assessing the extent to which religious ideals percolated downwards to the mass of the population is a problem which confronts Church historians of any period, as does the difficulty of evaluating the influence of women in a patriarchally structured society.

Institute of Historical Research,
University of London

---

[62] Colour illustrations in Harthan, *Books of Hours*, 134–5. See also Sheingorn, 'The wise mother', 76–7.

JEWELS FOR GENTLEWOMEN: RELIGIOUS BOOKS AS ARTEFACTS IN LATE MEDIEVAL AND EARLY MODERN ENGLAND

by ALEXANDRA WALSHAM

HISTORIANS tend to approach books primarily as vehicles for ideas, sources for the thought of the individuals and groups who wrote and read the words on the pages inside. They rarely pause to consider their significance as physical artefacts and items of material culture. This paper brings the format, appearance, and practical function of Bibles, prayer books, and other small devotional works to the very centre of our attention. It suggests that close scrutiny of the diminutive size and artistically crafted covers of some of the copies that survive yields fresh insights into the shape and texture of piety in late medieval and early modern England. The following investigation is heavily indebted to the findings of researchers in the specialized field of the history of bookbinding, a field once light-heartedly described as 'a humble auxiliary discipline . . . not entirely useless and undoubtedly innocuous'.[1] Yet, as we shall see, situated against the backdrop of developments in Tudor and Stuart embroidery and jewellery, domestic furnishing and female fashion, decorated bookbindings provide us with a unique and interesting reflection of the values and preoccupations of pre- and post-Reformation society.

* * *

Medieval book covers were often richly embellished: elaborately wrought in silver and gold, ornamented with enamel, inlaid with ivory, and encrusted with jewels.[2] Such treasure bindings were the products of an age in which books were rare and precious, calligraphic masterpieces whose very creation was an act of worship and veneration. Designed to be transferred from book to book, they were generally

---

[1] E.P. Goldschmidt, 'The study of early bookbinding', in *The Bibliographical Society 1892–1942. Studies in Retrospect* (1949), 175; Mirjam Foot, *The History of Bookbinding as a Mirror of Society*, The Panizzi Lectures (1997).
[2] E.g. the binding on an Anglo-Saxon copy of the Gospels reproduced in Paul Needham, *Twelve Centuries of Bookbindings 400–1600* (New York, 1979), xxi.

attached to liturgical texts owned by monasteries, cathedrals, and collegiate churches: missals, pontificals, graduals, and versions of the Holy Scriptures. A 1511 inventory of St Margaret's Westminster describes 'a gospeler garnysshed w^t a crucyfyx Mary & John w^t iiij cristall stones quadrant sette', while in 1536 Lincoln Cathedral listed a copy decorated with a metalwork image of the risen Christ surrounded by the Evangelists and four glorious angels.[3] Placed on the altar in close proximity to the consecrated host, such books were receptacles of numinous power. Kissed in the course of the service, they were crucial pieces of equipment for the celebration of the miracle of the Mass – in at least one case a resplendent binding was redeployed as the pax itself.[4] Often enclosing fragments of the bones and other remains of martyrs and saints, book covers were sometimes indistinguishable from reliquaries. An early thirteenth-century example, commissioned by Berthold, Abbot of Weingarten, to encase an illuminated manuscript missal, is engraved with an inscription proclaiming the relics it contains.[5] In Ireland, sacred books were kept in a special box called a *cumdach*: hung around the neck of a warrior as he went into battle, the Word of God served as a breastplate, protecting the wearer both physically and spiritually.[6]

This sense of the inherent sanctity of books persisted even after more efficient techniques of manuscript copying led to their near mass production and the mechanized printing press democratized access to and ownership of them. To echo Margaret Aston, texts, like letters, often remained 'symbols that enclosed a mystery rather than transmitting a message'.[7] This is evident when we look at the biggest bestseller of the the late Middle Ages, the Book of Hours.[8] The bindings of these private prayer manuals, no less than their illuminated pages, were frequently ornate and expensive: covered in velvet and silk, secured with gilt and silver clasps, and decorated with miniature images of the suffering Christ, Paschal Lamb, Holy Trinity, Virgin Mary, John the

---

[3] Cited in Howard M. Nixon and Mirjam M. Foot, *The History of Decorated Bookbinding in England* (Oxford, 1992), 21–2.

[4] Yvonne Hackenbroch, *Renaissance Jewellery* (Munich, 1979), 139–40 and pl. 353.

[5] Foot, *Mirror*, 60.

[6] P.J.M. Marks, *The British Library Guide to Bookbinding: History and Techniques* (1998), 56.

[7] Margaret Aston, 'Devotional literacy', in eadem, *Lollards and Reformers: Images and Literacy in Late Medieval Religion* (1984), 108.

[8] What follows is indebted to John Harthan, *Books of Hours and their Owners* (1977); Janet Backhouse, *Books of Hours* (1985); and Eamon Duffy, *The Stripping of the Altars: Traditional Religion in England, c. 1400–c. 1580* (New Haven, CT, and London, 1992), chs 6–8.

Baptist, and the Apostles. Like the famous fourteenth-century psalter which belonged to Anne Felbrigge, a nun in the convent of the Minoresses at Bruisyard in Suffolk, they could also be decorated with embroidered representations of the Annunciation and Crucifixion.[9] Cultivating lay devotion of a quasi-monastical kind, primers were cherished objects carried in special bags called chemisettes, preserved from grubby hands by the use of cloths known as forels, and laid on cushions in the private chambers and closets of the affluent and devout. Frequently passed down to relatives and friends as heirlooms, such books were symptomatic of the laity's increasingly introspective relationship with the written word. However, they also functioned in pre-Reformation religious culture in ways which had relatively little to do with the growth of literacy and the rise of silent reading. This was inextricably linked with the fact that they were mostly written in Latin. As Eamon Duffy has emphasised, primers were commonly conceived of as channels of supernatural energy independent of the texts they encompassed. This tendency was probably compounded by the inclusion in early sixteenth-century editions of the Sarum horae of rubrics advertising indulgences attached to their recitation.[10] Just as scraps of paper inscribed with verses from the Bible, pouches containing splinters of the True Cross, and jewelled pendants wrought in the shape of the holy letters IHS were supposed to safeguard the body and soul of whoever wore them, so too were Books of Hours regarded as communicating blessing in and of themselves. Like the little reliquaries which members of both sexes placed around their necks or fastened to their belts, they were effective talismans and amulets warding off evil and disease. No less than phials of holy water, wax tablets of the *agnus dei*, and objects which had come into contact with special hallowed places, they might be seen as sacramentals.[11]

This should not eclipse the fact that Books of Hours were pre-eminently mnemonic aids to prayer and meditation. Here their tactile

[9] BL, MS Sloane 2400. P. Wallis, 'The embroidered binding of the Felbrigge Psalter', *British Library Journal*, 13 (1987), 71–8. Cf. the Vaux Psalter (Lambeth Palace Library, MS 233), described in *Opus Anglicanum: English Medieval Embroidery* (1963), 64.

[10] Duffy, *Stripping*, 214, 289–90.

[11] For examples, see Ronald W. Lightbown, *Medieval European Jewellery with a Catalogue of the Collection in the Victoria and Albert Museum* (1992), 67–8, 96–9 and pl. 68–9, 79, 130, 137; Hackenbroch, *Jewellery*, 276–80, 313–16; Diana Scarisbrick, *Tudor and Jacobean Jewellery* (1995), 42–5. See also Colin Richmond, 'Religion and the fifteenth-century English gentleman', in Barrie Dobson, ed., *The Church, Politics and Patronage in the Fifteenth Century* (Gloucester, 1984), 193–203.

bindings bear comparison with beautifully carved rosaries and prayer nuts in the shape of medallions and pomegranates, which opened to reveal tiny intaglios of the Visitation, Annunciation, or Crucifixion.[12] Indeed, probate records suggest that they were usually grouped with devotional items of this type. Katherine Kerre, a Norwich widow who died in 1498, for instance, bequeathed to her friend Dame Joan Blakeney a book about St Catherine, together with a pair of amber beads with gilt paternosters and 'a gold rynge y^t towched our lordys grave'.[13] All three need to be recognized as devices to help laypeople achieve that deep, sensual apprehension of the passion of Christ which was the highest aspiration of the fervently pious. They also closely resemble tablet-shaped icons designed to hang from a girdle.[14] It is not insignificant that the Image of Pity, the Mass of St Gregory, and Veronica's Veil can all be found on leather and metalwork bindings from this period: printed paper versions formed a focus for devotion and fostered 'habits of visualisation' and techniques of 'mystical seeing' that were central to late medieval religious experience. Book covers may well have operated in a similar way, as a pathway and ladder to 'inward sight and feeling'.[15]

At the same time, it would be wrong to ignore the way in which elaborately bound books could function as fashion accessories and insignia of social status. We catch a glimpse of this in fifteenth-century paintings of well-dressed ladies perusing primers or kneeling in front of prayer desks on which they are reverently laid.[16] As early as AD 384 St Jerome was inveighing against the avarice and pride of wealthy people who stained the leaves of their books purple and adorned their

[12] For examples, see Hackenbroch, *Jewellery*, 280, fig. 751; 316, figs 822a and b, 823.

[13] Cited in Mary C. Erler, 'Devotional literature', in Lotte Hellinga and J.B. Trapp, eds, *The Cambridge History of the Book in Britain, vol. 3 1400–1557* (Cambridge, 1999), 523–5.

[14] See Lightbown, *Jewellery*, pl. 130, 137. In the case of several devotional diptychs in the collection of Philip the Good, Duke of Burgundy, image and book are quite literally indivisible: Dagmar Eichberger, 'Devotional objects in book format: diptychs in the collection of Margaret of Austria and her family', in Margaret M. Manion and Bernard J. Muir, eds, *The Art of the Book: Its Place in Medieval Worship* (Exeter, 1998), 291–323.

[15] See Andrew Taylor, 'Into his secret chamber: reading and privacy in late medieval England', in James Raven, Helen Small, and Naomi Tadmor, eds, *The Practice and Representation of Reading in England* (Cambridge, 1996), 45, 51 and passim; R.W. Scribner, *For the Sake of Simple Folk: Popular Propaganda for the German Reformation* (Cambridge, 1981), 3–4. For examples of medieval bindings with these images, see W.H. James Weale, *Bookbindings and Rubbings of Bindings in the Victoria and Albert Museum* (1898), 178, 115, 169 respectively.

[16] See Sandra Penketh, 'Women and Books of Hours', in Lesley Smith and Jane H.M. Taylor, eds, *Women and the Book: Assessing the Visual Evidence* (1977), 266–81.

covers with precious gems and stones while Christ, 'in the person of the poor, lies naked and dying at their door'.[17] Specially commissioned by the gentry and nobility, costly bindings were obviously intended at least partly to make a public impression. Even so it is difficult to draw a definitive line between genuine devotion and social pretension in assessing their significance for our understanding of pre-Reformation religion. What they do cast into sharp relief is the curious mixture of intense reflection and magical manipulation, of affective and wonder-working piety, which it has been argued was its most salient characteristic.[18]

The advent of Protestantism is often alleged to have precipitated a major paradigm shift from a culture revolving around images, rituals, and symbols to one that converged upon the abstract, invisible, and didactic word. It is also credited with eroding features of contemporary practice and belief which we would now label 'superstitious'. The rest of this paper adds to a growing body of scholarship suggesting that this stark contrast is rather misleading.

* * *

The first observation that might be made is that primers persisted after the Reformation in a different but still familiar guise. Helen White and Eamon Duffy have demonstrated how traditional materials were adapted in line with new Protestant priorities, both in the official collections of private prayers issued by Henry VIII, Edward VI, and Elizabeth I, and the many similar handbooks compiled by reformed ministers and publishers to meet the perennial need for pious words appropriate for every occasion. Distinctly Catholic ingredients and aggressively Protestant elements co-exist in works like Henry Bull's *Christian Prayers and Holy Meditations* (1568), Richard Day's *Booke of Christian Prayers* (1578) and the anonymous *Godlie Gardeine*, a tiny sextodecimo first issued in 1569 which was still being reprinted eighty years later.[19] Dozens of portable prayer books were produced in 16mo, 32mo, and even smaller formats – surviving copies and fragments

---

[17] Cited in Weale, *Bookbindings*, viii.
[18] Duffy, *Stripping*, 295–6.
[19] Helen C. White, *The Tudor Books of Private Devotion* (Madison, WI, 1951), and Eamon Duffy, 'Continuity and divergence in Tudor religion', *SCH*, 32 (Oxford, 1996), 189–205. For the books mentioned, see *STC* 4028–4037.3, 6428–32, 11554.5–11561.5. Day's book was first published in 1569 under the title *Christian Prayers and Meditations*. Many of the items cited in nn.19–23 were frequently reprinted before 1640.

surely represent only a fraction of the output of items so easily mislaid and lost. Typically they contain supplications and graces to be said on rising from sleep and retiring to bed, when dressing, washing, and sitting down to a meal, before receiving communion and on returning home from church, for patience in sickness, forbearance in childbirth, and continued good health. Close scrutiny of the quaint titles of these palm-sized artefacts is extremely instructive. Alongside numerous *Preparatives* and *Pathways* is a whole group of such miniature books which describe themselves as pomanders of prayer and posies and garlands of spiritual flowers, not to mention *A Bundle of Myrrhe* (1620) and *A Beautifull Bay Bush to shrowd us from the Sharpe Showers of Sinne* (1589).[20] These metaphors remind us of the prophylactic properties contemporaries attached to aromatic spices and leaves they kept in bags and balls about their persons, and underline the fact that such books were intended to be slipped into a capacious pocket or suspended by a chain from the waist. Titles like *The Diamond of Devotion*, *A Spyrytuall and moost Precyouse Pearle*, *A Tablet of Devout Prayers and Godly Meditations*, and *A Jewel for Gentlewomen* invite us to compare these minute volumes with precious stones and gems imbued with propitious and therapeutic properties.[21] Another cluster of compilations issued by mainstream Protestant publishers hark back even more explicitly to the patterns and appurtenances of medieval Catholicism. Thus the London pamphleteer Philip Stubbes published *A Rosarie of Christian Praiers and Meditations* in 1583, and in 1601 the poet and antiquary John Weever prepared an anthology of devotional verse entitled *An Agnus Dei,* printed on pages the size of a postage stamp.[22]

There are some grounds for thinking that there was a particular market for this genre of diminutive literature among women. In fact, a number have been attributed to female writers. Anne Wheathill's *Handfull of Holesome (though Homelie) Hearbs, gathered out of the Goodlie*

---

[20] See, e.g., Robert Hill, *The Pathway to Prayer, and Pietie* (1609), STC 13472.7; Thomas Becon, *The Pomander of Prayer* (1565), STC 1747; Nicholas Themylthorp, *The Posie of Godly Prayers* (1611), STC 23934.2; Thomas Twyne, *The Garlande of Godly Flowers* (1574), STC 24408; William Innes, *A Bundle of Myrrhe* (1620), STC 14090 and *A Beautifull Bay Bush* (1589), STC 1599.

[21] Abraham Fleming, *The Diamond of Devotion* (1581), STC 11041; Otto Werdmueller, *A Spyrytuall and moost Precyouse Pearle* (1550), STC 25255; [*A Tablet for Gentlewomen*] (1574), STC 23640; *A Tablet of Devout Prayers and Godly Meditations* (1571), STC 23641; *A Jewel for Gentlewomen* (1624), STC 14578; William Worship, *The Christians Jewell* (1617), STC 25985.

[22] Stubbes's book is now lost but is listed in Andrew Maunsell, *The First Part of the Catalogue of English Printed Books* (1595), 87. John Weever, *An Agnus Dei* (1601), STC 25220. This book was 128mo.

Garden of Gods most Holie Word (1584) and Elizabeth Joceline's *The Mothers Legacie, to her Unborne Childe* (1624) may be cited alongside the prayers of Queen Catherine Parr and Marguerite of Angoulême's *Godly Meditations*, both of which were initially published in the 1540s, but were still in print several generations later. Another example is *Morning and Evening Prayers* compiled by Elizabeth I's governess, Lady Tyrwhit.[23] The sole surviving copy of the 1574 edition of this 32mo volume is now preserved in a remarkable gold girdle book binding from which it is likely to have displaced an earlier and more traditional set of devotions (Fig. 1). Probably wrought by the Dutch craftsman Hans of Antwerp after designs by Holbein, it is decorated with depictions of Moses and the Brazen Serpent and the Judgement of Solomon, and engraved with the texts of Numbers 21.8 and I Kings 3.27, according to the wording given in the Great Bible of 1539. Another set of covers dating from *c.*1525–35 pairs the Judgement of Solomon with an image of Daniel defending Susannah from the accusations of the elders.[24] The iconography of these bindings is not unequivocally Protestant, though they do seem to be indicative of the biblical and evangelical brand of piety that became fashionable in Henrician court circles. Certainly one tablet in the collection of Queen Catherine Howard was overtly anti-Catholic: it apparently showed a 'pycture of the Bishop of Rome runnyng away Lamentyng and divers other persons[,] one settyng his fote upon the busshop overthrown'.[25] Lady Jane Grey reputedly went to her execution in 1554 with 'a black velvet book hanging before her' and royal inventories from the 1530s, 1540s, and 1550s record similar items set with diamonds and rubies.[26] These books were not only elegant accessories of aristocratic ladies, as revealed by John Foxe's vivid cameo of Hugh Latimer's appearance before the ecclesiastical commissioners in September 1555, 'wearing an old thread-bare Bristowe frieze gown

[23] Anne Wheathill, *A Handfull of Holesome (though Homelie) Hearbs* (1584), STC 25329; Elizabeth Joceline, *The Mothers Legacie, to her Unborne Childe* (1624), STC 14624; Catherine Parr, *Prayers stirryng the Mynd unto Heavenlye Medytacions* (1545), STC 4818; Marguerite of Angoulême, *A Godly Medytacyon of the Christen Sowle*, repr. as *Godly Meditations* (1548, [1568?]), STC 17320–1; Lady Elizabeth Tyrwhit, *Morning and Evening Prayers* (1574), STC 24477.5.

[24] Anna Somers Cocks, ed., *Princely Magnificence: Court Jewels of the Renaissance, 1500–1630* (1980), 48–51; Hugh Tait, 'Historiated Tudor jewellery', *Antiquaries Journal*, 42 (1962), 232–6; idem, 'The girdle-prayerbook or "tablett": an important class of Renaissance jewellery at the court of Henry VIII', *Jewellery Studies*, 2 (1985), 29–57.

[25] BL, MS Stowe 559, fol. 14r.

[26] Cited in Therle Hughes, *English Domestic Needlework 1660–1860* (1961), 96.

Fig. 1 Girdle prayer book, attributed to John of Antwerp, showing the Judgement of Solomon and Moses with the Brazen Serpent, c.1540. By permission of the British Museum.

girded to his body with a penny leather girdle, at the which hanged by a long string of leather his Testament'.[27] As Mirjam Foot has commented, 'wearing a book as part of one's apparel indicates a greater intimacy between the owner and the text, than if it had been merely put on a shelf, suggesting an appropriation or incorporation of the Word of God into the body and soul of the wearer.'[28] Miniature devotional books suspended from ribbons or chains are still visible in paintings completed towards the end of the sixteenth century, including a portrait of Dame Philippa Speke dated 1592,[29] and they also merit a mention in John Lyly's *Euphues* (1580), tied to the girdles of 'Englysh Damoselles' who are 'as cunning in the scriptures' as their Italian counterparts are in Ariosto and Petrarch.[30] Re-attached to impeccably Protestant collections of prayers, such bindings seem to have weathered the storm of the Reformation very successfully, becoming exquisite emblems of continuity absorbing, embracing, and mediating change.

Girdle books disappeared when changes in female dress made them something of an inconvenient appendage. Yet the decorative bindings of the early seventeenth century are no less effective as mirrors of English society than those which preceded them. Many examples of elaborately tooled leather and fine textile covers survive, alongside books adorned with delicate brass, gold, or silver clasps. A little octavo Bible covered with 'greene say' belonging to his daughter Nelly was among the books stolen from the kitchen window of Thomas Crosfield's Yorkshire rectory in 1653, and Samuel Bellingham listed a copy of Bishop Lewis Bayly's *Practice of Pietie*, bound in red and fixed with clasps, in a memorandum of 'Bookes in my wives box' written around 1672.[31] A silver-mounted book cover enclosing a 1631 edition of John Downame's *Brief Concordance of the Bible* is engraved with ovals containing the seven moral Virtues and the figures of Faith, Hope, and

---

[27] G.E. Corrie, ed., *Sermons and Remains of Hugh Latimer, sometime Bishop of Worcester, Martyr 1555*, PS (Cambridge, 1845), 279. I owe this reference to Dr Susan Wabuda. See also the comments of Patrick Collinson, 'Windows into a woman's soul: questions about the religion of Elizabeth I', in idem, *Elizabethan Essays* (1994), 92–3.

[28] Foot, *Mirror*, 63.

[29] See Somers Cocks, *Princely Magnificence*, 106; Roy Strong, *The English Icon: Elizabethan and Jacobean Portraiture* (1969), figs 46, 51, 79.

[30] John Lyly, *Euphues and his England* (1580), in R. Warwick Bond, ed., *The Complete Works of John Lyly*, 3 vols (Oxford, 1902), 2:199. [See also n.62 below.]

[31] Frederick S. Boas, ed., *The Diary of Thomas Crosfield* (1935), 99; BL, MS Sloane 647, fol. 26v.

Charity, while minute medallion portraits of Noah and Moses, David and Saul, are etched on the clasps that fastened an edition of Nicholas Themylthorpe's *Posie of Godly Praiers* (1619).[32] By the mid-seventeenth century those of more humble means could wrap their devotional works in paper covers printed with woodcut images of stories such as the raising of Lazarus.[33] As the printed price list of one Jacobean bookbinder shows, there was also a vogue for pricking and gilding the foredges and embellishing the corners of small format Bibles, Prayer Books, and Sternhold and Hopkins's version of the metrical Psalms.[34] The edges of one example in the Bodleian are painted with the exhortation 'Search the Scriptures 1692'.[35]

But above all the early Stuart period was the heyday of the embroidered bookbinding. Perhaps because of their novelty, needlework covers have been preserved in public libraries and private collections in relatively large numbers. Before examining some of these bindings in more detail, we need to establish by whom they were made. In the Middle Ages the art of embroidery had been monopolized by male master craftsmen who belonged to the Broderers' Guild. Rehabilitated in 1561 as a livery company, by 1580 it had eighty-nine members, though we know little of their activities since the records of the society were destroyed by the Great Fire of London.[36] Some scholars are nevertheless confident that the vast majority of needlework bindings are the work of professionals.[37] This finds some support in a petition presented to Archbishop Laud in 1638 by the milliners of the Royal Exchange, who spoke up on behalf of 'Imbroderers working in their own homes' who had for many years produced 'rare and curious covers' for the Bibles and Psalm books of the 'nobility and gentry of this kingdome'.[38] However, there are enough instances of bindings incorporating the initials of the women who stitched them to

[32] Anthony Wells-Cole, *Art and Decoration in Elizabethan and Jacobean England* (New Haven, CT, 1997), 205; Howard M. Nixon, *Five Centuries of English Bookbinding* (1978), no. 26.

[33] Mirjam M. Foot, 'An English woodcut binding, 1647', in eadem, *Studies in the History of Bookbinding* (Aldershot, 1993), 286–7.

[34] Eadem, 'Some bookbinders' price lists of the seventeenth and eighteenth centuries', ibid., 26–32.

[35] *Fine Bindings 1500–1700 from Oxford Libraries. Catalogue of an Exhibition* (Oxford, 1968), 129.

[36] George Wingfield Digby, *Elizabethan Embroidery* (1963), 29.

[37] E.g., ibid., 33.

[38] Bodley, MS Tanner 67, fol. 33r, printed in H.R. Plomer, 'More petitions to Archbishop Laud', *The Library*, ser. 3, 10 (1919), 129–38.

bear out the alternative claim that, along with samplers and caskets, pillows, bedcaps, and pictures, they were largely amateur pieces, the end products of a young girl's education in a craft intimately associated with the inculcation of feminine virtues.[39] The distinction between cottage industry and genteel recreation breaks down in the case of Damaris Pearse, daughter of a late seventeenth-century Devon Dissenting minister, who plied her needle for both private edification and a modest profit.[40] Books bound in covers of this kind were particularly suitable as new year's gifts and wedding and engagement presents. In 1544 and 1545, at the age of eleven and twelve, Princess Elizabeth worked embroidered bindings to enclose a manuscript collection of prayers and her own translation of Marguerite of Angoulême's *Miroir de l'âme pechereuse*, intended for presentation to her father and stepmother Queen Catherine Parr respectively. Annotations in a 1640 Bible reveal that it was a keepsake given to Mrs Mary Bradley by her 'dear and tender mother', her grandmother having lovingly worked the cover.[41]

Indeed, most surviving examples of embroidered bindings are to be found on small Bibles, Prayer Books, and volumes of the Psalms, sometimes ingeniously conjoined in a style of back to front double binding technically known as dos à dos. However, they also appear on a variety of other popular portable books of devotion, including Lewis Bayly's *Practice of Pietie* (1649), Richard Bernard's *The Way to True Happinesse* (1639), Thomas Sorocold's *Supplications of Saints* (1630), and Edmund Bunny's purged edition of the Jesuit Robert Persons's famous *Book of Christian Exercise* (1598).[42] Patriotic celebrations of England's providential deliverances such as George Carleton's *Thankfull Remembrance of Gods Mercie* (1627) and Michael Sparke's bestselling *Crums of Comfort* (1628) sometimes received similar treatment.[43] Other items for

---

[39] Articulated most clearly by Rozsika Parker, *The Subversive Stitch: Embroidery and the Making of the Feminine* (1984), esp. chs 4–5.

[40] Xanthe Brooke, 'Tales in thread', *The Antique Collector* (Nov. 1990), 119.

[41] Cyril Davenport, *English Embroidered Bookbindings* (1899), 32–6, and pl. 4–5; idem, 'Embroidered bindings of Bibles in the possession of the British and Foreign Bible Society', *Burlington Magazine*, 4 (1904), 277, 279.

[42] See Sotheby and Co., *Catalogue of an Extensive Collection of Decorated Book Bindings with a Few Manuscripts* (1951), 8; Davenport, *Embroidered Bookbindings*, 99–101 and pl. 46; Frederick A. Bearman et al., eds, *Fine and Historic Bookbindings from the Folger Shakespeare Library* (Washington DC, 1992), 140; Mirjam M. Foot, *The Henry Davis Gift: A Collection of Bookbindings*, vol. 1 (London, 1978), 92.

[43] *Fine Bindings*, 100; Michael Sparke, *The Crums of Comfort* (1628), bound dos à dos with *The Whole Booke of Psalmes* (1627): BL, C.65.i.7(2).

which needlework covers were made include the sermons of Samuel Ward and George Herbert's *The Temple* (1641), bound with Christopher Harvey's *The Synagogue* (1647), as well as a scattering of secular literature including the essays of Francis Bacon and the works of James I.[44]

There was undoubtedly a fashionable aspect to the production and possession of such bindings. The proliferation of domestic embroidery was an index of the downward diffusion of wealth and the rise of a culture of luxury and comfort in which the home became the chief site for social display. Zealous piety itself was evidently rather trendy. To carry a book conspicuously to church was to court charges of pride and hypocrisy. Dozens of preachers echoed Lancelot Dawes's complaint that too many laypeople bore Bibles in their hands but Mammon in their hearts, and John Earle's acid sketch of the She-Puritan captures her sitting at a sermon, ostentatiously 'turning down the leaf in her book when she hears named chapter and verse'.[45] We may perhaps envisage her garbed in the pair of embroidered gloves the British Library acquired along with a tiny copy of the Psalms and a bag in which to place it (Fig. 2).[46] At the same time, the sincerity of those who stitched beautiful needlework covers and protective cloths for religious books they treasured should not be underestimated. Carefully preserved in bed chambers, closets, and boxes, and laid like medieval primers on cushions worked in coloured silks, Protestant Bibles and Prayer Books came close to being regarded as sacred artefacts. Kept in a pocket from which they could readily be extracted for reference, they might be compared with phylacteries: the little leather boxes containing Hebrew texts written on vellum worn by the Jews to remind them of the Law. At least one bears a very faint resemblance to some of the mnemonic devotional aids designed to be fingered which we have already examined. Bound into a cover embroidered with the pious image of a pelican pecking its breast, it is still accompanied by a book marker comprising twelve strings ending in tassels, each one representing the Apostle whose name has been intricately woven into it (Fig. 3).[47]

---

[44] Davenport, *Embroidered Bookbindings*, 41–2, 76–7 and pl. 9, 31; Foot, *Henry Davis Gift*, 130–1; *Fine Bindings*, no. 171.

[45] Lancelot Dawes, *Gods Mercies and Jerusalems Miseries. A Sermon preached at Pauls Crosse, the 25. of June. 1609* (1609), sig. E5v; John Earle, *Microcosmography*, ed. Harold Osborne (n.d.), 73.

[46] Foot, *Mirror*, fig. 46.

[47] Davenport, 'Embroidered bindings', 275, 279.

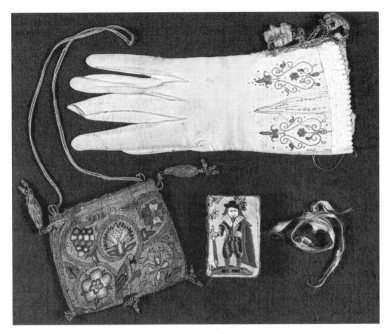

Fig. 2   English embroidered binding on *The Whole Booke of Psalmes*
(London, 1633), with bag and gloves. British Library Shelf-mark: C.17.b.11.
By permission of the British Library.

It is now time to turn to the designs sewn on to these bookbindings.
Many are decorated with stylized insects, birds, animals, fruit, leaves,
and flowers copied from contemporary pattern books.[48] Others depict
allegorical figures such as the Seasons, Senses, Peace, and Plenty. Faith
and Hope appear against an idyllic rural backdrop on a New
Testament and Psalms dating from the mid 1630s, while a copy of
Samuel Smith's *Davids Repentance* (1637) portrays a lady with a serpent
and dove, together with the text from Matthew 10.16: 'Be as wise as
serpents and innocent as doves . . .' (Fig. 4).[49] Figures from classical
mythology, which were popular subjects for tapestry hangings, rarely
feature on bookbindings, presumably because it was considered
inappropriate to mingle the pagan and profane with the pious. But

[48] E.g. the binding on a copy of Joseph Henshaw, *Horae Successivae, or Spare-houres of
Meditations* (1632): Davenport, *Embroidered Bookbindings*, 90–1 and pl. 40.
[49] Ibid., 42–3 and pl. 10; Foot, *Henry Davis Gift*, 123.

Fig. 3   English embroidered binding on a copy of the Bible bound with
the Psalms (London, 1632), in the British and Foreign Bible Society
collection (H478). The binding shows a Pelican in its Piety. The twelve
tassels are stitched with the names of the twelve apostles.
By permission of the Syndics of Cambridge University Library.

Fig. 4   English embroidered binding showing the figures of Faith and
Hope, on *The New Testament* (London, 1625) bound with *The Whole Booke
of Davids Psalmes* (London, 1635). British Library Shelf-mark: C.46.a.19(1–2).
By permission of the British Library.

it is quite common to find miniature portraits of members of the
Stuart Royal Family, mainly James and Charles I and their queens
Anne of Denmark and Henrietta Maria. The embroidered bag in
which Mary Moone kept her Book of Common Prayer after 1677
neatly fused piety with patriotism in a picture of Charles II in the guise
of King David with his lyre.[50]

Most pictorial bindings, however, depict stories from Scripture,
predominantly the Old Testament and Apocrypha. A cover for a
Geneva Bible worked by Elizabeth Illingworth in 1613 combines Jonah
and the whale with Abraham about to sacrifice Isaac (Fig. 5). Jacob
wrestling with the angel and taken up to heaven in a dream feature on
a 1643 copy of the Psalms (Fig. 6), another shows Abraham summoning
Hagar and Ishmael back from the wilderness, and a third the youthful
David with his slingshot and the head of Goliath.[51] Often quaintly

[50] See *The Whole Booke of Psalmes* (1643) – BL, C.17.a.25; G.D. Hobson, ed., *English
Bindings in the Library of J. R. Abbey 1490–1940* (1940), no. 35.
[51] John L. Nevinson, *Catalogue of English Domestic Embroidery of the Sixteenth and
Seventeenth Centuries [in the Victoria and Albert Museum]* (1938), pl. XXXIV; Davenport,
Embroidered Bookbindings, 105–6 and pl. 49; Preston Remington, *English Domestic Needlework
of the XVI, XVII and XVIII Centuries* (New York, 1945), pl. 23; Marks, *British Library Guide*,

[cont. on p. 140]

Fig. 5   English embroidered binding worked by Elizabeth Illingworth 1613, showing Jonah and the whale and Abraham and the Sacrifice of Isaac, on a copy of the Geneva Bible (1610).

Fig. 6   English embroidered binding, showing Jacob's Dream and Jacob Wrestling with the Angel, on *The Whole Booke of Davids Psalmes both in Prose and Meeter* (London, 1643). British Library Shelf-mark: C.17.a.24. By permission of the British Library.

dressed in contemporary costume and surrounded by butterflies, squirrels, strawberries, and lions, other favourites which found their way on to bookbindings and cushions include Esther interceding with her husband Ahasuerus on behalf of the Jews, Solomon and the Queen of Sheba, Judith decapitating Holofernes, and chaste but naked Susannah watched by the lecherous elders while bathing. The main sources for these frequently repeated designs were Flemish picture Bibles such as those produced by Bernard Saloman, Jost Amman, Maarten de Vos, and above all Gerard de Jode, and broadside prints based on the plates sold by London stationers like Peter Stent and John Overton.[52]

In her book *The Subversive Stitch*, Rozsika Parker suggested that the frequent depiction of female biblical figures engaged in heroic action might be interpreted as 'an assertion of women as active beings in the very medium intended to teach obedience and passivity'. The evidence for reading these embroideries as 'weapons of resistance to the constraints of femininity'[53] is slender, but what they do reveal clearly is the profound influence which Protestant abhorrence of idolatry exercised on every aspect of English culture in this period. In this regard the studied avoidance of anthropomorphic images of God the Father and of episodes in the life of Jesus Christ described in the Gospels and Acts is very striking. John Calvin and his followers drew a careful distinction between narrative pictures and static icons: the latter were inherently dangerous invitations to popish veneration but the former had a legitimate didactic function.[54] To echo a character in Joseph Mayne's 1639 comedy *The Citye Match*, it is almost as if these book covers could be cited as edifying texts 'by some Pure

fig. 47. See also *The New Testament* (1625) – Bodley, Douce Bib.Eng. N.T. 1625 g.1. One example of Moses and Aaron bearing the tables of the Ten Commandments has been detached from the book it originally covered and mounted in a frame: Yvonne Hackenbroch, *English and other Needlework Tapestries and Textiles in the Irwin Untermeyer Collection* (1960), pl. 36.

[52] Nancy Graves Cabot, 'Pattern sources of scriptural subjects in Tudor and Stuart embroideries', *Bulletin of the Needle and Bobbin Club*, 30 (1946), 3–57; Margaret Swain, *Figures on Fabric: Embroidery Design Sources and their Application* (1980), ch. 4; Wells-Cole, *Art and Decoration*, 27, 104, 121–2, and ch. 14; J.L. Nevinson, 'Peter Stent and John Overton, publishers of embroidery designs', *Apollo*, 24 (1936), 279–83.

[53] Parker, *Subversive Stitch*, 96, vi, respectively; cf. 102, 107. See also Ruth Geuter, 'Reconstructing the context of seventeenth-century English figurative embroideries', in Moira Donald and Linda Hurcombe, eds, *Gender and Material Culture in Historical Perspective* (Basingstoke, 2000), 97–111.

[54] John Calvin, *Institutes of Christian Religion*, ed. John T. McNeill, 2 vols (1961), bk 1, ch. 11, §12.

Instructer'.[55] Reinforcing the findings of Tessa Watt and Anthony Wells-Cole concerning other spheres of exterior and interior domestic decoration, they add weight to suggestions that the iconophobia of post-Reformation English society has been greatly exaggerated.[56]

It is probable that the shift in aesthetic priorities linked with the rise of the Laudian programme for the 'beauty of holiness' left its mark on the practice of embroidering bookbindings. The 1630s witnessed a revival both of ecclesiastical needlework and of the iconographical motifs associated with the ancient school of English embroidery known as the *Opus Anglicanum*. Edmund Harrison, bookbinder to King Charles I, produced wall panels depicting the Visitation and Betrothal of Mary and the Adoration of the Shepherds, and the elaborate concordances produced by the Ferrars and Collets at Little Gidding reflect the same set of developments. Significantly, these 'sublimations of scissors and paste' were sumptuously bound: the king described one presented to him in 1635 as 'a precious gem, and worthy of his cabinet'.[57] When Richard Cosin published his *Collection of Private Devotions* in 1627, with the letters IHS incorporated into the title-page, William Prynne called it 'an undoubted Badge, and Character of a Popish, and Jesuiticall Booke' and said that it bore 'the very Marke, and Seale of the Beast upon its Fore-head'.[58] It is certainly true that most bindings on which it can be found emblazoned cover foreign and clandestine Catholic publications.[59] These were too much like medieval icons to be acceptable to zealous Protestants.

And yet there was a sense in which richly decorated Protestant books were perceived as precious holy objects. In Lutheran Germany hymnals, prayer books, and Bibles were believed to be incombustible, like the relics of saints and some portraits of the Wittenberg reformer himself. Perhaps it should not surprise us that Luther and Melanchthon were often tooled on to sixteenth-century leather

[55] Joseph Mayne, *The Citye Match. A Comoedye* (Oxford, 1639), 11.

[56] Tessa Watt, *Cheap Print and Popular Piety, 1550–1640* (Cambridge, 1991), 134, 136 and chs 4–5; Wells-Cole, *Art and Decoration*, 296, 300. Cf. Patrick Collinson, *The Birthpangs of Protestant England* (New York, 1988), 115–21.

[57] Margaret H. Swain, *Historical Needlework: A Study of Influences in Scotland and Northern England* (1970), 59–60 and Nevinson, *Catalogue*, 39 and pl. XXVIII; George Henderson, 'Bible illustration in the age of Laud', *Transactions of the Cambridge Bibliographical Society*, 8 (1982), 185–96, quotations at 185, 187, 190.

[58] William Prynne, *A Briefe Survay and Censure of Mr Cosen his Couzening Devotions* (1628), 4.

[59] See, e.g., Sabine Coron and Martine Lefèvre, *Livres en broderie: reliures françaises du Moyen Âge à nos jours* (Paris, 1995), nos 23, 37.

bindings from that country.[60] In England, cases can be cited of the Bible being used as aid to divination and decision making, as a magic talisman imbued with medical powers, and as an amulet affording supernatural protection. During the Civil War, it was reported that bullets had miraculously bounced off the pocket Gospels carried by Parliamentary soldiers.[61] These compelling examples of the syncretism that could occur between traditional and Reformed belief may be unusual, but even in everyday use religious books were items of material culture which served a variety of purposes other than reading. As shown here, they might still be regarded residually as devotional devices and jewels. Whereas medieval craftsmen had concentrated on individualizing the illuminated pages inside, early modern ones, faced with uniform printed texts, turned them into special personal possessions by embellishing their covers. Symbols not of the separation, but the continued interweaving, of image and word, embroidered and other decorative bindings add a new dimension to the commonplace that sixteenth- and seventeenth-century Protestantism was a religion of the book.[62]

University of Exeter

[60] Robert W. Scribner, 'The Reformation, popular magic, and the "disenchantment of the world"', *Journal of Interdisciplinary History*, 23 (1993), 484; Weale, *Bookbindings*, 37, 41, 44, 273, 278, 286, 289, 299.

[61] David Cressy, 'Books as totems in seventeenth-century England and New England', *Journal of Library History*, 21 (1986), 92–106; Richard Baxter, *Reliquiae Baxterianae* (1696), pt I, 46.

[62] Addendum to n.30: In *An Apology for Women* (1609), 35–6, William Heale also disparaged those 'too too holy women-gospellers, who weare their testament at their apronstrings . . .'.

TRIPLE-DECKERS AND EAGLE LECTERNS: CHURCH FURNITURE FOR THE BOOK IN LATE MEDIEVAL AND EARLY MODERN ENGLAND[1]

by SUSAN WABUDA

'THE spirit of the Lord God is upon me: because the Lord hath anointed me to preach good tidings unto the meek.' When Jesus stood up to read these verses from Isaiah at the start of his public ministry, as he began to reveal himself as the Word in the synagogue of Nazareth, the book 'he had opened' at the reading desk was one of the Torah scrolls, brought out for him from the Ark of the Law, the imposing reserve which is, from age to age, the most sacred part of any synagogue.[2] Holy Scripture has always been a public book, a treasure for each synagogue, and for the commonwealth of the Christian community sacred as text and object. But the mystical sanctity of the Bible, and holy books in general,[3] has raised a perennial problem. Precious books have usually been hedged round by restrictions to protect them from the profane, even at the cost of obscuring the public approach which is a necessary part of assembled worship. In this episode in the life of Christ, when the listeners grew too 'filled with wrath' for him to continue, we meet the deep and recurrent tension between the community's need to hear the Word, and the conflicting desire to shield its essential sanctity, which accompanied the book from Judaism in transition to the Christian Church.

Some of the conflicting dynamics between the sacred and the profane, access and reserve, have been addressed (if not always

---

[1] Some of the themes of this paper are amplified in my monograph *Preaching during the English Reformation* (Cambridge, 2002). Continued thanks are due to Prof. Patrick Collinson, Maria Dowling, and Alexandra Walsham (for suggesting this topic).

[2] Isa. 61.1–2, 58.6; Luke 4.16–30; *Encyclopedia Judaica* (Jerusalem, 1971), *sub* 'Ark', 'Torah Ornaments', 'Word', and 'Yad'.

[3] Margaret Aston, 'Devotional literacy', in her *Lollards and Reformers: Images and Literacy in Late Medieval Religion* (1984), 101–33, esp. pp. 108–113; David Cressy, 'Books as totems in seventeenth-century England and New England', *Journal of Library History*, 21 (1986), 92–106; Keith Thomas, *Religion and the Decline of Magic* (New York, 1971), 45–6, 118–19, 214; Susan Wabuda, 'The woman with the rock', in Susan Wabuda and Caroline Litzenberger, eds, *Belief and Practice in Reformation England* (Aldershot, 1998), 43; Alexandra Walsham, *Providence in Early Modern England* (Oxford, 1999), 332.

resolved) through the Church's furniture for the book. In serving as evocative settings, meeting-places between heaven and earth, the lectern and the pulpit have represented the struggles to find a fit balance between availability and restraint, especially when the meaning of the book itself was challenged and redefined in the sixteenth century. The furniture associated with books, and with the exposition of the meanings of books (or, more particularly, sacred scriptures), is therefore an intimate and important element in the overall relationship between 'the Church and the book'. While the main focus of this essay will be English church furniture, occasional glances further afield will begin to suggest how the tensions between availability and access were played out on the continent.

In the greater scheme of things, the part played by the pulpit seems immutable. But in reality, the worth of the pulpit as an article of church furniture has changed drastically in the effort to redefine the holy. Before the Reformation, as rests for the book, the pulpit and the lectern were subordinate to the high altar. They had their own modest place in the economy of salvation when parishioners donated them for the good of the parish.[4] The ritual presentation and reading of the Epistles and Gospels were important, but less so than the celebration of the Eucharist. In the course of the sixteenth-century reforms, once the tenet of *sola scriptura* provided the new standard for salvation, the place of the book was enhanced as the Eucharist was redefined. Correspondingly, the position of the pulpit became more central in Protestant regions, more imposing, and its meaning became even more abstract at the same time that it lost much of its importance as a good work in the great process of salvation.

During and after the Middle Ages, the Catholic Church drew an exacting parallel between the sacrament of the altar and the Word. The Church maintained that the Bible was food for the soul, and like the sacrament of the altar, had to be administered properly, by priests who taught orthodox views and interpreted Scripture properly. In the Middle Ages, under the pressure of Lollardy, these requirements led to the withholding of the vernacular Bible under the terms of the anti-heresy statutes that were unique to England. These laws were removed

[4] Subordination: Joseph A. Jungman, *The Mass of the Roman Rite*, tr. Francis A. Brunner, rev. edn (New York, 1980), 53, 269–73. Donations of pulpits: J. Charles Cox, *Pulpits, Lecterns, and Organs in English Churches* (1915), 42, 62, 70, 80; Eamon Duffy, *The Stripping of the Altars: Traditional Religion in England, c. 1400–c. 1580* (New Haven, CT, and London, 1992), 110–16, 124–5, 134, 153–4, 334–5.

under Henry VIII, but reimposed under Mary Tudor. For the theologian John Standish, writing in 1554, the restrictions that governed the laity's decorum as they received the Host also determined their reception of the gospel, and ruled out any existing English translation of the Bible. God had designed Scripture to be obscure, and the clergy had to serve as intermediaries in teaching its mystic truths. The laity should no more take the Scripture into their own hands than they should handle the Host itself. In *The Stripping of the Altars*, Eamon Duffy has established that the laity would have been able to appreciate the gospel readings on many levels, and that Latin was no insurmountable impediment. Still, it would also be true to say that the Word was protected from the congregation, which Standish argued was for their own good. The placement of the rood screen also served to veil the gospel book in many parishes, much as it did the Host.[5]

The placement of the church's furniture for the book symbolically re-enacted the book's relation to the Host, and the life and sacrifice of Christ. During the Mass, the reading of the gospel, with the homily, represented Christ as a teacher, and together these events provided important tableaux as the ritual rose to the culmination of the eucharistic miracle. In great churches, like the monastic cathedral of Durham, the gospel book, which might be bound with precious stones and images of the saviour, resided on its cushion on the high altar for much of the Mass. Usually the lectern remained in the choir. The pulpit was often fixed to the rood screen (which it could be carved or ornamented to match) on the north side of the church, which was associated with the gospel, a liminal placement, straddling the boundary between the clergy and the laity.[6]

Pulpits were select, semi-enclosed podiums or platforms, small stages suspended between heaven and earth, not only raised, but encompassed by a railing or enclosure to increase the dignified

[5] [John Standish], *A Discourse wherin is Debated whether it be Expedient that the Scripture shoulde be in English* (1554), STC 23207, sigs E5r-E9r, K3v-K4r; Duffy, *Stripping*, 53–130, 157–60, 213–32; Patrick Collinson, 'The coherence of the text: how it hangeth together: the Bible in Reformation England', *Journal for the Study of the New Testament*, Supplement series, 105 (Sheffield, 1995), 84–108, esp. 84; Aston, 'Devotional literacy', 109; Anne Hudson, *The Premature Reformation: Wycliffite Texts and Lollard History* (Oxford, 1988), 278–389; Wabuda, 'Rock', 46.

[6] Jungmann, *Mass*, 273–5, 283–92; *Rites of Durham*, ed. J.T. Fowler, Surtees Society, 107 (1903), 8–9; Margaret Aston, 'Segregation in church', *SCH*, 27 (1990), 237–94, esp. 242–50. For much of what follows, Cox, *Pulpits*, esp. chs 3–4, 8–9. See also the paper by Alexandra Walsham elsewhere in this volume.

aspect of the structure, as well as to protect the preacher from falls. A rest for the book or the preacher's sermon notes often projected from the side facing the congregation. Embroidered or painted banners, which hung down the front, under the bookrest, added an air of dignity to the structure, and drew attention to the book and face above it. Over the preacher's head, an ornate canopy served as a sounding board to project his voice. Most parish churches in England were equipped with a pulpit before the Reformation.[7]

Lecterns too were extremely common in the late Middle Ages, from the simple desk-shaped variety (whose gable form could accommodate codices or unfurled scrolls), to the elaborate pedestal, topped with a generous bookrest resembling the outstretched wings of an eagle (the symbol of St John the Evangelist). Less commonly, the great bird was a pelican, the symbol of Christian suffering and sacrifice. Norwich Cathedral still has its superb pelican lectern. At Durham, the pelican lectern (esteemed as the finest in the country) was matched by a pelican pyx that hung over the high altar. The ancestor of the lectern and pulpit was the ambo of the early Church, a book desk developed from its predecessor in the synagogue, its name derived from the Greek, meaning to climb.[8]

Of course the use of height to set the Word apart and amplify its dignity has been among the oldest practices associated with Holy Scripture. The main altar usually stood higher than the pulpit, and higher still than the lectern.[9] Elevation too was a necessity for seeing and hearing the preacher. When St Augustine preached from his throne in Hippo, he was at a higher physical remove than those who stood before him, but close enough for the first row of listeners to be able to look him in the eye.[10] The very act of ascending the short flight of steps into the medieval pulpit was a sacred statement of authority.[11]

Metaphorically, the preacher speaks as he sits 'in Moses' seat', in the sense that his words were to emanate ultimately from the law of Moses, as in Nehemiah, when Ezra the Scribe read the book of the law from a pulpit of wood 'above all the people', who bowed their heads

[7] Cox, *Pulpits*, 36–81.

[8] Pelicans: *Rites of Durham*, 1–9; Cox, *Pulpits*, 163–5; J.W. Blench, *Preaching in England in the Late Fifteenth and Sixteenth Centuries: a Study of English Sermons, 1450–c.1600* (Oxford, 1964), 16; Miri Rubin, *Corpus Christi: the Eucharist in Late Medieval Culture* (Cambridge, 1991), 310–12. For the ambo, see Cox, *Pulpits*, 28; Jungmann, *Mass*, 269–73.

[9] Cox, *Pulpits*, 28; Jungmann, *Mass*, 53, 269–73.

[10] Peter Brown, *Augustine of Hippo: a Biography* (Berkeley, CA, 1967), 251.

[11] William Lyndwood, *Provinciale* (Oxford, 1679), III.4 (133, f); Cox, *Pulpits*, 32.

and worshipped the Lord with their faces to the ground. In stonework at Rochester cathedral, the prophets bridge the gap over the doorway to the chapter room, rising between the triumphant *Ecclesia* and the broken-staffed *Synagoga* (a theme repeated over the famous south door of Strasbourg cathedral). They are portrayed in the act of preaching from Moses' seat, pulling long scrolls from the multi-tiered lecterns by their sides.[12] When Jesus finished his reading in Nazareth, he sat to conduct his lesson with every eye upon him. Standing was gradually adopted during the Middle Ages, especially to make the preacher more visible and audible, at outdoor pulpits in cemeteries and church-yards (like Paul's Cross in London, or the surviving example next to the ruins of the Dominican house in Hereford). Mindful of ancient tradition, but adapting it to suit his humility and increasing age, Bishop John Fisher preached from a simple chair, a rare example of authority without pomp.[13]

The special concerns, taste, patterns of devotion, the relative wealth of every parish, and the generosity of its members, were expressed through the lectern and pulpit, as much as any other part of the church's fabric, its vestments, chalices, statues, or lights. Usually the parish was equipped with its own free-standing lectern, though this was not exclusively so. The indefatigable J. Charles Cox estimated in 1915 that no fewer than two hundred medieval pulpits had survived to his day, their original aspects sometimes lost to us through the conversions and rebuilding that many churches endured from the sixteenth century.[14] He counted nearly thirty-five medieval brass eagle lecterns, including the magnificent example at Clare in Suffolk. East Anglia still has so many eagle lecterns (including those at the church of St Margaret and the chapel of St Nicholas in Lynn), that they could be mistaken for being a regular fixture. But Clare's neighbouring village of Kedington (one of those few parish churches to avoid Victorian refurbishment) does not have an eagle lectern, and never needed one.

---

[12] My thanks are due to the staffs of the cathedrals at Rochester and Strasbourg for my visits in the summers of 2000 and 1978.
[13] Matt. 23.2; Neh. 8.1–5; *Sermons by Hugh Latimer*, ed. George Elwes Corrie, PS (Cambridge, 1844), 85–6, 206–7; Collinson, 'Coherence of the text', 107; H. Leith Spencer, *English Preaching in the Late Middle Ages* (Oxford, 1993), 64; Damian Riehl Leader, *A History of Cambridge, 1, The University to 1546* (Cambridge, 1988), 100; Maria Dowling, *Fisher of Men: a Life of John Fisher, 1469–1535* (1999), 76. My thanks also to Fr Louis Pascoe, S.J.
[14] Cox, *Pulpits*, chs 3–4, 8–9; Duffy, *Stripping*, 57–8, 334. See also Francis T. Dollman, *Examples of Antient Pulpits* (1849); G.R. Owst, *Preaching in Medieval England* (Cambridge, 1926), 199.

The fragment of the rood screen that survives (as ornamentation decorating the elaborate pew for the Barnardiston family) still has its built-in book rest at the eastern side, the chancel side, of the screen. At the reading of the gospel, the priest would have come up to the screen and been framed by it, like a living saint. Here the congregation would have been able to see the gospel book every Sunday.[15]

The books that were brought to the pulpit were the manifest sign of divine sanction, and the obvious token of the priest's learning. The founder of a late fifteenth-century London chantry specified that he wanted the priest who served it to be able to 'deliver sermons from notes', the notes themselves being important as the visible manifestation of God's word, witnesses to the truth of their utterances. For emphasis, preachers displayed their books to inspire their hearers much as they would raise a crucifix aloft.[16]

Like the altar, the pulpit and the lectern belonged to the use of the clergy, and they stood in the holiest part of the church in the symbolic space that was set apart from the laity. In the dim interiors of many English churches, crowded with competing attractions for the eye and mind – the great rood with its screen, the candles flickering before the statues of the saints, and the stained glass – the pulpit tried to hold its own as an important focal point. But the churchgoers often paid for the pulpit, and the names of donors were often inscribed upon it, with pleas to onlookers to pray for their souls.[17] Building a pulpit was a good work that assisted the soul of the donor, and it was meant to form a perpetual legacy for the entire community, most notably apparent in the bidding prayer that was delivered for 'all Christian souls' suffering in purgatory, led by the priest from the pulpit during the Mass or sermons, and especially at the regular reading of the parish bede-roll. Part of the public struggle for salvation was waged from the pulpit, as prayers were marshalled from the entire parish, or many parishes. For the welfare of his soul, John Lane of Cullompton in Devon left

---

[15] Cox prints a finer example at Monksilver in Somerset, *Pulpits*, 162–3. Also, Eamon Duffy, 'Holy maydens, holy wyfes: the cult of women saints in fifteenth- and sixteenth-century England', *SCH*, 27 (1990), 175–196; idem, *Stripping*, 110–16; Peter E. McCullough, *Sermons at Court* (Cambridge, 1998), 23–4; Aston, 'Devotional literacy', 109. My thanks to the parishes of Clare and Kedington for my visits in 1997.

[16] Pulpit notes: *The Records of Two City Parishes*, ed. William McMurray (1925), 1–14, 22. Crucifix: see Iris Origo, *The World of San Bernardino* (New York, 1962), 11–42, or *The English Works of John Fisher*, ed. John E.B. Mayor, EETS, e.s., 27 (1876), 388–428.

[17] Cox, *Pulpits*, 42, 62, 70, 80; Duffy, *Stripping*, 110–16, 124–5, 134, 153–4, 334–5; J.J. Scarisbrick, *The Reformation and the English People* (Oxford, 1984), 45.

bequests to one hundred neighbouring parishes to have his name added to their bede-rolls 'to pray for me in their pulpits'.[18]

In practice, however, just as lay people were not usually permitted to intrude upon the most sacred space of the church, they were forbidden to meddle with the pulpit. Most pulpits were outfitted with doors that locked. When Erasmus placed his Folly in a pulpit, he played upon the implausibility of a woman annexing the most public of priestly offices for herself.[19] Nor were unlicensed or unorthodox clerks permitted access. The angry friars who pulled Thomas Bilney out of the pulpit by his ears in the late 1520s intended to protect the sanctity of the pulpit from the pollution of heresy as much as they wanted to stop the spread of his ideas.[20]

Attitudes changed as the sixteenth century proceeded. Evangelical reformers beheld the pulpit in a welter of contradictions resulting from their understanding of the nature of salvation and the changing role of the clergy. Once the tenet of purgatory and votive Masses began to be criticized, and the bidding prayer came under increasing attack from the 1530s, the traditional purpose of the pulpit was undermined. 'Preachers, belike, were sitters in those days', remarked Hugh Latimer in 1549 of Christ's example in Luke 5.3, when Jesus sat in Simon Peter's ship to preach to those who gathered by the lakeside. 'I would our preachers would preach sitting or standing, one way or other.' He never tired of expounding from Romans 10.8–17 that preaching was the true ladder of salvation. Spiritual regeneration was possible only through the faith that came by the hearing of the Word of God and preaching. Even though he referred to the well-worn commonplace that the pulpit was a bell, the preacher was the clapper, and woe to the parish who had let the pulpit remain silent, the structure itself smacked of popish trappings. Remembering Bilney, who had preached 'in the open fields' in emulation of Christ, Latimer argued that the pulpit might be 'superstitiously used', and wondered if it were not better to have a sermon occasionally in a 'profane place'. Unconsciously he echoed the peripatetic Thomas Man, that great fifteenth-century champion of Lollardy, who attacked clerical privilege by dismissing

---

[18] Fisher, *Works*, 281. Lane: PRO, PROB 11/23, fols 29r-v; Robert Whiting, *The Blind Devotion of the People: Popular Religion and the English People* (Cambridge, 1989), 19–20, 237.

[19] Aston, 'Lollard women priests?' in *Lollards and Reformers*, 49–70; Wabuda, 'Rock', 55.

[20] John Foxe, *Acts and Monuments*, ed. George Townsend, 8 vols (1843–9), 4:627; and similarly for Hugh Latimer in Exeter: *Gleanings from the Common Place Book of John Hooker*, ed. Walter J. Harte (Exeter, nd), 13–14.

pulpits as nothing more than 'priests' lying stools'. Latimer argued that a 'good preacher may declare the word of God sitting on a horse, or preaching in a tree', though he conceded that this idea might be so lacking in essential dignity that it might be laughed 'to scorn' for all of its enthusiasm. Many of the pulpits Latimer knew were so closely associated with the doctrines and practices he was working to overturn that it is hardly surprising that he wished the simplicity of 'Christ's chair' could be revived.[21]

For, with Reformation, why keep the pulpit at all? Why not convert it to some less elaborate seat, or do away with pulpits altogether, just as altars were demoted and communion tables set up in their stead? Here we meet the paradox of the public nature of learning from the book, in contrast to private reading, and of the unavoidable implications of the tenet that faith cometh by hearing.[22] For the evangelical reformers kept the notion of a spiritual elite, a special tier among the greater body of all believers, priests though all might be in some sense. Once the Bible was translated and placed openly on desks for all to read in the parish churches from 1536, the common men or women could now hold the most sacred scriptures in their own hands and read it to others. But the public assembly, during the liturgy, still provided necessary direction in the correct understanding of what the Word meant. And here the pulpit, sanctioned by biblical precedents, still proved useful, in a humbler capacity as a support for the teacher and his book.[23]

Under Edward VI and again under Elizabeth, the naves of churches became preaching spaces, and chancels were opened for communicants in accordance with the 1552 Book of Common Prayer. The communion table dominated the chancel, and the pulpit, detached from its rood screen, pushed into the body of the church. The medieval pulpit was now sometimes an odd, even flamboyant, survivor.[24] The smallest pulpit in England, at the church of Stoke-by-Clare in Suffolk, is a good example. Only twenty inches across, it was probably brought by

---

[21] Latimer, *Sermons*, 85–6, 206–7; Matt. 23.2; Neh. 8.1–5. Man: Foxe, *Acts and Monuments*, 4:209. Bilney: ibid., 4:642. Legend suggests that St Bernardino delivered one of his first sermons from the branches of an olive tree: Origo, *San Bernardino*, 26.

[22] Rom. 10.17.

[23] Euan Cameron, *The European Reformation* (Oxford, 1991), 111–49; Diarmaid MacCulloch, 'The myth of the English Reformation', *JBS*, 30 (1991), 1–19; Wabuda, 'Rock', 40–59.

[24] Diarmaid MacCulloch, *Thomas Cranmer: a Life* (New Haven, CT, and London, 1996), 508–11; Duffy, *Stripping*, 473–5.

Matthew Parker, possibly salvaged from the dissolution of Stoke College nearby after the original furnishings, including the rood screen, were removed.[25] In time, as the Book made way for the Word, the latter took precedence even over the Eucharist, and the most eye-stopping feature of church furniture became the pulpit. In the eighteenth century, the book desk, lectern, and pulpit were all combined together into one imposing structure, the triple-decker pulpit, each section graduated in size, with the pulpit supreme at the highest part, placed to obscure the altar or table. These towering triple-deckers could bristle with useful accessories: candle-rests, an hour-glass, and at Kedington, even a stand for the preacher's wig. The style of the carving and wood-work became more abstract, with Renaissance arches or strap-work as common motifs, or even raised dots, as in the case of the pillars of the Jacobean pulpit at All Saints, Rotherham. Figurative carving never completely disappeared, though paint may not have been much used. Verticality was extreme and more essential than ever, as pulpit builders endeavoured to instil a sense of awe in the onlookers. And in contrast to medieval pulpits, with their entreaties to pray for the souls of the donors, seventeenth-century patrons had their gift inscribed with their name and the date without an invitation for the audience to do more than to show due appreciation. 'Faith is by hearing' reads one inscription at Lyme Regis.[26]

Something even more pronounced occurred in Calvinist churches in Geneva, Scotland, and the United Provinces in the Netherlands. The pulpit was moved out into the body of the church, and away from its old association with the high altar. The direction of worship was reassigned, from the east end of the church to the middle of the nave, where the pulpit now commanded the centremost position, a fitting symbol of the new centrality that the Bible and the sermon took in the life of the congregation.[27]

Cox called the pulpit's triumphant new position in English churches

[25] My thanks to Maria Dowling for advice on this point, and to the parish for the opportunity for a close inspection of the pulpit in 1997. John Strype, *The Life and Acts of Matthew Parker*, 3 vols (Oxford, 1821), 1:15–18, 44–5.

[26] Cox, *Pulpits*, 62, 80, 94, 106, 134, and ch. 7. Also Diarmaid MacCulloch, *Tudor Church Militant: Edward VI and the Protestant Reformation* (1999), 162. My thanks to Prof. Collinson for our visit to Rotherham in 1999.

[27] Andrew Spicer, 'Rebuilding Solomon's Temple? The architecture of Calvinism', *SCH*, 36 (2000), 275–87.

an 'odious arrangement'.[28] Elsewhere on the continent, in Catholic countries, the relationship between the high altar and the pulpit was retained, but simplified following the Council of Trent, as a mirror of the traditional association between the Eucharist and the Word. The problem of how to allow the laity an unhindered view of the high altar (now provided with a tabernacle for the reserved sacrament) and the gospel book was solved by forfeiting the screen. The visibility of the priest, as preacher and in presiding at the sacrifice, was now paramount. Churches built in Catholic regions, especially in the eighteenth century (including Vienna and Krakow) were designed with uninterrupted sight-lines. Cluttering distractions, like pillars and tall pews as well as rood screens, were avoided. Ingenious architectural solutions created seamless, oval spaces. The pulpit was brought forward, away from the altar, and given an enhanced position (on the north side of the aisle). Although it might be heavily ornate, especially in the baroque period, its role was essentially supplementary to the altar, as it had been in the Middle Ages. Now church buildings themselves were meant to evoke the protective mantles of the Torah scrolls, and veils for the sacrament of the altar.[29]

The deferential reserve accorded to the book and to the Word in public worship has proved to be something of a constant in English church furnishings, regardless of doctrinal change. The various paradoxical manifestations of the pulpit have been created to heighten and enhance the congregation's appreciation for the authority and the mystic power of the text, as well as the preacher, who walks in the footsteps of Christ and his apostles. Interpretations of holy writ may change, and the pulpit may grow, shrink, or move. But through the ages, the most consistent pattern of all has been the clustering of the faithful around the preacher, learning from a living man reading and teaching from a living text.

Fordham University

---

[28] Cox, *Pulpits*, 96.

[29] Anthony Blunt, *Borromini* (1979), 67. 114–18; Thomas DeCosta Kaufman, *Court, Cloister, and City: the Art and Culture of Central Europe 1450–1800* (Chicago, 1995), 217–18.

PIETY, PENANCE, AND POPULAR READING IN DEVOTION TO THE VIRGIN MARY AND HER MIRACLES: ITALIAN INCUNABULA AND EARLY PRINTED COLLECTIONS

by RUTH CHAVASSE

'THOSE folk are all men [and women] of my kidney who delight in miracles and fictitious marvels, whether hearing or telling about them', exclaimed Erasmus's Folly. As for saints,

> Each one of these is assigned his [or her] special powers . . . so that one gives relief from toothache, another stands by women in childbirth. . . . There are some whose influence extends to several things, notably the Virgin, mother of God, for the common ignorant man comes near to *attributing more to her than to her son.*[1]

Reformers saw such cults as detracting from the centrality of Christ in Christian devotion. One of the reforming factors of anticlericalism in the early sixteenth century was the search for a more direct route to salvation, a more direct line to God than through the mediating authority of the perhaps all too earth-bound priest. Increasingly often in pre-Reformation Europe the mediating influence of Mary or of a favourite saint was felt to be more effective than that of the priest. Both lay and religious found Mary, the mother of God, more accessible than a judgemental Christ. Despite the teaching of the Church, Mary did appear to come between Christ and his people, as often illustrated by the iconography of the Madonna of Mercy upon whose mantle the arrows rained down by Christ or God the Father were broken.[2]

This escalating devotion not only to Mary but to her miracles was a Europe-wide phenomenon in the late fifteenth century. It was evidence of an obsessively penitential culture, seen especially in the activities of confraternities. Confraternities put great effort into saving not only the souls of brothers and sisters but, for example,

---

[1] D. Erasmus, *Praise of Folly*, tr. B. Radice (1971), 125–9 (emphasis added).

[2] See Ruth Chavasse, 'The Virgin Mary: consoler, protector and social worker in Quattrocento miracle tales', in Letizia Panizza, ed., *Women in Italian Renaissance Culture and Society* (Oxford, 2000), 154, 158, 159 fig.10.

the souls of those whom the law had condemned to die.[3] The emphasis on penance was also evident in personal piety and in the moral exhortations of sermons, where examples drawn from miracle stories furnished readily understood moral precepts. Society as a whole absorbed a vast number of posthumous miracles attributed to the Virgin Mary. Can they only be understood as 'an exercise in piety where to believe even the most doubtful and extravagant legends' was proof of faith?[4] A telling confirmation of this faith is found in a manuscript addition at the close of a 1545 edition of a collection of Marian *Miracles*, which ends (as most of the collections do) by announcing 'The end of the Miracles of the Madonna': below, 'without end' has been inserted to emphasise that Mary's miraculous power continues.[5] After a millennium and a half of Christianity, the miracle was a form of 'seeing salvation' in everyday life better understood by Erasmus's ordinary man or woman than through the life of Christ.[6]

In 1918 Ezio Levi wrote that 'Italian miracle books shed a revealing light on many mysteries.' He was referring to the explosive publishing phenomenon which followed rapidly in the wake of the arrival of printing with movable type in Italy in the 1460s – thirty-four editions of *Miracles of the Virgin Mary* by 1500, and more in the early years of the new century.[7] They were not the only books of popular vernacular religious literature being widely published, but considering the number of editions, neglect of their significance is surprising.

Moreover, the Marian miracle volumes have considerable significance for the iconology of Marian altarpieces in central Italy, works which were being painted in great numbers at the same time as the

---

[3] C.F. Black, *Italian Confraternities in the Sixteenth Century* (Cambridge, 1989), 217–23; Ezio Levi, 'I miracoli della Vergine nell'arte del medio evo', *Bolletino d'arte*, 12 (1918), 24 and fig. 20, showing confraternity participation in the final journey of the accused to the gallows in the story of 'Il miracolo del ladro Elbo', who was saved by the intervention of the Virgin. This miracle is also depicted in the cycle of Marian miracles in the Lady Chapel, Winchester Cathedral.

[4] M. Levi d'Ancona, *The Iconography of the Immaculate Conception in the Middle Ages and the Early Renaissance* (New York, 1957), 57.

[5] *Miracoli della gloriosa Vergine Maria* (Florence, 1545): BL, 4823.a.43, MS interlinear addition, no pagination.

[6] 'Seeing Salvation', London, National Gallery exhibition, 2000; catalogue published as Gabriele Finaldi, ed., *The Image of Christ* (2000).

[7] Levi, 'Miracoli', 25; *The Illustrated Incunabula Short-Title Catalogue* (CD-ROM: BL, 2000) lists known incunabula editions.

miracle books were appearing.[8] This paper deals with the books, with their content and the light they throw on the piety and morality of a wide spectrum of pre-Reformation society, mainly but not exclusively in Italy. The opening story of every Italian edition of *Miracles of the Virgin Mary* concerns a wealthy knight who, losing his money, made a pact with the devil, exchanging his wife for the restoration of the riches which he had lost. Its continuation, as the Virgin intervenes to rescue the wife and save the rich man's soul, was depicted in the Lady Chapel of Winchester Cathedral about 1500, and also opens the English version of *Miracles of Our Lady* printed by Wynkyn de Worde in 1496.[9] The present discussion is based on an examination of the often single remaining copies of volumes of miracle tales; to date seventeen Italian editions have been examined.[10]

The format of the editions of *Alcuni miracoli della Virgine Maria* is remarkably similar. They are slim quarto volumes without pagination but with chapter or story headings which are also collected in a table of contents, found usually at the beginning (but later at the end) of the book. A colophon rather than a title page gives publishing information; from the 1490s, when woodcut illustrations were introduced, an illustration may serve as a title page.[11] Wynkyn de Worde's edition took a scene of the crucifixion as its title page, from Caxton's *The Fifteen Oes and other prayers* (printed in 1491), affirming the status of the *Miracles* as a book of prayer. None of the editions examined carries a printing privilege. Surprisingly for popular religious literature, the type used was nearly always Roman, clearly set with wide margins. One Venetian edition has Roman for the main text and Gothic for titles; the two Bologna editions are in Gothic, with that of 1495 printed in two columns – these two editions are inferior in quality, especially in the

---

[8] Compare *Miracoli* (Florence, 1495), fol. f2; BL, IA 27465. Florence, church of Santo Spirito, Velluti chapel, 'Madonna del Soccorso' (unknown Florentine artist, ?1490s).

[9] M.R. James and E.W. Tristram, 'The wall paintings in Eton College chapel and in the Lady Chapel of Winchester cathedral', *Walpole Society Proceedings*, 17 (1929), 1–43; *The Treasures of Eton*, ed. James McConnell (1976), 116–30. Wynkyn de Worde, *The Miracles of Our Lady* (Westminster, 1496): Glasgow, University Library, Bv.3.4.

[10] For BL and Italian library copies see *Illustrated Incunabula Short-Title Catalogue*, and *Indice generale degli incunaboli*, vol. 4 (Rome, 1965).

[11] Examples are *Miracoli* (Venice, 1491): BL, IA 22345 (title page 'Annunciation' and 'Christ raising Lazarus'); *Miracoli* (Brescia, 1496), title page 'The Holy House of Loreto'. See Ruth Chavasse, 'Latin lay piety and vernacular lay piety in word and image: Venice, 1471-early 1500s', *Renaissance Studies*, 10 (1996), 330–1. Margaret M. Smith, *The Title Page: Its early Development, 1460–1510* (2000) was published after this paper was completed, but is relevant for my comments on illustrations as title pages.

quality of their paper. Milan and Vicenza production were closely related, as were Florentine editions.[12] New editions were no doubt soon printed from existing printed texts. The sources of this literature were widely known throughout Europe in the later Middle Ages, in collections such as the *Speculum historiale* of Vincent de Beauvais (d.1264), *The Golden Legend* of Jacopo da Varazze (d.1298), and Jean Mielot's *Miracles de Nostre Dame* (*c.*1456).[13] As yet no manuscript source contains the number and order of stories consistent with the almost uniform format of the Italian incunabula.[14] The Italian printed collections include several stories with a specifically Italian context, as well as the legends well-known throughout Europe. The text of the stories is remarkably similar throughout all editions, which would seem to indicate a well-known manuscript source rather than oral tradition, but visual traditions might also contribute. The story of the knight who made a pact with the devil (a most pernicious error condemned by the Council of Paris in 829 to be severely punished) was carved on a holy water stoup in Modena in the early twelfth century.[15] The mounted knight and devil of the Modena stoup are close to woodcut illustrations of the opening story of the later printed collections.[16] Transmission of legends by word and image were closely linked over several hundred years, and their persistence shows the proximity of the religious and secular worlds. The Vicenza publisher Leonardo d'Achate, composing his verse colophon to describe the

[12] Milan and Vicenza editions published by Lavagna, Achate, and da Reno have a verse colophon where in similar wording the publisher claimed to be 'master of these sweet songs'. Florentine editions are characterized by a larger number of legends, 75 rather than 61-2.

[13] See Levi, 'Miracoli', esp. 1-3. I am also indebted to research carried out by Anna Frost on literary sources while she was a postgraduate student at King's College London, and presented in an unpublished paper at the Institute of Historical Research, 1990, which supported my research into the iconography of the Madonna del Soccorso altarpieces.

[14] The possibility remains of discovering Italian MS sources. Since presenting and submitting this paper I have received references to MSS in Florence from Catherine Lawless, for which I am most grateful: Florence, Biblioteca Riccardiana, MS 1408 (15th century), fol. 108v, has the opening story of the printed editions; ibid., MS 1451 (15th century), fol. 62v, has the same opening miracle story. These and other Florentine MSS have yet to be checked for their precise relation to the printed editions.

[15] Modena, Museo Civico, Sala dell'arte sacra: three sides of 'acquasantiera' decorated with scenes from the legend of the knight and the devil, probably work of Niccolò, younger assistant to Wiligelmo. Adolfo Venturi, *Storia dell'arte italiana, 3: L'arte romanica* (Milan, 1904), 157-60.

[16] Esp. *Miracoli* (Florence, 1545), fol. Aii[r]; also *Miracoli* (Milan, 1496), opening story (no foliation).

sweet miracle chants, must have referred to their popularity in the *piazze* of northern Italy where they would have been recounted not by *giulliari*, the minstrels of the courts, but by *cantastorie*. The colophons of the early Milan and Vicenza editions associated reading, singing or chanting, and praying. The printer/publisher's offerings were to rise in prayer to the Queen of Heaven as Mediatrix, and return to earth in granting the supplicant's request; with the corollary that the devotee, whose soul had been saved by Mary's intercession, thereafter celebrated Mary's feasts, especially that of her Conception. Devotion to the Immaculate Conception became the main cult of the altar of the Madonna del Soccorso in the Augustinian Santo Spirito in Florence by the end of the sixteenth century, thereby justifying the iconography of a popular altar which could have appeared dubious in the atmosphere of Catholic reform.[17]

The miracle stories were not only popular stories worth telling or chanting to those who could not read; they were also offered as prayers. As moral precept or as prayer, each story ends with 'Amen' in every printed edition apart from the single more sophisticated edition produced by Achate of Vicenza for a different readership.[18] These examples of confession, penance, penitence, and forgiveness were used as books of intercession, and in one example structured an individual's daily prayer, with the day of the week inserted by hand.[19] The numbered story or chapter heading made the collection convenient for daily prayer or for easy reference when using examples for preaching. The woodcut decoration of the opening page of the Florentine 1495 edition suggested use for intercession by depicting a monk at prayer. Ownership of these books indicates that they were as popular with religious as with lay people, and the content of the stories confirms that the appeal was to the whole community whether lay men and women, rich or poor, and to priests, monks, hermits, or nuns.

Such popular early books have literally been read to dust: editions survive often in single copies, making it difficult to reach general

---

[17] Florence, Archivio di stato, Corporazioni religiose soppresse dal governo francese, 122, pezzo 37, Memoriale G, tavola di Santo Spirito, 1598, fols 9r–v refers to masses to be said or sung especially for the feast of the Immaculate Conception and most often sponsored by women.

[18] See n.21 below.

[19] *Miracoli* (Florence, ?1482): Poppi, Biblioteca Comunale, Inc. 701. See Chavasse, 'The Virgin Mary', 140, 158 n.3.

conclusions about who owned and read them. At the time multiple ownership was common, and evident from two of the volumes examined: the Stonyhurst copy of the Vicenza 1476 edition is inscribed 'Est mei A.F. et amicorum'; a copy of the 1491 Venice collection has a manuscript list of names on the title page, perhaps members of a confraternity, an association known to act as a lending library.[20] Evidence of their popularity is found in the fact that these books were sold or passed on, not discarded. The first owner of the Stonyhurst 1476 copy to inscribe his name in 1479 was Victor, a Camaldolesian monk of Murano, Venice – appropriate ownership of precepts which make frequent reference to the problems of withdrawal from the world. Achate's edition published to celebrate the Jubilee of 1475 survives in two copies of contrasting ownership, one hand-rubricated and still in excellent condition, the other much handled and distinguished in 1493 by a poor signature with two hearts pierced by an arrow. Achate's publications were of high quality, and he is better known for his classical publications and correspondence with humanists. His decision to publish such a popular vernacular religious text at first seems surprising. It is of considerable significance that in 1481 he published an upmarket edition of the miracle stories within a larger collection of works of devotion. It is the only folio edition seen so far, printed clearly in Roman type in two columns on good paper, a characteristic of Achate's production. This version opens with lives of Christ and the Virgin Mary; its second book or section is a life of John the Baptist; the third comprises Mary's miracles after the death of Christ, which were also well-known at the time; finally come the posthumous miracles, containing sixty-two stories, as in his 1475 edition. The examined copy has its original tooled binding with one clasp remaining and the whole is in excellent condition. It is inscribed with a humanist hand, 'This book is of the monastery of S. Maria Magdalena of Padua and that of the monk Ezirado of that monastery. 1502'. This was certainly no longer a book for the popular market but a quality production. Was it a step towards sophistication that it is the only edition which omits 'Amen' after each miracle? 'Amen' simply

[20] *Miracoli* (Vicenza, 1476) – Stonyhurst College, BV VIII 10 (I am grateful to the Revd F.J. Turner, S.J., for enabling me to consult this copy); *Miracoli* (Venice, 1491) – BL, IA 22345. Catherine Gill, 'Women, texts, and religious culture in Trecento and Quattrocento Italy', paper delivered for session 'Women and Devotional Books in Late Medieval and Renaissance Europe' of The Renaissance Society of America conference, Florence 2000, refers to confraternities or churches acting as lending libraries.

closes the volume.[21] It is likely that our popular miracles of the Virgin were often included in such larger books of devotion, at least during the first half of the sixteenth century. Some miracle stories are included in English Books of Hours and therefore had the same association with daily prayer.

The pitfalls of life which required intercession and penance as illustrated in the miracle stories divide into categories of natural disasters or accidents which might lead to untimely physical death, and spiritual dangers which led to serious sins and (frequently) to damnation or spiritual death. An analysis of the stories, which vary little from edition to edition, establishes subject and social groups, although the order in publication made no attempt to group the stories. The stories are about lay men, women, and children throughout society, and about priests, monks, and nuns. What is revealing is the persistence of and emphasis on contemporary problems and concerns. Herein lay their relevance for their devotees and for our understanding of fifteenth-century piety and its dependence on the doctrine of merit and belief in the saintly treasury of merits. Every disaster, physical or spiritual, demanded penance and/or good works to gain salvation in the world to come through the merits of the Blessed Virgin Mary.

The opening story of every edition, as if to set the moral tone of what is to follow, is the legend of that wealthy knight who sold his soul and his wife to the devil. After the intervention of the Virgin Mary, the knight lived contentedly with his wife without his former wealth. They both did much good in the world, which merited them eternal salvation. Usually there are about ten stories on the theme of greed for wealth and its consequences of misfortune or evil befalling men. A solution is offered to those whose materialistic ambitions have spiralled out of control.

The largest category of examples deals with family problems and sexual misdemeanours: adultery, incest, broken vows of chastity, blasphemy, or pacts with the devil. It is always stated that such sins were the work of the devil, whose hold over humankind has to be broken by the heavenly power of the Mother of God. Many of these transgressions fell into the category of reserved sins beyond the jurisdiction of the parish priest. The late edition of 1545 illustrates the story of the woman wrongly accused of adultery, whose husband

---

[21] Vicenza, 1481: Verona, Biblioteca Civica, Inc. 644.

RUTH CHAVASSE

was misled by the devil disguised as a travelling hermit. The month-
old baby's plea to his father to believe in his paternity is illustrated in a
small woodcut at the point in the story when the enraged father
returned home determined to kill both mother and child.[22]

A large and diverse category of miracles concerns the clerical and
monastic professions, with the greater number describing the pitfalls
and a smaller number pointing up the good side of the profession.
These legends were based on common temptations of priests and
religious, but they also show understanding of the frailty or human
side of religious life. It is not surprising that the books were owned by
monks and monasteries. Eremitical withdrawal from the world was
increasingly practised in the fifteenth century, so it is significant that
these *exempla* emphasised the attendant problems of such a way of
pious life, as well as lay people's tendency to mistrust their motives.
Nuns and abbesses were vulnerable to temptation and to abuse. An
abbess could be a powerful woman, whose authority far exceeded that
of a married woman, and the closing story of most collections is a jibe
at such a woman whose bearing and power in her convent was greatly
resented by her nuns. She fell resoundingly far, but with the help of the
Virgin (and, of course, her contrition) both she and her community
were saved.[23]

The meritorious qualities of the religious profession fall into the
category of stories which emphasise the importance of good works and
devotion both lay and religious. The moral is straightforward: good
works will be rewarded. Some examples refer to ecclesiastical patronage, building a church or monastery, others to devotion to the Virgin
Mary, applauding the frequency, repetition, and decorum of salutation
and prayer. Apart from penance, which underlies the whole, there is
little reference to the sacraments.

Many stories reflect ordinary everyday life without reference to
specific social status or profession. They reflect the culture of the time
and the problems which arose within it when Christian morality was
inseparable from day to day living. There are references to widespread
problems such as the plague (illustrated by a hospital ward), and
considerable preoccupation with anti-Semitism, which was increasingly widespread toward the end of the fifteenth century and during

[22] Florence, 1545: BL, 48.a.43.
[23] Giovanni Maria del Basso, 'Il sigillo delle monache: autorita e modello', in Gabriella
Zarri, ed., *Donna, disciplina, creanza christiana dal XV al XVII secolo* (Rome, 1996), 347–66, and
my review in *Renaissance Studies*, 12 (1998), 604.

the sixteenth century. Mary certainly came to the help of Jews, but the corollary was always conversion to Christianity. Other ethnic groups in Europe were acknowledged, as in the example of a Christian woman married to a 'pagan'. There were enough Moslems in Italy for their presence to be recognized; solutions to problems which arose would hardly now be considered politically correct. A Narni wife who gave birth to a very black child called upon the Virgin, who interceded with God to effect a miracle for all to see and the child 'which was so black became white and beautiful through the merits of Our Lady'! The problem of poverty was recognized but strictly in forms accepted by the Church as such, as in the case of the poor widow whose only son, her only source of livelihood, was imprisoned. The story tells how the widow removed the Christ Child from a sculpture of the Virgin and Child in her church and took it home with her, whereupon the Virgin appeared to the son in prison and told him to go to his mother and return the Christ Child to the church. The outcome benefited both mother and son. The story of the painter challenged by the devil was popular throughout Europe, not just in Italy of the Renaissance; it reflected the value attached to the artistic expression of divine grace.[24] The purpose of these legends as they developed was 'seeing salvation' through Mary and her miracles. Their precepts were understood as prayers for all seasons and for many conditions of men and women.

The exceptionally large number of editions of Marian *Miracoli* deserves attention in the history of printing and the book. They tell us much about the printer/publisher's choice of text, and show that publishing was not exclusive or intellectually elitist, even in such a centre as Venice.[25] Their sparse survival is a guide to the popularity of reading or reciting miraculous explanations of disasters in a pre-scientific age. Publication fell off with the onset of religious reform, although there was the edition from Florence as late as 1545, and the miracle tales may well have been included in other devotional books. The images of the Madonna with which they were closely associated survived, especially in central Italy, often inscribed 'ora pro nobis';

[24] For the Narni story see *Miracoli* (Venice, 1491), ch. xxx, for the widow ch. xlvii. The painter story is usually ch. 9 or 10 in Italian collections; it was also depicted in the Lady Chapel of Winchester cathedral: Chavasse, 'Latin lay piety', 331, illustrated at 341 fig. 13 from *Miracoli* (Venice, 1505).

[25] Examples are Bernardino Benali and Matteo Codeca da Parma (Venice, 1491) – BL, IA 22345; Lazzaro Suardi (Venice, 1490) – Verona, Biblioteca Civica, Inc. 168; and Achate of Vicenza.

many of these altars still have an active devotion to Mary. The cross-fertilization of literature and art in Italy, France, and England in the late Middle Ages is affirmed in the printing and depicting of these miracles in woodcuts, painting, or sculpture. The opportunities which print offered to give expression to the deep-seated penitential culture of the middle years of the second Christian millennium had been eagerly grasped. The Italian Marian miracle books, despite the small numbers which now survive, are vital witnesses to characteristics of popular Catholicism, even as the piety and devotion which they reflected were being challenged and overthrown elsewhere in sixteenth-century Europe.

LAP BOOKS AND LECTERN BOOKS:
THE REVELATORY BOOK IN THE REFORMATION

by MARGARET ASTON[1]

(Presidential Address)

THE size of books has always mattered – for manuscript books as well as printed books. It makes a great difference to the fate of its contents and eventual influence whether the page is in a heavy folio or a portable pamphlet. Differences of format affected authority and influence and had a direct bearing on the circulation of ideas, the critical lift-off that could take place when vocalization took the silent word into mouths and minds away from the lettered page. This may seem self-evident, but even so, given the recognized role of the book in the Reformation (or reformations) of the sixteenth century, some reflections on this aspect seem worthwhile. The revelatory quality of the book in this period is here approached first by looking at the role of small lap books, and then by considering the challenge in England to the accepted order of books, when the great lectern book of Scripture was first laid open for general reading in church naves.

* * *

Some years ago Armando Petrucci wrote an article on the origins of the modern book in which he distinguished three types. First the massive scholastic folio, the product of the university world, the *libro di banco*, which demanded a desk or lectern for use; second the medium-sized book, quarto or small folio, more portable but destined in the main for libraries; and thirdly the popular text that was small enough to carry in pouch, or pocket, the *libro da bisaccia* that would fit into the friar's scrip, the compact handbook (*libretto da mano*) which was the model for Aldus Manutius' innovatory octavos with their economic italic type. Here I follow a bipartite scheme that subsumes under the heading of lap books some of Petrucci's second type, treating quarto, octavo, and smaller publications together, in that readers of all kinds could appropriate such texts to informal reading in a variety of

---

[1] I am very grateful to Elizabeth Eisenstein for reading and improving the full delivered text of this essay.

163

locations. The primers that an Italian visitor in 1500 noticed English women taking to church, and which we see depicted in so many Books of Hours, were portable texts that could rest on a lap. Church service books were different. For most lay people of that time lectern books were clergy books; volumes that they could see and hear used but not expect to handle. The massive antiphonals and graduals (those coucher books whose name described their natural state of lying on the reading desk) were for clerical use in the choir, 'wrytt with gret hand' (as a 1455 inventory describes a large matins book), even with letters an inch high to facilitate group reading.[2] A built-in authority belonged to the very format of *libri di banco*, the authority of *literati* and the associations of liturgy and sacrament: the authority of the lectern. Parishioners might corporately own the books in the choir that were needed for their services; they were not expected to use them, and even though the parishioners were not excluded from the chancel, it was not their part of the church.

Lectern and lap books belonged to different spheres. The large book which had to be 'couched' was elevated by its lectern position. Little books and pamphlets, by contrast, were easily portable, mobile, and texts on the move increased in number and influence with the growth of literacy. Small books in lesser hands and lower positions, as some manuscript illuminations suggest, might challenge that clerical world by an inversion of the solemnities of the page, by turning reading into gossip or satire – or worse, into subversion or heresy. What we might call the proprieties of texts could be undermined by newcomers to the page. Perhaps there was always an insidious element in the small pocket book, those texts whose dagger-like properties (that gave the name *enchiridion* to a number of works besides those of St Augustine and Erasmus) were not merely personally protective, but also potentially aggressive: pocket books like pocket knives.[3] Private lay reading, especially where vernacular biblical texts were concerned, was dangerous and closely watched, and before the Reformation, as during it, the

[2] A. Petrucci, 'Alle origini del libro moderno; *Libri da banco, libri da bisaccia, libretti da mano', Italia Medioevale e Umanistica*, 12 (1969), 295–313; J. Milsom, 'Music', in L. Hellinga and J.B.Trapp, eds, *Cambridge History of the Book in Britain, vol. III: 1400–1557* (Cambridge, 1999) [hereafter *CHBB3*], 542–8; C. Wordsworth and H. Littlehales, *The Old Service-Books of the English Church* (1904), 104–7, 203–6; M. Aston, *Lollards and Reformers* (1984), 123–4; *The Church Book of St. Ewen's, Bristol 1454–1584*, ed. B.R. Masters and E. Ralph, Publications of the Bristol and Gloucestershire Archaeological Society, Records Section, 6 (1967), 9.

[3] The Greek word had the meaning of hand-knife as well as handbook, and Erasmus's *Enchiridion* (*STC* 10480) was presented as 'The Handsome Weapon of a Christian Knight'.

books that worried church authorities were specially small works of portable form – Petrucci's *libretti da mano.*

The reading-matter of the Lollards is of some interest here. Wycliffite books covered a wide range from great tome to pamphlet, and it is surely important to bear in mind the differences of format when thinking about official reactions to Wycliffite lay readers. There was all the difference in the world – one might almost say there were different worlds – represented by the two huge illuminated volumes containing the early version of the Wycliffite translation of the Bible, which belonged to Thomas of Woodstock, Duke of Gloucester (d.1397), and the quire of eight leaves containing a dialogue between a clerk and a knight, written about 1400, that survives at Durham.[4] The former could only be a lectern book, and has to be envisaged as belonging to a lordly chapel. Official watchfulness increased, but a folio Bible such as this, or the comparable one owned by Thomas of Lancaster, Duke of Clarence (d.1421),[5] were arguably always less likely to attract inquisitive notice from the authorities than books of lower status and busier use. And the differences in survival rates of tomes and pamphlets may be seen as a reflection of their differing circulation and usage and perceived danger, as well as resulting from the perennial vulnerability of small formats.

It was the larger Wycliffite books, both quarto and folio, carrying scriptural texts and glossed gospels, the possessions of respectable and respected hands, which survived in large numbers. Folios of the whole Wycliffite Bible, such as one owned by Henry VI and given to the London Carthusians, or the copy which belonged to the Bowyer family through the sixteenth century, seem to have remained in gentry possession untroubled by the regulations issued by Archbishop Arundel in 1409. Cranmer, while conscious of these restrictions, was familiar with this still circulating version, made so that 'folk should not lack the fruit of reading', as he put it in his preface to the 1540

---

[4] Anne Hudson, *Lollards and their Books* (1985), 183–4, 192–200; eadem, *The Premature Reformation* (Oxford, 1988), 12, 112, 205, 247. On BL MSS Egerton 617–618 see J. Forshall and F. Madden, eds, *The Holy Bible, containing the Old and New Testaments, with the Apocryphal Books, in the Earliest English Versions made from the Latin Vulgate by John Wycliffe and his Followers*, 4 vols (Oxford, 1850), 1:xliii, no. 32; S.L. Fristedt, 'A weird manuscript enigma in the British Museum', *Stockholm Studies in Modern Philology*, ns 2 (1964), 116–21.

[5] Wolfenbüttel, Herzog August Bibliothek, MS Aug. A. 2; Forshall and Madden, *Holy Bible*, 1:lxi, no. 153; Hudson, *Premature Reformation*, 115, 233 (see 199 for the observation that many Wycliffite biblical manuscripts seem intended for church use and can be seen as lectern books).

Great Bible, and of which 'many copies remain and be daily found'. These numerous copies included the smaller New Testaments, such as the copy that Dame Anne Danvers gave to Syon in 1517, or that owned in 1547 by William Carter, rector of Bishop Wearmouth (Co. Durham).[6]

The smaller, shorter texts which carried the word into the under-world of late medieval England have mostly vanished. The records of their proscription use various terms suggestive of the nature of these ephemera which existed in paper as well as parchment. We hear of quires and schedules as well as of books and tracts. The small format address included single sheets as well as gatherings of a few pages. The royal order of 1388 directing seizure of Lollard books (the first alarm signal of how books were endangering religion) listed books, booklets (*libri* and *libelli*), schedules, and quires; in 1395 the summary document addressed to Parliament and Convocation by Lollards (extracted, at least in part, from a fuller book which the king had heard read) was called a *libellus*; and the scriptural texts that were subjected to control by Arundel's Constitutions of 1409 were in the form of book, booklet, or tract (*liber, libellus, tractatus*). It is worth listening to this terminology. It seems to be specific, and the specifics may be related to context. If we can assume that the *liber* was something of substance to be envisaged in the hands of clerks and university men, its derivatives were aimed at readers of other kinds. Significantly Reginald Pecock, the only bishop brave enough to think of responding to heretics in their own coinage, was said to have compiled booklets, tracts, and quinternions for the people.[7] The *libellus* features prominently in these developments and implies something more than a schedule and less than a book or tome. It has resonances to which I shall return.

It seems not wholly unrealistic to see these book distinctions as reflecting an age-old ecclesiastical attitude towards learning and instruction, which was geared to the respective needs and capacities of laity and clergy. In the seventh century Isidore of Seville had

---

[6] Ibid., 233 n.34; Forshall and Madden, *Holy Bible*, 1:xliv–v, xlvii, lxi–ii, nos 39, 60, 154, 156; Thomas Cranmer, *Miscellaneous Writings*, ed. J.E. Cox, PS (Cambridge, 1846), 119.

[7] Hudson, *Lollards and their Books*, chs 11, 12; idem, *Premature Reformation*, 200–4, 249; *Knighton's Chronicle 1337–1396*, ed. G.H. Martin (Oxford, 1995), 438–43; M. Aston, *Faith and Fire: Popular and Unpopular Religion, 1350–1600* (1993), 88 n.62, 113; 'Introduction', in M. Aston and C. Richmond, eds, *Lollardy and the Gentry in the later Middle Ages* (Stroud, 1997), 3–4; F. Somerset, 'Answering the *Twelve Conclusions*: Dymmok's Halfhearted Gestures towards Publication', ibid., 53; D. Wilkins, ed., *Concilia Magnae Britanniae et Hiberniae*, 4 vols (1737), 3:317.

proposed a threefold division of book production which consisted of collections that were appropriate for scholastic instruction; homilies suitable for preaching to the people; and lastly great works of learning 'tomes which we call books or volumes'. Obviously there were many changes in book production and readers over the centuries, but the distinction between texts and smaller works suited to lay people, and the 'tomes or volumes' that were repositories of divinity, remained. There was a solemnity and weightiness in the great book that expressed its content – sometimes literally. The early eighth-century Codex Amiatinus needs two people to move it, and provides an example of a book that had the character of a treasure chest of mysteries rather than that of an instrument of reading. Vast tomes could be the focus of veneration, more than tools of learning and sacramental service. A book which effected miracles (as was believed of a ninth-century Greek codex) was an object whose credal content resided in something far removed from any individual's understanding of its words.[8] There were senses in which sixteenth-century reformers reformed (among all else) the idea of the book.

Paul Saenger has pointed to the fact that the 'large, cumbersome' Bibles printed in the early incunable period show few signs of use – either in liturgical service or for *lectio divina* during conventual meals. Their primary function, beautifully produced and often sumptuously illuminated as they were, was iconic: to stand as imposing presences witnessing to the revelation of the word.[9] The big and heavy decorated manuscript Bibles that the first Mainz printed Bible imitated may also be seen in this light, as objects of display whose presence on a lectern in cathedral or monastic church was a means of representing God's presence, comparable to the carved or painted crucifixion. This is not, of course, to say that we should think of the largest, most unman-oeuvrable church books merely as items of display, to be looked at

[8] 'tomi, quos nos libros vel volumina nuncupamus', quoted in Armando Petrucci, *Writers and Readers in Medieval Italy*, tr. C.M. Radding (New Haven, CT, and London, 1995), 39–40, from *Etymologiarum sive originum libri XX*, ed. W.M. Lindsay (Oxford, 1911), 6.8.1–2; see also Petrucci, *Writers and Readers*, ix, 59, 118, 123, 129, 137–9. On the Codex Amiatinus (written at Jarrow) and a huge fifteenth-century Latin antiphoner, see R.L.S. Bruce-Mitford, 'The art of the Codex Amiatinus', *Journal of the Archaeological Association*, ser. 3 (1969), 1–25; A. Galeazzi, *Biblioteca Medicea Laurenziana* (Florence, 1986), 60, 218, tav. xi–xii, clxiv.

[9] P. Saenger, 'The impact of the early printed page on the reading of the Bible', in P. Saenger and K. van Kampen, *The Bible as Book: The First Printed Editions* (1999), 32–3; and on the condition and survival rate of larger books in libraries see E. Leedham-Green, 'University libraries and book-sellers', in *CHBB3*, 340–3; H.-J. Martin, *The French Book: Religion, Absolutism, and Readership, 1585–1715* (Baltimore, MD, 1996), 59.

rather than used. But this aspect of the largest format Bibles is important in that it draws to our attention the fact that the scriptural text that scholars used and worked on was in a more serviceable smaller and portable form. And ordinary lay readers, those who were interested in direct and cheap access to the word without learned apparatus, wanted yet another format.

If large books had sacral qualities the small book had revelatory ones. One might even suggest that some special resonances attached to the word *libellus*. The 'little book' or *libellus* belongs to the Book of Revelation, the biblical book which has most to say about the role of the book in divine illumination. 'What thou seest, write in a book' (Rev. 1.11). St John's visionary experience is related in terms of the opening of the book 'written within and on the backside, sealed with seven seals' (Rev. 5.1). Then in chapter 10 appears the mighty seventh angel, clothed in a cloud, rainbowed, with feet like pillars of fire, who 'had in his hand a little book, open', and the seer was commanded to take and eat it. The little book that appears at this point differs from the closed sealed book of protected mysteries, in that it was delivered *open* by angelic mission and was at once devoured, an ingestion that was both sweet and bitter which was immediately followed by further prophesying.[10]

Revelation was the most illustrated book of the entire Bible, and it is interesting to see how representations of the book in these depictions are related to the scriptural text. Dürer's influential series of Apocalypse woodcuts (first published in 1498) deftly brought together passages of the textual narration in single images so that, for instance, the appearance of the angel with the little book is also the scene (portrayed here for the very first time) of St John devouring the book. The scene (in chapter 4) of the door opening in heaven, introduces from the following chapter the book with seven seals and the lamb with seven horns and seven eyes which opened them. This procedure involved Dürer in taking some liberties with the text. The opening woodcut of St John's vision of the seven candlesticks (Rev. 1.10–16) shows not only the 'one like unto the Son of man' in the midst of the candlesticks, sword in mouth, with a handful of stars, but also as seated on a rainbow – like Christ in judgement – and holding a written book, neither of which is referred to in the text at this point. Dürer has elided several passages, taking the throne and rainbow from chapter 4 and the

---

[10] Rev. 10–11.

Fig. 1   St John eating the Book: woodcut illustrating Revelation 10 in
Albrecht Dürer's 1498 *Apocalypse*.

Fig. 2 St John's Vision of the Seven Candlesticks: woodcut illustrating
Revelation 1 in Albrecht Dürer's *Apocalypse*.

open book in hand from chapter 10.[11] Lucas Cranach the Elder, however, did quite otherwise. His *Vision of the Seven Candlesticks*, illustrating Luther's German New Testament in 1522, evinced a new concern for a more careful, indeed literal, representation of the words of the text. Here is no throne, no rainbow, no book, and St John no longer kneels but lies prone on the ground, true to the words 'when I saw him, I fell at his feet as dead' (Rev. 1.17). This scrupulosity is also to be seen in later Lutheran illustrated Bibles, such as Matthaus Merian's in the early seventeenth century. The reformers' closer fidelity to the scriptural text had a direct effect on representations of the revelatory book.

Fig. 3   Matthäus Merian's engraving for Revelation 1, used in the 1630 folio Bible and the *Icones Biblicae*, both published in Strasbourg. Photo: Warburg Library.

---

[11]   Peter Parshall, 'The vision of the Apocalypse in the sixteenth and seventeenth centuries', in Frances Carey, ed., *The Apocalypse and the Shape of Things to Come* (1999), 100–6, and catalogue entries at 129–39. The Vulgate uses the word 'devora', where the AV has 'eat'.

If reading is a kind of consuming, the consumption of books took different forms and was related to their format. The digestion of texts (scriptural and others) could be meditative or ruminatory, as well as inducing prophecy, discussion, and controversy.[12] But arguably, whether it was the book-on-lap in the cell or study, or the smuggled pamphlet shared in group discussion, the *libellus* played a special role. Much ardour attached to the small books of the Reformation period, and it was to small books that an influential segment of the period's readership was attached.[13]

From the initial rush of Luther's quarto pamphlets in the 1520s,[14] small books can be seen making an enormous contribution to the religious mentality of readers and hearers across Europe. Small format booklets and broadsheets travelled light with advantages of speed and concealment. Dürer knew about Luther from reading his pamphlets, and during the last decade of Dürer's life the authorities in England were feeling threatened by the clandestine importing from abroad of Lutheran texts and Tyndale's New Testament translation.[15] The appearance of printed pamphlets was a phenomenon of German-speaking lands, but the spread of new-style evangelism and reforming ideas was accomplished through much of the sixteenth century by means of the small book – both illicit and official.

Counter-reforming enquiries into the ownership of forbidden books in the Austrian Tyrol in the late 1560s revealed that much the most common category of such religious works was small tracts, followed by prayer books, Gospels, and books of psalms and hymns. The advantages of the *libellus* in carrying messages in the vernacular to

[12] On the metaphor of reading and eating, the text as nourishment, see Michael Camille, 'Visual signs of the sacred page: books in the *Bible moralisée*', *Word and Image*, 5 (1989), 114, 117–18; B. Smalley, *The Study of the Bible in the Middle Ages* (Oxford, 1952), 178–9, 242, 282 (Peter Comestor or Manducator = the one who had chewed up and digested Scripture).

[13] Recent works on German pamphlet literature include R.G. Cole, 'The Reformation pamphlet and communication processes', in H.-J. Kohler, ed., *Flugschriften als Massenmedium der Reformationszeit*, Tübingen Symposium, 1980 (Stuttgart, 1981), 139–62; Paul A. Russell, *Lay Theology in the Reformation: Popular Pamphleteers in Southwest Germany, 1521–1525* (Cambridge, 1986); Miriam U. Chrisman, *Conflicting Visions of Reform: German Lay Propaganda Pamphlets, 1519–1530* (Atlantic Highlands, NJ, 1996). For remarks on pamphlet reading through the period see Martin, *French Book*, 12, 23, 38–9.

[14] Euan Cameron, *The European Reformation* (Oxford, 1991), 101–2, summarizes this output.

[15] J.C. Hutchison, *Albrecht Dürer* (Princeton, NJ, 1990), 165–6, 217 n.4; W.M. Conway, *Literary Remains of Albrecht Dürer* (Cambridge, 1889), 107, 123, 156–9; David Daniell, *William Tyndale* (New Haven, CT, and London, 1994), 108–11; J.F. Mozley, *William Tyndale* (1937), 70–1.

new readers and learners perpetuated manuscript practices of the fifteenth century. An itinerant bookseller recommended to Zwingli in 1519 was reported to be selling nothing but writings of Luther from door to door in towns and villages, as John Hacker (with a more assorted pack) may have done in England around this time, following the practice of Lollard evangelists who had left congregations copies of their sermons.[16] The unbound brochure or handbook of doubtful or heterodox character could be hidden in a bale of cloth or an individual's sleeve, whether it was a printed Protestant text (witness a carpenter of Bruges and a man of Louvain) or a written Wycliffite 'schedule' (witness Sir John Oldcastle and William Taylor, both of whom produced such at their trials, the latter's being a list of authorities written on paper).[17] And of course print facilitated the disguise of false appearances, like the Protestant message masquerading as an indulgence. Heroic deeds and ingenious escapades were undertaken to transmit reforming texts. On the eve of fierce persecution of Protestant teaching in Spain in the late 1550s, Julián Hernández carried copies of this false indulgence and other small Calvinist books all the way from Geneva, where he had worked as a proof-reader, to Seville, where he was burned as a Lutheran in 1560. Philibert Hamelin of Tours, who was burned at Bordeaux in 1557, had become a printer after taking refuge in Geneva, and then travelled through France as missionary colporteur, distributing the Bibles and prayer books he had printed. And presumably it was the slimness of printed booklets that facilitated a daring night-time propaganda mission accomplished in 1565 by men of Geneva, who succeeded in dropping their 'little books' down air vents into the cellars and basements of houses in the city of Laon – reportedly resulting in increased enthusiasm for reform.[18]

---

[16] J.L. Flood, 'The book in Reformation Germany', in J.-F. Gilmont, ed., *The Reformation and the Book* (Aldershot, 1998), 44–5, 56, 77–8; idem, 'Subversion in the Alps: books and readers in the Austrian Counter-Reformation', *The Library*, 6th ser., 12 (1990), 198–9; Hudson, *Premature Reformation*, 464–5, 471, 474–5, 477–8, 486–7; Aston, *Lollards and Reformers*, 204–5.

[17] A.G. Johnston, 'Printing and the Reformation in the Low Countries, 1520–c.1555', in Gilmont, *Reformation and Book*, 163; Hudson, *Premature Reformation*, 201–2, 312–13 (examinations of 1413 and 1421). A paper pamphlet of several leaves ('*certa folia papiri scripta*'), confessed as written in his own hand, formed part of Taylor's 1423 trial and we know its length since it was transcribed in the record, and filled about three folio pages in Chichele's register (fols 58v–60r): *The Register of Henry Chichele*, ed. E.F. Jacob, 4 vols, Canterbury and York Society, 42, 45–7 (Oxford, 1938–47), 3:162–6.

[18] J.E. Longhurst, 'Julián Hernández Protestant martyr', *Bibliothèque d'Humanisme et Renaissance*, 22 (1960), 90–118; F.M. Higman, 'French-speaking regions, 1520–62', in

Small books continued to play a critical role in building up and serving the faith of reformed churches. Robert Kingdon has shown the importance of the vernacular psalter of Clément Marot and Theodore Beza in establishing Calvinist congregations, aided by a planned campaign of production by printers of Paris, Lyons, Geneva, Antwerp, and elsewhere, which succeeded in getting vast numbers of copies on to the market in the 1560s.[19] Psalm-singing nurtured congregational activities in England too, and the printed editions of Sternhold and Hopkins's metrical version (mostly quarto, with and without tunes) between 1549 and 1599 amount to over a hundred and fifty. Huge numbers of individuals and households were enabled by this means to become vocal participants in a new form of actively shared worship: men and women singing together, sometimes with an exultation that led to violence and image-breaking, and which held enormous potential for strengthening bonds of congregational solidarity. Prayer books and psalm books clearly must be set alongside vernacular Bibles in the forging of new confessional loyalties,[20] and when it comes to Bibles the success of the Geneva version in sixteenth-century England is itself proof of the influence of a comfortably sized book in domesticating reading and the hearing of reading.

The 'little book' of Revelation 10 often proved revelatory in practice. Life-transforming experiences that came from the page were far more likely to be found in small than in great books. One might expect it to be a New Testament, as it was in the case of Thomas Bilney, whose purchase and reading of Erasmus's new Latin text first brought him the exhilaration of spiritual comfort. But conversion

Gilmont, *Reformation and Book*, 143; A.G. Kinder, 'Printing and Reformation ideas in Spain', ibid., 312–13; N.Z. Davis, *Society and Culture in Early Modern France* (1975), 202–3; Paul Chaix, *Recherches sur l'imprimerie à Geneve de 1550 à 1564* (Geneva, 1954), 194; Jean Crespin, *Histoire des Martyrs*, ed. D. Benoit, 3 vols (Toulouse, 1885–9), 2:468–71. Longhurst, 'Julián Hernández', 99, shows how the printers prepared smuggled texts to evade suspicion, and this included removing Geneva from the title-page of the *Imagen del Antechristo*.

[19] Robert M. Kingdon, 'Patronage, piety, and printing in sixteenth-century Europe', 1964 paper reprinted in his *Church and Society in Reformation Europe* (London, 1985), ch. 17, 27–31 (I thank Elizabeth Ingram for this reference); Davis, *Society and Culture*, 4–5, 86–7, 168–9, 171–2, 184, 189; idem, 'The Protestant printing workers of Lyons in 1551', in H. Meylan, ed., *Aspects de la propagande religieuse* (Geneva, 1957), 247–57.

[20] *STC* 2419–2498.5, 2499.9–2500, and 2375–2402.5 for prose edns; N. Temperley, *The Music of the English Parish Church*, 2 vols (Cambridge, 1979), 1, chs 2, 3. For the Prayer Book see Judith Maltby, *Prayer Book and People in Elizabethan and Early Stuart England* (Cambridge, 1998), esp. 24–30, 44–5 on ownership of the book; eadem, ' "By this Book": parishioners, the Prayer Book and the Established Church', in Kenneth Fincham, ed., *The Early Stuart Church, 1603–1642* (Basingstoke, 1993), 115–37.

could just as easily come from a modern pamphlet. The humble Widow Sneesby of Over in Cambridgeshire whom Margaret Spufford found to have been converted to the Quakers from the Baptists in the 1650s, reached her new faith through reading the books of a visiting apostle. And we know from his own words that Richard Baxter's soul was (as he put it) awakened by means of 'an old torn book' which was lent to his father by a poor day labourer – this being one of the many editions of the work known as *Bunny's Resolution* (Edmund Bunny's version of a work by the Jesuit Robert Parsons).[21]

* * *

The matter of book formats and the role of the large lectern book may have some bearing on the phase of English reform that saw the arrival of open vernacular Scripture. The order for the Great Bible to be placed in all churches for universal reading was such a major change of policy that it could be seen in apocalyptic terms. According to the 1538 royal Injunctions, 'one book of the whole Bible of the largest volume in English' was to be 'set up in some convenient place within the . . . church' where 'your parishioners may most commodiously resort to the same and read it'. Nobody was to be ticked off for turning the pages. 'Ye shall discourage no man privily or apertly from the reading or hearing of the said Bible', but everyone was to be stirred and encouraged to read it. A few years later John Bale, commenting on the little open book which the angel gave to St John to eat (Revelation 10.8–10), equated this 'sweet little book' with the opening of Scripture, 'to be received of all men, in faith devoured, and in a pure love digested'.[22] The seventh age had arrived with the seventh-seal opening, seventh-trumpet sounding, and opening of the book.

The first edition of 'the whole Bible of the largest volume' appeared in 1539, but it was not until 1540–1, when seven editions were

---

[21] John Foxe, *Actes and Monuments* [hereafter *A&M*] (1563), 468; M. Spufford, *Contrasting Communities* (Cambridge, 1974), 216–17; *The Autobiography of Richard Baxter*, ed. N.H. Keeble (Letchworth, 1974), 7. For editions of Bunny's Protestant adaptation of Parsons' *A Booke of Christian Exercise, appertaining to Resolution*, 1584–1630s, including a Welsh version, see *STC* 19355–90.

[22] W.H. Frere and W.M. Kennedy, eds, *Visitation Articles and Injunctions of the Period of the Reformation*, 3 vols, Alcuin Club Collections, 14–16 (1910) [hereafter *VAI*], 2:35–6; *Select Works of John Bale*, ed. H. Christmas, PS (Cambridge, 1849), 376, from *The Image of Both Churches* [1548?]. On the Great Bible see L. Hellinga and J.B. Trapp, 'Introduction', in *CHBB3*, 27–8; L. Hellinga, 'Printing', ibid., 105–6; P. Neville-Sington, 'Press, politics and religion', ibid., 592–4.

published, that the possibility of churches at large buying and displaying the book became a reality, and even then purchasing was probably uneven. A proclamation issued in 1541 threatened to fine recalcitrant parishes, and according to a complaint of 1546 there was still 'no smale numbre' of churches that had no Bible, though it may be that by this time most parishes had in fact complied.[23] It is clear that many churches, parochial as well as cathedral, did buy Bibles, and it is worth thinking about the arrangements made for these books, and the impact of their arrival and use. What was the 'convenient place' in a parish church where parishioners could turn the pages and read, or listen to others reading, a large folio volume?[24] Lecterns or bookrests were not the kind of furniture that had ever been required for nave use; they were essentially items of the choir and chancel.[25] But it is hard to imagine how a book like the Great Bible could have been appointed for general use without some kind of stand or desk, and the nave reading-desk, whose appearance we may date to this critical phase, was something new.

We can learn a certain amount about the placing of church Bibles. Sometimes all we know is that the book was chained, as at Morebath in Devon, which in 1538 bought a cord to bind 'the churche boke callyd the bybyll' and then five years later paid for a new Bible and a chain. The splitting of the cost of the book between parishioners and incumbent still left the expense of installation to the former. In another Devon parish, Ashburton, the vicar paid more than half the 12s. spent in 1540–1 on a bound copy of a 'new book called a bybyll'; the parishioners paid 8d. for a chain and setting the book in place.[26]

[23] A Supplication of the Poore Commons (1546), STC 23435.5, sig. A6v; Four Supplications, ed. F.J. Furnivall, EETS, e.s. 13 (1871), 66–7; Robert Whiting, Local Responses to the English Reformation (Basingstoke, 1998), 197–8; D.S. Kastan, '"The noyse of the new Bible": reform and reaction in Henrician England', in C. McEachern and D. Shuger, eds, Religion and Culture in Renaissance England (Cambridge, 1997), 54, 66; M. Bowker, The Henrician Reformation (Cambridge, 1981), 170; J.F. Mozley, Coverdale and his Bibles (1953), 261–4; P.L. Hughes and J.F. Larkin, eds, Tudor Royal Proclamations, 3 vols (New Haven, CT, and London, 1964–9), 1:296–8.

[24] A.S. Herbert, Historical Catalogue of Printed Editions of the English Bible 1525–1961 (London and New York, 1968), 25–35, gives the sizes of the Great Bibles.

[25] Gerald Randall, Church Furnishing and Decoration (1980), 79–81; J.C. Cox, Pulpits, Lecterns, and Organs in English Churches (Oxford, 1915), 162–203; J.C. Cox and A. Harvey, English Church Furniture (1907), 78–81. I am very grateful here to Trevor Cooper for his generous help and stimulation.

[26] Accounts of the Wardens of the Parish of Morebath, Devon, 1520–1573, ed. J.E. Binney (Exeter, 1904), 103, 126, 133; Churchwardens' Accounts of Ashburton, ed. A. Hanham, Devon and Cornwall Record Society, ns 15 (1970), ix, 107.

Desks and chains (and in one case a candlestick) were bought for the great Bibles of the London churches of St Mary Magdalen in Milk Street and St Mary Woolnoth, and at Wimborne in Dorset; while at All Hallows, Staining, in Lancashire, an interesting entry records 16*d*. spent on a lock and two keys 'for the pew under the bybill', which is suggestive of something like a lectern.[27]

Cathedral churches which provided more than one copy might make more elaborate arrangements, seeing to the furnishing of books in different parts of the building. The dean and chapter of Lincoln bought two copies for the cathedral in 1540–1, and Edmund Bonner, still a zealous promoter of English scripture, lost no time after his appointment to the see of London about ordering that six Bibles should be placed in St Paul's cathedral. They were positioned (according to Foxe's account) on pillars in the church, attached with chains.[28] These Bibles may have been distributed between choir and nave, as was ordered by Edward VI's injunctions for cathedrals in 1547. Two English Bibles 'of the largest volume' were to be placed in the choir for ministers; two others in the body of the church 'in such meet and convenient places, as every person coming thither may have recourse to the same'.[29]

It was all-important for lay reading of the Bible that the book should be, in this novel fashion, placed in the church nave. A bishop who wholeheartedly believed in access to vernacular Scripture would have done as Bishop Shaxton did, explicitly ordering in 1538 that in every parish church of his diocese the Bible be 'chained to a desk in the body of the church; where he that is lettered may read, and other unlearned may hear wholesome doctrine and comfort to their souls'.[30] Parishioners were thereby invited to read by the physical presence of holy writ in their part of the building. Henry VIII's first set of injunctions in 1536 had included a direction for the provision of Bibles, both Latin and English, to be laid in the choir.[31] This points

---

[27] Mozley, *Coverdale*, 173, 261–2, 263; J.C. Cox, *Churchwardens' Accounts* (1913), 118, 120. I am grateful to Dr Nicholas Bennett for confirming that an 'ancient desk and chain in the library of Lincoln cathedral' surmised (by Cox and Harvey, *English Church Furniture*, 332) as probably that which housed the Great Bible, is a chimera.

[28] Bonner was elected bishop on 20 Oct. 1539 and made arrangements for setting up the Bibles before his departure for France in late Feb. 1540: *A&M* (1570), 2:1362, 1381; Susan Brigden, *London and the Reformation* (Oxford, 1989), 332.

[29] *VAI*, 2:137.

[30] Ibid., 2:59.

[31] Ibid., 2:9.

towards clerical control. Books in the choir (as the Edwardian injunctions indicate) were clerical books, and there were traditional inhibitions about access to chancels. It was a complaint of the 1546 *Supplication of the Poore Commons* that 'many of thys wycked generation as well pristes as other theyr faythful adherentes wold plucke [the Bible] other into the quire other else into some pue where poore men durst not presume to come'.[32] Also there was the matter of ease of actual reading. One enterprising individual who saw the importance of providing the right furniture for the Great Bible in the nave was John Uvedale, who wrote to Thomas Cromwell from York in May 1540, describing himself as 'youre oldeste disciple'. Congratulating the recently elevated earl with the gift of a sea urchin stuffed with down, Uvedale renewed his earlier suggestion that all the bishops should be instructed to set up two or three English Bibles in their cathedral and collegiate churches, 'as semely and as ornatly as they canne dekke them, with setis and formes for men of all agis to rede and studie on theim' – study centres for Bible reading, where parishioners could meet in comfort round the Great Bible text. And though this proposal does not say as much, it was to be assumed that the book itself had some sort of desk or lectern to rest on.[33]

Enthusiasts for opening the Great Bible to all comers were not lacking. But the book itself says something about the reservations and anxieties that hedged this development. The title page trumpeted the fame of the king as dispenser of the word of God, divinely sanctioned by GOD himself, who hovers almost like a protective angel in the clouds over Henry's head. The book passes down the page, hand to hand, from king to archbishop and clergy and to respective lay lords. But the applauding commoners shouting VIVAT REX at the bottom of the page do not read but hear the *verbum dei*. There are no books here (apart from that held by one layman in the finely illuminated copy of the 1539 edition in St John's College, Cambridge). The implication seems to be that the great book could not be expected to enter the hands and domestic possessions of ordinary lay men and women.[34]

---

[32] *Supplication*, sig. A6r; Furnivall, *Four Supplications*, 66.

[33] *Letters and Papers, Foreign and Domestic of the Reign of Henry VIII*, ed. J.S. Brewer, J. Gairdner, and R.H. Brodie, 21 vols (1862–1932) [hereafter *LP*], 15:308–9 (648); PRO, SP1/160/8; Mozley, *Coverdale*, 265.

[34] John N. King, *Tudor Royal Iconography* (Princeton, NJ, 1989), 70–4 (note comments at 72); Diarmaid MacCulloch, *Thomas Cranmer* (New Haven, CT, and London, 1996), 238–40.

Fig. 4   Title-page of the Great Bible, 1539.
Photo: Cambridge University Library, reproduced by permission
of the Syndics of Cambridge University Library.

Cranmer's prologue or preface to the Great Bible also sounded notes of carefully worded caution. The archbishop deftly reproved the extremists on both side of the vernacular Bible debate: on one side those who refused to read or hear English Scripture and (still worse) prevented or discouraged others from doing so; and on the other side those whose inordinate reading, indiscreet speaking, and contentious disputing slandered and hindered the word of God.[35] This sense of nervousness was given unusually open expression by Bishop Bonner, who went so far as to post a printed warning to readers over his Great Bibles in St Paul's. A copy of this 'admonicion and advertisement' survives in the Bible Society's copy of the April 1540 edition of the Great Bible. These three paragraphs forbade anyone to hinder Bible reading, and enjoined a proper sense of devotion and obedience in readers. In particular attention was drawn to the need for 'reverence and quyet behaveour'. People were not to 'be specyallye congregate therefore, to make a multitude'; there were to be no expositions that went beyond the book itself; in particular, 'no readinge therof be used (alowde and with noyes) in the tyme of any devyne service or sermonde'. However, while he was abroad in France in the spring of 1540, things went wrong, and on his return Bonner set up an additional advertisement 'renued agayne to the Reader of this Byble', warning 'wilfull and unadvysed personnes' that the Bibles would be taken down unless they stuck to his orders. His first 'frendely' admonition had made clear in what manner, 'ye and at what tymes', the Bible should be read. These conditions had been disregarded by rash unlearned individuals who 'have reede the same especyallye and chieflie at the tyme of devyne servyce'. Services in the cathedral choir and sermons at Paul's Cross must not be interrupted or disturbed. The Bible was to be read 'quyetlye and devoutely in tyme convenyent and agreeable'.[36]

One cause of this ultimatum seems to have been the case of John Porter, a London tailor, who was charged with heresy and died in

---

[35] Cranmer, *Miscellaneous Writings*, 118–25; MacCulloch, *Cranmer*, 258–60; D. MacCulloch, 'Henry VIII and the Reform of the Church', in idem, ed., *The Reign of Henry VIII* (Basingstoke, 1995), 175; S.E. Lehmberg, *The Later Parliaments of Henry VIII* (Cambridge, 1977), 229–31.

[36] The 'admonicion' (which measures about 217x174 mm) faces the title-page, mounted on modern paper, of the Bible Society copy in the Cambridge University Library, described by Herbert, *Historical Catalogue*, no. 52 (28–9), where the text is printed. Both Bonner's notices are printed from Bonner's register, London, Guildhall Library, MS 9531/12, pt 1, fols 26v–27r, in Foxe, *A&M*, ed. S.R. Cattley and G. Townsend, 8 vols (1837–41), 5, App. xiv.

¶An admonicion and aduertisement
geuen by the Byschop of London, to all readers of thys Byble in thenglysshe tounge.

TO thentent that a good and wholsome thynge, godlye and ver-teously (for honest entetes and purposes) set forth for many: be not hyndered, or malygned at, for the abuse, defaute, and euel behaue-our of a fewe. Who for lacke of dyscrecion and good aduisement commonlye (wythout respect of tyme or other dewe circumstaun-ces) procede rasshly and vnaduysedly therin. And by reason therof rather hynder, then set forwarde the thynge that is good of it selfe.

It shall therfore be very expedient that whosoeuer repayreth hether to reade thys booke (or any soche lyke in any other place) he prepare hym selfe chefelye and principally wythall deuocion, humilite and quyetnes, to be edefyed and made the better therby. Adioynynge thervnto his perfect and most bounden duetye of obe-dyence to the kynges maiestye our moost gracious and drad soueraygne Lorde & supreme heade: especiallye in accomplysshynge hys graces moost honorable in-iunctions and comaundementes geuen and made in that behalfe.

And ryght expedient, yee, necessarye it shalbe also that leauynge behynde hym vayne glorye, hypocresie, and all other carnall and corrupt affeccyons: he brynge with hym discrecion, honest intent, charyte, reuerence & quyet behaueour: to and for the edifycacyon of hys awne soule, wythout the hynderaunce, let, or distur-baunce of any other his chrysten brother. Euermore forsepnge, that no nombre of people be specpallye congregate therfore, to make a multitude. And that no exposition be made thervpon, otherwyse then it is declared in ý boke it selfe. And that especiall regarde be had, that no readinge therof be vsed (alowde & wyth noyes) in the tyme of any deuy-ne seruice or sermonde: or that in thesame the-re be vsed any disputacion, contencion, or any other mysdemeanour. Or fi-nallye that any man iustlye maye reken him selfe to be offended therby, or take occasyon to grudge or mali-gne therat.
✠

God saue the Kynge,

Fig. 5 Bishop Bonner's warning advertisement to Bible readers, posted in St Paul's Cathedral, London. Photo: Cambridge University Library, for the British and Foreign Bible Society.

prison in 1542, earning a place in Foxe's *Acts and Monuments* as 'cruelly Martyred for readyng the Bible in Paules'. Other evidence shows that Porter's story has more dimensions than the martyrologist allowed it (including a charge of sacramental error), though his activity as a reader in St Paul's is not in doubt. It seems clear that this 'gospeller' had transgressed the bounds set in Bonner's notice by attracting large crowds with his loud and very audible Bible readings in the cathedral which (it appears) may well have taken place during services.[37]

The passage in 1543 of the Act for 'thadvauncement of true Religion and for thabbolisshment of the contrarie' marked (despite its title) a major setback for English Bible reading, and was – as has been fully recognized – one of the planks of the scaffolding against reforming structures that Henry VIII put in place after the execution of Cromwell. But what exactly were the reasons for this backtracking? Attention has tended to focus on the social distinctions that allowed reading of Bible and New Testment to nobles and gentlemen (those of 'the highest and moste honest sorte') while denying it to working men and women, and those of the 'lower sorte' who in 'greate multitude' had lapsed into erroneous and divisive opinions. But it is important to notice that the Act also differentiates between different kinds of books and readings. Bible and New Testament apart, there were no limits on anyone of any social status reading and teaching at home on psalters, primers, Paternoster, Ave, and Creed – the vernacular teaching officially set forth. When it came to Scripture, the great dividing line that expressed the cause of current alarm was between innocuous quiet reading by respectable gentry (acceptable in house, orchard, or garden) and loud open reading or teaching that amounted to preaching in any open place or assembly.[38]

There was repeated harping at the time on the transgression of the condition which Bonner stressed in his advertisements: readings must not be timed to coincide with church services and sermons. The royal proclamation of May 1541 held the same warning: the 'commodity' of Bible-reading did not include reading 'with loud and high voices in time of the celebration of the holy mass and other divine services used in the church'. Contemporaries read the 1543 Act as putting a stop above all to Bible reading in service time. The bishops' order of the day was, according to William Turner, that 'while ye read in the quire the pope's service and the devil's service . . . no man should read the word

---

[37] A&M (1570), 1381, compare (1563), 621; Mozley, Coverdale, 265–9; Brigden, London, 333, 339–40; P. Janelle, 'An unpublished poem on Bishop Stephen Gardiner', BIHR, 6 (1928–9), 16–17, 167–72. According to this source (168), 'Every halydaye unto polys he wolde resorte / and redde some story of the bible openlye', at which he had a greater audience 'then we hadde to here our mummynge masse and matyns / whereat your canons of Poolis toke displeasure'.

[38] Statutes of the Realm, ed. A. Luders et al., 11 vols (1810–28), 3:896 (34–35 Henry VIII, c.1).

of God'. 'They have straitly forbidden the reading thereof for time of their Romish service', as Bale put it; the view of the *Supplication of the Poore Commons* being that 'they never rested tyll they had a commandement frome your highnesse that no man of what degree so ever he were should reade the Byble in ye tyme of goddes service (as they call it)'.[39]

By 1543 it had become very clear in some quarters (and even some erstwhile evangelicals had to acknowledge the risks) that giving open access to a potentially congregational tome in naves of parish church and cathedral was extremely difficult to control. Where readers read Scripture in places of worship, laymen were likely to take a lead, and hearers were likely to start listening to words other than those of the liturgy and clerical sermons.

The evidence of what was going on in Kent between 1538 and 1543 which was gathered as the result of the so-called Prebendaries' Plot against Archbishop Cranmer is suggestive of reactions to the arrival of the Great Bible in parish churches. Some incumbents were resolutely opposed to this leap into a new world. A chantry priest of Tenterden (where recollections of Lollard proclivities might well have died hard) was reported to have said 'there be heresies in the Bible'. William Kempe, the vicar of Northgate, Canterbury, had failed to read either the Bible or the injunctions to his parishioners. The vicar of Faversham had gone so far as to remove the Bible from his church, and the whole parish of St Peter's in Canterbury witnessed against Vincent Ingeam for having forbidden anyone to read or hear the Bible under pain of imprisonment and for having actually confined two who challenged him on this score.[40] Laying the English Bible 'of the largest and greatest volume'[41] open to all comers was an affront to the clergy, for whom this reversal of the traditional order of books, chancels, and naves, shockingly breached proper boundaries between ministry and congregation.

Entrenched views that holy writ was not for lay consumption were indeed most likely to be expressed by clerical voices. In Kent it seems clear that they were provoked by the existence of lay readers. Had

---

[39] Hughes and Larkin, *Proclamations*, 1:296–8; W. Turner, *The Huntyng & Fyndyng out of the Romyshe Fox* ([Bonn], 1543), sig. D8r (cited Mozley, *Coverdale*, 269); Bale, *Image of Both Churches*, in *Select Works*, 440; *Supplication*, sig. A6r; Furnivall, *Four Supplications*, 67.

[40] *LP*, 18/ii:294, 299, 300, 307–9, 318, 358; MacCulloch, *Cranmer*, 297–322, and on Christopher Nevinson at 204.

[41] The phrase used in the 1541 proclamation, cited in n.23 above.

Cranmer's commissary, Christopher Nevinson (husband of the Archbishop's niece), allowed a Canterbury tailor to hold open house for his reading and exposition of the Bible? Another such charge was laid against John Tofts, the decidedly evangelical and iconoclastic town clerk of Canterbury who, it was said, 'openly and with lowde voice red the bible in English in the church to his wife, Sterbleys wife, George Toftes wife, to the mydwife of the same parish, and to as many other as then were present'. (It sounds almost like a women's conventicle, and notice again the offensiveness of the loud lay voice.) And there was the case of the Canterbury barber, Thomas Makeblyth, who read the Bible instead of joining the Palm Sunday procession. Elsewhere, those who were represented as favouring 'evil opinions' were charged with being common readers of the Bible during service time.[42]

When the Great Bible appeared in naves of parish churches it arrived with inescapable associations. As a large, heavy folio, it was the kind of book requiring a lectern or stand that, like traditional service books, had previously belonged to clerical use and to the keeping of chancel and choir.[43] The very act of standing to read a tome at a lectern, above all in a church, was alien to lay persons – something that might well have seemed improper, if not intimidating, though that did not deter enthusiasts, whose loud voices seemed to proclaim their confident ability to rival professional churchmen. It amounted to taking the lectern book out of the hands of the clergy. It was particularly provocative that groups of hearers gathered at such readings during times of church services, when they inevitably seemed to constitute scriptural counter-celebrations, challenging the Mass and Matins being celebrated elsewhere in the building. The book service detracted from the altar service. One of the accusations against the evangelical curate of Lenham in Kent, Thomas Dawby, was that he had frequently procured parishioners of his and other parishes 'to read the Bible, even at the choir door where divine service was sung or said, from the beginning of the service to the ending, with as low a voice as they could'.[44] The Great Bible appeared to be promoting an alternative English form of service divorced from the clerical office. The lectern (or reading-desk) was opposing the altar.

---

[42] LP, 18/ii:300 (Cambridge, Corpus Christi College, MS 128, p. 31), 307, 315, 358.
[43] The First Churchwardens' Book of Louth 1500–1524, ed. R.C. Dudding (Oxford 1941), 152–3, 172–4, lists books belonging 'to the hey qwere'.
[44] LP, 18/ii:315. This related to Dawby's curacy of Lenham, before 1543.

The arrival of the lectern-book of Scripture seemed to prove the essential dangers of opening the English Bible to lay readers. Much could happen 'by way of reading', especially of a Bible laid open to all comers on a desk in church. The vernacular Bible created its own communities of hearers, like the small or not so small groups who gathered round men like John Porter, John Tofts, and Thomas Dawby, to listen to their readings of holy writ. This was inescapably challenging – quite apart from any undesirable disquisitions on the text – both to clerical authority and ultimately to the Church as a whole, since these developments revealed the inherent inconsistency of the Henrician position, the incompatibility of open vernacular Scripture and Latin rite. The new lay use of the lectern for the open English Bible could not happily coexist with traditional liturgy. It is hardly surprising that the King backed off as he did in 1543. Convocation's order of 1543 for English Bible readings at morning and evening prayer, chapter by chapter through both Testaments, may have been a success for Cranmer in sustaining the momentum started in 1538, but it was very different from unrestricted lay access. It could be seen rather as ensuring that the public voicing of Scripture in church emanated only from choir lecterns and clerical mouths. No more Henrician Bibles 'of the largest and greatest volume' were printed after December 1541; English adventuring into lay readership was effectively put on hold until the accession of Edward VI.[45]

Ultimately (and not so many years later) banishment of the Mass and the arrival of congregations who had their own books, transformed the concept of the large church book. Foxe's 'Book of Martyrs' is itself an outstanding example of the new role that could be played by the great tome, as an ecclesiastical book that was influential in forming its own community, well beyond the normal confines of an unwieldy lectern book. The books that appear in illustrations in this work fall into the category of lap, not lectern books, perpetuating an image that had gained wider currency and new resonances from the start of the

---

[45] Elizabeth L. Eisenstein, *The Printing Press as an Agent of Change*, 2 vols (Cambridge, 1979), 1:358; MacCulloch, *Cranmer*, 289–91, 301; Lehmberg, *Later Parliaments*, 184; Wilkins, *Concilia*, 3:863. Lay readings of Scripture in church were banned at once under Mary. See *VAI*, 2:354 for Bonner's London article of enquiry as to whether any layman had 'expounded or declared any portion or part of Scripture in any church or elsewhere', and Hughes and Larkin, *Proclamations*, 2:5–8, for Mary's 1553 proclamation forbidding anyone to presume 'to preach, or by way of reading in churches . . . to interpret or teach any Scriptures'.

Lutheran era. Reform and the book came together in woodcuts of seated listeners (often women) below the pulpit, open book on knees; the image of the living word of evangelical truth simultaneously heard and read. Such texts might be seen as instruments that banished false beliefs; books replaced beads for those whose faith came through hearing.[46] But the *Acts and Monuments* itself, having started life in a small format in Latin, found readers and made its enduring impact through the large folios of the English editions from 1563 on. In the first instance the officially sponsored readership was (more or less) of the traditional clerical kind. The 1571 canons ordered that archbishops and bishops, deans and archdeacons, should provide copies of the Bishops' Bible and of the *Monuments of Martyrs* (large folio books), both in their cathedrals and also in the hall or great chamber of their houses, for the use of ministers of the church, visitors, and servants.[47] But if at this stage the 'Book of Martyrs' was perforce limited in its outreach to readers, the author himself had a much broader vision, regarding printing as a revelatory art and aiming his own history at the entire true congregation of Christ's flock. Readers (and owners) were to be of all kinds.[48] Remarkably for such an enormous work this aim was achieved. And (also remarkably) unlike the scripture which it almost paralleled, it was not a work that also took off in small formats.[49] The 'Book of Martyrs' succeeded in making book history by taking the cumbersome folio effectively from church desks on to secular laps in domestic parlours. Such accessibility brought more than wear and tear to the volumes themselves. In the 1580s the copy which had cost St Andrew's, Holborn, more than 30s. to buy and set up on an iron desk was mutilated by 'some ungodly enemy', who 'lewdly' cut leaves out of

[46] See, for examples, Georg Pencz's 1531 contrasting sermons, Foxe's title-page, the woodcut prefacing book 6 of the *Acts and Monuments*, and Latimer preaching before Edward VI; J.N. King, 'The godly woman in Elizabethan iconography', *Renaissance Quarterly*, 38 (1985), 41–84; idem, *Tudor Royal Iconography*, 97, 100, 162, figs 25, 28, 52; M. Aston and E. Ingram, 'The iconography of the *Acts and Monuments*', in David Loades, ed., *John Foxe and the English Reformation* (Aldershot, 1997), 75–7.

[47] Gerald Bray, ed., *The Anglican Canons 1529–1947*, Church of England Record Society, 6 (Woodbridge, 1998), 176–9, 182–3; *VAI*, 3:321, 335–6, show the bishops of Winchester and Rochester seeing to this order. [See also no.52 below.]

[48] Susan Felch, 'Shaping the reader in the *Acts and Monuments*', in Loades, *John Foxe*, 57–60.

[49] Damian Nussbaum, 'Whitgift's "Book of Martyrs": Archbishop Whitgift, Timothy Bright and the Elizabethan struggle over John Foxe's legacy', in David Loades, ed., *John Foxe: An Historical Perspective* (Aldershot, 1999), 135–53; Jesse Lander, ' "Foxe's" *Books of Martyrs*: printing and popularizing the *Acts and Monuments*', in McEachern and Shuger, *Religion and Culture*, 69–92.

Fig. 6   Matthias Gerung, woodcut of *The Destruction of the Catholic Church*, *c.*1547. Department of Prints and Drawings, British Museum, London, 1867–7–13–107. Reproduced by permission of the Trustees of the British Museum.

it, leaving some 'uncaryed awaye' which were found and restored by the churchwarden.[50]

* * *

The text-based evangelism of the Reformation had a profound and far-reaching influence on the symbolism of the book. Scripture, the active agent of the word on the move, could be seen as a missile, effecting apocalyptic change. And the supreme validation of Scripture for ministry and sacrament became visible in changing artistic formulas, as a book took the place of a chalice on clerical funeral monuments, and of a crucifix at pious deathbeds. The book, great and small, was a visual as well as verbal messenger.

We may end, not wholly inappropriately, by giving the last word to a papal image. Michelangelo's astounding vision of the Last Judgement in the Sistine Chapel includes the central group of trumpeting angels in the lower register. On either side an open book is held out for display to the saved and damned, small on Christ's right and on his left so large that (like the enormous Codex Amiatinus) two pairs of hands are needed to support it. Can we read this as Vasari did as an Apocalyptic image? Why are there two books instead of the more usual 'book of life' mentioned in Revelation 12? And if this is a transposition of St Michael with the scales, why is the heavier book on the side of the condemned? Michelangelo's two books are unique, and call for an interpretation which looks beyond traditional imagery and takes account of the troubled years and troubled consciences preceding 1536–41 when the painting was executed. Michelangelo had his own spiritual anxieties and drew on scriptural and patristic knowledge. His two books may be seen to represent not the terrible tally of accounted sins weighed and pronounced on by the supreme judge, but rather the books of conscience of individual souls.[51] The open, outward-facing

---

[50] London, Guildhall Library, MS 4249 ('The Bentley Register'), fols 235r, 236v. In 1584 the churchwarden, enjoining better keeping of the church books, gave a copy of Jewel's works to replace the Calvin on Job (set up in 1580/1) that had been stolen.

[51] Leo Steinberg, 'A corner of the *Last Judgment*', *Daedalus*, 109 (1980), 260, 272–3, n. 90; idem, 'The *Last Judgment* as merciful heresy', *Art in America*, 63 (1975), 48–63; Charles de Tolnay, *Michelangelo*, 5 vols (Princeton, NJ, 1943–60), 5:33–4; Bernadine Barnes, *Michelangelo's Last Judgment* (Los Angeles and London, 1998), 60, 146 n.69. Rev. 20.12 speaks of the opening of books in the plural, but Last Judgement depictions, such as those of Jan Provost, represent the single opened 'book of life' mentioned in the same verse: Craig Harbison, *The Last Judgment in Sixteenth Century Northern Europe* (New York and London, 1976), 38, 115–16, figs 6, 57, 115.

Fig. 7   Michaelangelo Buonarotti: group of trumpeting angels from
the Last Judgement fresco (1536–41) in the Sistine Chapel.

large and small books, reflecting the gesturing hands of Christ above,
radiate the message of this ultimate jurisdiction. Heavier consciences
called for the heavier tome. The smaller book showed the culmination
of the revelatory page of salvation for the saved. The book great and
small was here, as it were, canonized in Christian iconography. It was
no accident that this happened at the time when Scripture reached out,
as never before, into the entire Christian community.[52]

---

[52] Addendum to n.47: For the recent discovery that there were at this time unrealistic
hopes of placing copies of Foxe's book in all churches see Elizabeth Evenden and Thomas S.
Freeman, 'John Foxe, John Day and the printing of the "Book of Martyrs"', in Robin Myers,
Michael Harris, and Giles Mandelbrote, eds, *Lives in Print: Biography and the Book Trade from
the Middle Ages to the Twenty-First Century* (2002), 30, 46.

THE CHRISTIAN BRETHREN AND THE
DISSEMINATION OF HERETICAL BOOKS[1]

by JAMES DAVIS

THE illicit influx of William Tyndale's vernacular New Testament and other reforming works into England in the late 1520s was considered an affront to the ecclesiastical authorities and an encouragement to lay heretical thought.[2] No one was more vitriolic in condemnation than Thomas More, the lawyer-turned-polemicist, who was to become Chancellor from 1529. He declared, 'Nothynge more detesteth then these pestylent bokes that Tyndale and suche other sende in to the realme, to sette forth here theyr abomynable heresyes.'[3] As Chancellor, More was renowned for his zealous persecution of heretics and booksellers, which he justified as a moral and legal imperative in order to uphold the Catholic faith. He also wrote several works, initially at the request and licence of Bishop Tunstall in March 1528, and thereafter in reply to the treatises of Tyndale and other Antwerp exiles. These writings provide tantalizing insights into the activities of Tyndale and the Christian Brethren as seen through the eyes of their chief protagonist. It was not only the New Testament, emanating from Cologne and Worms, that worried More, but Tyndale's polemical works from the printing press of Johannes Hoochstraten in Antwerp, especially *The Parable of the Wicked Mammon*, *The Obedience of a Christen Man*, and *The Practice of Prelates*. Fellow exiles, such as George Joye, John Frith, and Simon Fish, were

---

[1] James Davis, 'The smuggling, dissemination and burning of heretical books, 1470–1540' (Cambridge University M.Phil. thesis, 1997) gives further detail about issues discussed below. I would like to thank Peter Spufford, Margaret Aston, Richard Rex, and Kaele Stokes for their advice.

[2] The English episcopal authorities feared that an unauthorized translation of the New Testament would encourage unorthodox thinking. On 14 May 1530 Bishop Nix of Norwich remarked, 'It passeth my power, or that of any spiritual man to hinder it now, and if this continue much longer it will undoe us all': BL, MS Cotton Cleopatra E.v, fol. 360r. See also M. Bowker, *The Henrician Reformation: the Diocese of Lincoln under John Longland, 1521–1547* (Cambridge, 1981); P. Gwyn, *The King's Cardinal: the Rise and Fall of Thomas Wolsey* (1990), 347–51, 479–99.

[3] *The Confutation of Tyndale's Answer*, in G.L. Carroll and J.B. Murray, eds, *The Complete Works of St Thomas More*, 15 vols (New Haven, CT, and London, 1963–97) [hereafter *CWM*], 8:27 ll.32–5.

also writing popular and doctrinal works, including *A Disputation of Purgatorye, The Revelation of Antichrist, David's Psalter*, and *A Supplication for the Beggars*.[4] Thomas More regarded William Tyndale, the Antwerp exiles, and their 'Brethren' in England as the most active producers and distributors of vernacular heretical books. However, his perceptions of the Brethren, their sympathizers, and their organization have been under-utilized by historians, who often rely more on the post-contemporary reflections of John Foxe.[5] There perhaps remains the suspicion that More was conveniently coalescing all sedition under a single banner as a rhetorical device, or due to prejudice and unfounded conspiracy theories. Indeed, *The Confutation of Tyndale's Answer* outlined a smuggling network as an attempt to demoralize Tyndale's supporters, by describing how various individuals had renounced their doctrines and betrayed their fellows. These were his tools of polemics, but More's testimonies should not be dismissed as the mere delusions of a staunch anti-heretical zealot. He had studied the reforming works and interrogated significant figures in the Brethren. His conspiracy theories, it can be argued, were based on fact.[6]

Historians have been divided on the composition and definition of the 'Christian Brethren' in pre-Reformation England. E.G. Rupp saw them as a kind of heretical book society which provided a vital connection between reforming evangelicals in England and their exiled compatriots.[7] Recently, Susan Brigden identified a large number of London merchants, clerics, lawyers, and apprentices who could be classified as Brethren, though she did not amplify the provincial and overseas linkages.[8] The term 'Christian Brethren' itself is a terminological conundrum, and has led to several tenuous connections. John F. Davis suggested that cells of the Christian Brethren were hinted at

---

[4] *STC*, nos 24454, 24446, 24465, 11386.5, 11394, 2370, 3036, 10883.

[5] Several historians, such as J.F. Davis, A.G. Dickens, and C. Haigh, make little use of More's writing when discussing the Christian Brethren: J.F. Davis, *Heresy and Reformation in the South-East of England, 1520–1559* (1983), 27–95; idem, 'Lollardy and the Reformation in England', *Archiv für Reformationsgeschichte*, 73 (1982), 217–36; A.G. Dickens, *The English Reformation* (rev. edn, 1967), 104–16; idem, 'The early experiences of English Protestantism', *Archiv für Reformationsgeschichte*, 78 (1987), 187–222; C. Haigh, *English Reformations: Religion, Politics and Society under the Tudors* (Oxford, 1993), 51–71. By contrast, Susan Brigden's excellent study includes many references to More's work and his remarks about the Brethren: S. Brigden, *London and the Reformation* (Oxford, 1989), 82–128, esp. 111.

[6] *Confutation*, 11–27.

[7] E.G. Rupp, *Studies in the Making of the English Protestant Tradition* (Cambridge, 1947), 6–7, 13–14.

[8] Brigden, *London*, 82–128.

by the names Lollards used for each other, such as 'brother in Christ' and 'known men'.[9] Anne Hudson has rightly argued that the wide use of the term 'brethren' within Lollard communities, as well as among the larger remit of readers of Holy Scripture, means that it is hazardous to regard 'brethren' in an exclusive sense.[10] Nevertheless, Davis further proposed that the Christian Brethren was an organization based on middle-class Lollard support and propagation, a connection supported by A.G. Dickens, who posited that Lollard communities 'created a ready-made organization for the distribution and reception of Lutheran books'.[11] Conversely, Rupp warned against over-emphasising the role of Lollards, while Richard Rex minimized their role in the new reforming atmosphere.[12]

The writings of Thomas More corroborate the lesser role of Lollardy within the Christian Brethren. He made no mention of Lollards when discussing the book-smuggling of the late 1520s, though did mention John Tewkesbury, who was a known Lollard from the 1528 abjurations. He was burnt in 1531, having been found with a number of Lollard works and Tyndalian treatises. However, More made no overt attempt to identify him as a colporteur of continental works, merely stating that Tyndale saw him as a martyr.[13] Tewkesbury was no different to other Lollards caught with Tyndalian works, such as Thomas Harding of Chesham, Buckinghamshire, or John Tyball and Thomas Hilles from Essex.[14] Their purchase of New Testaments from Robert Barnes in August 1526 is a frequently recited tale, and is often quoted in the context of Lollard and Brethren associations.[15] Yet these works were purchased through the indirect means of precocity and serendipity. Indeed, when the Essex and London Lollards faced the mass trials of Bishop Tunstall in 1528, the evidence reveals a distinct lack of anything but traditional Lollard texts.[16] The Lollards were avid

---

[9] Davis, *Heresy and Reformation*; idem, 'Lollardy and the Reformation', 217–36.

[10] A. Hudson, *The Premature Reformation: Wycliffite Texts and Lollard History* (Oxford, 1988), 482.

[11] Dickens, *English Reformation*, esp. 60.

[12] Rupp, *Studies*, 6–7, 14; R. Rex, *Henry VIII and the English Reformation* (1993), 136–9.

[13] *Confutation*, 20 l.37–22 l.37; Maidstone, Kent Record Office, DRb/Ar 1/13, fols 135v–136r; BL, MS Harley 421, fol. 12v.

[14] Lincoln, Lincolnshire Archives Office, Ep. Reg. 26, fols 228r-v; John Foxe, *Actes and Monuments*, ed. G. Townsend, 8 vols (1843–9) [hereafter *A&M*], 4:123–4, 219–46, 580–1.

[15] J.S. Brewer, J. Gairdner, and R.H. Brodie, *Letters and Papers, Foreign and Domestic of the Reign of Henry VIII*, 21 vols (1862–1932) [hereafter *L&P*], 4/ii, nos 4218, 4850; BL, MS Harley 421, fol. 35r.

[16] Ibid., fols 11r–35r.

readers and receptors of the new literature, but there is scant evidence that they were active distributors through organized trading networks or via missionaries such as John Hacker.

The heart of the Christian Brethren lay elsewhere, and More wrote of a distinct group of 'euangelycall brethren' who disseminated heretical books, with the impetus deriving from the Tyndalian exiles in Antwerp: 'the captayns be prestes, monkes, and freres.'[17] He justified his use of the terminology, 'as for to call them by the name of the bretherne, is nothynge of my bryngynge vppe, but a worde walkyge in euery mannes moth . . . and bygonne by the good blessed bretherne them selfe'.[18] William Tyndale and John Frith were known to use 'brethren' extensively in their works and communications to sympathizers.[19] More further distinguished them from the Lollards and identified the reformers and colporteurs as 'this new bretherhed'.[20] These smugglers and colporteurs can thus be distinguished from the more amorphous and ambiguous 'brethren' in the Lollard conventicles and parish gilds.

Thomas More regarded Tyndale as one of his most dangerous foes, and as a leading light among English reformers. He also recognized that the exiles and printers in Antwerp needed finance to exist: 'There is beyond the sea, Tyndale, Ioye, and a great many mo of you. I know thei cannot liue without helpe, some sendeth theim money and succoureth theim.'[21] It is well known that English merchants at home and abroad figured largely in Tyndale's life, from the patronage of Humphrey Monmouth to Thomas Poyntz who allowed Tyndale to live in the house of the Merchant Adventurers in Antwerp. On 14 October 1531 John Coke, secretary to the Merchant Adventurers, was imprisoned in the Fleet by More for owning a New Testament, but in 1533 was still in touch with 'Brother William'.[22]

However, Tyndale's involvement in the English distribution networks may have been even more significant than once thought. An article by J.L. Douthit-Weir postulated that Tyndale himself may have been in England in 1527 to have *The Obedience of a Christen Man* and

---

[17] *Confutation*, 12 l.23.

[18] *The Debellacion of Salem and Bizance*, in *CWM*, 10:28 ll.12–17.

[19] John Frith, *A Disputation of Purgatory* (Antwerp, 1531); *The Apology*, in *CWM*, 9:91 l.11.

[20] Ibid., 116 l.34; *Debellacion*, 29 l.2.

[21] Edward Hall (ed. H. Ellis), *Chronicle* (1809), 763.

[22] BL, MS Harley 425, fols 8r–12v; *A&M*, 4:617–19, 5:121–6; F.J. Youngs, 'The Tudor government and dissident religious books', in C.R. Cole and M.E. Moody, eds, *The Dissenting Tradition* (Athens, GA, 1975), 170; *L&P*, 4/ii, no. 4260, 6, nos 402–3.

The Parable of the Wicked Mammon surreptitiously published by John Rastell, before hastily returning to the Continent in early 1528 to have them reprinted properly in octavo with the distinctive Hans Luft colophon. Tyndale's movements for that period are certainly unknown, and the theory is based upon a codicological study of surviving quartos (previously assigned as 1550s reprints) and Rastell's typeface, water-mark, woodcuts, and capitals.[23] The notion is, however, somewhat undermined by Rastell's own orthodoxy and his *New Boke of Purgatory* which shows him still committed to the Catholic faith in 1530.[24] But there is an alternative, for in 1528 Wolsey heard a Chancery suit brought by Rastell against a young printer, Laurence Andrewe, who had borrowed 'certeyn printyng stuff to the valew of xx li and above', and failed to return it before fleeing abroad. It is possible that Andrewe printed Tyndale's works, and an apology in *Mammon* underlined the difficult conditions that surrounded this printing: 'For verily the chance was such, that I marvel that it is so well as it is.'[25] A letter of Edward Lee had reported rumours in December 1526 that Tyndale was carrying New Testaments into England.[26] If he did so, this presents a new angle on the creation of the book networks and the Christian Brethren. The Brethren do not appear in the records before 1527, when any evidence suggests that Tyndale's Cologne New Testaments were largely distributed through ad hoc means, such as the Frankfort fair and the Steelyard.[27] After that date, Forman's cell appears, and then the cells that Thomas More uncovered. Even if it was not Tyndale himself, there were seemingly contacts trying to establish a nascent distribution network, probably with the help of his merchant financiers.

This embryonic Christian Brethren was first seen in Oxford in 1528, when Thomas Garrett, curate of All Hallows Honey Lane in London, was discovered to have 'a great numbre of corrupt bokes and secretly dydd destribute them amonge his new acquayntans in sondry colleges

---

[23] J.L. Douthit-Weir, 'Tyndale's The obedyence of a Chrysten man', *The Library*, 5th ser., 30 (1975), 95–107; D. Daniell, *William Tyndale: a Biography* (New Haven, CT, and London, 1994), 155.

[24] H.R. Plomer, *Wynkyn de Worde and his Contemporaries from the Death of Caxton to 1535* (1925), 202.

[25] PRO, C1/564/27; H. Walter, ed., *Doctrinal Treatises and Introductions to Different Portions of the Holy Scriptures by William Tyndale*, PS (Cambridge, 1848), 126.

[26] *L&P*, 4/i, nos 1802–3.

[27] E.F. Rogers, ed., *The Letters of Sir John Hackett, 1526–1534* (Morgantown, WV, 1971), no. 37; *L&P*, 4/ii, no. 3132.

and hallys.'[28] Many books were found in scholars' homes and nearby monasteries, including six New Testaments and books by Luther, Melanchthon, Francis Lambert, and Hus. The book network itself spread from Garrett to Dr Thomas Forman (rector at Honey Lane), his servants John Goodale and Geoffrey Lome, and two printers, John Gough and Sygar Nicholson, who had distributed works in the universities and monasteries of south-east England.[29] Thomas More accused Forman of being a leading corrupting force and was astonished at Wolsey's lenient penalty of penance. However, Forman was to die in mid-1528, and this book network seems to have disintegrated after its discovery.[30] The links with the later Christian Brethren nevertheless suggest that they were not entirely an ad hoc organization. John Frith was an Oxford scholar who fled to join Tyndale in Antwerp, while John Gough continued to be an active reformer and a friend of *John* Tyndale, who was caught by More distributing books in October 1530.[31]

Others were arrested that year with John Tyndale, including Thomas Patmore, a priest, John Purser, Thomas Somer, and Richard Hilles, all merchants, who together had circulated some three thousand copies of *The Practice of Prelates* in London. Tyndale, Patmore and Hilles were also accused of spending £1,840 10*d.* on purchasing two thousand New Testaments and other books. All were ordered to do penance, and paraded through the streets on horseback, facing back-to-front, with 'their gownes or clokes to be tacked or pynned thick with the sayd new testamentes.'[32] John Tyndale had previously abjured for 'sending five marks to his brother William Tyndale beyond the sea, and for receiving and keeping with him certain letters from his brother'.[33] Brigden doubts that they were more than evangelical brothers, and points to Martin Tyndale, fellow of King's, Cambridge,

[28] Ibid., no. 3968.

[29] Ibid., nos 3962–3, 4004, 4017, 4074; W.T. Mitchell, ed., *Epistolae Academicae, 1508–1596*, Oxford Historical Society, ns 26 (1980), 217–19, 223–4; *A&M*, 5:5, 421–7.

[30] *A Dialogue Concerning Heresies*, in *CWM*, 6:269–70; *Confutation*, 379 ll.11–17; London, Guildhall Library, MS 9531/10, fols 126v–37r.

[31] Frith, *Disputation*, sigs Avii^r–Aviii^r; London, Guildhall Library, MS 9171/11, fols 132v–3r.

[32] Youngs, 'Books', 170; R. Brown and A.B. Hinds, eds, *Calendar of State Papers and Manuscripts – Venice*, 38 vols (1869–1947), 4, no. 642; G.A. Bergenroth, P. de Gayangos, and M.A.S. Hume, eds, *Calendar of Letters, Despatches and State Papers, relating to the Negotiations between England and Spain*, 13 vols (1862–1954), 4/i, nos 509, 539; BL, MS Harley 425, fol. 15r; *L&P*, 6, nos 39, 99, 100.

[33] *A&M*, 5:29, 34–6.

as John's real brother. However, Foxe was using a Star Chamber deposition, and Chapuys and Scarpinello both state that one of the penitents was 'a brother of its author'.[34] Whatever their fraternal status, the link with William Tyndale remains. Similarly, John Purser later stood surety for John Birt in 1531, which allowed Birt to escape to the Low Countries, and Hugh Latimer spoke up for the penitents.[35]

Thomas Patmore's name recurs in a statement of Sebastian Newdygate in 1531 concerning conversations with Thomas Keyle, a mercer of London who owned dissident books and had connections in Antwerp.[36] Patmore, Parker, and Mershall, all priests, and Shreve, a barber surgeon, had two thousand books against the Sacrament in circulation as well as other works, which may refer to the episode above or additional book distribution. J.F. Davis interpreted a further passage of Newdygate's as illustrative of the Christian Brethren collecting money from Lollard cells, but in fact it merely demonstrates the organized financial basis of the Brethren:[37]

> Thomas Keyle mercer of London shewid me that there was made for the Augmentacion of Christen brethren of his sorte, Auditours and Clerkes within this Citie. And that every Christen brother of their sorte shulde pity it certayn summa of money to the aforesaid Clerke which shulde goo in to all quarters of this Realme and at certayn tymes the Auditors to take Accompte of them.[38]

Money was obviously collected from patrons, as well as from the sale of books, which demonstrates the financial backing the Christian Brethren enjoyed. Thomas More certainly recognized the Brethren's need for financial support:

---

[34] S. Brigden, 'Thomas Cromwell and the Brethren', in C. Cross, D. Loades, and J.J. Scarisbrick, eds, *Law and Government under the Tudors* (Cambridge, 1988), 36–7; *L&P*, 6, no. 751. See also n.28 above.

[35] *Apology*, 90 ll.12–18; G.E. Corrie, ed., *Sermons and Remains of Hugh Latimer*, PS (Cambridge, 1845), 306. Preachers like Latimer and Thomas Bilney provided a sympathetic and evangelical force to the activities of the booksellers.

[36] Sebastian Newdygate was a Carthusian monk, executed in 1535 as an intransigent Catholic: Rupp, *Studies*, 8. For Thomas Keyle see *L&P*, 4/i, nos 787(18), 3008(9), 4594(20). London, Metropolitan Archives (formerly Greater London Record Office), DL/C/330, fols 83v, 123r.

[37] J.F. Davis, 'Joan of Kent, Lollardy and the English Reformation', *JEH*, 33 (1982), 228.

[38] PRO, SP1/237, fol. 95r; *A&M*, 5:34–6, app. xiii; *L&P*, Addenda, 2 parts (1929), 1, no. 752.

There ys no small noumber of suche erronyouse Englyshe bookes prented of whyche, yf fewe were boughte, there wolde not of lykelyhed so many be putte in prente – sauynge that some brethren there are in this realme that of theyr zele to theyr sectes, beyng of such substance that they may forbere yt, geue some money therto beforehande, content to abyde thaduenture of the sale, or geue the bokes aboute for nought to brynge men to the deuyl.[39]

More also claimed that heretical books were freely available in Bristol, where they were 'throwen in the strete and lefte at mennys dores by nyghte that where they durst not offer theyr poyson to sell, they wolde of theyr cheryte poyson men for nought'.[40] The free distribution of Simon Fish's *Supplication of the Beggars* was organized for maximum dramatic impact, with tracts scattered in the streets of London on the day that Parliament opened on 3 November 1529.[41] Fines identified a similar short tract that probably came from the Tyndalian group, pungent and satirical in style and attacking the banning of the vernacular Bible.[42] Such pamphlets and ephemera were the apparatus of propaganda, and Tyndale and the Christian Brethren were using such material and financial support to great effect.

The Tyndalian exiles also seemed to be in regular contact with the Brethren in England, as exemplified in the letters that were discovered by the English authorities. A member of the Merchant Adventurers known to have distributed books was Richard Harman, who was arrested by John Hackett, Wolsey's agent, in July 1528 for selling Cologne New Testaments, but later released. Four letters to Harman were discovered. Those from John Saddelere, draper of London, and Thomas Davy and John Andrews, both clothiers of Cranbrook, complained of the burnings of New Testaments. Another from Richard Hall, ironmonger of London, requested 'two new books of the New Testament in English'.[43] Thomas More discusses similar letters between the Brethren which were conveyed by Thomas Hytton between the Netherlands and England, 'wryten from euangelycall brethren here, vnto the euangelycall heretykes beyonde the see'. One

---

[39] *The Answer to a Poisoned Book*, in *CWM*, 11:6 ll.21–9.
[40] *Confutation*, 813 ll.16–20.
[41] *A&M*, 4:659, 666; *L&P*, 4/iii, no. 5416.
[42] J. Fines, 'An unnoticed tract of the Tyndale-More dispute?', *BIHR*, 42 (1969), 220–30.
[43] Rogers, *Letters of Hackett*, nos 67–9, 72, 75, 78–80, 82, 95, 98, 115.

can only surmise the links between Hytton and the Christian Brethren, but George Joye included Hytton in a calendar of saints, and Tyndale mentions him in *Practice and Answer*. Hytton claimed to have only crossed the sea once before with two New Testaments and a primer in English, but it is possible he had been asked to convey messages between the Christian Brethren.[44] He was caught in February 1530 with such letters upon him, and it is interesting that it was at this time that John Hackett was asked to help catch George Constantine before he could return to England with more books.[45]

The eventual capture of Robert Necton and George Constantine by More and Bishop Stokesley in late 1531 was a major coup for the authorities. More claimed he was given significant information regarding the distribution of books, and several were consequently arrested. He also stated that Constantine 'shewed me the shypmannes name that had tham and the markes of the ferdellys.'[46] Such was the anxiety among the Brethren that John Birt wrote to Constantine, cryptically trying to encourage him to keep the faith and not disclose any more information. Constantine eventually escaped in December 1531 from More's Chelsea house and fled to Antwerp, like so many other Brethren.[47]

The provincial and Continental links are seen through the activities of Constantine, Necton, and Bayfield. Constantine travelled to Shropshire for customers, and in May 1528, Richard Cotton, curate of Atcham near Shrewsbury, confessed to disputations, 'mainly with a certain George Constantine'.[48] In Bristol there was a thriving book trade with Richard Webb, who had close connections with Necton and Tyndale.[49] Robert Necton sold illicit books throughout London and East Anglia. The purchasers of his stock included London merchants and priests in East Anglia, and he also left some fifteen New Testaments and twenty-three *Oeconomica Christiana* with William, a merchant of Lynn.[50] He acquired them from various Christian

---

[44] *Confutation*, 11–17; *A&M*, 4:619, 8:712–15.

[45] Rogers, *Letters of Hackett*, no. 78.

[46] *Confutation*, 20 ll.21–2.

[47] Ibid., 17–20; *Apology*, 118–19; *L&P*, 4/i, nos 1802–3.

[48] Lichfield Record Office, B/A/1/14i, fols 51r–2r; J. Fines, 'An incident of the Reformation in Shropshire', *Transactions of the Shropshire Archaeological Society*, 57 (1961–4), 166–8.

[49] *Confutation*, 813–16.

[50] *L&P*, 4/ii, nos 4029, 4030; *A&M*, 4:680–2; John Strype, ed., *Ecclesiastical Memorials*, 6 vols (Oxford, 1822), 1/ii:63–4.

Brethren, including George Constantine, Geoffrey Lome, and Simon Fish. Indeed, it was Constantine who introduced Necton to Fish, who had acquired New Testaments from Harman.[51] When Necton was later approached by a certain 'Duche' with New Testaments, he returned the favour by passing them on to Fish, assuming he would have the capital to buy them.[52] This 'Duche' was Hans van Ruremund, who was producing pirate copies of Tyndale's New Testament with his brother, Christoffel, declaring; 'what is so litle a noumber for all englond? And we wil sel ours beter cheape.' They were a separate operation to the Brethren, and perhaps working for profit as much as religious zeal. But the Brethren took a pragmatic view of their activities and were seemingly prepared to buy their stock to supplement their own.[53]

Richard Bayfield, an ex-monk of St Edmunds, was the most active colporteur whom More apprehended, having smuggled a variety of books into London and Colchester in 1530 and 1531. He had apparently been converted by Robert Barnes in 1523, and Necton sold him two New Testaments in 1527. When forced to abjure his beliefs in 1528, Bayfield fled to Antwerp, where he was enlisted as a courier for the next few years: 'many of those books also [he] hast dispersed and given unto divers persons dwelling within our city and diocese of London'. Eventually his luck ran out and he was discovered with books and a list of fifty-four titles, including books by Luther and Melanchthon, and was burnt as a relapsed heretic on 4 December 1531.[54]

By the beginning of 1532, Thomas More had achieved remarkable success in restraining the dissemination of dissident books. John Frith secretly returned to England in Lent 1531, probably to reorganize the decimated Brethren, but he too was captured in October 1532, and Tyndale wrote to Frith in prison declaring: 'all the brethren loke what shall become of hym'.[55] More's zeal in rooting out the Christian Brethren was founded upon an effective combination of ecclesiastical heresy procedures and royal proclamations which allowed cases to be brought before Star Chamber. He also felt that Wolsey and Tunstall

---

[51] Ibid., 1/ii:54–5, 63–5.

[52] *A&M*, 4:656–66, 698–9.

[53] George Joye (ed. E. Arber), *An Apology* (1535) (Birmingham, 1883), 20–1; Rogers, *Letters of Hackett*, nos 27, 29, 30; *A&M*, 5:27, 37.

[54] *A&M*, 4:680–8; London, Corporation of London Record Office, Journal 13, fol. 289v.

[55] *A&M*, 5:5–6; *Apology*, 91 l.11.

had been too tolerant, perhaps illustrated by their lack of burnings in the 1520s. More's frustration in attempting to stem the flow of books led him to excesses, if not the beatings he denied, then certainly fabrication of evidence, such as the imprisonment in 1531 of John Petye upon the supposed evidence of a 'lytle old preest', after no heretical texts could be found in Petye's home.[56] It is certainly arguable that More, with the help of agents and confessions, had broken the back of the Christian Brethren by 1532. Nevertheless, the Brethren had laid the foundations for the belligerent native printers who were to produce books in even greater numbers in the late 1530s, as well as the official English Bible of Miles Coverdale.

Much more could be said about the Christian Brethren and Thomas More's persecution of them. What this paper has sought to stress is the core aspects of the distribution of Tyndalian books. At the heart was a group, referred to by Thomas More and William Tyndale as the 'euangelycall brethren', with its main adherents among merchants, academics, and clergy, as well as eminent sympathizers and preachers. The movement and production of books, after a false start and the establishment of support, grew into a well-organized network of popular propaganda and financing. At the core were Antwerp exiles who supplied the texts, and particularly William Tyndale whose mercantile and clerical links seem to have been vital. By 1530 Thomas More recognized the effectiveness and threat of this group. It is his zealous application to the task of disrupting the distribution networks that provides many of the insights into the Christian Brethren, who might otherwise have remained clandestine.

Wolfson College, Cambridge

---

[56] Brigden, *London*, 184–5; *A&M*, 4:586.

BERNARDINO OCHINO'S BOOKS AND ENGLISH RELIGIOUS OPINION, 1547–80

by M.A. OVERELL

ERNARDINO Ochino was one of the less famous and more
unpredictable of the Protestant refugees whom Thomas
Cranmer invited to England in 1547. He remained in the
limelight throughout Edward VI's reign, largely because of his writing.
A study of the English publication of his works throws some light on
the complex interaction between English books and European
Protestantism. Collinson's comment that 'English theologians were as
likely to lean on Bullinger of Zurich, Musculus of Berne or Peter
Martyr as on Calvin or Beza' is important here.[1] In Edward VI's reign
they leant quite confidently on more unsteady props, of whom Ochino
was one.

Ochino, who was born in Siena about 1487, had a long career as a
Catholic religious, then as a Protestant minister and preacher. First he
held high office as a Franciscan Observant and then as General of the
more austere Capuchins. Already in great demand as a preacher, in the
later 1530s he came under the influence of the Spanish religious
teacher Juan de Valdés, and the group of reformers known as the
'*spirituali*'. Although their emphasis on the Bible and on salvation by
faith alone resembled Protestant teaching, many of them, notably
Cardinals Contarini, Morone, and Pole, thought that such beliefs were
not in conflict with loyalty to the Catholic Church. Ochino, however,
moved to the opposite conclusion and, expecting persecution from the
traditionalists, fled from Italy to Protestant territory in the company of
the more famous reformer, Peter Martyr Vermigli. In 1547 imperial
victories forced them both to flee again, Ochino from Augsburg and
Vermigli from Strasbourg. By the end of that year, they were in
England, having been invited by Archbishop Cranmer.[2] At this point
Ochino was already about sixty, and had over twenty publications to

---

[1] Patrick Collinson, 'England and international Calvinism, 1558–1640', in Menna
Prestwich, ed., *International Calvinism: 1541–1715* (Oxford, 1985), 214.

[2] Dermot Fenlon, *Heresy and Disobedience in Tridentine Italy* (Cambridge, 1972), 50, 97,
220–2. For general information on the Italian Reformation, see Salvatore Caponetto, *The
Protestant Reformation in Sixteenth-Century Italy* (Kirksville, MO, 1999).

his name, mostly dialogues and collections of sermons. Usually he chose dialogues – the quintessential humanist form, a verbal tennis match. For the Italian '*spirituali*' it became a favourite Nicodemite way of avoiding saying what you meant. Juan de Valdés, Ochino's mentor, used it a lot.[3] In the hands of skilled exponents, it is clear who is supposed to be the winner. Unfortunately, in much of what Ochino wrote, it is not. The difficulties which that ambiguity might cause were not immediately appreciated.

We do not know exactly how Cranmer knew of Ochino and of his need for a safe refuge in 1547. The archbishop's humanism, his ability to read Italian, and his extensive network of contacts among continental reformers, were all reasons why he should have had some knowledge of the Italian's career, but detailed evidence is missing. Cranmer's sanguine hope was that his guests would 'do away with doctrinal controversies and establish an entire system of true doctrine'.[4] A sour Spanish ambassador described Ochino and his more famous companion-exile, Peter Martyr Vermigli, as the 'pet children' of the archbishop. Ochino's record did not justify Cranmer's expectations. He had in his employ not a systematic theologian but a popular ex-Capuchin preacher, who, according to Charles V could make the very stones weep with his oratory.[5] Yet during his exile in England in Edward VI's reign, Ochino's books were central to his popularity. He did not speak English and was much more at home in his native Tuscan than in Latin, so writing was his chief occupation. In 1549 Francis Dryander recorded that 'Bernardine employs his whole time writing and this too with a force and rapidity, as tells he me beyond what he ever did before.'[6]

The six publications of Ochino's work in Edward VI's reign were the work of three translators. John Ponet, Cranmer's chaplain, was a competent Italianist and a friend of both Ochino and Vermigli.

---

[3] Bernardino Ochino, *Seven Dialogues*, tr. Rita Belladonna (Toronto, 1988), xxv; M.A. Overell, 'Vergerio's anti-Nicodemite propaganda and England: 1547–1558', *JEH*, 51 (2000), 296–7.

[4] Cranmer to Henry VIII, 18 Nov. 1536, Cranmer to Hardenberg, 28 July 1548: *Miscellaneous Writings and Letters of Thomas Cranmer*, ed. J.E. Cox, PS (Cambridge, 1846), 330–2, 423; M.A. Overell, 'Edwardian court humanism and *Il beneficio di Cristo*, 1547–1553', in Jonathan Woolfson, ed., *Reassessing Tudor Humanism* (2002), 151–73.

[5] Van der Delft to the Emperor, 16 May 1548: *Calendar of State Papers, Spanish, 1547–9* (1912), 266; G. Rosso, *Historia delle cose di Napoli sotto l'imperio di Carlo Quinto* (Naples, 1760), 70.

[6] Dryander to Bullinger, 3 Dec. 1549: *Original Letters Relative to the English Reformation*, 2 vols, PS (Cambridge, 1847), 1:353.

Richard Argentyne was worthy if dull, and Anne Cooke, one of the bluestocking daughters of Sir Anthony Cooke, produced lovely Tudor prose. She was fast off the mark. Her first volume, *Sermons [five]*, appeared in July 1548, a bare eight months after Ochino's arrival, and Argentyne's *Sermons [six]* came out in the same year.[7] Ponet's version of Ochino's *A Tragoedie or Dialoge of the Uniuste Primacie of the Bishop of Rome* appeared in two different versions in 1549. Anne Cooke's *Fouretene Sermons . . . Concernyng the Predestinacion and Eleccion of God* were printed in 1550 or 1551. It was followed by a composite volume containing all these sermon translations.[8] In addition, Ochino produced a dialogue about the 1549 rebellions, which was not printed.[9]

The speed and quantity of publication is proof that Ochino was in vogue and the stationers knew he would sell. The humanist court and the group of classical scholars known in their own day as 'the Athenian tribe' and to historians as 'the Cambridge Connection' were the motivating force behind this Ochino industry.[10] He was a stranger from Italy, the first home of humanism. Despite his inability to speak English, preaching in Italian was one way he could earn his royal pension and Canterbury prebend. Through Cranmer's influence, Ochino was catapulted into a preaching post at the Italian church in London a month after his arrival in December 1547. The Duchess of Suffolk and the Marquess of Northampton were among his listeners.[11] Others close to the court were also fluent in Italian, among them Richard Morison, John Ponet, William Thomas, and Thomas Hoby. Cranmer could translate, and by 1551 the king was learning the language.[12] At the centre of the group was the great humanist John

[7] *Sermons [five] of Barnardine Ochine of Sena* (1548), STC 18764; *Sermons [six] of the Right Famous and Excellente Clerke Master B Ochine* (Ipswich, 1548), STC 18765.

[8] *A Tragoedie or Dialoge of the Uniuste Primacie of the Bishop of Rome*, tr. John Ponet (1549), STC 18770–1; *Fouretene Sermons . . . Concerning the Predestinacion and Eleccion of God* ([1551?]), STC 18767; *Certayne Sermons of the Ryght Famous and Excellent Clerk* ([1551?]), STC 18766.

[9] Philip McNair, 'Ochino on sedition', *Italian Studies*, 15 (1959–60), 46–9. For Ochino's unpublished 'Dialogo de Peccato' [1549], in BL, MS Add. 28,568, see McNair, 'Ochino's Apology: three Gods or three wives', *History*, 60 (1975), 353–73 (369); Daniel Bertrand-Barraud, *Les Idées philosophiques de Bernardin Ochin* (Paris, 1924), 123–9.

[10] Winthrop Hudson, *The Cambridge Connection* (Durham, NC, 1980).

[11] Cranmer to Bonner, 27 Jan. 1547/8: London, Guildhall Library, MS 9531/12 pt 1, fol. 117r, cited by Diarmaid MacCulloch, *Tudor Church Militant: Edward VI and the Protestant Reformation* (1999), 79; Van der Delft to the Emperor, 23 Feb. 1548, *Calendar of State Papers, Spanish, 1547–9*, 253.

[12] 'Mémoires de la vie de François de Scepeaux, sire de Vieilleville', in *Collection complète de memoires relatif à l'histoire de France*, ed. C-B Petitot, 52 vols (Paris, 1822), 26:339–41, cited

Cheke, the king's tutor. He was now free to reveal the Protestant sympathies he had kept private during Henry VIII's reign, and he was a patron of Ochino.[13]

Titles and dedications in the translations of his works treat Ochino's exile status as his main credential. What he was mattered as much as what he wrote. He was 'borne [sic] within the University of Siena . . . now also an exile for the faithful testimony of Jesus Christ', 'persecuted of Paul III', 'the most notable preacher of all Italy', according to Argentyne's *Six Sermons.*[14] The idea of exile, like the idea of martyrdom, had immense power. Ochino's exile was his 'proteccion' in all his contacts with England. He had suffered for his faith and so he was revered. According to his best translator, Anne Cooke, his sermons 'proceeded from the happy spirit of the sanctified Bernardine [of Siena]'. Her editor's preface added that Ochino was 'a man whose life without words were a sufficient proteccion to his worke'.[15] Yet, in other circumstances, Ochino's opinions would have caused concern. It was conventional to say that faith was more important than learning, but Argentyne had to cope with whole sermons attacking 'human sciences'. Ochino has, he says, some 'compassion of them that rest blinded' with learning because he was once 'in that error'. He was probably the least learned of Cranmer's exiles and his tendency, already evident in 1548, to toss about theological arguments and end with mockery was to cause offence later on.[16] By Elizabeth's reign the 'proteccion' had worn off somewhat, but not completely.

Death and the devil, traditional themes of the mission preacher, were Ochino's forte. Satan appears, full of gusto, in dialogues with the soul in Anne Cooke's 1548 collection of sermons, but Ochino's

---

in Jennifer Loach, *Edward VI*, ed. George Bernard and Penry Williams (New Haven, CT, and London, 1999), 13; Jonathan Woolfson, *Padua and the Tudors* (Cambridge, 1998), 246–7, 258, 276; Maria Dowling, 'Cranmer as humanist reformer', in Paul Ayris and David Selwyn, eds, *Thomas Cranmer: Churchman and Scholar* (Woodbridge, 1993), 89–114.

[13]   Caelio Secundo Curione, *Selectarum Epistolarum*, 2 vols (Basle, 1553), 1:287; John F. McDiarmid, 'John Cheke's Preface to De Superstitione', *JEH*, 48 (1997), 100–19.

[14]   *Sermons [six]* (*STC* 18765), title page and prefaces, sigs aiii–v.

[15]   Bernardino Ochino, *Fouretene Sermons*, tr. by Anne C[ooke, Lady Bacon], ed. G.B. (1551), sigs Aii–v; see also *Certayne Sermons*, where Anne Cooke's *Fouretene Sermons* on predestination appear as Sermons 12–25.

[16]   Sermon XX in *Sermons of Bernardine Ochyne to the Number of .25 Concerning the Predestination and Election of God*, tr. A. C[ooke, Lady Bacon and R. Argentine] (1570), *STC* 18768, sig. Lviii (all subsequent references are to this composite edition). Bertrand-Barraud, *Les Idées philosophiques*, 96.

diabolic talents were really shown off when Lucifer, Beelzebub, and 'the council of devils' had all the best lines in Ponet's translation of the *Tragoedie or Dialoge*. The book became embroiled in the tortuous politics of that year. Two versions appeared. The edition before Somerset's fall contains flattering references to him. In the second, the part played by Somerset is cut and 'the Counseill' is substituted.[17] These interlinked short plays are about the overthrow of the kingdom of Satan and the pope by that godly troop, Henry VIII, Thomas Cranmer, Edward VI, and his 'counseill'. Ochino's dedication to the King declared that he had driven out Anti-Christ 'being yet but almost a babe'.[18] Actually Edward was eleven, and Diarmaid MacCulloch has argued that he took ideas from the earlier pro-Somerset version for his own composition on the papal supremacy, written in French for Jean Belmain between December 1548 and August 1549.[19] If so, Ochino had become a royal crib soon after his arrival. A splendidly bound copy of his *Tragoedie* went into the royal library and another is in the inventory of Northumberland's library.[20]

At the time of the unrest in summer 1549, the government seems to have requested that several of the exile theologians should produce writings and sermons against the rebellions; but huge risks were attached to using Ochino as a propagandist. His 'Dialogue between the king and his People' gave the rebels' economic grievances far more of an airing than was circumspect:

> King: But everyone has to bear his own cross, remembering that God has given it to him for his benefit.
>
> People: If in that case he does not have enough to live on, what then?
>
> King: Then you must do as God commanded . . . without going outside the law in order to find food.
>
> People: And what if that is not enough. Have we got to allow ourselves to die of hunger?

---

[17] Sermon XXII in *Sermons to the Number of .25*, sigs Ni–ii; *Tragoedie*, STC 18770–1.

[18] For Ochino's possible use of Kirchmayer's *Pammachius*, see Roland H. Bainton, *Bernardino Ochino: esule e riformatore senese* (Florence, 1940), 96; P. McNair, 'Bernardino Ochino in Inghilterra', *Rivista Storica Italiana*, 103 (1991), 237–9; *Tragoedie*, STC 18770, Ochino's preface, sig. ?Ai.

[19] MacCulloch, *Tudor Church Militant*, 26–7.

[20] *Literary Remains of Edward VI*, ed. J.G. Nichols, 2 vols, Roxburghe Club (1857), 1:cccxxv–cccxxxiii; Bodley, MS Add.C.94, fol. 13r, cited by MacCulloch, *Tudor Church Militant*, 53, 230.

King: Definitely you must do so when you have no other alternative.

Ethan Shagan's recent research has shown that Protector Somerset, too, advertised his sympathies for the people. Possibly he put Ochino up to it. But Somerset did not survive and the translation of Ochino's 'Dialogue' was not printed.[21]

About 1551, the stationer John Day brought out two further books of Ochino's sermons: a collection on predestination and a composite volume containing all the twenty-five sermons translated between 1548 and 1551.[22] Anne Cooke, dedicating *Fouretene Sermons . . . Concerning the Predestinacion and Eleccion of God* to her mother, claimed that she had been taught the doctrine from her infancy, and she praised Ochino for 'the high style of his theologie'. But on predestination Ochino was elusive and in one sermon someone – possibly the editor, whose initials in the preface ('GB') may stand for William Baldwin[23] – entered two marginal warnings. Sermon 3 was entitled, 'If we may know in this present life whether we be in the grace of God or not'. But 'this must be warily read', thought the editor. Ochino makes a typically extravagant comment about the fate of the elect: 'he [Christ] will conduct them to salvation although they, as much as lieth in them, were continually prompted to all evil'. Set beside it is the marginal entry, 'This is not spoke to declare that it is possible for god's elect to be wholly given to sin, but if it were possible yet should they recover that pestilence.'

It would be wrong to read too much theology into these brief marginal inscriptions but it looks as if English sensitivity on the indefectibility of grace was involved. Yet, having done his bit with the red pen, the editor lets pass many other inconsistencies. Ochino asserts the inevitability of suffering for God's chosen, and then suddenly retracts this orthodoxy in favour of a eulogy of the elect's happy state both on earth and in heaven. 'They have the honour of every enterprise they take in hand, they cannot be letted or resisted no more than God.'[24] Sixteenth-century religious thought, Protestant or Catholic,

[21] McNair, 'Ochino on sedition', 37, 47; MacCulloch, *Tudor Church Militant*, 44–5, 121–2; Ethan Shagan, 'Protector Somerset and the 1549 rebellions', *EHR*, 114 (1999), 34–63.

[22] *STC* 18767, 18766: see n.15 above.

[23] J.N. King, 'John Day: master printer of the English Reformation', in P. Marshall and E. Ryrie, eds, *The Beginnings of English Protestantism* (Cambridge, 2002), 195.

[24] *STC* 18768, Preface, sig. Av; Sermon III, sigs Cii–iii; Sermon VII, sig. Eiiii; and Sermon XIV, sig. Ki.

did not usually promise earthly bliss to anyone. On free will and predestination, there is the statement, 'None is in hell but by his own wickedness.' This is followed rapidly by, 'but it may truly be said that [God] doth harden and blind the hearts of sinners'. Having meandered around reprobation, Ochino then throws in the sponge. 'Of the reprobate I intend not to dispute wherefore God hath cast them off.' At this relatively early stage of the predestinarian debates, such knotty questions produced mental contortions even in systematic thinkers, but Ochino's were of a rare order.[25]

Apart from marginalia on that one sermon, there is no record of concern that Ochino might not be a reliable theologian. Calvin warned against him and against Italians in general but Court interest was undiminished.[26] The Princess Elizabeth tried her hand at translating his 'De Christo Sermo' from Italian into Latin. The royal library contained Ochino's *Prediche* with the king's initials.[27] When Richard Morison was involved in a diplomatic scuffle at the imperial court for staging 'preachings' in his household, his own devil-may-care account was this: 'I did but read them Machiavel and Bernardine [Ochine] Prediches for the tongue.'[28]

Ochino's success owes much to the vogue for Italian Reformation exiles and literature in Edward's reign. He could bask in the glory reflecting from his countryman Vermigli's significant contribution to English Reformation theology.[29] The king read Edward Courtenay's translation of the Italian Reformation's bestseller, *Il Beneficio di Cristo*; Latimer preached to the court about its morality tale, the *Tragedy of*

---

[25] Ibid., Sermon IX, sig. Gi; Sermon XI, sig. Gviii.

[26] Calvin to M. de Falais, March 1546, in *Opera Calvini* in *Corpus Reformatorium*, ed. William Baum, Edward Cunitz, and Edward Reus, 58 vols in 25 (Brunswick, 1863–1900), 12, no. 784 (319–23), cited by Bertrand-Barraud, *Les Idées philosophiques*, 19; J. Calvin, 'Praefatio in Libellum de Francisco Spiera', tr. into English in *A Notable and Marvailous Epistle*, by E[dward] A[glionby] (Worcester, 1550), STC 12365.

[27] Bodley, MS Bodl. 6; Nichols, *Literary Remains*, 1:cccxxx.

[28] *Calendar of State Papers, Spanish, 1550–2* (1914), 349–52; *Calendar of State Papers, Foreign, 1547–1553* (1861), 216.

[29] Vermigli's influential eucharistic work was printed in Latin, *Tractatio de sacramento eucharistiae, habita in universitate Oxoniensi* (1549), STC 24673, and translated the following year as *A Discourse or Traictise of Peter Martyr Vermill* (1550), STC 24665; MacCulloch, *Thomas Cranmer* (New Haven, CT, and London, 1996), 467–9, 501, 511–12; Alan Beesley, 'An unpublished source of the Book of Common Prayer; Peter Martyr Vermigli's "Adhortatio ad Coenam Domini Mysticam"', *JEH*, 19 (1968), 83–8; James Spalding, '"The Reformatio Legum Ecclesiasticarum" and the furthering of discipline in England', *Church History*, 39 (1970), 162–71; M. Anne Overell, 'Peter Martyr in England 1547–1553: an alternative view', *Sixteenth Century Journal*, 15 (1984), 87–104.

Francesco Spiera; and the Italian enthusiast, William Thomas, became Edward's close mentor and adviser.[30] It is probable that humanism played as large a part as Protestantism in all this, and indeed that the two were inextricable. It is also significant that John Cheke was in contact with Basel radicals Caelio Secondo Curione and the Franco-Italian Sebastien Castellio, who were Ochino's friends. There was a steady stream of gifts, dedications, and letters, and Castellio was suggested as Bucer's replacement. This raises the question whether Ochino was in favour because radicals in general were attracting a lot of interest. Diarmaid MacCulloch has commented that 'Prominent Edwardians could afford to take a generously wide view of what a Reformed identity might mean.'[31] It seems tenable that the success of Ochino and his books was another symptom of that 'generously wide view'.

The predestination sermons had honourable mention in the controversy between Predestinarians and Freewillers in the King's Bench prison in 1555–6.[32] John Clement wrote, 'whose heart soever God moveth to be desirous to know further in the truth of this matter, let him read that godly boke of Bernardine Ochine's'. When he gets to reprobation he almost reproduces Ochino's words: 'As for reprobation I have nothing to say of it.'[33] Clement may have been introduced to Ochino's writing by John Bradford, but more probably his confession was actually written by one of the group's leaders.[34] This prison tribute formed an appropriate coda to Ochino's English exile.

When Ochino fled abroad at Mary's accession, English admiration for him was put under strain from all sides. He arrived in Geneva on 28 October 1553, the day after the burning of Michael Servetus. The tradition that Ochino joined in the outcry in which Italians were prominent is uncertain but likely. Calvin's suspicions of Italian

---

[30] CUL, MS Nn.4.43; M.A. Overell, 'The exploitation of Francesco Spiera', *Sixteenth Century Journal*, 26 (1995), 633; eadem, 'The Reformation of death in Italy and England: circa 1550', *Renaissance and Reformation*, 23 (1999), 5–21; E.R. Adair, 'William Thomas; a forgotten Clerk to the Privy Council', in R.W. Seton-Watson, ed., *Tudor Studies Presented to A.F. Pollard* (1924), 133–60.

[31] MacCulloch, *Tudor Church Militant*, 174. [See also n.41 below.]

[32] D. Andrew Penny, *Freewill or Predestination* (Woodbridge, 1990), 158; N. Pococke 'The condition of morals and religious belief in the reign of Edward VI', *EHR*, 10 (1895), 433.

[33] Clement's 'Confession', in J. Strype, *Ecclesiastical Memorials*, 3 vols in 6 (Oxford, 1822), 3/ii, no. 61 (446–67, esp. 463).

[34] Bradford certainly knew Ochino and was familiar with the Spiera story, John Bradford, *Writings*, 2 vols, PS (Cambridge, 1848–53), 1:433, 2:80, 352–3. I am grateful to Dr Tom Freeman for his scholarly insights about the background to Clement's confession.

Protestants turned to resentment at the very moment when Genevan power was established. Moreover, Ochino and Vermigli lost an influential friend when Ponet's resistance theory brought him into disfavour, followed rapidly by his death.[35] Last, the Italianiate Princess Elizabeth turned into a queen suspicious of Italian reformers, who resisted inviting even the revered 'Doctor Peter Martyr' to return to England. Experience of the troubles in the Strangers' Churches served to confirm her prejudices. In 1561, in the midst of this frosty displeasure, Ochino dedicated to her the most perverse of all his books, *The Labyrinths of Free Will*. He recalled his conversations with her about predestination when Edward was king. *The Labyrinths* exposed every possible viewpoint in the predestination/free will debate, and came to absolutely no conclusion. Ochino ended by recommending 'learned ignorance', just as he had in 1548.[36]

Predictably, Queen Elizabeth ignored the dedication and, in 1563, Zurich's leaders asked that any further books should be handed in for checking. Then came the big explosion. The *Thirty Dialogues* of 1563 were published in Basel, and there was yet another English dedication, this time to Francis Russell, Duke of Bedford, the well-known patron of Italian reformers. The Zurich censors condemned the three dialogues on the Trinity, Toleration, and Polygamy.[37] The last caused the biggest scandal and, once again, the problem arose from the dialogue form. It was not clear who was the winner: Telipolygamus (who wanted to marry more wives), or Ochino (who was ostensibly trying to dissuade him). Ochino's final capitulation goes like this: 'If you then do that to which God shall incline you, so that you are led by Divine Instigation, you shall not err. For it can be no error to obey God. Other advice I cannot give you.' He was banished from Zurich and died towards the end of 1564, in exile in Moravia. The Protestant bush telegraph buzzed with condemnations, and continental publications seem to have stopped.[38]

---

[35] Winthrop Hudson, *John Ponet* (Chicago, 1942).

[36] Andrew Pettegree, *Foreign Protestant Communities in Sixteenth Century London* (Oxford, 1986); Patrick Collinson, *Archbishop Grindal* (1979), 125–52; Overell, 'Peter Martyr', 103–4; *Labyrinthi, hoc est de libero aut servo arbitrio* (Basle, [1561]).

[37] For Ochino's plagiarism of the *Dialogus Neobuli* (1541), probably by Johannes Lening, see Mark Taplin, 'Bernardino Ochino and the Zurich polygamy controversy of 1563' (University of St Andrews, M.Litt. thesis, 1995), 26–46. I am grateful to Dr Bruce Gordon for alerting me to this valuable study. [See also n.41 below.]

[38] McNair, 'Ochino's Apology', 364. For a list of Ochino's publications after he left England, see Karl Benrath, *Bernardino Ochino von Siena*, 3rd edn (Nieuwkoop, 1968),

The two further printings of Ochino in England in Elizabeth's reign therefore need examination. Why go on publishing him? About 1570 there was a reissue of the 1551 composite edition of his sermons. The printer was that same respectable Protestant stationer, John Day, who brought out the first edition. The adulatory prefaces were reprinted, and Ochino's name appeared in the title.[39] It is impossible to know why the project went ahead. Ignorance is a possibility at this date; 'little England' defiance cannot be ruled out; business sense probably indicated that predestination would sell. But it is significant that England was doing its own thing, not toeing the line, after a very public continental drama had revealed a heterodoxy so profound that Ochino's earlier writings were rendered suspect. Geneva, Zurich, even Basel, had condemned Ochino, yet London went on printing him. In 1580 William Phiston, 'student', translated the less controversial *Sermons of Faith, Hope and Charitie*. These sermons date from Ochino's exile in Geneva and Basel in the 1540s, when he was less at odds with the continental reformers, despite Calvin's doubts about him. The subject matter sounded innocuous enough. Yet the characteristics which finally got Ochino into trouble were already evident, albeit in a more moderate form: interlocutors, inconsistencies, and extravagant statements like 'thou might better choose to have committed all the sins in the world' than 'to distrust in God'. Although Phiston was playing safe to some extent in choosing his material, he knew it had become combustible, and he came out with the uncomfortable facts about Ochino's disgrace in his dedication to Archbishop Grindal. 'Only this is reported of him that in his latter years, howsoever it fell out I wot not, but he by his fall declared manifestly what and how vehement the frailty of human nature is . . . but yet it is certain that once he was zealous . . . nothing inferior . . . in perfect judgement', Phiston said, excusing what Europe had condemned.[40]

I have suggested that the admiration given to Ochino in Edward VI's reign was due to a 'generously wide view' of Protestantism. Humanism and sympathy for all exiles made contemporaries overlook Ochino's inconsistencies and keenness to expose all the different arguments, usually in dialogue form. He was surrounded by patrons

320–3. The late date sometimes given to the Italian version of the *Labyrinths* (i.e., 1569) appears to be a mistake: ibid., no. 42 (322).

[39] *STC* 18768, reprinted from 18766.

[40] *Certaine Godly and Very Profitable Sermons, of Faith, Hope and Charitie*, tr. William Phiston (1580), 1–2, 59–60, *STC* 18769.

more concerned to praise his courage than to follow through the implications of his theology. English Protestantism was still at the experimental stage. The 1551 volume contained mild warnings, but Protestant theology books were still, relatively, a novelty to be prized rather than censored. The expanding book market and consequently greater theological sophistication contributed to some 'narrowing' under Elizabeth. But why should Ochino's works have been published at all after Europe's condemnation in 1563? England warmed to him fast and went off him slowly. It seems that in neither process were the attitudes of Calvin or Bullinger particularly decisive. Phiston's open reference to Ochino's 'fall' and 'frailty' shows that ignorance was not the whole story. Sturdy independence, a sense of loyalty to exiles, safe distance, and relatively weak censorship until 1580, may all have played their part. Certainly the Edwardian 'wide view' did not continue to the same degree in Elizabeth's reign. But this sideshow of Reformation history suggests that English attitudes remained wider, for longer, than those of the continent.[41]

The Open University

---

[41] Addendum to n.31: See also Hans R. Guggisberg, *Sebastian Castellio: Humanist and Defender of Religious Toleration in a Confessional Age*, ed. and tr. Bruce Gordon (Aldershot, 2003), 56–61, 172–3.

Adendum to n.37: See also Mark Taplin, *The Italian Reformers and the Zurich Church* (Aldershot, forthcoming).

DRESSED IN BORROWED ROBES: THE MAKING AND MARKETING OF THE LOUVAIN BIBLE (1578)

by ELIZABETH MORLEY INGRAM

THIS paper examines the transformation of a Protestant Geneva Bible into a widely used Catholic one. This surprising metamorphosis occurred in two stages: first, the publication in Paris in 1566 of a French Bible for Catholics by René Benoist, a member of the Paris Faculty of Theology; second, the marketing of this Bible as a product of the Louvain Faculty of Theology by the famous Antwerp printer, Christopher Plantin. While the relationship between the Paris and Antwerp editions is known to French specialists, the origin of the Antwerp edition has been (understandably) misdescribed in several English reference works.[1] The relationship between the two editions seems worth rehearsing here for it touches on more general issues of Catholic attitudes towards vernacular Scripture, the migration of texts across confessional lines, and the power of printers.

By the second half of the sixteenth century, most European Protestants had access to Bibles in their own language. For the Catholic Church however, the question of permitting Catholics to use vernacular translations was problematic. For many – perhaps most – Catholics, vernacular Scripture was analogous to heresy because of its close associations with heterodox movements past and present. Yet within the sixteenth-century Church, continuing debate on the issue kept alive arguments supporting vernacular Scripture, arguments raised by the example and precepts of Scripture itself, and by the work of Catholic humanists. The issue became urgent in face of the huge production and popularity of Bible translations emanating from the Reform centres of Europe.[2] At the fourth session of the Council of

---

[1] T.H. Darlow and H.F. Moule, *Historical Catalogue of the Printed Editions of Holy Scriptures in the Library of the British and Foreign Bible Society*, vol. 2: *Polyglots and Languages other than English* (1911), 394, no. 3734. R.A. Sayce, 'Continental versions to *c.*1600: French', in S.L. Greenslade, ed., *The Cambridge History of the Bible*, vol. 3: *The West from the Reformation to the Present Day* (Cambridge, 1963), 121. Both authorities, misled by the title of Plantin's 1573 New Testament, describe his editions as revisions of the Louvain French translation of 1550.

[2] For the arguments, see Guy Bedouelle, 'Le Débat catholique sur la traduction de la Bible en langue vulgaire', in Irena Backus and Francis Higman, eds, *Théorie et practique de l'exégèse* (Geneva, 1990), 39–59; Guy Bedouelle and Bernard Roussel, 'La Lecture de la Bible

Trent in March 1546, the question of whether the translation of Scripture into national tongues constituted an 'Abuse' intensely engaged the delegates. Unable to agree after protracted discussion and unwilling to promulgate a divisive decision, the Council simply dropped the matter and issued no recommendation. It went on to affirm the authority of the Vulgate Bible and called for its revision, the equal authority of Scripture and Church Tradition, and the sole authority of the Church in the interpretation of Scripture.[3]

The official position of Rome was promulgated in the early editions of the Papal Index of Prohibited Books. The first edition (1559) flatly prohibited the printing and reading of any vernacular Bible without written permission from the Roman Office of the Inquisition. The Tridentine edition (1564) softened this somewhat by spelling out, in an appended set of *Rules*, conditions for granting laymen such permission. According to Rule 4, the translation had to be by a Catholic, and a bishop or inquisitor needed to be persuaded by a pastor or confessor that the reader's faith would suffer no harm.[4] Although these requirements did not altogether proscribe vernacular Bibles, they set up obstacles that produced the same dampening effect.

A major problem was the lack of a widely approved revision of the Vulgate to serve as the basis of an acceptable Catholic translation. An early attempt to provide one had been made by the Theological Faculty of the University of Louvain in response to an imperial command to prepare a corrected edition of the Vulgate from which French and Flemish translations might be made. This Louvain Vulgate, edited by Jean Henten, duly appeared in 1547, followed three years later by the Louvain French translation by Nicolas de Leuze (1550). Henten's Vulgate achieved notable circulation much later when re-edited as part of Plantin's 1574 Polyglot. However, the French translation did not survive past its first edition, presumably a victim of subsequent debate within the Louvain Theological Faculty (1554–6) which decided against the legality of vernacular Scripture.[5] In Paris, the publication of any form of Scripture in French had been prohibited

---

en langue vivante au XVIe siècle: chronologie de quelques textes et faites marquants', ibid., 61–76.

[3] Robert E. McNally, S.J., 'The Council of Trent and vernacular Bibles', *Theological Studies*, 27 (1966), 205–27; V. Coletti, *L'Éloquence de la chaire: victoires et défaites du latin entre Moyen Âge et Renaissance* (Paris, 1987), chs 9–11.

[4] McNally, 'Council of Trent', 226–7.

[5] Bedouelle, 'Le Débat', 48–9.

since 1525 by the censoring authority, the Theological Faculty. The close association of heresy with vernacular Bibles tainted the whole enterprise.

As a result, no Catholic vernacular Bible had emerged in France by the middle of the sixteenth century to counter the flood of Geneva French Bibles, especially inexpensive New Testaments and Psalms, that poured into France during the 1550s and 1560s in a concerted effort to convert France to Calvinism. Geneva printers deliberately made these Calvinist Bibles attractive to a wide lay readership by adding helpful aids to understanding, such as book and chapter summaries, marginal annotations, historical charts, definitions of difficult terms, and often diagrammatic pictures and maps, all designed to help ordinary readers understand the text and, not incidentally, to absorb the desired doctrinal slant.[6]

During these unsettled decades in France, when the Reform seemed ascendant and political-religious tensions were exploding into civil war, a prominent member of the Paris Faculty of Theology, René Benoist, was persuaded that Catholics needed a vernacular Bible that might strengthen lay resistance to the Reform, and he determined to provide one.[7] He was well placed and well connected for such an undertaking. Under the protection of the Cardinal of Lorraine (brother of the Duc de Guise), he had been appointed confessor to Mary Stuart, whom he accompanied to Scotland for two years. There he briefly met several Scots divines, whom he failed to convert, and experienced at first hand the religious upheaval that he saw infecting his own land on his return to Paris in 1562. He became curate of St Eustâche, where he was a much admired preacher popularly known as 'le Pape des Halles', and was eventually appointed Counsellor of State and confessor to Henry IV. His biographer records Benoist's authorship of more than 130 items, mostly of religious polemic championing the Catholic cause and lambasting 'heretics'.

In the 1560s, Benoist was keenly aware of the popularity of Genevan Bibles with his parishioners. Deciding to fight fire with fire, he

---

[6] Bettye Thomas Chambers, *Bibliography of French Bibles*, 2 vols (Geneva, 1983–94) [hereafter Chambers]. Reader aids in Geneva Bibles are described at 1:xiii–xiv.

[7] For Benoist's biography and bibliography, see Emile Pasquier, *Un curé de Paris pendent les guerres de religion: René Benoist, le Pape des Halles, 1521–1608* (Paris, 1913), and Carlo de Clercq, 'La Bible française de René Benoist', *Gutenberg Jahrbuch* (1957), 168–74. A detailed history of the Benoist-Plantin editions appears in Pierre-Maurice Bogaert, ed., *Les Bibles en français: histoire illustrée du moyen âge à nos jours* (Turnhout, 1991), 91–101.

published in 1566 a folio Bible in French and a separate, small-format New Testament with parallel French and Vulgate texts.[8] These would defend against heresy by answering it in marginal annotations, as announced in his subtitle: 'Avec . . . expositions contenantes briefves et familieres Resolutions des lieux qui ont esté depravés et corrompus par les heretiques de nostre temps.' The Bible's preliminaries include an item of unusual interest, a series of six 'Advertissemens apologetiques', or explanatory notes, in which Benoist explains and justifies his work.[9] In the first he declares his fidelity to the Catholic Church. In the second, he argues for the present necessity of vernacular translations, and states (perhaps on the basis of Rule 4 of the 1564 *Index*) that the pope and his councils support them. His Bible is especially needed, he claims, now that the heretics have persuaded nearly everyone that they must have, and read, Scripture. In the fourth note, he explains that because the heretics have corrupted the text, he will restore it by translating from the Vulgate.

Against these claims, Benoist's fifth *Advertisement* surprises. Here he declares that his translation and notes often follow the Bible of the heretics, that is, the Geneva version. Anticipating objections, he argues that the Holy Spirit guides Catholics to embrace truth wherever it is found; heretics must sometimes tell the truth, for even the devil speaks true at times, and so (he declares) we take back from them what is good and true, which is properly ours, and leave them what is theirs, which is lies and corruption. They have stolen the Bible from us, so it is only just that the Church Militant despoil her enemies as the Israelites did in Egypt; and since spiritual warfare has opened between us and the heretics, he concludes, am I not permitted to pillage them?

Benoist's new Catholic Bible is in fact a Geneva Bible with occasional changes in text and marginal notes to align it with Catholic doctrine. It also copies the illustrations of the Tabernacle and Temple and the ancillary texts habitually published in Genevan Bibles. The most obviously Reformist of these is a two-page text titled 'La Somme de tout ce que nous enseigne la Saincte Escriture' (sigs +7^{r-v}). This is a summary of Reformist faith that serves to ground Calvinist doctrine in Scripture. Originating in a Latin Bible of 1532 and revised by Calvin

---

[8] For Benoist's editions of 1566, see Chambers, 1, nos 371–3 (Bible), 378–9 (New Testament).

[9] Sigs +5^v–+6^v. See the analysis by Francis Higman, 'Les *Advertissements* des Bibles de René Benoist (1566, 1568)', in his *Lire et découvrir: la circulation des idées au temps de la Réforme* (Geneva, 1998), 563–71.

and others, it became a standard feature of Geneva Bibles for the next two centuries.[10] Benoist appropriated it for Catholic readers by making (among minor changes) two substantive additions: first, to the statement that we are sanctified and justified by faith, he added 'comme aussi par la reception des saincts sacrements & obeissance a Dieu et son Eglise'; and to the text's final statement that the only foundation of the Church is the faith and salvation proclaimed by Jesus Christ, Benoist added 'en l'Eglise Catholique'.

Other material that Benoist lifted unchanged from the Geneva editions he opposed is less overtly Calvinist, though typical of Reformist interests in history and philology. There are chronological tables, a list of correspondences between the Old and New Testaments, an index of Hebrew and Greek names with their meanings, and one of difficult or controversial words defined from a Calvinist viewpoint, such as 'Priest. . . . the pastors and ministers who are responsible for teaching the people by the Word of God'. Benoist also included an orthodox Epistle of St Jerome frequently printed with the Vulgate, and a table of liturgical readings for feast days.

Although Benoist arranged the books of his Bible in Vulgate rather than Geneva order, his 'translation' is mostly a word-for-word reproduction of current Geneva versions, including book and chapter summaries, with a light sprinkling of Vulgate readings. For instance, when Moses descends from Sinai with the tablets (Exodus 34.29), Benoist restored the Vulgate's description of Moses's face as *horned* (French 'cornue') in place of the Geneva reading *shining* ('luisante'). However, it is typical of Benoist's hasty work that he ignored the chapter summary printed on the same page that retains the Geneva reading 'ayant sa face luisante'.

As one would expect, most of Benoist's changes were made in the many notes that fill the margins of his Geneva source, primarily those that touch on doctrinal differences concerning the nature of the Eucharist, good works, clerical celibacy, justification by faith, and idolatry. These changes take two forms. Sometimes Benoist inserted a new note of his own differentiated by an asterisk or dagger from the series of letter-keyed Genevan notes. For example, where God warns against adding to his Word (Deuteronomy 4.2), Benoist added a note stating that heretics abuse this text in order to reject the ceremonies of the Catholic Church. More frequently Benoist appended his answering

---

[10] Chambers, 1, no. 167.

comment directly to the original Genevan note, with nothing to signal change of authorship apart from content and tone. Thus when the Genevan note on the Tower of Babel (Genesis 11.4) points out the builders' pride, Benoist's unmistakable voice adds that such are the heretics who proudly forsake God's commandments to wander among their own inventions. The Protestant notes and Benoist's Catholic responses are undifferentiated. Readers must carefully follow the cramped marginal notes to discover Benoist's comments, and in so doing, they will absorb a good dose of Genevan commentary.

And much slid past Benoist's attention. Many notes no less Genevan than those he answered remained untouched on the page. No wonder, then, that within a few months of the Bible's publication in 1566, the Paris Theological Faculty had drawn up a list of thirty heretical statements in the Old Testament, all but two in the notes, condemned Benoist's Bible, and ordered it suppressed. Benoist resisted, offered to make changes if the Faculty would show him their list of errors (they refused), and vainly hoped that a second edition of his Bible two years later would improve his position with his critics. This 1568 edition differs from the first primarily by printing the Latin Vulgate in parallel columns with the French text, perhaps to strengthen a sense of orthodoxy. However, the French text and notes, including the condemned points, is virtually unchanged, though an errata list (sigs &3^v-&4^v) asks readers to substitute some doctrinally significant Vulgate terms for Genevan ones throughout, such as Vulgate *penitence* (*poenitentia*) for Genevan *repentance*, *images* (*imago*) for *idoles*, *prestre* (*sacerdos*) for *sacrificateurs*.

Benoist was now plunged into a bitter quarrel with his colleagues that raged for nearly thirty years. In response to this second edition, the Paris Theological Faculty ratified its earlier condemnation, and successfully appealed for a royal decree to suppress both editions. Benoist, in turn, petitioned the Paris Parlement to compel the Faculty to reveal its list of errors so that he might correct them. The theologians again refused on the grounds that the errors were too many, and in 1572 expelled Benoist from the Faculty. Benoist further aggravated the dispute by circulating anonymously in Paris a 'Juste & nécessaire complainte' against 'ses Confreres Docteurs en Théologie' claiming, among much else, that his Bible had been read and approved by the papal nuncio in Paris. The faculty, at the end of its tether, submitted the whole affair to Rome in August 1574, where the following year Pope Gregory XIII condemned Benoist's Bible for errors and heresies. Benoist again refused to submit. He maintained his popularity with his parishioners, and enjoyed royal favour. He played a role in the conversion of Henry IV (1593), who made Benoist his confessor and appointed him Bishop of Troyes. Benoist's elevation was blocked, however, by the pope's refusal to send the necessary documents. The long dispute was resolved only in 1598 when Benoist signed a half-hearted submission to the pope in return for being made Dean of the Paris Faculty of Theology, the very body that had so opposed his Bible.[11]

The scene now shifts to Antwerp, where the first appearance of Benoist's Bible and New Testament in 1566 caught the eye of Christopher Plantin. Plantin was in difficulty. His finances were stretched, and he feared that his business ties to anti-Catholic printers in a nearby town might compromise his good standing with the Catholic authorities of Philip II, whose financial backing he needed for his ambitious polyglot Bible. The reprinting of a French Catholic Bible would be opportune financially and a means of strengthening his Catholic credentials with the king.[12]

Plantin worked quickly. The royal privilege he obtained indicates his intention to publish Benoist's Bible in full. By the end of February 1567 the text of the Bible had been reviewed and approved by Jean Henten, editor of the Louvain Vulgate already mentioned, who declared it to be of great use to all Catholics and to the confusion of heretics. Three more members of the Louvain Faculty signed their agreement. However, six months later only the French New Testament had emerged from Plantin's press, not the whole Bible.[13] In a prefatory Address 'au Lecteur Catholique', Plantin explained that he had already begun printing the text of the full Bible when some (unnamed) authorities persuaded him to publish first a separate New Testament in order to save Catholic readers from editions that were suspect and depraved. It seems probable that these 'suspect' editions refer to Benoist's Bible and the storm that had already broken over it in Paris. Because Benoist's New Testament had escaped mention in the Paris condemnation, Plantin evidently felt secure enough to publish it.

[11] Bogaert, *Les Bibles*, 93–102; De Clercq, 'Bible française', 169–74.
[12] Leon Voet, *The Golden Compasses: The History of the House of Plantin-Moretus*, 2 vols (Amsterdam, 1969), 1:54–8.
[13] Chambers, 1, no. 385; Leon Voet and Jenny Voet-Grisolle, *The Plantin Press (1555–1589)* (Amsterdam, 1980), no. 724; Carlo de Clercq, 'Les Éditions bibliques, liturgiques et canoniques de Plantin', *De Gulden Passer*, 34 (1956), 161–70.

The title page shows Plantin cautiously backing away from Benoist's book and taking the first steps toward its transformation. From the title Plantin eliminated Benoist's abrasive reference to 'places . . . depraved and corrupted by the heretics'. He identified Benoist as author ('par M. René Benoist, Angevin, docteur, etc.') but gave equal billing to the corrector ('Le tout revue par F. Jean Henten, docteur en Theologie'). There is no title-page mention of Paris or Louvain or their Faculties of Theology: Plantin apparently wanted to attract as little attention as possible to his source. And he succeeded. No objections to his New Testament were raised, though it reproduces Benoist's text and notes, with minimal editing by Henten.

Six years later, in 1573, Plantin issued a second edition of Benoist's New Testament despite the further condemnation in Paris of Benoist's 1568 Bible. This time Plantin made crucial changes that decisively distanced his book from Benoist's. Most importantly, all marginal notes were expunged. The title was further shortened to read simply 'Le Nouveau Testament de nostre Seigneur Jesus Christ, Traduict de Latin en François Par Les Theologiens de Louvain'. That last phrase is a fiction by which Plantin promoted the members of the Louvain Theological Faculty who merely approved his earlier edition to the role of anonymous translators. The translation remains the Geneva–Benoist–Henten version just as it appeared in Plantin's first French New Testament of 1567.[14]

Plantin finally printed Benoist's full Bible in 1578.[15] He again suppressed Benoist's name and all marginal commentary except biblical cross-references. The Bible's title is even less informative than that of Plantin's previous New Testament, though more strictly correct: *La Saincte Bible, contenant le Vieil et Nouveau Testament, traduicte de Latin en François. Avec les Argumens sur chacun livre declarans sommairment tout ce y est contenu.* The title page makes no mention of Louvain, but two members of its Theological Faculty approved the text, one of whom, Jacques de Bay, provided a short Latin preface. This enhances the Bible's seeming orthodoxy by describing it as the work of Louvain theologians charged (by an unspecified authority) to produce a French translation based faithfully on the Vulgate, so that bishops and inquisitors could be satisfied that the faith of its readers would suffer no harm. Plantin is praised for volunteering to print their work, and in

---

[14] Chambers, 1, nos 430–1.
[15] Chambers, 1, no. 439; De Clercq, 'Éditions bibliques', 169–70.

closing, de Bay refers to the great labour of completing this translation ('translationem hanc', sig. +2r^r). Paris and Benoist are of course not mentioned. Even a cautious reader of the preface might well assume that the entire edition had been conceived and carried out by the Louvain theologians, with Plantin graciously stepping in at the end to publish it. Yet the text closely follows Benoist's 1568 edition, and incorporates his errata. It reproduces the same peripheral texts, including the Genevan summary of faith with Benoist's changes, and copies the same illustrations of Tabernacle and Temple popularized by Geneva Bibles.

It was this Plantin edition of the French Bible that came to be identified as the 'Louvain' version on the title pages of its many subsequent editions, thus lending it the full authority of one of Europe's pre-eminent Catholic institutions and too easily confusing it with the earlier, unrelated Louvain French translation of 1550. This Benoist–Plantin text became the accepted vernacular version for French Catholic readers throughout the seventeenth century. Some twenty editions of these 'Louvain' Bibles and New Testaments appeared before the end of the sixteenth century, and nearly two hundred more in the next. Many include the Reformist summary of faith, de Bay's preface, and the attribution 'by the Theologians of Louvain' printed on the title page.

The text was revised at least three times in the seventeenth century, notably by the Jesuit controversialist François Véron in 1646.[16] Recognizing the Genevan matrix of the Louvain Bible (this 'vaisseaux d'or d'Egypte', sig. A2^r), Véron revised Plantin's New Testament of 1573 to purge its remaining Genevan errors, especially those affecting faith. The resulting New Testament was frequently reprinted to the end of the century. And this was not the end. A Bible historian writing in the mid-nineteenth century reported that the Louvain Bible crossed confessional lines once more from Catholicism back to Protestantism, and could still be seen on the pulpits of Reformed churches in northern France until the early 1800s.[17]

This brief outline of the transformation of a Genevan Bible into the Catholic Louvain Bible and its long afterlife points up the extent to which texts could penetrate confessional divides in the sixteenth century. A parallel and better-known transformation occurred earlier

---

[16] Chambers, 2, no. 1227.
[17] Emmanuel Pétavel, *La Bible en France* (Paris, 1864), 126.

in Saxony when in 1527 the Catholic divine Jerome Emser edited Luther's New Testament for Catholics in order to discourage their eager reading of Luther's original. Shortly after Emser's death, his name appeared as author on the title page, much to Luther's disgust.[18] Francis Higman has brought to light the wide circulation of what he calls 'trans-confessional texts'. Translations of Luther's devotional works were absorbed anonymously into Catholic pietistic literature, and part of a Calvinist confession of faith found its way into a book of Catholic instruction. A book of religious consolation in French by a member of the Paris Faculty of Theology, which was printed several times in Paris during the 1540s, was discovered by Higman to be a translation of a work by Luther that was, during the same decade, twice condemned by the same Faculty.[19] Against these border crossings, the Geneva–Louvain migration may seem less an aberration than an extension of established (though not dominant) cultural practice.

That such blurring of borders, deliberately or accidentally, also caused anxiety about Scripture is amply shown in a Louvain Bible edition of 1621. Here the learned editor from the Paris Faculty, Pierre Frizon, who well remembered the turmoil Benoist's Bible had caused, included an appendix titled 'How to tell a French Catholic Bible from a Protestant one'. He first advises readers to observe whether the Apocryphal books are distributed throughout the Old Testament (Catholic) or gathered at the end (Protestant), and concludes with a long list of contested Catholic/Protestant readings against which readers should check their text.[20]

But clearly the many readers who bought the Louvain Bibles and New Testaments were unconcerned about such doctrinal distinctions. Like Benoist's parishioners and Emser's before them, they wanted a Bible in their own language like their Protestant neighbours. Plantin made this possible by dressing Benoist's Geneva-based text in a robe of Louvain-based orthodoxy. Perhaps because these Bibles borrowed the robes of both Geneva and Rome, they were particularly well dressed for success.

---

[18] H. Volz, 'Continental versions to c.1600: German', in Greenslade, *Cambridge History of the Bible*, 3: 107–8.

[19] Francis M. Higman, *Bibliographie matérielle et histoire intellectuelle: les débuts de la Réforme française*, The Cassal Lecture, 1986 (1986), 7–10.

[20] 'Les Moyens pour discerner les Bibles Françoises Catholiques d'auec les Huguenotes' is advertized on the title page and printed at the end of the text. Frizon discusses Benoist's Bible in the preface, 'Advertisement au benin Lecteur': Chambers, 2, no. 1107.

LUTHER AND THE BOOK: THE ICONOGRAPHY OF THE NINETY-FIVE THESES

by BRIAN CUMMINGS

L UTHER'S Ninety-Five Theses are not perhaps the book of the millennium, but they have some claim to being one of the books of the half-millennium. Few books in Church history can have had as much effect as this single-page broadsheet. Through this text, or so it is sometimes represented, Western Christianity was cut in two. The Ninety-Five Theses heralded the new age of print, with its capacity to transform culture in ways which have a strong resonance with our own 'age of information'. The theses, it was said, were known throughout Germany in a fortnight and Europe in a month.[1] With some justice, the theses have been described as the publishing event of the sixteenth century, and the first media sensation of the modern era.[2]

Nevertheless, at least in the popular imagination, the history of the publication of the theses has been suppressed in favour of the image of the lonely monk nailing his radical principles to a church door.[3] The significance of the theses as a textual artefact, or even as a writing or reading process, has been displaced into an event which is more existential or psychological. In particular, this has deflected attention from the material nature of the theses as a text, and from the processes of the text's dissemination, with the effect that the significance of the theses for a history of the Church and the book has diminished or even disappeared. This paper aims to restore some sense of the theses as a book, of the book as revolutionary object, and of Luther as a revolutionary bookman.

All kinds of ambiguity surround the original promulgation of the

---

[1] Friedrich Myconius, *Historia reformationis* (Leipzig, 1718), 23, writing in the 1530s. Luther's own account, written in 1541 in *Wider Hans Worst*, makes the same claim: *D. Martin Luthers Werke*, Kritische Gesamtausgabe, 60 vols (Weimar, 1883–1997) [hereafter WA], 51:540.

[2] Famous statements of this kind occur in A.G. Dickens, *The German Nation and Martin Luther* (1974), 102–15, and Elizabeth Eisenstein, *The Printing Press as an Agent of Change*, 2 vols in 1, pbk edn (Cambridge, 1980), 306–13.

[3] The first reference to the event is in Melanchthon's preface to *Omnia opera Martini Lutheri*, 7 vols (Wittenberg, 1546), 2, sig. *iv^{r-v}: 'Et has publice Templo, quod Arci Witenbergensi contiguum est, affixit.'

theses. Recent debate has centred on whether the theses were in fact posted, but other obscurities are equally important.[4] The theses stand at the intersection of many of the most important tensions in the early modern book. They represent both an oral university disputation and a written text; a local, perhaps manuscript, promulgation in Wittenberg university itself, and a printed version for dissemination throughout Europe.[5] Printed versions vary between broadsheet examples, which survive in copies from various cities; a unique blockbook copy also dated 1517 from Basel; and a later full-length quarto version with commentary by Luther which was reprinted widely.[6] Along similar lines, the theses ambiguate between the learned culture of the academy or the bishop's court, and the popular sphere of broadsheets and invective. Copies were read carefully by scholars, prelates, and ambassadors, but were also pasted on to noticeboards in public squares. Written in cryptic theological Latin, the theses were nonetheless produced also in at least one unofficial translation into the vernacular.[7]

The textuality of the theses thus crosses the boundary between written book and oral event, print and manuscript, Latin and vernacular, lay and clerical, learned and popular, open and closed, at this crucial moment in ecclesiastical and cultural history. It may well be because of, rather than despite, these textual complexities, that it was so radically successful. This is not the place for a full examination of the bibliographical problems of the theses. Instead, this paper first reclaims the image of Luther the writer above that of Luther the lonely monk. To do so, it examines what is, it seems, the earliest, and arguably also the most striking, image ever made of the posting of the theses. This image strikingly reflects the impact of this particular 'book'. Indeed, it demonstrates the way in which the theses were apprehended

---

[4] Erwin Iserloh, *Luthers Thesenanschlag: Tatsache oder Legende?* (Wiesbaden, 1962), has spawned a large bibliography in response. For a summary, see Richard Marius, *Martin Luther* (Cambridge, MA, 1999), 137–9.

[5] The context of the disputation is recounted by Ernest Schwiebert, 'The Theses and Wittenberg', in C. Meyer, ed., *Luther for an Ecumenical Age* (St Louis, MO, 1967), 120–43.

[6] Josef Benzing, *Lutherbibliographie: Verzeichnis der gedruckten Schriften Martin Luthers bis zu dessen Tod* (Baden-Baden, 1966), nos 87–9; the *Resolutiones disputationum de indulgentiarum virtute* appeared in 1518 in Wittenberg and Leipzig (ibid., nos 205–8). Klemens Honselmann, *Urfassung and Drucke der Ablaßthesen Martin Luthers und ihre Veröffentlichung* (Paderborn, 1966), gives a full description of the early imprints.

[7] A translation by Caspar Nützel was printed in Nuremberg, but does not survive. It is mentioned in letters between Luther and the Nuremberg humanist Christoph Scheurl in early 1518.

in their own time as a publication phenomenon rather than as a personal drama. It powerfully evokes the idea of the printed book as an agent of social transformation. In graphic terms, it illustrates the origins of the Reformation as a textual event.

This copper-plate engraving (Fig. 1) is from Leipzig, by the artist Conrad Grahle (active 1615–30).[8] It was produced in 1617 for the Luther *Jubel Jahr*, a self-conscious celebration of German Protestantism which proclaimed Luther's theses as the origin of the Reformation.[9] On the hundredth anniversary, 31 October 1617, the townspeople of Wittenberg marched in a procession, not unlike a Corpus Christi procession, to the door of the church to celebrate the hallowed day. A large variety of these one-sheet posters were made, in different parts of the empire and surrounding Protestant cities: examples survive from Ulm, Leipzig, Nuremberg, Strasbourg, Stettin, and elsewhere.[10] There is also a parallel version to Grahle's engraving, this time in woodcut, place and printer unknown.[11] Although there is less detail on the woodcut print, the overall design is clearly identical and must have been based on the same drawing. Both are accompanied by texts which are printed under the image: in the case of Grahle's Leipzig version, 292 rhyming couplets by Peter Kirchbach (1590–1638); on the woodcut, a prose narrative of the dream and its interpretation in German.[12]

At first sight, the engraving confirms the modern iconography of the theses. All of the elements of the Luther myth are in place, so much so that the engraving shows a considerable amount of narrative sophistication and obliquity, for all its stark grandeur. At the extreme left, the church stands massively, indeed too large for the frame, which cuts the door in half. In small letters it is marked *schloßkirch zu*

---

[8] *Göttlicher Schriftmessiger woldenckwürdiger Traum* (Leipzig, 1617). The printer was Johann Gluck.

[9] A survey of the Jubilee is given by Ruth Kastner, *Geistlicher Rauffhandel: illustrierte Flugblätter zum Reformationsjubiläum 1617* (Frankfurt, 1982).

[10] The posters are listed in full in Kastner, *Illustrierte Flugblätter*, 343-62; there is a *catalogue raisonée* of examples from the Herzog August Bibliothek in Wolfenbüttel in Wolfgang Harms, ed., *Deutsche illustrierte Flugblätter des 16. and 17. Jahrhunderts*, 4 vols (Munich, 1980–9), 2:202–33.

[11] *Göttlicher Schrifftmessiger woldenckwürdiger Traum* (n.p., 1617), described and reproduced in Harms, *Illustrierte Flugblätter*, 2:222–3. W.A. Coupe, *The German Illustrated Broadsheet in the Seventeenth Century*, 2 vols (Baden-Baden, 1966), 1:72, perhaps influenced by the archaic style, accepts the date in the chronogram of 1568, which is, however, false.

[12] See Hans Volz, 'Der Traum Kurfürst Friedrichs des Weisen vom 30./31. Oktober 1517. Eine bibliographisch-ikonographische Untersuchung', *Gutenberg Jahrbuch*, 45 (1970), 174–211.

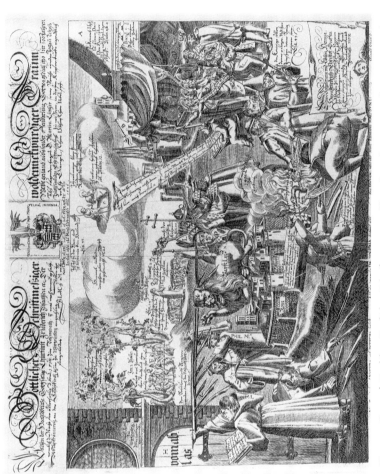

Fig. 1 Conrad Grahle, *Göttlicher Schriftmessiger woldennckewürdiger Traum* (Leipzig, 1617). Nuremberg, Germanisches Nationalmuseum, HB 51 (detail). Reproduced by permission of the Germanisches Nationalmusem.

Wittenberg. The monk's cowl is inscribed with the letters D.M.L. (Doctor Martin Luther). He holds a book in his left hand, and in his right a gargantuan quill with which he inscribes, directly into the wood of the door, in giant letters, 'VOM ABLAS' ('Of Indulgence'). The other end of the quill skewers the head of a lion (again marked, helpfully, 'Papst LEO X'); the quill goes in one ear and out the other, finally knocking the tiara off the head of the pope, who is surrounded by a useless posse of a king, a bishop, and a cardinal. Underneath, Rome stands ready to be sacked.

However, the engraving is considerably more complex than this, and follows a double narrative. Balancing the scene of revolutionary zeal on the extreme left of the picture is a scene on the far right of serene tranquillity. It is here that the reading of the image properly begins, marked by the letter (A), set in a huge canopy, under which a ruler lies sleeping. This scene explains the short-title of the engraving, 'The Dream of Frederick the Wise at Schweinitz'. The townscape of Schweinitz can be seen in the background behind the canopy (B). A date on the canopy sets the dream in the night before All Hallows' Eve, 1517, and a verse from the Book of Joel provides the clue to the meaning: 'your old men shall dream dreams, your young men shall see visions'. Frederick the Wise, Elector of Saxony, is dreaming a dream, as rulers traditionally do when they fall asleep on the eve of great events.[13] Displayed before Frederick's eyes is the grand narrative of the Reformation: the burning of heretics, the indulgence crisis, the Ninety-Five Theses, the schism of the Church. Above, a verse from Psalm 4 predicts the arrival of Luther: 'But know that the Lord hath set apart him that is godly for himself: the Lord will hear when I call unto him.' A sequence of letters is picked out in capitals: unscrambled they spell out a chronogram, DDDLLVVIIIIIII: 1617.

As the full title of the Leipzig engraving announces, it was never meant to be read as an eyewitness account of the proceedings at Wittenberg, but as a *Göttlicher Schriftmessiger woldennckwürdiger Traum*, an outlandish dream with a divine text-message. It is a full-scale prophetic Dream-Vision in the scriptural vein of Joseph or Daniel. The engraving recounts how Elector Frederick, lying in Schweinitz (A–D), dreamt not just one dream, but three rolled into one. The dream is recounted with exuberance in the prose narrative accompanying the woodcut version, with Luther playing a full part as

---

[13] Obvious scriptural parallels are Gen. 37, 40, 41, and Dan. 2.

Frederick's irrepressible daemon. Each time Frederick wakes into groggy consciousness he drops off again, and back comes the daemonic monk. There is a vivid sense of the drama of conscious and half-conscious states. Frederick has to be reassured by various interpreters of the dream that it is a revelation and not a nightmare on a European scale.

The three dreams are all different and yet the same. In one, represented just to the left and under the canopy (E–G), a monk sits at his scriptorium. From the clouds above, where can be seen the Father and the Son, the Dove of the Holy Spirit delivers a text, which flows directly into the book in Luther's lap. To the right side Luther, surrounded by apostles, presents his book in person to Frederick. This part of the dream gives Frederick the *bona fide* he needs that the monk is indeed, in the interpretation given in the woodcut prose gloss, *S. Pauli des lieben Apostels natürlicher Sohn*.[14] In the second dream (H–I), the monk is revealed as writing his script on the church door of Wittenberg, in letters so big, the text tells us, they could be read in Schweinitz (about twenty miles away). As the Elector drifts further into hallucination (K–P), he sees the feather of the quill stretching all the way to Rome, wreaking almighty havoc in its trajectory. It skewers through the head of a gigantic lion, who lets out such an unearthly scream (*so grewlich brüllete*) that it is heard not only through the city but throughout the Holy Roman Empire. Frederick, as he gropes back into consciousness, is not surprisingly apprehensive about the state of his unconscious. But before he can recover, the monk is at it again. Now Frederick is shown, in a third and final dream, the origin of the apocalyptic quill (T–X). In this sinister scene in the right foreground, a feather is being plucked from a goose. The same goose is being roasted in a fire outside the city walls. It is from this source that the pile of pens being stocked at Luther's feet on the left of the picture is derived, ready for him to wage war in Wittenberg.

Although the Dream of Frederick is mentioned in one or two sermons before 1617, there is no record of it before the third quarter of the sixteenth century.[15] It is not described in any of the early sources on Luther such as Melanchthon or Johannes Cochlaeus. There is a nice reference to it in one of the plays performed for the Jubilee, *Indulgentiarius confusus*, by Martin Rinckhart, where Friedrich proudly

---

[14] 'Somnium Friderici sapientis Electoris Saxoniae' (woodcut prose-text), col. 1.
[15] Kastner, *Illustrierte Flugblätter*, 281–2.

tells 'Mein Wundertrawm' to Luther himself.[16] More significant is the afterlife of the dream in the form both of the engraving and its iconography. The engraving itself was reprinted later in the seventeenth century and, in a cruder version, into the middle of the eighteenth. In a curious turn on the central image of Luther writing on the church door, a 1724 emblem book took the motif of Frederick's dream, but replaces Luther with Christ writing on the heart of the believer.[17]

The dream narrative of these engravings, like all good dream narratives, is clever about the conditions of truth and fiction. It bears some curious claims to authenticity. In a Latin postscript to the woodcut, one D.K. declares himself to have transcribed the dream from a manuscript in the possession of Magister Bartholomäus Schönbach of Rochlitz. The manuscript is the autograph of one Antonio Musa; Musa heard the story from none other than Georg Spalatin himself. Spalatin, as any Lutheran knows immediately, was the Elector's secretary, and a correspondent of Luther from even before the Indulgence crisis: he provides the ultimate imprimatur of authenticity. D.K. reverently copied the manuscript in 1591 – on the eve of All Saints, naturally.

It is, as the modern scholars say, pure conceit.[18] But this conceit is typical of the engraving as a whole. It is a telling example of the way the engraving continually rides the edge between historicity and prophesying, evidence and fabulation, dream and primal scene. The frame is crammed full of verifiable historical detail, presented with a considerable concern for accuracy and, more importantly, recognizability. The facial portraits of Frederick, Luther, Melanchthon, Erasmus, Pope Leo, are carefully based on original sources. The figure of John Tetzel and the scene of indulgence-selling, the cityscapes, the braziers and wood-cutting, the elaborate use of headgear to signify rank and identity, all give the scene the mark of truth.

---

[16] Quoted in ibid., 284.

[17] Ibid., 287; Harms, *Deutsche illustrierte Flugblätter*, 2:222. A copy of Grahle was printed in Strasbourg in 1668 for the 150th anniversary; see Wolfgang Harms, *Illustrierte Flugblätter aus den Jahrhunderten der Reformation and der Glaubenskämpfe* (Coburg, 1983), 90–1. A full bibliography of versions of the 'Dream' is given in Kastner, *Illustrierte Flugblätter*, 353. The 19th-century iconography surrounding the theses, beginning in 1807 with Johann Hummel (1769–1852), is described in Joachim Kruse, ed., *Luthers Leben in Illustrationen des 18. and 19. Jahrhunderts* (Coburg, 1980), 65, 124, 160, 193.

[18] Nevertheless, all of the protagonists in this scholarly ruse can be identified; Harms, *Deutsche illustrierte Flugblätter*, 2:222.

Above all, the church door of Wittenberg, and the massive, upright, unbending figure of Luther himself, stand out in their brooding, material presence. The posting of the theses, like the huge gothic letters *vom ablas*, is established as ineradicable visible fact.

At the same time, the frame of reference is visionary and apocalyptic. The accumulation of contingently knowable events is grafted in every detail to a narrative that is consciously ideological and iconoclastic. Perhaps the key example of this is the burning of the Czech martyr John Hus, which is placed programmatically in the lower foreground, in the immediate line of view of the imagined spectator. This scene shows an interpretative economy which is highly allusive to the central theme of Luther's prophetic status. Hus is not shown: he is the one historical figure in the picture who is given an entirely allegorical iconic status. He does not need to be shown, because everybody knows that Hus is a goose, since Hus is the Czech word for 'goose'. Everybody knows it because Luther had made the reference himself. It is a strain of prophetic thinking in the engraving which can be traced to the master himself.[19] An old prophecy stated that a goose would be burned, but in a hundred years he would be replaced by a white swan who would fulfil God's will. Luther retold the story on more than one occasion: interestingly, one of them is his preface to the Book of Daniel, in a passage on the interpretation of visionary dreams. The goose/swan trope is found almost immediately in early Lutheran iconography, and can be seen still in other early seventeenth-century examples.[20] In the 1617 Leipzig engraving, its use is brilliantly compact: a goose is roasted, but from his wing a feather is taken. The goose feather is of course the essential ingredient of penmaking (indeed, *Gansefeder* is the German word for a pen). The transference from Hus to Luther takes place not only in the metamorphosis of the swan, but in a direct physical lineage from the martyrdom of the heretic to the triumph of the word in the pen of God's writer. At the same time, the reference completes the chronology or chronography which is central to the picture's occasion. One hundred years after Hus dies, Luther's Theses are given their

---

[19] WA 30/iii:387. The woodcut also makes a reference to another prophecy (concerning Frederick the Wise) alluded to by Luther in 1521 (WA 8:561).

[20] Jutta Strehle gives a comprehensive survey of the motif in *Luther mit dem Schwan* (Wittenberg, 1996), 81–118. The swan was a common figure in commemorative medals produced in 1617: see R.W. Scribner, *Popular Culture and Popular Movements in Reformation Germany* (1987), 343, 345.

miraculous birth, and one hundred years after this, it is celebrated in this image.[21] The Protestant theocracy is established *in saecula saeculorum*.

This brings us to what seems to be the most striking iconographic feature of the engraving, one which makes it an intensely interesting index for the reception and meaning of the Ninety-Five Theses themselves. The picture is saturated with images of writing as a medium, and of its physical modes of production. Luther's pen spans more than half of the total frame. It bisects the image, cutting across the line of vision as brutally as it pierces the lion's contorted head. It is an image full of the overbearing presence of Luther, but most of all of Luther as writer. Indeed, even he is dwarfed by his pen. The prose-text accompanying the woodcut, too, is mesmerized by this '*lange Schreibfeder*' and the path it drives through Frederick's dream. The pen is the unstoppable engine of Reformation. In a strange pastoral scene in the left background of the picture, the pope and his prelates sit with the giant pen across their laps, hapless as to what to do with it. The pen provided by the martyred Hus/goose is declared to be *unzerbrechlich*, unbreakable. Its mark is permanent, indelible. The rest of the scene is littered with spare quills. They lie at Luther's feet, where an assistant is helping to gather Luther some more. The resources of writing are in endless supply: '*unzehlich viel andere Schreibfedern hier zu Wittenberg gewachsen*' ('countless more quillpens are provided here to Wittenberg').[22]

Further warrant of the power of writing is given by the way that the copperplate image itself swarms with physical texts. Seventeen scriptural citations, in the German text of Luther's Bible, are placed around the engraving, giving it context and meaning. They provide the message contained within the image with its endorsement. Some are illustrative, such as the text from Joel about the old men dreaming dreams. Others are exemplary and epiphanic, such as the text which lies in the middle of the cloud in the centre of the picture: 'Heaven and Earth shall pass away, but my words will not pass away.' Of considerable interest are those which pertain to the figure of Luther himself. On the page in front of him as he writes on the door is a text from Paul's letter to the Ephesians. In the book which he holds as the

---

[21] The Grahle engraving proclaims this chronology in graphic form by containing three chronograms, 1416 [sic], 1517, 1617.

[22] 'Somnium Friderici sapientis Electoris Saxoniae', col. 2.

scripture flows down from heaven to meet him is a text even closer to the heart of the Lutheran canon: Romans 3. On the shaft of the pen itself is a text from Judges 5, which manages to conjoin in remarkable juxtaposition the iconic status of Luther as the divinely inspired writer with the physical image of the pen itself: '*von Sebulon sind Regierer geworden durch die Schreibfeder*' ('Out of Zebulun come they that wield the pen of the writer'). But the scriptural citations have more than a textual presence. They are part of the visual grammar of the picture, so much so that the woodcut version, which is pictorially almost identical, looks denuded and almost simplistic without them. The textual imprints which float between the images render a physical presence to writing itself as a medium. This is a world invaded by, incorporated with, texts.

In other Jubel Jahr *Flugblätter*, too, Luther is commonly shown with a book.[23] In another example from Leipzig, again the work of Grahle, Luther is portrayed as a monk standing in a monastery doorway, which can be presumed to be Wittenberg.[24] Outside the walls Tetzel, his head buzzing with hornets, skulks off followed by dogs wearing cardinals' caps. Luther is being attacked by a pope, this time portrayed as a griffin wearing a tiara. Luther holds a book in his left hand, bearing the simple text 'SCRUTAMINI SCRIPTURAS'. In his right he holds a torch, which the griffin in vain attempts to extinguish by vomiting.

Luther and the book provide a central iconographic figure of the 1617 Jubilee. At the same time the book is connected inextricably with violence. Here the pen is used as a shield against the draconian pope. In a Stettin woodcut bearing the epigraph *Tandem triumphat veritas*, Luther stands on a book, bearing a shield and sword of truth, with the papal regalia crushed underneath and Tetzel fleeing for his life.[25] The pope, once more a lion, is lying prone, crushed beneath the weight of Luther's book, skewered once more by a quill, this time through the sockets of both eyes.

[23] For instance, the examples in Harms, *Deutsche illustrierte Flugblätter*, 2:203 (Ulm, 1616), 211 (Nuremberg?, 1617), 217 (Amsterdam, date unknown), 219 (Nuremberg, 1617), 221 (place unknown, 1617), 225 (Leipzig, 1617), 227 (Stettin, 1617), 229 (Stettin, 1617), 233 (place unknown, 1618).

[24] *In Lucis evangelicae auspiciis divi Martini Lutheri* (Leipzig, 1617). The design is signed 'Johann Deperr'. There is a description and reproduction in Harms, *Deutsche illustrierte Flugblätter*, 2:224–5. A cruder version, in reverse, of the same design occurs in a woodcut by Johan Bader (Stettin, 1617).

[25] *Emblema auff das Erste Evangelische Jubel Jahr* (Stettin, 1617), described and reproduced in Harms, *Deutsche illustrierte Flugblätter*, 2:228–9.

Most of all, Grahle's 'Dream of Frederick the Wise' is remarkable for its extreme zest for violence, for violence as transcendence. The central image is of the lion's head impaled like a kebab on the quill's point. The phallic energy of this primal scene hardly needs stating. The connection between writing and violence is made more widely significatory by the quills which bristle all over the picture. These are weapons close to hand, and can be plucked at will. The iconography is central to the image's message. The violently penetrative pen is a witness to the perceived power of the letter. God wages revolution through writing, through texts, through books.

The engraving is witness in its every trace to the stupendous power of Luther as writer, and of writing as a medium. All of this energy and violence is then inflected back into the historical moment which forms the overt subject of the engraving and of the festival which it is produced to celebrate: the act of writing and publication contained in the Theses themselves. In a brilliant but also particularly brutal visual trope, the sharp point of the quill is wielded by the monk to incise his giant letters directly into the wood of the door. By this means, the engraver creates a graphic icon of the historical moment of revolutionary writing.

With hindsight, the Reformation has come to be seen as inextricably connected with the coming of the printed book. Although the relationship between the revolution in religion and the revolution in media has sometimes been overstated, there can be no doubt that the book played a powerful part in this decisive moment in Church history. Luther's own extraordinary output as an individual producer of books on an industrial scale transformed Germany as a centre of print as well as a centre of the new religion. As a result the obscure town of Wittenberg became, for a time, one of the cultural capitals of Europe. The role of the Ninety-Five Theses as a prototype for the cultural force of print has become obscured by the perhaps more anecdotal question of whether or when Luther nailed them to the church door. The 1617 image by Conrad Gahle, by contrast, makes the inscription on the door part of a much wider history. It acknowledges how the story of Luther and the book, and of the Church and the book in the sixteenth century, are caught in the same violent history.

University of Sussex

'THE GOOD OLD WAY': PRAYER BOOK PROTESTANTISM IN THE 1640s AND 1650s

by JUDITH MALTBY

Between 1640 and 1642 the Church of England collapsed, its leaders reviled and discredited, its structures paralysed, its practices if not yet proscribed, at least inhibited. In the years that followed, yet worse was to befall it. And yet in every year of its persecution after 1646, new shoots sprang up out of the fallen timber: bereft of episcopal leadership, lacking any power of coercion, its observances illegal, anglicanism thrived. As memories of the 1630s faded and were overlaid by the tyrannies of the 1640s . . . the deeper rhythms of the Kalendar and the ingrained perfections of Cranmer's liturgies bound a growing majority together.[1]

PROFESSOR John Morrill, quoted above, has rightly identified a set of historiographical contradictions about the Stuart Church in a series of important articles.[2] Historians have until recently paid little attention to the positive and popular elements of conformity to the national Church of England in the period before the civil war. The lack of interest in conformity has led to a seventeenth-century version of the old Whig view of the late medieval Church: the Church of England is presented as a complacent, corrupt, and clericalist institution, 'ripe' – as the English Church in the early sixteenth century was 'ripe' – to be purified by reformers. However, if this was the case,

---

[1] John Morrill, 'The attack on the Church of England in the Long Parliament', in idem, *The Nature of the English Revolution: Essays by John Morrill* (1993), 89. I am grateful to Elizabeth Clarke, Arnold Hunt, Elizabeth Macfarlane, and Alison Shell for comments on this essay.

[2] 'The religious context of the English Civil War' (1984); 'The attack on the Church of England in the Long Parliament' (1984); 'The Church in England 1642–1649' (1982), republished in Morrill, *Nature of the English Revolution*. See also the introduction to that volume, 'Introduction: England's wars of religion'. There are useful discussions of the Church of England in the 1640s and 1650s in John Spurr, *The Restoration Church of England 1646–1689* (New Haven, CT, 1991), ch. 1, and Robert Ashton, *Counter-Revolution: the Second Civil War and Its Origins, 1646–8* (New Haven, CT, 1994), ch. 7. The most thorough treatment in print of the Church of England in this period, however, remains W.A. Shaw, *A History of the English Church During the Civil Wars and Under the Commonwealth 1640–1660*, 2 vols (1900).

how does one account for the durable commitment to the Prayer Book demonstrated during the 1640s and 1650s and the widespread – but not universal – support for the 'return' of the Church of England in 1660? This paper contributes to the larger exploration of the theme of 'the Church and the book' by addressing in particular the continued use by clergy and laity alike of one 'book' – the Book of Common Prayer – after its banning by Parliament during the years of civil war and the Commonwealth.

* * *

In April 1660, three weeks before the Declaration of Breda and proclamation of Charles II, Easter, a forbidden Festival, was celebrated in most parish churches up and down the country. It was the collapse of the old church which presaged the downfall of the monarchy· and it was to be the church's survival which was to herald the Restoration.[3]

These are remarkable claims about a Church which in its pre-1642 historiography was dominated until recently by widespread acceptance of the critique of the godly.[4] We can speak of a set of religious attitudes, practices, and beliefs which found authenticity, comfort, and renewal in conformity to the official and lawful forms of the Christian religion as offered by the Church of England. As civil war descended on the English portion of the British Isles, one could speak of a religious tradition which was firm in its loyalty to the Church of England, expressed principally in support for the liturgy and episcopacy, but unhappy about the Laudian innovations of the 1630s. This tradition found a voice in a series of petitions in support of episcopacy and the liturgy to the Long Parliament in the months leading up to the outbreak of the civil war. Although it is reasonable to assume that the tribulations of the middle of the century created marriages of convenience between Laudians and Prayer Book Protestants – indeed redrew some boundaries – it would be a mistake to see the views under

---

[3] Morrill, 'Attack on the Church of England', 89–90.

[4] For a historiographical critique, see Judith Maltby, *Prayer Book and People in Elizabethan and Early Stuart England* (Cambridge, 1998), 1–19. The work of Professor David Underdown is also critical to our concerns. Perhaps more than any other historian, Underdown has uncovered the *popular* elements of conservative or traditional politics in the 1640s–50s and has alerted us to the existence of considerable attachment to the 'Old Church', to the Prayer Book and Church festivals: see idem, *Revel, Riot and Rebellion: Popular Politics and Culture in England 1603–1660* (Oxford, 1987), esp. chs 5, 8, 9, 10.

examination in this essay as evidence of the 'popularity' of pre-civil war Laudianism. As Professor Robert Ashton has rightly remarked, 'Royalism was in fact a far more common Anglican characteristic [in the late 1640s] than ritualism.' Placing the early Stuart Church in a longer-term perspective of the events of the turbulent middle decades of the seventeenth century troubles some historiographical waters and raises some important questions about the popular life of the Church of England on either side of 1642.[5]

What to call the set of religious convictions explored in this essay is more than a problem of semantics or an excuse for pedantry. Terms like 'Prayer Book Protestants', 'Church of England loyalists' and 'followers of the "Old Church"', however long-winded, are to be preferred to the term 'Anglicans'. To single out Prayer Book loyalists as *the* Anglicans' before the Restoration begs enormous scholarly and historical questions as it treats the emerging multi-denominational character of English Christianity after 1660 as a foregone conclusion.[6] Further, it implies 'ownership' of a Church by particular groups within it and 'unchurches' sets of individuals who were as much a part of the *ecclesia anglicana* as those retrospectively canonized as the 'true Anglicans', as Professor Diarmaid MacCulloch has so rightly warned us, by the highly successful revisionists of the Oxford Movement.[7]

---

[5] Ashton, *Counter-Revolution*, 230, though see below, 253–5, for caution about the shades of Royalism amongst Church of England loyalists. Maltby, *Prayer Book and People*, ch. 3; eadem, 'Petitions for Episcopacy and the Book of Common Prayer 1641–1642', in Stephen Taylor, ed., *From Cranmer to Davidson: a Church of England Miscellany*, Church of England Record Society, 7 (Woodbridge, 2000), 105–67; David Underdown, *A Freeborn People: Politics and the Nation in Seventeenth-Century England* (Oxford, 1996), 56–7. Cf. Christopher Haigh, 'The Church of England, the Catholics and the people', in Peter Marshall, ed., *The Impact of the English Reformation 1500–1640* (1997), 253–4 (first published 1984); Alexandra Walsham, 'The parochial roots of Laudianism revisited: Catholics, Anti-Calvinists and "Parish Anglicans" in early Stuart England', *JEH*, 49 (1998), 620–51.

[6] By the end of the eighteenth century the range of religious options available created, despite the existence of two established Churches in Britain, a pluralism more akin to the new United States than to much of the rest of Europe: James Obelkevich, 'Religion', in F.M.L. Thompson, ed., *Cambridge Social History of Britain 1750–1950* (Cambridge, 1990), 311 and passim.

[7] Diarmaid MacCulloch, 'The myth of the English Reformation', *JBS*, 30 (1991), 1–19. See also Maltby, *Prayer Book and People*, 233–7; Peter Lake and Michael Questier, 'Introduction', in Peter Lake and Michael Questier, eds, *Conformity and Orthodoxy in the English Church, c.1560–1660* (Woodbridge, 2000), xix. However, see e.g. Christopher Haigh, *English Reformations: Religion, Politics and Society under the Tudors* (Oxford, 1993); Walsham, 'Parochial roots'; Morrill, 'Church in England'; Ashton, *Counter-Revolution*, for the use of the word 'Anglican' in this period.

If we may now accept the existence of English Christians before 1642 whose religious identities and loyalties were formed and became *in*formed by conformity to the established Church of England, yet can be properly distinguished from the Laudian agenda, a simple but important question emerges. What happened to that set of religious convictions in the face of a Parliamentary onslaught? In the 1640s, Parliament embarked on a series of legislation which achieved far more than the taking away of the Church of England's historic privileges and placing it on an equal footing with its emerging competitors in the religious marketplace. Rather, it was not disestablishment which was the aim but the proscription and suppression of what was to many the Church of England's most defining and best loved features: the Book of Common Prayer, the church year, and episcopacy.[8] To call the suppression of the Church of England systematic would imply greater consensus and coherence among Parliamentarians, even amongst moderate presbyterians, than is likely. The attack on the Church of England managed to be both haphazard and thorough. While recent criticisms that too much coherence has been ascribed to pre-1642 Prayer Book Protestantism need to be taken seriously, it is nonetheless striking to note the specific and carefully chosen targets of the contemporary Parliamentary reformers: the Prayer Book, its calendar, and episcopal polity.[9]

* * *

The theological case against the Book of Common Prayer centred on more than concerns about its residual popery. To some more precise Protestants, the very idea of a *set* form of liturgy was unacceptable, though this was not a view held in any sense by all we might categorize as 'puritan'. Parliamentary reformers were faced with a problem not shared by the Tudor architects of the Church of England. Thomas Cranmer saw positive good in *set* forms of liturgy, though he saw many errors in the medieval rites that the Prayer Book replaced. One of the objectives of Common Prayer, after all, was to provide uniformity of practice throughout the country. The group of divines and others brought together as the Westminster Assembly by parliamentary

[8] Morrill, 'Church in England', 149–54; Shaw, *English Church*, 1:337–57; Paul Hardacre, *The Royalists During the Puritan Revolution* (The Hague, 1956), 39–44; C.H. Firth and R.S. Rait, eds, *Acts and Ordinances of the Interregnum 1642–1660*, 3 vols (1911), 1:582, 607.
[9] Lake and Questier, 'Introduction', xv–xvi. Cf. Marshall, *Impact of the English Reformation*, 232–3.

ordinance in 1643 were divided on this very notion of 'set' and 'free' prayer. To some of the moderate presbyterian view, their original intention was to reform, not suppress, the Book of Common Prayer. To more radical Protestants, however, any notion of set forms of public prayer smacked too much of incantation rather than of intercession. In the end, the result owed much to Scottish presence and influence in the Assembly.[10]

A Directory for the Public Worship of God was first authorized for use in 1645 and was largely what it proclaimed itself to be: not a liturgy but a set of *directions* for the conduct of public worship in England.[11] Given the abuse heaped upon the authorized liturgy for decades by the godly, the *Directory*'s 'Preface' was surprisingly civil and even respectful of the landfalls that the Prayer Book represented on the larger journey to a properly reformed Church. 'The Preface' maintained that the Book of Common Prayer was, without a doubt, an improvement on the 'Vain, Erroneous, Superstitious and Idolatrous' worship of the medieval Church.

> This occasioned many Godly and Learned men to rejoyce much in the Book of Common-Prayer at time set forth; Because the Masse, and the rest of the Latine-Service being removed, the Publique Worship was celebrated in our own Tongue.[12]

However useful in the early days of the Reformation, the Prayer Book had proved itself to be at odds with many other Reformed Churches, full of popish ceremonies, and a stumbling block to otherwise honest Christians who could not in conscience conform. The sheer familiarity of the Prayer Book turned it into something

> no better than an Idol by many Ignorant and Superstituous people, who pleasing themselves in their presence at that Service, and their Lip-labour in bearing a part in it, have thereby hardened

---

[10] Horton Davis, *The Worship of the English Puritans* (Glasgow, 1948), 98–114. For a detailed discussion of the formation of the *Directory*, see Bryan Spinks, *Freedom or Order? The Eucharistic Liturgy in English Congregationalism 1645–1980* (Allison Park, PA, 1984), 14–15, 31–51 (I am grateful to Prof. Spinks for his assistance); Peter King, 'The reasons for the abolition of the Book of Common Prayer in 1645', *JEH*, 21 (1970), 335–7; Shaw, *English Church*, 1:337–49.

[11] Morrill, 'Church in England', 152–3; Shaw, *English Church*, 1:353–4.

[12] *A Directory for the Public Worship of God, Throughout the Three Kingdoms of England, Scotland and Ireland* (1645), 1–2.

themselves in their ignorance and carelesnesse of saving knowledge and true piety.[13]

Further, the *Directory*'s authors denied that they were motivated by a
'love [of] Novelty'. They also strongly denied that their work represented any 'intention to disparage our first Reformers' who, if they were
still alive, 'The Preface' maintained, would of course be on the side of
further reform. Engaging in a difficult balancing act, they acknowledged that the Edwardian Reformers were

> Excellent Instruments raised by God to begin the purging and
> building of His House, and desire they may be had of us and
> posterity in everlasting Remembrance, with thankfulnesse and
> honour.

But that was then, this is now: providence called 'upon us for further
Reformation'.[14]

To those more familiar with the Prayer Book, the *Directory* reads
like a set of stage directions without the speaking parts. E.C. Ratcliff
notes that the *Directory* needs to be seen as a compromise between
moderates and radicals in the Westminster Assembly; nonetheless it
was largely a victory for the latter as he notes that the *Directory* was
'not so much a prayer book as a rubric book'.[15] It provided the
minister with guidance on what he should say at various services but
almost never provided the actual words. Significant exceptions to this
general rule include the words to be used at the precise moment of
baptism, which are firmly Trinitarian, and the marriage vows.[16]
Nonetheless, the use of godparents in baptism and the ring in
marriage – both prohibited practices in the *Directory* – appears to
have been widespread.[17]

---

[13] Ibid., 4.

[14] Ibid., 6. Petitions defending the Prayer Book early in the Long Parliament made much
use of the honoured status of the Edwardian bishops and martyrs who championed the
Prayer Book: Maltby, *Prayer Book and People*, ch. 3; eadem, 'Petitions', 113–67.

[15] E.C. Ratcliff, 'Puritan alternatives to the Prayer Book: the *Directory* and Richard
Baxter's *Reformed Liturgy*', in Michael Ramsey, ed., *The English Prayer Book 1549–1662* (1963),
64; Davis, *Worship*, 127–42; Spinks, *Freedom or Order?*, 31–6.

[16] *Directory*, 45, 62–3. Ironically it paraphrases the Prayer Book in several places. For
example, in the directions for baptism the minister is reminded that those baptized are
'bound to fight against the Devill, the World and the Flesh' – a paraphrase of the Book of
Common Prayer (ibid., 42, see also 49–50).

[17] David Cressy, *Birth, Marriage and Death: Ritual, Religion, and the Life-Cycle in Tudor and
Stuart England* (Oxford, 1997), 153, 347.

We await a major study of the English *Directory*, but it does seem not to have been a best-seller. There is little evidence in church-wardens' accounts for its purchase across a geographically diverse set of counties.[18] There must have been considerable confusion in the localities, however, as in 1648 six clergymen in Cambridgeshire were indicted for 'refusing to administer the sacrament but according to the Directory'.[19] Simply, the *Directory* appears not to have met the fundamental needs of many English Christians. Sir Henry Turner, the Speaker of the House of Commons, when introducing the Uni-formity Bill in 1662, spoke for many when he attacked the suppression of the Book of Common Prayer and its replacement by the *Directory*. He remarked that the Prayer Book was 'decried as superstitious, and in lieu thereof nothing, or worse than nothing was introduced'.[20] It has been noted that in the post-Reformation Church, one of the attractive things about the Prayer Book to the laity was that it curtailed overly enthusiastic clergy from endlessly chopping and changing the church service as the fancy took them.[21] To many Prayer Book Protestants the *Directory* must have looked like the worst of all possible worlds: it prohibited many popular rituals of the reformed English rite while at the same time giving ministers far too much liberty in their verbal expression. The Prayer Book may have smacked of popery to some, but the *Directory* was itself intensely clerical. Apart from psalm singing, active participation in the service for the laity was virtually eliminated. Even the Lord's Prayer, if it was to be said, was to be said by the minister alone.[22] The 'sacred dialogue' between clergy and people – the disparaged 'lip-labour' of ordinary men and women which marked conformist worship – was firmly rejected.[23] In the interests of freeing up the Holy Spirit, the laity were now not to be spared the full blast – in Richard Hooker's cutting phrase – of those 'voluntary dictates proceeding from' a

---

[18] Based on my survey of extant Cheshire churchwardens' accounts; Morrill, 'The Church in England', 152–3, 156, 164–7; Linda York, '"In dens and caves": the survival of Anglicanism during the rule of the Saints, 1640–1660' (Auburn University, AL, Ph.D. thesis, 1999), 100–1; Underdown, *Revel*, 255–6; Cressy, *Birth*, 175; King, 'Reasons for Abolition', 337; Ashton, *Counter-Revolution*, 230–1.

[19] Morrill, 'Church in England', 168.

[20] *Journal of the House of Lords*, 11:470.

[21] Maltby, *Prayer Book and People*, 44–5.

[22] Ratcliff, 'Puritan alternatives', 72.

[23] Parishioners took offence when clergy did not allow them to make the authorized responses in the Prayer Book. Maltby, *Prayer Book and People*, 40–4.

clergyman's 'extemporal wit'.[24] No wonder Sir Henry Turner saw the *Directory* as 'worse than nothing'.

* * *

Despite the prolonged attack over several generations by elements within the established Church, the Book of Common Prayer proved harder to sink than might have been expected from the puritan critique of it. Evidence for the liturgy's buoyancy abounds, and despite its prohibited status, some English Christians continued to use it for worship. Further, the Prayer Book provided more than a framework for the hour or two spent inside a church building for public worship or a structure for household use and the solitary prayer of individuals. Through Morning and Evening Prayer it gave shape to the day; though one suspects, apart from a few exceptions, that Cranmer's intention that the offices become the daily prayer of all the people of God rather than simply a monastic and clerical elite was never realized.[25] The Prayer Book helped to mark immense and universal moments in the life cycle, such as birth and death. Common Prayer also structured and shaped the year, providing days and seasons of solemnity and celebration. Although one may see it as a very impoverished cousin to the riches of the fifteenth-century world portrayed in *The Stripping of the Altars*, nonetheless the Prayer Book provided over thirty saints' days and other festivals of the Christian year based on the life of Christ.[26] Yet another popish remnant in the eyes of some, holy days were banned shortly after the book which directed their use.[27]

Provision of Prayer Book rites was experienced in this period as, at best, episodic. The layman John Evelyn, failing in 1652 to find any services at all on Christmas Day, at other times succeeded in finding

[24] From Book V.xxv.4 in Richard Hooker, *Of the Laws of Ecclesiastical Polity*, in *The Works of Richard Hooker*, ed. W. Speed Hill, 7 vols (Cambridge, MA, 1977), 2:116.

[25] See George Guiver, *Company of Voices: Daily Prayer and the People of God* (1988), 115–26.

[26] However impoverished the Protestant liturgy was, compared to its late medieval counterpart, Eamon Duffy has admitted that 'Cranmer's sombrely magnificent prose, read week by week, entered and possessed their minds, and became the fabric of their prayer, the utterance of their most solemn and vulnerable moments': idem, *The Stripping of the Altars: Traditional Religion in England 1400–1580* (New Haven, CT, and London, 1992), 593.

[27] On 8 June 1647 Parliament abolished church festivals, though the *Directory* had already ordered their extinction: Firth and Rait, *Acts and Ordinances*, 1:954, 607. A further proclamation against the observance of Christmas was issued on 24 Dec. 1652: R.S. Steele, *A Bibliography of Royal Proclamations of the Tudor and Stuart Sovereigns 1485–1714*, 2 vols (Oxford, 1910), 1:360 (no. 2981).

churches in London itself which used the banned Prayer Book. On another Christmas Day, in 1657, Evelyn and other devotees of the Prayer Book were attacked by Parliamentary troopers. He recorded in his famous diary:

> I went with my wife &c: to Lond: to celebrate Christmas day. . . . Sermon Ended, as [the minister] was giving us the holy Sacrament, The Chapell was surrounded with Souldiers: All the Communicants and Assembly surpriz'd & kept Prisoners by them. . . . [They] examined me, why contrarie to an Ordinance made that none should any longer observe the superstitious time of the Nativity (so esteem'd by them) I durst offend, & particularly be at Common prayers, which they told me was but the Masse in English.

Evelyn and his fellow communicants then proceeded to make their Christmas communions under testing circumstances.

> These wretched miscreants, held their muskets against us as we came up to receive the Sacred Elements, as if they would have shot us at the Altar, but yet suffering us to finish the Office of Communion, as perhaps [it was] not in their Instructions what they should do in case they found us in that Action.[28]

Coolness in the face of armed troopers was sometimes required of the clergy as well. According to his contemporary biographer, John Hackett (later Bishop of Coventry and Lichfield in 1661) calmly continued to read divine service even when a Parliamentary soldier of the Earl of Essex had a pistol pointed at him. Hackett and another future bishop, George Bull (consecrated to St David's in 1705), each committed to memory the funeral service and the baptismal services respectively so that they would appear to be praying extempore. The ruse worked, as this account of a funeral of a prominent puritan conducted by Hackett at the end of the Interregnum relates:

> there being a great concourse of men of the same fanatical principles [as the deceased], when the company heard all delivered by him [Hackett] without book, and, with free readiness, and

---

[28] 'Christmas day no sermon anywhere, so observed it at home, the next day we went to Lewisham, where was an honest divine preach'd on 21 Matt: 9 celebrating the Incarnation, for on the day before, no Churches were permitted to meet &c; to that horrid passe were they come': John Evelyn, *The Diary of John Evelyn*, ed. E.S. de Beer, 6 vols (Oxford, 1955), 3:78–9, 203–4.

profound gravity . . . they were strangely surprised and affected, professing that they had never heard a more suitable exhortation, or a more edifying exercise even from the very best and most precious men of their own persuasion!

The assembled godly were aghast when Hackett revealed to them that not one syllable had been his own and how 'all was taken word for word out of the very office ordained for that purpose in the poor contemptible Book of Common Prayer'.[29] Examples of such Prayer Book use can be multiplied from around the country.[30]

The attack on the festivals of the Christian year was perhaps one of the Parliamentary government's greatest misreadings of the religious sensibilities of many English people.[31] Indeed, not only in England, but in seventeenth-century Virginia it has been recently noted how popular the reformed calendar was among the colonists – providing not only a system for dating letters but even for attending Church.[32] It is worth remembering in current discussions about secularism that there was a debate in the seventeenth century as to how 'religious' a festival Christmas was as well. Richard Baxter was clear that the observance of Christmas had no place in a properly reformed Church. In a sermon preached in 1657 he remarked:

> Tomorrow . . . is the day called Christmass day, and many days called Holy days do follow it. . . . There is no proof that ever I saw . . . that the Church observed any of these days, of many hundred years after Christ.[33]

---

[29] Thomas Plume, *An Account of the Life and Death of the Right Reverend Father in God, John Hackett, Late Lord Bishop of Lichfield and Coventry*, ed. Mackenzie M.C. Walcott (1865), 64–6. This incident dates from just after the Restoration but illustrates the point. John Evelyn was able to give his mother-in-law a traditional Prayer Book funeral in 1652: Cressy, *Birth*, 416.

[30] Morrill, 'Church in England', 164–8; Spurr, *Restoration Church*, 16–17; Ashton, *Counter-Revolution*, 230–4, 247, 259–61.

[31] Ibid., 238–41.

[32] Virginians modified the Prayer Book calendar as well to take into account the different rhythms of the colony's agriculture and of its premier crop, tobacco. Local events led to the development of additional days along the lines of Armada Day or the Fifth of November, such as the designation of 22 March as a day of thanksgiving for the deliverance of the colony from an Indian massacre in the 1620s. The Assembly ordered that day 'be yeerly Solemnized as [a] holydaye': Edward L. Bond, 'Religion in seventeenth-century Anglican Virginia: myth, persuasion, and the creation of an American identity' (Louisiana State University, Ph.D. thesis, 1995), 188–95. For more on colonial 'Anglicanism', see below, 244–5.

[33] Cited in Geoffrey Nuttall, *Richard Baxter* (1965), 54. Baxter did defend the keeping of

Yet to many contemporaries, clergy and laity alike, the government's continued observance of national 'feast days' such as Armada Day or the discovery of the Gunpowder Plot contained a bitter irony.[34] The laywoman, Elizabeth Newell, approved of a theological critique of this state of affairs in a series of poems she collected in honour of the banned feast of Christmas from 1655 into the 1660s. The following poem purports to be written for Christmas Day 1658:

> What! the messias born, and shall a day
> Bethought to much expensiveness to pay
> To that memorial; shall an Anniversie
> Be kept with ostentation to rehearse
> A mortal princes birth-day, or defeat
> An Eighty Eight, or powder plots defeat[?]
> . . . . . .
> And shall we venture to exterminate
> And starve at once the memory and date
> Of Christ incarnate, where in such a store
> Of joy to mortals lay, as never before
> The sun beheld, a Treasury of Bliss,
> The birth day of the world as well as his[?]

To Elizabeth Newell, her opponents lacked any proper understanding of Christology, or indeed, a proper understanding of the relationship of the incarnation to salvation: 'Ingrateful Man; It was for only thee/ And for thy Restitution, that he/ Did stoop to wear thy raggs . . . was content/ Thus to affirme thy nature'.[35] It should be noted how *theologically* informed are the poems she collected, not simply 'spiritual'.

Discussion of the tribulations of John Evelyn, John Hackett, Elizabeth Newell, and other members of the gentry and clergy could, however, give the impression that adherence to the Prayer Book was a preoccupation of the better sort and the religious professionals. On the contrary, it has been shown that fidelity to the

---

Easter Day, as the evidence was much stronger for its observation by the earliest Christians, and commended the celebration of the Lord's Supper on that day: ibid., 55.

[34] Evelyn, *Diary*, 3:47–8, 144, 235, for Gunpowder Plot celebrations in the 1650s; Ronald Hutton, *The Rise and Fall of Merry England: the Ritual Year 1400–1700* (Oxford, 1994), 212, 221–2.

[35] New Haven, CT, Beinecke Library, Osborn MS b.49: Elizabeth Newell, 'Collection of devotional verse, *c.* 1655–1668', 12–13. I am grateful to Dr Elizabeth Clarke for bringing this manuscript to my attention and for other helpful discussions concerning Newell.

liturgy was also to be found further down the social ladder. In March 1648, violence erupted in Blandford in Dorset when a group of locals rescued a minister who had been arrested for using the proscribed liturgy.[36] Support for the Prayer Book was an element in the complex set of component parts that made up the popular uprisings by the Clubmen Associations in counties like Dorset and Wiltshire.[37] Newell's preservation of theologically sophisticated verse gives expression to views held more widely across the social spectrum. In 1647 indignation turned to violence in Canterbury when local people resisted the Kent Committee's attempt to suppress Christmas celebrations. The few shopkeepers who did open on Christmas Day were attacked by a mob. Significantly, the law-breaking soon took on political as well as theological overtones, as the crowd 'were soon shouting royalist slogans, "crying up King Charles, and crying down the Parliament . . .", assaulting Roundheads, and consuming the free beer offered by citizens who set up holly-bushes at their doors.'[38] Professor Underdown also notes evidence of continued celebration of Christmas in the 1650s in Cornwall and Devon. He maintains that where Christmas was, Royalism was likely to be present as well.[39] It must be remembered that the Prayer Book was 'common prayer' – a 'levelling text' – which provided some common culture across social and gender divisions. Even illiteracy did not close one off from the culture of the Prayer Book. To its hotter Protestant critics, the familiarity of the Prayer Book was its fatal flaw, turning it into an 'idol'. To the liturgy's adherents, its familiarity was its greatest aid to devotion.[40]

Prayer Book loyalism was to be found not only cutting across social and educational divisions but crossing an ocean as well. Thousands of miles to the west, without benefit of bishops or ecclesiastical courts, conformity to the Prayer Book appears to have been widespread in the lay-dominated Church of colonial Virginia. The mid-seventeenth-

---

[36] Underdown, *Revel*, 230. See also King, 'Reasons for abolition', 338–9; John Morrill and John Walter, 'Order and disorder in the English Revolution', in Richard Cust and Ann Hughes, eds, *The English Civil War* (1997), 315 (first published 1985). For widespread support for the Prayer Book across social divisions in the pre-civil war period, see Maltby, *Prayer Book and People*, 80–1, 181–227.

[37] Underdown, *Revel*, 156–9, 180, 226, 255; idem, 'The chalk and the cheese: contrasts among English Clubmen', in Cust and Hughes, *English Civil War* (1997), 295 (first published 1979).

[38] Underdown, *Revel*, 260.

[39] Ibid., 256–63, 267.

[40] See above, 237–8.

century Virginian Church managed to be a broad Church, its lay leaders winking at puritan infractions as adeptly as any moderate Jacobean bishop. Indeed it would appear that the general 'external' – and significantly non-Christian and 'savage' – threat provided to the colonists by America's first inhabitants made many of the theological disputes of the mother Church seem somewhat arcane. Only in the 1640s, and only after the threat from the indigenous population was reduced, did Virginian authorities turn to suppressing groups that would not use the Prayer Book, and then generally only moving against the most radical forms of nonconformity. In 1649, Norfolk county authorities banished to Maryland a group of individuals who would not conform to the Prayer Book – the same book which had been banned several years before in England. Local authorities seemed to have taken particular delight in sending such godly zealots to a colony renowned for its popery. Eventually even Cromwell had to strike a deal with the Virginians. Following a visit by his commissioners in the early 1650s, the colonists were given a general amnesty and permission to use the banned Prayer Book for another year provided the prayers for the king and royal family were omitted. In fact, it is likely they simply continued to use the old liturgy throughout the rest of the Interregnum – a speculation strengthened by the 'Cavalier' clergy who took up livings in Virginia in the 1650s.[41] It is intriguing to speculate further that a Book of Common Prayer, shorn of its royalist references, provided a precedent in the late 1780s as the new Episcopal Church revised its Prayer Book to remain distinctively Anglican yet thoroughly republican.[42]

In his diary, Evelyn provides numerous examples of both the use of the Book of Common Prayer and widespread observance of the holy days of the Prayer Book calendar. At certain times government zeal was such that the Evelyn family, as others, had to make do with the private use of the Prayer Book at home.[43]

---

[41] Conformity to the Prayer Book was also enforced in Barbados during the 1650s: Larry Gragg, 'The pious and the profane: the religious life of early Barbados planters', *The Historian*, 62 (2000), 269–70, 271–2, 275–7. Between 1637 and 1660, nearly 30 ministers migrated to the island: ibid., 268, but cf. 281–2.

[42] Bond, 'Religion in seventeenth-century Anglican Virginia', 186–222; George MacLaren Brydon, *Virginia's Mother Church and the Political Conditions under which it Grew*, 2 vols, Virginia Historical Society (Richmond, VA, 1947–52), 1:122–3, 129–31. I am grateful to Prof. Robert Prichard for this reference and for the possible connection made to the development of Anglicanism in America in the late eighteenth century.

[43] Evelyn, *Diary*, 3:2034, see also 3:978, 144, 225.

I Jan [1653]: I set a part in preparation for the B: *Sacrament*, which the next day *Mr. Owen* administered to me & all my family in *Says-Court*, preaching on: 6: John 32.33. shewing the exceeding benefits of our B: Saviours taking our nature upon him.[44]

The minister in question, Richard Owen, also ministered other important rites for the household, baptizing the Evelyn children and churching their mother at home according the Prayer Book.[45] Alongside such explicit acts of dissent as that Christmas Communion, there developed among Church of England loyalists an inward and quietist spirituality focused on the home and the interior religious life.[46]

It is tempting to see the domestication and 'privatizing' of Prayer Book Protestantism in this period as a parallel to the experiences of recusants under Elizabeth and the early Stuarts. There were no Church of England equivalents of the Jesuits, but there were plenty of obstructive and uncooperative clergy and laity. As with Roman Catholicism, the customs of the 'Old Church' often survived in the household, sponsored by gentry who had the social standing to reduce their personal risk and the finances to support sympathetic clergy. Women too emerge as important actors in the maintenance of proscribed observances kept alive in the domestic sphere. It is surely right, as has been argued, not to see Roman Catholicism as 'hermetically sealed' in post-Reformation English society.[47] There is a sense as well that this particular comparison can be overdone.[48] Overall, there is little evidence of a widely-held view among Church of England loyalists that they saw themselves as a 'continuing' or 'true' Church in struggle with a 'false' one. The mindset appears – especially as one moves to less public (and polemical) reflections on the state of the Christian faith in England – of *the* Church under the influence of a misguided or even wicked leadership. For example, take Evelyn's account of attending his own parish church in 1653:

---

[44] Richard Owen, D.D.: ibid., 3:79.

[45] Ibid., 3:75, 76, 89, 90, 147, 195. For home churchings see Cressy, *Birth*, 225; idem, 'Purification, thanksgiving and the churching of women in post-reformation England', *Past and Present*, 141 (Nov., 1993), 140–1.

[46] Spurr, *Restoration Church*, 21–2.

[47] Walsham, 'Parochial roots', 651.

[48] Cf. Claire Cross, 'The Church in England 1646–1660', in G.E. Aylmer, ed., *The Interregnum: the Quest for Settlement 1646–1660* (1972), 114.

30. [January, 1653] At our own *Parish Church*, a Stranger preached
on I *Apoc.* 5.6 describing the greate benefits don us by our B: Lord:
Note, that there was now & then, an honest orthodox man gotten
into the Pulpet, and though the present *Incumbent* were somewhat
Independent; yet he ordinarily preachd sound doctrine, & was a
peaceable man, which was an extraordinary felicity in this age.[49]

These are not the reflections of a Christian who has 'unchurched' his
theological and ecclesiological antagonists. However deep in error the
mainstream Protestant opponents of the Church of England might be,
it was in a sense a family quarrel, whereas the Church of Rome was
seen as outside the household. It is always worth remembering, of
course, that most violence is precisely domestic violence. The
influence of the religious upheavals of the middle of the century
on Protestant ecclesiology deserves much more scholarly attention, as
does a consideration of these events on England's Roman Catholic
community.[50]

*   *   *

Elizabeth Newell, John Evelyn, and John Hackett are examples of
individuals who negotiated the new religious order to some extent.
Others did not. Figures are not certain but between two and three
thousand clergy were ejected from their livings during this period by
agencies such as Parliament's Committee for Plundered Ministers.
Such figures could represent an ejection rate as high as twenty-five per
cent, although there was considerable regional and local variation as
the initiative passed from Westminster to the localities, and the figure
is mitigated by the hundreds of clergy who achieved preferment to
another parish after ejection. Clergy lost their livings or other forms of
preferment for a variety of offences including Royalism, the use of the
Prayer Book, failure to preach, moral offences, or simply over-
frequenting the ale house – or some fascinating combination of all
these things.[51] Although this does not diminish the ferocity with which

---

[49] The incumbent in Evelyn's description was Thomas Malory, deprived in 1661: Evelyn,
Diary, 3:80–1, 81 n.5.
[50] This issue will be explored with others in a forthcoming volume of essays edited by
Christopher Durston and Judith Maltby, *Religion and Society in Revolutionary England*
(Manchester University Press).
[51] Cross, 'Church in England', 110–14; Susan Doran and Christopher Durston, *Princes,
Pastors and People: the Church and Religion in England 1529–1689* (1991), 154–7; Anne
Laurance, '"This sad and deplorable condition": an account of the sufferings of northern

roughly a thousand clergy were ejected at the Restoration for their failure to conform to a new Act of Uniformity, it does put it in some perspective, and indeed goes part of the way not to justify such actions but to make them understandable. Professor Ivan Roots's assessment of the political settlement of 1660 is apposite for the church as well: 'there was only a smear of blood at the Restoration, but a whole streak of meanness'.[52]

*   *   *

One of the striking things about the survival of features of the Old Church in this period is the lack of leadership provided by members of the episcopate. Outlawed practices, such as the use of the Prayer Book or the observation of holy days, survived in large part due to the courage of clergy and laity, not due to any overt leadership provided by the bishops. In fact, the bishops in England ignored repeated requests from the exiled court in the 1650s to consecrate more of their order to make up for diminishing numbers.[53] That said, bishops did not disappear from the scene. By 1650, only a third of English and Welsh sees were vacant, and a third of the bench at the start of the civil war survived to be restored to their privileges in the 1660s.[54]

If bishops provided little public leadership to their flocks during this time of trouble, they did respond to requests for secret ordinations. A number of younger clergy (we do not know how many), often with no first-hand experience of episcopal government, sought out a second ordination from the hands of these 'redundant' bishops. It was, in truth, a sort of 'top-up' view of ordination, as these younger men appear to have continued to serve in the Interregnum Church. Such evidence again argues against the notion of the Church of England as a kind of

clergy families in the 1640s and 1650s', in Diana Wood, ed., *Life and Thought in the Northern Church c. 1100–1700*, SCH.S, 12 (Woodbridge, 1999), 465–7. Prof. Green estimates around 2,780 clergy were deprived: Ian Green, 'The persecution of "scandalous" and "malignant" parish clergy during the English civil war', *EHR*, 94 (1979), 508. See also Clive Holmes, ed., *The Suffolk Committees for Scandalous Ministers 1644–1646*, Suffolk Records Society, 13 (1970), 10–14, 18–20. Dr Holmes notes that charges of 'popish innovation' were more common that accusations of dissent from Calvinist orthodoxy (ibid., 19). J.W.F. Hill, 'Royalist clergy of Lincolnshire', *Lincolnshire Architectural and Archaeological Society, Reports and Papers*, 40 (1935), 34–127.

[52] Ivan Roots, *The Great Rebellion 1642–1660* (1966), 261.

[53] Ronald Hutton, *The British Republic 1649–1660* (1990), 91–2, 97; Cross, 'Church in England', 110–14.

[54] Nigel Yates, Robert Hume, and Paul Hastings, *Religion and Society in Kent, 1640–1914* (Woodbridge, 1994), 5–6.

'recusant' or 'underground' Church.[55] What motivated them to seek such episcopal alternatives? Presumably it was a variety of factors, including a search for stability in a period of uncertainty and change in many areas of English life. Jeremy Taylor dryly observed of these youngsters that never had the excellency of episcopal government been so obvious now that it was lacking.[56]

*   *   *

In what ways did individuals make sense of – construct a theology of – what was to them a catastrophic religious experience? The Warwick-shire clergyman Christopher Harvey, like others, used the imagery of the Exile. His popular collection of religious verse written in imitation of George Herbert's *The Temple* was significantly entitled *The Synagogue*. For the Jews of the Babylonian captivity and later of the Diaspora, without access to the Temple, the place of sacrifice and access to God, synagogues became a way of remaining faithful in the face of the ungodly. Harvey stayed in his benefice from his institution in 1639 until his death in 1663, and in that sense qualifies as a 'survivor' not a 'sufferer'. Nonetheless, he had a strong sense of living in a state of internal exile.[57] By the third edition of *The Synagogue*, published in 1657, Harvey had become, in the words of the one admirer of his verse, a prophetic voice reminding his readers not to forget 'Israel' in the midst of ungodliness.

> Sir,
> While I read your lines, methinks I spie
> Churches, and churchmen, and the old hierarchie:
> What potent charms are these! you have the knack
> To make men young again, and fetch back time.
>
> .   .   .   .
>
> The mid-space shrunk to nothing; manners, men,
> And times, and all look just as they did then;

[55] See above, 246–7.

[56] Spurr, *Restoration Church*, 9, 141–3 (Jeremy Taylor paraphrased ibid., 142); Cross, 'Church in England', 110–14; Hutton, *British Republic*, 91–2; Doran and Durston, *Princes, Pastors and People*, 156–7. For examples of episcopal ordinations in the 1650s, see Evelyn, *Diary*, 3:8–9 (in Paris), 172 and n.1. For the question of what should replace ordination by bishops in England, see Shaw, *English Church*, 1:243, 320–37.

[57] Judith Maltby, 'From *Temple* to *Synagogue*: "old" conformity in the 1640s-1650s and the case of Christopher Harvey', in Lake and Questier, *Conformity and Orthodoxy*, 94–103, 114–16.

Rubbish and ruin's vanisht, everywhere
Order and comliness afresh appear.
What cannot poets do? They change with ease
The face of things, and lead us as they please.
Yet here's no fiction neither: we may see
The poet, prophet; his verse, historie.[58]

Prayer Book Protestants attempted to make sense of their suffering Church in time-honoured ways: as identification with the sufferings of Christ, or as divine judgement for sin. In a fascinating set of correspondence with a puritan friend called Lang, the Sussex gentleman John Martin rejected the view that the degraded state of the Church of England in the 1650s was in any sense a sign of judgement on its liturgy or polity. In 1656 he wrote:

> For my owne part, I cannot be of your mind, who judge our Church Forsaken of the Lord, because Afflicted by men; when I consider, that Our Saviour himselfe was a man of Sorrowes, & therefore will never be angry with His Spouse, when she is made like Him. I am rather confirm'd we are the True members of Christ our Head, because there are so many in combination, that endeavour our Extirpation.[59]

Nothing, not even the 'wild extravigancies' of his own side, maintained the Sussex layman, would drive him 'out of the Good Old Way'.[60] Biblical paradigms of Hebrew exile or identification with the redemptive sufferings of Christ helped some to make sense of the collapse of their religious tradition.

Inevitably in the Christian psyche, however, some saw the miseries of the 1640s and 1650s as divine punishment. As an earlier generation interpreted the persecutions of Mary I as divine disapproval of the half-heartedness of the Edwardian reformation, so too the destruction of the Church of England by Parliament was seen by subsequent Protestants also as an expression of divine wrath for past errors and

---

[58] Christopher Harvey, *The Complete Poems of Christopher Harvey*, ed. A.B. Grosart (The Fuller Worthies' Library, privately printed, 1874), 88–9. The poem was reportedly written in 1654(/5?). See Maltby, 'Temple to Synagogue', 114–15, 120.

[59] Washington DC, Folger Shakespeare Library, MS V.a.454: 'The Letterbook of John Martin', 18. I am grateful to Mr David Cleggett, the Archivist of Leeds Castle Foundation, and Miss Laetitia Yeandle, the Archivist of the Folger Shakespeare Library, for their assistance with this manuscript.

[60] Ibid.

sins.[61] The religious drivers were the same, one might reflect, but the conclusions were strikingly different. The Norfolk gentleman Clement Spelman (1598–1679) raised these very issues in a draft letter written at the Restoration to the new Bishop of Durham, John Cosin. Spelman related to Cosin that while he was part of the Royalist garrison at Oxford he caused a tract by his father Sir Henry Spelman (1564?–1641) defending tithes to be re-published in 1646 with an extensive introduction by himself.[62] Charles I asked to see Clement, having read his father's tract, and 'afterwards said when god pleased to restore him, hee would restore his impropriacions to the church'. 'A resolution', reflected Spelman, 'befitting so pyous a prince.'[63] But monarchical devotion would not be the over-arching theme of the layman's letter to the new bishop. Spelman embarked on a fascinating theological and historical analysis of England's and the Church of England's ills over the past two decades. Cataloguing the long dynastic troubles of the Tudors and Stuarts, he placed the woes firmly as a result of the seizure of Church property by the crown. He concluded that this seizure of Church property, not the destruction of the monastic life – there is no hint of remorse for the latter – was a great sin:

> for gods punishment never exceed[s] the offence, and since the punishment was nationall I must beleeve the sinne soe too, and I know noe nationall sinne in England but that of Sacrilidge committed as a Law by act of parliament, whereto everyone is Cosentinge eyther actually by himselfe or implicitively by his Representative in parliament.[64]

---

[61] See the oration of John Hales to Elizabeth I in 1559 in John Foxe, *Acts and Monuments* (1576), 2005–7. Also Catherine Davis, '"Poor persecuted little flock": Edwardian protestant concepts of the church', in Peter Lake and Maria Dowling, eds, *Protestantism and the National Church in Sixteenth-Century England* (1987), 78, 81, 94–5. I am grateful to Dr Tom Freeman for these references. For the attempts by English radicals to make sense of their defeat in 1660, see Christopher Hill, *The Experience of Defeat: Milton and Some Contemporaries* (New York, 1984).

[62] This is likely to be Henry Spelman's *De non tenerandis ecclesis* (1st edn 1613). Clement's letter is almost certainly to John Cosin and dated *c.*1660–2: Durham, Durham University Archives [hereafter DUA], Cosin LB 1b, no. 94. See also 'Clement Spelman' and 'Sir Henry Spelman' in *New DNB* (on-line, 1995).

[63] DUA, Cosin LB 1b, no. 94.

[64] Ibid. Clement was very much his father's spiritual and intellectual heir. Sir Henry's extensive treatment of his theme in *The History and Fate of Sacrilege* was not published until 1698. He provided a gazetteer of former monastic lands in Norfolk and catalogued a variety of terrible fates which befell the families that turned church property to secular

That the destruction of the Church of England, its liturgy and festivals, and the years of civil war and unrest were God's wake-up call to the new regime, Spelman was in no doubt:

> And when wee observe gods method in our punishment, wee have reason to beleeve that, that Sacriledge drue on us this punishment, for the same order the King & Kingdome tooke to Robb god and the Church, the same methode god observes to punish the King and Nation.

Constructing an eerie symmetry, Spelman noted that Henry VIII used Parliament, sitting in St Stephen's Chapel, to rob the Church one November. So God, to punish both the king and nation, used Parliament again sitting in St Stephen's Chapel, again in November, to pass an Act to dissolve the monarchy: an eye for an eye, or a dissolution for a dissolution.

> The Kinge makes use of a Crumwell to Dissolve the Monastryes, and god of a Crumwell borne in a dissolved Monastrye to punish the Kinge, thus our punishment sprang from our Sinnes.

In the mind of Spelman this relentless divine punishment for sacrilege pursued Charles I to his last sacramental act:

> King Henry 8 had taken all the Challices from the Alters of the Dissolved Monasterys and the parliament and Crumwell seise all the Kings plate soe that the day before that his Majestie dyed hee was necesitated to send to the Taverne at Charing-Cross to borrow a Cup wherein to receive his last Communion at St James a disolved hospitall his prison, whence the next daye his Majestie goes to Whitehall the place of his murder first a Religious house one of the 40ty dissolved, and given to Cardinall Wosley by him built for the ArchBp of Yorke, but againe torne from the Church by King Henry 8: and made his Court.

Spelman suggested that funds could be annexed to impoverished dioceses like Chester and Peterborough (significantly both cathedral churches are former monastic houses) to help 'expiate a Continued Sacrildge'. The devout layman urged the new bishop to encourage Charles II to 'religously pay what his father piously promised to the

uses: ibid., 243–82; Alexandra Walsham, *Providence in Early Modern England* (Oxford, 1999), 109–10.

Church' making Cosin a 'Nathan to our David'.[65] Sadly among Cosin's papers in Durham there is no reply.

*   *   *

This raises another emerging theme which can only be touched on here: the real ambivalence towards the monarchy and the Supreme Governorship of the Church of England. We are familiar with the 'cult' of Charles I, a king far more impressive and useful in his death to co-religionists than he ever was in life. John Spurr has written powerfully of the psychological effect on the nation, shared by Laudian and puritan and those in between, of the execution of the king.

> To many this was not simply the nadir of a cause, but the beginning of the end: God had removed the English Josiah, and the ruin of Judah herself could only be a matter of time. . . . The anniversary of the regicide and the expiation of the nation's guilt now became central motifs in the prayers of intercession used by the 'mourners in Sion'.[66]

Ironically, given the suppression of the Church calendar and the Prayer Book by Parliament, Charles's death created a new 'holy day' and a market for new liturgies. In the royal chapel in Paris, John Cosin adapted the daily offices of the Book of Common Prayer to provide a service to be used every Tuesday – the day of Charles's execution. Morning and Evening Prayer began with the verse 'Enter not into judgement with thy servants O Lord, for no flesh is righteous in thy sight' and instead of the more upbeat *Venite*, Psalm 121 ('I will lift up mine eyes') was to be used. The portion of the psalms appointed to be read antiphonally reveals a sense of desolation. The appointed readings from Scripture also matched the mood: for Morning Prayer, Genesis 28.10–22 (God's promise to Jacob in a dream to be with him) and Luke 21.1–21 (foretelling by Christ of the sufferings of his followers and the destruction of Jerusalem); and for Evening Prayer, II Chronicles 20.1–21 (the prophet Jahaziel tells the people of Judah that God is with them in the face of a much larger enemy) and I Peter 2 (identification with Christ as the rejected stone and a call to accept the proper political and social order). The psalm appointed was, appropriately, *De profundis*,

---

[65] DUA, Cosin LB 1b, no. 94. This remarkable description of Charles's last hours is not mentioned in the classic account by C.V. Wedgewood, *The Trial of Charles I* (1964), 177–82.

[66] Spurr, *Restoration Church*, 20–1; Maltby, 'Temple to Synagogue', 115.

Psalm 130, 'Out of the deep'. The responses were re-drafted and emphasised the need for divine protection in the present and divine intervention to secure the restoration of Charles II in the future. Additional material for Holy Communion reflected these concerns as well.[67]

None the less there is a striking undercurrent of unease and discontent among Church of England loyalists about Charles himself and more significantly, about basing the claims of authenticity for the established Church on arguments around the Supreme Governorship. In the 1647 edition of *The Synagogue*, Harvey included a poem extolling every Church officer of the now defunct Church of England from the parish sexton to bishop. In Harvey's construction, the top of the ecclesiastical totem-pole was the bishop; there is no poem called 'The Supreme Governor'. In fact, Harvey contrasted unfavourably the precious metals of the Communion plate to the gold of a royal crown:

> Never was gold or silver gracèd thus
> Before:
> To bring this Body and this Blood to us
> Is more
> Then to crown kings.

As I have commented elsewhere, it is very tempting indeed to see this as a veiled, though rather thinly veiled, criticism of Charles's Supreme Governorship. Harvey continues:

> A King unto Whose Cross all kings must vail
> Their crowns
>   .   .   .   .   .
> Whose frowns and smiles
>   .   .   .   .   .
> doom them either unto weal or woe.
> A King Whose will is justice, and Whose word
> Is pow'r
> And wisdom both; a King, Whom to afford
> An hour

---

[67] DUA, Cosin Library B.IV.4: *A Forme of Prayer, used in the King's Chapel upon Tuesdayes, in these Times of Trouble and Distresse* (?Paris, 1649).

Of service truly
Perform'd and duly,
Is to bespeak eternity of bliss.[68]

Even Cosin's customized Prayer Book appointed as the first collect at
Morning Prayer one for the Church, not for the sovereign:

Lord, we beseech thee, let thy continuall pity cleanse and defend
thy Church: and because it cannot continue in safety without thy
succour, preserve it evermore by thy help and goodness, through
Jesus Christ our Lord.[69]

This became, in fact, the collect for Trinity 16 in the 1662 Book of
Common Prayer. The collect also appeared in the pre-civil war Prayer
Books, but in 1662 the word 'Church', as in this post-regicide rite,
replaced the more 'godly' term 'congregation'.[70] For many Church of
England loyalists the Stuarts were at best a mixed blessing.[71]

*   *   *

The period of England's brief (to date) experiment with religious
localism and republicanism saw the suppression of the Book of
Common Prayer, episcopal polity and (perhaps most unpopular of
all) the reformed ritual year. These experiences of suppression helped
to form an 'Anglican' identity, though even in this period 'Anglican' is a
problematic word to use with any degree of historical and scholarly
integrity. We must always remember that it was little used by
contemporaries. In many ways, 'episcopalian' is a better term, though
ironically the fact that it is so is due more to lay and clerical
faithfulness than to episcopal leadership. What we observe in the
1640s and 1650s is the hardening of certain religious traditions *within*
the larger pre-civil war Church of England and their emergence as *the*
Church of England. The formation of this religious identity was
greatly aided by the retrospective spin doctors of the Restoration
Church of England; the biographer Izaak Walton being both the most

---

[68] Harvey, *Poems*, 26–7; Maltby, '*Temple* to *Synagogue*', 115.

[69] DUA, Cosin Library, B.IV.4.

[70] F.E. Brightman, *The English Rite: Being a Synopsis of the Sources and Revisions of the Book
of Common Prayer*, 2 vols (1921), 2:516–17; Marion J. Hatchett, *Commentary on the American
Prayer Book* (San Francisco, 1995), 190.

[71] For a discussion of earlier ambivalence towards the royal supremacy, see Davis,
'Edwardian protestant concepts', 78–9.

notable and engaging of them. Walton, not Richard Hooker, in many ways deserves the title of the inventor of Anglicanism.[72] As Professor John Morrill has remarked: 'religious commitment is best observed in periods of persecution'.[73] Before the civil war, religious identities invested in the liturgy, the calendar, and episcopacy formed a flexible and considerable strand *within* the larger national Church. In Cromwell's England it was the suppression of these same key components of a religious tradition, in particular the attempt to suppress the Book of Common Prayer, rather than the abolition of the monarchy, that helped paradoxically to create a self-conscious 'Anglicanism'.

Corpus Christi College, Oxford

---

[72] See Jessica Martin's excellent study, *Walton's Lives: Conformist Commemoration and the Rise of Biography* (Oxford, 2001); Peter Lake, *Anglicans and Puritans? Presbyterian and Conformist Thought from Whitgift to Hooker* (1988), 225–30; Maltby, *Prayer Book and People*, 235–7.

[73] Morrill, 'Church in England', 150.

PROVISION OF BOOKS FOR POOR CLERGY PAROCHIAL LIBRARIES IN THE BRITISH ISLES AND THE NORTH AMERICAN COLONIES, 1680–1720

by W.M. JACOB

FOR ministers of Word and sacraments in a reformed Church, books were part of their stock-in-trade. By the late seventeenth century books were widely available, and theological books were the staple of the publishing trade. Possession of books distinguished the inventories of deceased clerics whose wills were proved in consistory courts from their lay neighbours, but books were still too expensive for poorer clergy to buy.

A learned as well as a godly ministry was the ideal of the first wave of English reformers. By the 1640s the Church of England had achieved a largely graduate clergy, except in south-west Wales and north-west England.[1] The restored bishops in 1660 recognized that much was still to be achieved in reforming the Church and its ministry, but for a generation they and their lieutenants were pre-occupied with restoring the Church, physically, financially, and in the affections of the people. The second generation of restored bishops began on a second stage of reform to ensure that the Church and people were strong in the paths of righteousness against the wiles and errors of dissent on the one hand, and a resurgent, counter-reformed Roman Catholic Church, on the other.

William Sancroft, Archbishop of Canterbury 1678–90, began sketching plans to reform and strengthen further the pastoral role of parish clergy. His successor, John Tillotson, took up these plans in a circular letter to the bishops in 1692. In concert with this, a galaxy of distinguished bishops and churchmen acted to put flesh on these bones. Bishops, notably Gilbert Burnet of Salisbury and Simon Patrick of Ely, produced charges for their clergy describing the pastoral tasks of parish priests. Burnet and Archbishop Sharp of York persuaded Queen Anne to restore to the Church the proceeds of two taxes specific to the clergy, to be administered by the Governors of Queen Anne's Bounty

---

[1] Rosemary O'Day, *The English Clergy: the Emergence and Consolidation of a Profession, 1558–1642* (Leicester, 1979).

and used to augment poor livings. Henry Compton, Bishop of London, made proposals for integrating the Anglican congregations in the North American colonies with the mother Church. The Society for the Promotion of Christian Knowledge (SPCK) was founded to promote Christian knowledge among children and adults. Numerous local initiatives sought to re-invigorate spiritual and moral life. Proposals were made for the continuing education and encouragement of the clergy by appointing rural deans, with regular deanery meetings of clergy to review and discuss their pastoral work, especially preaching and catechizing. It is this last aspect of this second wave of reform in the Church of England which this paper will discuss, by examining the attempts to increase clerics' theological awareness by providing libraries for their use. Chronologically, this survey covers the last decades of the seventeenth century, and the first quarter or so of the eighteenth. It deals primarily with England and the North American colonies, but also considers the movement in other parts of the British Isles.

Study for three or five years at one of the universities might have provided a good start for a teaching and preaching ministry, but continuing engagement with the tradition and with contemporary thought was also important. However, in a poor living a man with a growing family might not have spare money to buy books to stimulate and re-invigorate his teaching, preaching, and pastoral ministry. Nor were there many libraries outside the universities. Surviving evidence suggests that in 1680 there were perhaps forty-four 'parochial' libraries in England and Wales.[2]

One such library was at St Peter Mancroft in Norwich. Thomas Tenison, later to become Archbishop of Canterbury, was 'upper minister' there from 1673 to 1680, and donated some books.[3] Subsequently, as vicar of St Martin's in the Fields, Tenison pointed out to his vestry in March 1684 that in London there was not

> one shop of a stationer fully furnished with Books of various Learning or any noted Library (except that of St James which belongs to his Ma[jes]tie and to which there is no easy access) and

[2] All statistics, unless otherwise stated, are derived from *The Parochial Libraries of the Church of England: A Report of a Committee Appointed by the Central Council for the Care of Churches to Investigate the Number and Condition of Parochial Libraries Belonging to the Church of England* (1959).

[3] Edward Carpenter, *Thomas Tenison: Archbishop of Canterbury, His Life and Times* (1948), 10.

that of Sir Robert Cotton (which consists mostly of books relating to the antiquities of England) and the Library of the Dean and Chapter of St Peter at Westminster which is inconvenient by reason of remote situation.[4]

The previous month Tenison had mentioned to John Evelyn that

> there were thirty or forty Young Men in Orders in his Parish, either Governors to young Gentlemen or Chaplains to Noblemen who being reproved by him upon occasion for frequenting Taverns or Coffe-houses told him they would study and employ their time better, if they had books. This put the pious Doctor upon this designe ['of erecting a Library at St Martin's parish for the publique use'].[5]

Tenison offered to build and stock a library himself, and to provide an endowment for a librarian and the repair of the books, to which the vestry 'heartily concurred'. Tenison commissioned Sir Christopher Wren to design the library. On 15 July 1684, when the Library was opened, Evelyn noted 'The Books with backs gilt are set on shelves: there be divers tables set in convenient places for the use of such as read or transcribe.' As it comprised six thousand printed volumes, numerous medieval manuscripts, and, 'A Collection of Greek Liturgies and Liturgy in 38 volumes', this library should have distracted able young clergy from taverns and coffee houses. Tenison also provided for its future management by establishing a trust with nine trustees, including the vicar and churchwardens of St Martin's *ex officio,* and the Archbishop of Canterbury as visitor, but he left no funds for the purchase of new books. Few books, it seems, were added to the library after Tenison's death in 1715.[6] Surprisingly, Tenison does not appear to have encouraged the establishment of libraries in his dioceses as Bishop of Lincoln (1692–5) or as Archbishop of Canterbury (1695–1715). Perhaps four libraries were established during his time in Lincoln, and none in his time in Canterbury.

The issues facing those proposing to establish parochial or deanery libraries for the use of clergy were the long-term security of the books, their management, and the addition of new books. Security of books

---

[4] Westminster City Archives, St Martin's in the Fields Vestry Minute Book, 1683–1716.
[5] *The Diary of John Evelyn*, ed. E.S. de Beer, 5 vols (Oxford, 1955), 4:367.
[6] Lambeth Palace Library [hereafter LPL], MS 1708: Catalogue of the Library of Archbishop Tenison.

was a major concern. When, in 1686, William Stone, vicar of Wimborne Minster in Dorset, persuaded local clergy and gentry to donate books or funds for a parochial library, Roger Gillingham, a lawyer, refused to give any books until they were chained to prevent their removal.[7] In 1690 Thomas White, the deprived Bishop of Peterborough, and a former vicar of Newark, bequeathed all his printed books to the mayor, aldermen, and vicar of Newark, provided they created a room

> with a Lock and Key thereto, which Key if required shall be kept by the Vicar . . . for the time being hee first giving security of a thousand pounds to the said Mayor and aldermen never to embezzle the said Bookes not to lend any booke out of the Library either to his own house or to others, and I do appoint that when the accounts of the towne shall be made up every year the whole library shall be called over in the presence of the Mayor and aldermen, and if any book be wanting the vicar shall lay down the price of it presently or have the key taken from him, and his bond be sued for reparation.

If the vicar failed, the schoolmaster was given responsibility on the same terms, and if he failed, the keys would be forfeit to White's executors.[8]

Barnabas Oley (1602–86), fellow of Clare College Cambridge, prebendary of Worcester, and vicar of Great Gransden in Huntingdonshire, attempted to provide a modicum of reading matter for poor clergy in the north-west by requiring his executors to provide collections of sixteen volumes for ten poor vicarages in the diocese of Carlisle: 'The several books . . . to be kept within the church . . . for the use of the vicars there for the time being and their successors for ever'. Sets of books, costing £10 10s. 8d. each were sent to ten parishes in the diocese of Carlisle in 1687. In 1703, when Bishop Nicolson visited all the parishes in his diocese, he required information about the books, and the articles of agreement drawn up at the time of their distribution so that he could check in each parish whether any books were missing. He was not impressed with what he found.[9]

[7] Helen Hixson, *Chains of Knowledge: Wimborne Minster Chained Library* (nd), no pagination.
[8] Quoted in Brenda M. Park, *The Bishop White Library of Newark Parish Church* (Newark, 1999), no pagination.
[9] *Miscellany Account of the Diocese of Carlisle*, ed. R.S. Ferguson (Carlisle, 1877), 7.

There were a number of initiatives in dioceses in the 1690s and early
1700s to establish deanery libraries and clerical societies, to encourage
higher standards of clerical learning and pastoral care. In May 1697
Abraham de la Prynne, then curate of Broughton in Lincoln diocese,
noted that at the visitation 'there is a project come out for a lending
library in every deanery. I subscribed 5s towards the first trial of it.'[10] On
14 April 1701 the Bishop of Chester was reported as suggesting Kendal
as 'the most proper place for a Lending Library within the Archdeaconry
of Richmond, there being twelve chapels of Ease belonging to the
Vicarage of Kendall, the curates of which are all very meanly provided
for.'[11] From Northamptonshire it was reported in November 1701 that
'the neighbouring clergy give each other catalogues of their libraries
instead of lending libraries'.[12] The library at St Mary's Warwick,
established in 1701, was 'for the use of theological Readers in Warwick
and its Neighbourhood', which was reportedly encouraged by 'Dr Bray
of Sheldon', and was contributed to by local gentry and clergy.[13]

Dr Bray (1658–1730), as well as being rector of Sheldon in
Warwickshire from 1690, was, in 1696, appointed commissary for
Maryland by Bishop Compton of London. Bray accepted the appointment on condition that Compton and the other bishops would support
his plan for libraries for the clergy in the colony. In recruiting clergy
for Maryland Bray found that only the 'poorer sort' were willing to go
to North America, clerics who had no money to buy books to equip
themselves as catechists and preachers.[14] He intended that his libraries
should be used by parishioners as well as clergy.

A man of entrepreneurial vision and energy, Thomas Bray
recognized that money was required to buy books for libraries, and
that criteria were required for their selection. He started at the top,
approaching Princess Anne, proposing to name the capital of Maryland
'Annapolis', and outlining plans for a library, to which she subsequently donated forty guineas.[15] He drew up a proposal for

[10] *Diary of Abraham de la Prynne,* Surtees Society, 54 (1869), 133.

[11] *A Chapter in English Church History: being the Minutes of S.P.C.K. 1698–1704, together with
an abstract of Correspondents' Letters,* ed. Edmund McClure (1888), 128.

[12] SPCK Abstract Letter No 360, 10 Nov. 1701, in BL, MS Harley 7190, fol. 13, quoted in
Dudley W.R. Bahlman, *The Moral Revolution of 1688* (New Haven, CT, 1957), 73.

[13] *Parochial Libraries of the Church of England,* 103.

[14] *Publick Spirit: Illustrated in the Life and Designs of the Revd Thomas Bray D.D., late Minister
of St Botolph without Aldgate* (1746), 10.

[15] Charles T. Laugher, *Thomas Bray's Grand Design: Libraries of the Church of England in
America 1695–1785,* ACRL Publications in Librarianship, 35 (Chicago, 1973), 10.

fund-raising among the 'Nobility, Clergy and Gentry about London
. . . and . . . among the Merchants and Traders in the foreign
plantations . . . as persons principally concern'd to encourage this
Design', for 'the more plentifully they have reaped of their Temporal
things the more Liberally they should sow to them in Spiritual
things'. Bishops were requested to recommend clergy to solicit the
gentry in their parishes; donations were to be forwarded to
archdeacons and thence to bishops, and finally to the bishop of
London. Booksellers and authors were invited to donate books. Books
were to be stamped with a donor's name, and a list of benefactors
would be kept for posterity in 'the Colledge in Virginia'. The advice
of the bishops, professors of both universities, and 'some of the
Eminent London Divines' was to be sought in drawing up lists of
stock for the libraries, and commissioners were to be appointed by
the Archbishop of Canterbury and the Bishop of London to purchase
books at favourable prices.[16] By 1697 sixteen libraries had been
despatched to Maryland. In late 1699 Bray himself set out to visit the
colony. He was much delayed on the voyage, and, recognizing that
this was a common occurrence, and that naval chaplains and clergy
en route to America might be left in idleness, he established libraries
for their use at Gravesend and Deal, and reformed the library at
Plymouth.[17]

Bray himself produced proposals for the library stock, and for the
care and maintenance of libraries.[18] Catalogues of the colonial libraries
were to be deposited with the bishop of London, the appropriate
colonial commissary, in the library, and with the parish vestry as
trustees of the library. The incumbent was held responsible for the
library; churchwardens were required to inspect it annually; and the
commissary was required to check on his triennial visitation that no
book was 'imbezzl'd or lost'.[19] Bray recommended that each colonial
assembly pass an Act making clergy responsible for any books lost
through their own carelessness. Loss of books, and lack of care of them,
emerged as major problems. In 1696 the Maryland House of Burgesses
agreed that a law be made 'to secure the Libraries that are to be
bestowed upon the parishes'. Subsequently a law of 1699 made the

---

[16] LPL, Gibson MS 933/36: 'Means for Raising a fund for purchasing of the aforesaid
General and Parochial Libraries'.

[17] Laugher, *Thomas Bray's Grand Design*, 11.

[18] Published as *Bibliotheca Pariochialis* (1697).

[19] Laugher, *Thomas Bray's Grand Design*, 19.

minister of a parish responsible for the library.[20] In 1700 the South Carolina Assembly passed an Act for Securing the Provincial Library at Charles Town. The North Carolina Assembly passed a similar law in 1705. There is a striking similarity between these pieces of legislation, and Bray may be the common source.

Between 1695 and 1704 Bray raised over £5,000 for libraries in North America. He established five provincial libraries, thirty-eight parochial libraries, and thirty-seven 'laymen's libraries' there, plus six libraries in Newfoundland, and several in the West Indies.

Care for clerical reading matter also extended to the Celtic fringe. Neglect of the poverty-stricken marginal areas of the British Isles during the Reformation was not repeated in the second wave of reform. In 1695 the governor of the Isle of Man appealed to Archbishop Tenison for funds to complete Isaac Barrow's design for a library on the Isle for poor clergy.[21] In 1699 Bishop Wilson of Sodor and Man began to establish clerical and parochial libraries on the Isle, modelled on Bray's plan, with about twenty-five books in each library.[22] Also in 1699 there was a proposal to establish 'Libraries in the Highlands of Scotland, for the use chiefly of Ministers and Probationers'. The depressed economy in the Highlands was noted, as well as 'The great industry of the Romish Missionaries'. A library was proposed for each county. Money or books were 'to be put into the hands of Mr Taylor, a Bookseller at the Ship, or of Mr Robinson at the Golden Lion in St Paul's Churchyard'. It was noted that 'a scheme for the future preservation of libraries' was being prepared.[23] This may have been the work of the Revd James Kirkwood, a non-juror, who in 1699 published *An Overture for Forwarding and Maintaining the Bibliotecks in every Parish through out this Kingdom* [Scotland] which was laid before the General Assembly of the Church of Scotland. In 1702 Kirkwood published a *Letter anent a Project for Erecting a Library in every Presbytery or at least County in the Highlands*, which was approved by the General Assembly. In 1703 he was reported to have collected 'upwards of 12,000 Merks in Books and Money for erecting Libraries in the highlands, in London'. Kirkwood's trustees and treasurers included members of the SPCK. His proposed rules for preserving

---

[20] Ibid., 31.

[21] LPL, Gibson MS 941/74, Letter from William Sacheverell.

[22] John Keble, *The Life of the Rt Revd Father in God Thomas Wilson, Lord Bishop of Sodor and Man* (Oxford, 1863), 148, 251.

[23] LPL, Gibson MS 938/34.

libraries passed by the General Assembly were modelled on Bray's proposed legislation for the colonies.[24]

In Ireland, Bishop Otway of Ossory founded a diocesan library at Kilkenny cathedral in 1693. Archbishop Narcissus Marsh of Dublin, a correspondent of Tenison, in 1701 commissioned Sir William Robinson to design a building for his library, and in 1707 an Act was passed by the Irish Parliament for 'Settling and Preserving a Publick Library for ever'. Diocesan libraries were established by bishops at Cork (1720), Derry (1726), Cashel (1730), and Raphoe (1737). A parochial library was founded at Cork in 1723.[25]

In 1705 Bray turned his attention from the North American colonies to Wales, with which James Kirkwood, who had taken the Scottish initiative, was also involved. In March 1705 a special committee of the SPCK was set up to develop libraries in Wales. It recommended that libraries be established in each Welsh diocese at Carmarthen, Bangor, Cardiff, and Denbigh. Cowbridge and St Asaph were subsequently substituted for the latter two. A receiver of money and books was nominated for each county.[26] In 1707, fifty thousand proposals were distributed in England and Wales advertising plans for lending libraries in market towns and parochial libraries for poor ministers in each impoverished Welsh living. In March 1708 expenditure on books for the lending libraries was set at £50 each. By the constitutions and rules drawn up for the Welsh libraries, books were to be available for loan 'to any clergyman or schoolmaster inhabiting within ten miles of the said town . . . or to any trustees . . . or to any . . . who shall contribute the sum of 10s or give any books of that value to or for the use of the said library'.[27] In June 1710 the books for the Bangor library were despatched from London, and in October 1711 it was noted that the four Welsh lending libraries had cost £194 17s. 1d.[28]

By 1708 forty-five libraries had been established in England since 1684, nine of which had been set up in the previous four years, perhaps encouraged by Bray's establishment in 1705 of 'Trustees for erecting

---

[24] W.K. Lowther Clarke, *A History of the SPCK* (1959), 103–4.

[25] Muriel McCarthy, *Archbishop Marsh and his Library* (Dublin, nd); Maura Tallon, *Church of Ireland Diocesan Libraries* (Dublin, 1959).

[26] Mary Clements, *The S.P.C.K. and Wales 1699–1740* (1954), 43.

[27] Geraint H. Jenkins, *Literature, Religion and Society in Wales 1660–1730* (Cardiff, 1978), 52.

[28] *Correspondence and Minutes of the SPCK Relating to Wales 1699–1740*, ed. Mary Clements (Cardiff, 1952), 267, 270, 273, 276.

Parochial Libraries and promoting Charitable Designs'. Robert Nelson, the devotional writer, and Henry Hoare, whose Bank held Bray's account for the libraries in the colonies, were among the Trustees. Between 1706 and 1710, £1,738 was collected for libraries, Nelson and Hoare being substantial contributors to the fund. Hoare collected the subscriptions. Bray secured a list of parishes estimated to have incomes under £20 a year, but it was decided to offer libraries to parishes with incomes under £30 a year. The libraries were to be for reference only, to ensure that they were not 'dissipated or used for other purposes'. The trustees were adamant that they were not to be lending libraries. Their secretary, Henry Newman, explained to the Bishop of Bangor:

> These libraries consist of a collection adapted to the use of a country clergyman that is destitute of books or ability to buy them; and if the collection be not kept entire . . . they will not be useful to him, and if lending were allowed they would be in danger of being embezzled and the incumbent would have a good excuse to his diocesan if upon a visitation they should be half wanting.

Incumbents of parishes receiving libraries were required to catechize the children every Sunday. Each parish receiving a library, which comprised sixty-seven or seventy-two books, was required to pay a premium of £5. The aim was 'to furnish a man with the knowledge necessary to undertake a parochial charge'.[29] Four years were spent in preparing the project. Initially the trustees proposed to establish five hundred libraries, but sights were lowered to two per diocese, 'as a Specimen of the Charity they intended'. Even this was not achieved, because of 'some Bishops entertaining the Proposal very coldly'. Authors gave large numbers of their books, and bulk purchases were made. Incumbents of parishes receiving libraries were required to give a bond of £30 to the diocesan bishop to observe the rules prescribed by the 'Act of Parliament'.[30]

A major preoccupation of the Trustees was the long-term care of the libraries. Bray was well aware, from his experience of establishing libraries in the American colonies, how easy it was for books to be 'imbezzled'. Bishop Nicolson, who was of their circle, would have reported the fate of the books donated by Benjamin Oley to Cumbrian parishes. Chaining books to shelves or desks was still current practice.

---

[29] L.W. Cowie, *Henry Newman: An American in London 1708–1743* (1956), 53–4.
[30] CUL, SPCK Archives, EL1CS/1, pp. 201, 205.

The last library founded with its books chained to the shelves was at All Saints Hereford in 1715. Bray and his associates, building on experience in the colonies, the Irish Parliament, and the General Assembly of the Church of Scotland, sought parliamentary protection for parochial libraries. They may have been influenced by replies to a printed advertisement by a 'Divine of the Church of England' inserted at the foot of a brief of 28 February 1705 issued to raise money to rebuild All Saints Oxford, addressed to the 'Minister of every Parochial Church and Chapel in England'. Among other questions, this asked: 'What library is settled in your Parish and by whom?' Most respondents ignored this question, but thirty-one gave positive answers.[31]

Early in 1709, a Bill for the 'Better Preservation of Parochial Libraries' was steered through the House of Commons by Sir Peter King, subsequently Lord Chancellor. It was amended in the Lords by Archbishop Tenison, and received the Royal Assent in April. This required incumbents of livings with libraries to give security for the preservation of the library at the direction of the bishop; bishops and archdeacons were required to inspect libraries at their visitations; incumbents on entering a living were required to make a catalogue to be sent to the bishop and to keep a register of benefactions; no book might be alienated without the consent of the bishop, and then only if a duplicate copy; churchwardens were required to lock libraries during interregna.[32]

In the following ten years, 1710–20, at least sixty-seven new libraries were established, fifty-three of them under the auspices of the SPCK Trustees. There is little evidence, however, for the enforcement of the Act, although in 1750 Bishop Secker of Oxford asked the rector of Henley, 'why have you not yet, after repeated Admonitions for twelve years past, given no security for the Preservation of your Parochial Library and delivered me a Catalogue of it as the Law directs?'[33] The Act has never been repealed.

Although modest, and in the end more modest in their outcome than had been hoped, the efforts in the period after 1680 to make books available to poor clergy in the British Isles (especially in the

---

[31] *Parochial Libraries of the Church of England*, 22. The returns were bound in 6 volumes as *Notitia Parochialis*: LPL, MSS 960–5.

[32] For the full text of the Act see *Parochial Libraries of the Church of England*, 48–50.

[33] *Correspondence of Bishop Secker*, ed. A.P. Jenkins, Oxfordshire Record Society, 57 (1991), 195.

poorer and more remote areas), and in the colonies, were significant developments. Although the aspirations were somewhat undermined by the lack of provision for subsequent addition of new books, the attempt to establish parish libraries and ensure their maintenance was a clear recognition of the importance of access to books to the pastoral and teaching roles of the Anglican clergy in the late Stuart and early Hanoverian years.

WRITING THE HISTORY OF THE ENGLISH BIBLE IN THE EARLY EIGHTEENTH CENTURY[1]

by SCOTT MANDELBROTE

The letter of Scripture suffering various Interpretations, it is plain that Error may pretend to Scripture; the antient Fathers being likewise dead, and not able to vindicate themselves, their writings may be wrested, and Error may make use of them to back itself; Reason too being bypassed by Interest, Education, Passion, Society, &c. . . . Tradition only rests secure.[2]

THE 1680s were a difficult decade for the English Bible, just as they were for so many of the other institutions of the English Protestant establishment. Roman Catholic critics of the Church of England, emboldened by the patronage of James II and his court, engaged in controversy over the rule of faith and the identity of the true Church, much as they had done in the early years of the Reformation or in the 1630s.[3] Nonconformists and freethinkers deployed arguments drawn from Catholic scholarship, in particular from the work of the French Oratorian Richard Simon, and joined in ridicule of the Bible as a sure and sufficient foundation for Christian belief. As one son of the Church of England, who later repented of his errors in these years, put it:

to obtain ye reputation of wit & learning wch is now much esteemed in ye World, I was so unhappy to engage my self in ye sentiments & principles of ye Author of the Critical History of the Old Testament which yet I plainly perceived did directly tend to overthrow al ye belief which Christians have of ye truth & Authority of ye Holy Scriptures.[4]

[1] I am grateful to Jeremy Catto and Martin Kauffmann for assistance in the writing of this essay.
[2] [Joseph Johnston, OSB], *A Reply to the Defence of the Exposition of the Doctrine of the Church of England* (1687), 133.
[3] See Georges Tavard, *La Tradition au XVIIe siècle en France et en Angleterre* (Paris, 1969), 244–486; John Miller, *Popery and Politics in England 1660–1688* (Cambridge, 1973), 239–49; Henry G. van Leeuwen, *The Problem of Certainty in English Thought 1630–1690*, 2nd edn (The Hague, 1970), 13–48; Michael C. Questier, *Conversion, Politics and Religion in England, 1580–1625* (Cambridge, 1996), 12–39.
[4] Nottingham University Library, MS PW Hy 228 (declaration of John Hampden, 15

The insults that were levelled at Protestant faith in the Bible were compounded by the threat posed to the integrity and availability of the text of Scripture itself by the King's Printer, Henry Hills, who had recently converted to Catholicism.[5] Throughout the 1680s, Hills engaged in a battle with the University of Oxford in an attempt to prevent the University's newly established press or its London partners from printing or selling Bibles. He argued that the plan proposed by John Fell, Bishop of Oxford, to finance a learned press through the sale of cheap, well-printed Bibles infringed the patent granted to the University, which limited it to printing only larger and more expensive texts. He therefore claimed that the University's actions breached the terms of the King's Printer's general monopoly over the production of Bibles in England, whilst engaging all the while in a furious war of price-cutting with the Oxford press. Trying to defend the University, Fell argued that it 'will be of great importance to let men see how unfit the King's printers are to be trusted with a monopoly of Bibles'. Despite his efforts to show that 'if we should be stopt from going on to Print, the former extortion would return' and to demonstrate the inferior quality of the King's Printer's publications, Fell's scheme seemed destined to failure with the issue of a Quo Warranto against the University in June 1688.[6]

* * *

Printing at Oxford may have been saved by the Revolution of 1688, which precipitated the fall of Hills from his positions of authority within the Stationers' Company, his removal from the office of King's Printer, and the expulsion of his younger son, Robert, from the demyship at Magdalen College into which he had been intruded in January of that year.[7] Yet neither the intellectual nor the material threat to the standing of the English Bible vanished with the arrival

April 1688); other copies at BL, MS Sloane 3229, fols 183r-6v; CUL, MS Mm I 40, p. 191. For some discussion of the translation and influence of Richard Simon's *Histoire critique du Vieux Testament* (Paris, 1678) in England, see Justin A.I. Champion, 'Père Richard Simon and English Biblical criticism, 1680–1700', in James E. Force and David S. Katz, eds, *Everything Connects: In Conference with Richard H. Popkin* (Leiden, 1999), 39–61.

[5] *A View of Part of the Many Traiterous, Disloyal, and Turn About Actions of H.H. Senior* (1684).

[6] Oxford University Archives, SEP/P/10–11, SEP/P/15–16 (quotations from SEP/P/15, fols 2–3), SP/D/2–3; Bodley, MS Ballard 49, fols 190r–209r, 233r–259v. See also John Johnson and Strickland Gibson, *Print and Privilege at Oxford to the Year 1700* (1946).

[7] J.R. Bloxam, ed., *Magdalen College and King James II, 1686–1688*, Oxford Historical Society, 6 (1886), 181, 194, 208, 225–6, 231–2, 252.

of William of Orange. Catholic mission activity continued in England and with it the arguments that had characterized the late 1680s.[8] These had reached their height in the controversies during 1688 which pitted Thomas Tenison, then rector of St Martin-in-the-Fields, and his young protégé, Henry Wharton, against the Jesuit Andrew Pulton and his ally, a Yorkshire convert to Catholicism, Thomas Ward.[9]

In November 1687, when 'Times now grew warm, and the Papists began to be very confident of their Cause', Wharton had rushed to Cambridge in order to make copies of the most precious manuscripts in the University Library, in Archbishop Parker's library at Corpus Christi College, and the library of Trinity College.[10] These included the materials out of which churchmen had constructed the myth of the antiquity of vernacular use of Scripture in England, supposedly stretching back to the time of the Anglo-Saxons if not of the ancient Britons themselves.[11] Wharton was a remarkably precocious scholar, born, it seems, with the gift of tongues, who as an undergraduate at Caius College, Cambridge, in the early 1680s had read a book a day and received private mathematical tuition from Isaac Newton.[12] The University to which he returned in 1687 was putting up a spirited resistance to the attempts of the Crown to force it to admit Roman Catholics. Newton was one of the leaders of its disobedience.[13] But Wharton found more than old friends there to assist his cause. Among

---

[8] Eamon Duffy, '"Poor protestant flies": conversions to Catholicism in early eighteenth-century England', *SCH*, 15 (1978), 289–304.

[9] [Henry Wharton], *The Pamphlet entituled, Speculum Ecclesiasticum, or an Ecclesiastical Prospective-Glass, considered, in its False Reasonings and Quotations* (1688); [Thomas Tenison], *An Answer to the Letter of the Roman Catholick Souldier* (1688).

[10] Henry Wharton, *Fourteen Sermons preach'd in Lambeth Chapel*, 2nd edn (1700 [1st edn, 1697]), sig. A6v; cf. Bodley, MS Gough Kent 14, fol. 119r. Wharton's transcripts are now in LPL, MSS 585, 593–4.

[11] [Matthew Parker], *De antiquitate Britannicae ecclesiae* (Hanau, 1605 [1st edn, 1572]); James Ussher, *Britannicarum ecclesiarum antiquitates* (Dublin, 1639); William Lloyd, *An Historical Account of Church-Government* (1684); Edward Stillingfleet, *Origines Britannicae* (1685). See also May McKisack, *Medieval History in the Tudor Age* (Oxford, 1971), 1–49; Glanmor Williams, 'Some Protestant views of early British Church history', in his *Welsh Reformation Essays* (Cardiff, 1967), 207–19.

[12] For an account of Wharton's life, see David Douglas, *English Scholars 1660–1730*, 2nd edn (1951), 139–55; 'Excerpta ex Vita Ms. Henrici Whartoni, A.M. a seipso scripta', printed in George D'Oyly, *The Life of William Sancroft*, 2 vols (1821), 2:105–54. Notes and exercises written by Wharton when an undergraduate may be found in LPL, MS 592.

[13] Richard S. Westfall, *Never at Rest. A Biography of Isaac Newton* (Cambridge, 1980), 475–80.

the manuscripts that he discovered at Trinity was the text of a work by Reginald Pecock, an early fifteenth-century Bishop of Chichester who had been forced to resign his bishopric in 1458 under suspicion of heresy. Wharton had soon transcribed and edited Pecock's *Treatise proving Scripture to be the Rule of Faith*, and equipped it with a lengthy preface that cleared Pecock of the charge of Lollardy and asserted the supremacy of the Bible over tradition as the rule of faith of both the primitive and the medieval Church.[14] Less than a month after the granting of the imprimatur for this work, permission was given for the publication of another book in which Wharton had a hand. This was the re-edition of Thomas James's *Treatise of the Corruption of Scripture, Councils and Fathers*, which had been written as a defence of his earlier *Bellum papale*, itself an attack on Tridentine attitudes to Scripture with reference to the supposed inaccuracies of the Sixtine and Clementine editions of the Vulgate.[15]

Responding to James, Thomas Ward drew attention to the inconsistency of the Protestant approach to the Bible as a rule of faith. He made fun of the differences to be found between the various vernacular translations of Scripture produced during the sixteenth and seventeenth centuries, highlighting passages that related to points of doctrinal conflict between Catholics and Protestants to suggest the appearance of a lack of certainty among the Reformers.[16] Although forced underground by political change, ideas like Ward's remained a threat to the image and doctrine of the Church of England. Indeed, Wharton soon ventured into print again to assert the antiquity of the practice of allowing the laity to read the Bible in the vernacular, and the consequent novelty and error of papal prohibitions on this activity. Editing and extending an unpublished manuscript by Archbishop James Ussher, which had been put into his hands by William Sancroft, Archbishop of Canterbury, Wharton claimed that their respective attitudes to Scripture marked out the

---

[14] Reginald Pecock, *A Treatise proving Scripture to be the Rule of Faith*, ed. Henry Wharton (1688), sigs A1–4v, pp. ix–xxii, xxxii–xl. The manuscript itself is described by Montague Rhodes James, *The Western Manuscripts in the Library of Trinity College, Cambridge*, 4 vols (Cambridge, 1900–4), I:452–3.

[15] Thomas James, *A Treatise of the Corruption of Scripture, Councils and Fathers, by the Prelats, Pastors and Pillars of the Church of Rome, for Meintenance of Popery* (1688 [1st edn, in 5 parts, 1611]); cf. idem, *Bellum papale, sive concordia discors Sixti quinti, et Clementis octavi, circa Hieronymianam editionem* (1678 [1st edn, 1600]).

[16] T[homas] W[ard], *The Errata to the Protestant Bible, or the Truth of their English Translations Examin'd* (1688).

Church of England as the embodiment of the primitive Church and Rome as its antithesis.[17]

Wharton's publication of Ussher signalled a turning-point in the writing of the history of the English Bible and its uses for Churchmen as well as for their critics. The events of the late 1680s and early 1690s led to divisions within the Church of England itself over the issue of whether it was possible in conscience to swear oaths to the new King and Queen, William III and Mary II. Wharton's loyalty to the idea of a national Church led to his banishment from the circle of Archbishop Sancroft, who eventually found himself among the non-jurors.[18] Nevertheless, Wharton inherited several of Sancroft's manuscripts, including the papers of William Laud, on the archbishop's death in 1694. Yet Wharton's authority as an advocate for his Church had by then been diminished by his partisan and xenophobic attack on Gilbert Burnet's *History of the Reformation*.[19] Moreover, some of the men who followed Sancroft into schism with the Church of England began to write their own histories of the English Bible which were markedly critical of the tradition of vernacular translation that Wharton had extolled.

Thus Jeremy Collier proclaimed that Archbishop Arundel, in his *Constitutions* (composed in 1407 and issued in 1409), 'was so far in the Right, as not to allow every private Person the Liberty of translating the *Scriptures*'. His defence of episcopal authority extended to an apology for the Tridentine doctrine of the equivalence of the standing of Scripture and Tradition as well as a hearty defence of the Authorized Version.[20] Other non-jurors attacked contemporary attempts to revise the Psalter, arguing for the continued use of the old translation of Cranmer's Great Bible (1539) which was retained in the Book of Common Prayer. John Johnson, a Kentish High Churchman who was sympathetic to the non-jurors, for example, suggested

---

[17] James Ussher, *Historia dogmatica controversiae inter orthodoxos & pontificios de scripturis et sacris vernaculis*, ed. Henry Wharton (1690), 97–192, 210–48; cf. Wharton's own *Auctarium historiae dogmaticae Jacobi Usserii* (1689), which was appended to the edition of Ussher.

[18] Cf. Wharton's grandest work, dedicated in part to Sancroft, *Anglia sacra*, 2 vols (1691).

[19] Anthony Harmer [i.e. Henry Wharton], *A Specimen of some Errors and Defects in the History of the Reformation of the Church of England* (1693). Cf. Gilbert Burnet, *The History of the Reformation of the Church of England*, 3 vols (1679–1714). At least one contemporary observer, who was well-placed to know, doubted that Harmer was Wharton. See CUL, MS Add. 3, no. 43 (Nicholas Battely to John Strype, 22 Feb. 1692/3), MS Add. 4, no. 27 (Wharton to Richard Chiswell, 28 Oct. 1693).

[20] Jeremy Collier, *An Ecclesiastical History of Great Britain*, 2 vols (1708–14), 1:635 (for the quotation); 2:iv, 869.

that 'there is reason to believe that nothing has more discouraged the Ruling part of Foreign Churches in Communion with that of *Rome*, from Translating the Bible into the Vulgar Tongues, than the Experience they have had of the ill use made of it here in *England*', attacking in particular dissenting authors 'whose Stomachs turn at that Bible, by which our Reformation was first wrought'.[21] Both Collier and Johnson wished to stress the origins of the Authorized Version, which was issued by royal command, in the episcopally-sanctioned translations of the sixteenth century. They denied that scholarly discoveries, for example of the meaning of Hebrew words, justified departure from traditional versions of Scripture, and were scornful of the notion that individuals might be free to interpret the Bible for themselves. By these arguments they suggested that the use of certain vernacular Scriptures might not pose any obstacle to reunion with Rome. This was an aim which seemed to both High Churchmen and non-jurors the fulfilment of an aspiration within some quarters of the Church of England, dating back at least to the 1630s, and their own best chance of political or ecclesiastical rehabilitation.

The argument that developed again embraced the mundane world of the printing and publication of the English Bible as well as the rarefied realms of history and scholarship. Johnson therefore approved of the plans that Arthur Charlett entertained for the Oxford University Press to publish a corrected edition of the Authorized Version, just as it had left the translators' hands. He rejected contemporary attempts to appease dissenting criticism by adding references and other paratextual material to editions of the English Bible.[22] In common with a number of others, he was also interested in the evidence that ancient copies of the English Bible, either in manuscript or from the early years of print, might yield about the history and context of its translation. The most successful exponents of research into the history of the printing of the English Bible, however, came to rather different conclusions from Johnson, although several of them shared his sympathy for the non-jurors.

Humfrey Wanley, the librarian to the Harley family, presided over a collection that would come to include the then only known copy of

[21] [John Johnson], *Holy David and his Old English Translators Clear'd* (1706), 2.
[22] Bodley, MS Ballard 15, fols 108–9 (Johnson to Charlett, [26 Dec.] 1713); cf. *The Holy Bible* (1701) (= T.H. Darlow and H.F. Moule, *Historical Catalogue of Printed Editions of the English Bible 1525–1961*, revised and expanded by A.S. Herbert (1968) [hereafter DMH], no. 868).

the first edition of William Tyndale's translation of the New
Testament (Worms, 1526).[23] Throughout the first decade of the
eighteenth century, he was active in buying early editions of the
English Bible and in collecting for himself books and fragments of
books that would cast light on their history.[24] Among those who
helped him to form his collection were John Bagford, a notable book
scout and historian of printing, and John Strype, the author of a
number of histories of the English Reformation that presented
Cranmer and others in a positive light for their work in promoting
the vernacular reading of Scripture and providing accurate printed
editions of the Bible.[25] Wanley in turn advised these and other authors
about the early printing history of the English Bible. In general,
Wanley sympathized with several of Johnson's opinions. He appears,
however, to have shared a rather different view of the Authorized
Version, which although largely excellent, 'has still many considerable
Faults, and very much needs another Review'.[26]

Wanley and his friends exploited opportunities provided by changes
in the market for rare books and in the collecting habits of their
patrons to bring new information to bear on the history of the English
Bible.[27] Their conclusions were often tentative and sometimes
erroneous but they were far better informed than any of their
predecessors or competitors. With the exception of Strype, however,
their work remained largely unpublished and unrelated to the printed
polemic about the translation of the English Bible. It laid the

[23] See DMH, no. 2, now BL, C.188.a.17, and Joseph Ames, *A List of Various Editions of the Bible and Parts thereof, in English from the Year 1526 to 1776* (1778), copy at Bodley, 258 e.104, manuscript on verso of titlepage. Ames secured access to the book for John Lewis: see Bodley, MS Don. d.89, fol. 72.

[24] See BL, MSS Harley 3781, fols 121–4; 5908, fols 5v, 60r–62v; CUL, MSS Add. 4, no. 103; Add. 6, nos 296, 305, 306, 333, 336; Bodley, MS Ballard 13, fol. 81.

[25] For Bagford, see Milton McC. Gatch, 'John Bagford, bookseller and antiquary', *British Library Journal*, 12 (1986), 150–71; idem, 'John Bagford as collector and disseminator of manuscript fragments', *The Library*, 6th ser., 7 (1985), 95–114; BL, MSS Harley 5908–9; Sloane 1378; Bodley, MSS Rawlinson Letters 20, fols 360–1; 21, fols 38–9; CUL, MSS Dd.X.56–7. On Strype, see John Joseph Morison, 'John Strype: historian of the English Reformation' (Syracuse University, Ph.D. thesis, 1976); CUL, MSS Add. 1–10; John Strype, *Memorials of the Most Reverend Father in God Thomas Cranmer* (1694), esp. 60, 443; idem, *The Life and Acts of Matthew Parker* (1711), esp. 205–9, 272–3, 399–404.

[26] 'An essay upon the English translation of the Bible', *Bibliotheca Literaria*, 4 (1723), 1–23, at 22. This piece refers frequently to Wanley's conclusions.

[27] See Anna Katherine Swift, 'The formation of the library of Charles Spencer, 3rd Earl of Sunderland (1674–1722): A study in the antiquarian book trade', 2 vols (Oxford University, D.Phil. thesis, 1986).

foundation, however, for the writings of the most prolific historian of the English Bible and for his engagement in argument with non-juring and Catholic opponents of the current practice of vernacular translation and dissenting critics of the accuracy of the Authorized Version.

* * *

The publications of John Lewis (1675–1747), rector of Margate in Kent, were one part of a campaign to buttress the status of the Authorized Version, encouraged by Whig bishops like Edmund Gibson of London or White Kennett of Peterborough and promoted by prominent divines such as Daniel Waterland. In 1724 Gibson was confronted by the accusation that the continued poor printing of the English Bible by the King's Printer, who by now also controlled the Oxford Bible Press, and the high prices that he charged, 'would help blind all the young and poor people in the Nation, and take the Bible out of their hands as much as the Church of Rome does'.[28] His solution was to obtain an Order in Council requiring that Bibles and Prayer Books be printed on paper and with type of an agreed standard, that the King's Printer employ adequate proof-readers, and that exact prices be set on the title-pages of these works.[29] Although it had only limited effect, this represented the first serious attempt by the hierarchy to regulate the monopoly on printing the English Bible. In the late 1710s, Kennett had already encouraged Lewis and another young divine, John Russell, to work on the life and writings of John Wyclif, and in particular on Wycliffite translations of the Bible.[30]

The status of the translations of the Bible by Wyclif and his followers had been debated from the time of the Reformation. Thomas James asserted that Wyclif's view of Scripture was compatible with that of the Reformers; and many earlier authors had used works that they supposed were by Wyclif to defend a Protestant interpretation of the Roman Catholic Church's recent fall into error.[31] Wharton, however, rejected Wyclif's authorship of the prefaces to the Wycliffite Bibles, and suggested that those Bibles that contained them were the

[28] LPL, MS 1741, fol. 28r (Edward Gee to Edmund Gibson, 6 May 1724).
[29] *The London Gazette*, 6262 (21–25 April 1724), fol. 2r; the order was noticed by John Lewis, see Bodley, MS Eng.Hist.c.313, p. 207.
[30] On Russell, see Bodley, MSS Rawlinson J fol. 4, fols 236r, 333–4; Rawlinson J fol. 7, fol. 93r; Rawlinson J 4° 1, fol. 214v; BL, MS Landowne 1038, fols 81–2. For Lewis's links with Kennett, see BL, MS Add. 28,651, fol. 27v; Bodley, MS Eng. Misc.c.273, p. 42a.
[31] Thomas James, *An Apologie for Iohn Wickliffe* (Oxford, 1608); Margaret Aston, *Lollards and Reformers* (1984), 243–71.

work of another translator.[32] Wharton's views were one reflection of
the confusion caused by the existence of multiple copies of the
Wycliffite translation of the Bible, in two versions.[33] A further
complication was the belief that there had been complete English
translations of the Bible before Wyclif.[34] Russell was among those who
asserted that there were surviving manuscripts of pre-Wycliffite
English Bibles.[35] This was a notion that Lewis, with the support of
Waterland, came to reject.[36] Unlike Russell, who had proposed to
prepare a version of the Wycliffite Bible, Lewis was successful in
raising sufficient subscriptions for the publication in 1731 of his
edition of Wyclif's New Testament.[37] For that edition, Lewis took
as his copy texts two manuscripts of what scholars now know to be a
later Wycliffite version of the translation of the New Testament,
claiming that they were by Wyclif himself.[38] In contrast to Russell,
who also used the later version for his collations, Lewis did not believe
that the disputed preface was by Wyclif, preferring to follow Waterland's advice and to ascribe it to John Purvey.[39] Lewis's own editorial
preferences seem to have been formed by the personal associations,
with Waterland in Cambridge and with the Dering family in Kent,
which gave him access to these copy texts. The particular manuscripts
that he used also lacked the material that Wharton had claimed
marked out the work of a later translator.

Whatever the reasons for his choice of texts, Lewis's work on the
Wycliffite New Testament formed part of a clear plan of scholarly but

---

[32] Harmer [i.e. Wharton], *Specimen*, 16–17.

[33] See Sven L. Fristedt, *The Wycliffe Bible*, 3 parts (Stockholm, 1953–73); Anne Hudson, *The Premature Reformation* (Oxford, 1988), 222–77.

[34] For example, James, *Treatise*, part 5, 30.

[35] See Jacobus Le Long, *Bibliotheca sacra*, 2 vols (Paris, 1723), 1:424–6.

[36] Bodley, MS Rawlinson d.376, fol. 63r; cf. John Lewis, *A Complete History of the several Translations of the Holy Bible and New Testament into English*, 2nd edn (1739), 17, 43–4.

[37] John Russell, *A Sermon preach'd in Lambeth Chapel* (1722), sig. E5v; idem, *Proposals for Printing by Subscription, the Holy Bible translated by John Wickleffe* (1719). Russell's transcripts are now BL, MSS Add. 5890–5902. Cf. *The New Testament*, tr. John Wyclif, ed. John Lewis (1731); an annotated list of subscribers is in Bodley, NT. Eng.1731 b.1.

[38] The copy texts used by Lewis can now be found at Bodley, MS Gough Eccl.Top.5 (for the Gospels) and CUL, British and Foreign Bible Society Library, MS 155 (for the Epistles, Acts, and Apocalypse). Cf. *New Testament*, ed. Lewis, 104–5. For descriptions of these manuscripts, see Josiah Forshall and Frederic Madden, eds, *The Holy Bible, containing the Old and New Testaments, with the Apocryphal Books, in the Earliest English Versions made from the Latin Vulgate by John Wycliffe and his Followers*, 4 vols (Oxford, 1850), 1:l, lxiv; Conrad Lindberg, 'The manuscripts and versions of the Wycliffite Bible', *Studia Neophilologica*, 42 (1970), 333–47.

[39] Lewis, *Complete History*, 35–40; cf. Bodley, MS Rawlinson d.376, fols 63–4.

polemical writing that was designed to dismiss the pretensions of Catholics, non-jurors, and Dissenters alike. Early in his career, he had attacked his former friend, Johnson, over his beliefs about the sacraments; in his later work, Lewis also dismissed non-juring views about the inappropriateness of private versions of Scripture and the divine inspiration of the English liturgy.[40] In the life that he published in 1720 and in his history of biblical translation, Lewis tried to clear Wyclif of Catholic accusations of heresy and to demonstrate that the Wycliffite translation of the Vulgate was more accurate than those produced by post-Reformation Catholics.[41] He treated scathingly contemporary Catholic criticism of English translators, in particular those of the Authorized Version, whilst being alive to the scholarly potential of the work of authors like Simon.[42] Although charitable towards moderate nonconformity, Lewis was sceptical of the claims of Dissenters that they had the right to revise passages of the Authorized Version that dealt with points of doctrine. He also demonstrated the usual anxieties of an Anglican parish priest towards the wilder interpretations of Scripture put forward by some of the sects.[43] Perhaps above all, Lewis cast himself as the heir of Henry Wharton, whose work he defended publicly in the second edition of his history of English translations of the Bible. Both Wharton and Lewis owed much to the patronage of Thomas Tenison, who had lent manuscripts to Wharton, and, as Archbishop of Canterbury, has encouraged Lewis in his earliest preferment. Wharton had preceded Lewis as the vicar of a living on the Isle of Thanet in Kent and had set a standard for scholarship and clerical behaviour to which he aspired. Like Wharton, Lewis also chose to work on Reginald Pecock, taking his testimony as proof of the way in which the Catholic Church had gone astray in the years before the Reformation, and deploying his 'Treatise of Faith' to argue that even opponents of the Lollards had endorsed doctrines similar to those of later Protestants.[44]

---

[40] [John Lewis], *A Vindication of the Right Reverend the Ld. Bishop of Norwich* ([1714]); cf. Bodley, MS Clarendon Press c.17; [John Lewis], *A Specimen of the Gross Errors in the Second Volume of Mr Collier's Ecclesiastial History* (1724), p. v; Manchester, John Rylands University Library, MS 47, esp. fol. 24r; Lewis, *Complete History*, 68–71.

[41] John Lewis, *The History of the Life and Sufferings of the Reverend and Learned John Wicliffe* (1720); idem, *Complete History*, 23–5.

[42] Ibid., 44–5, 356–65, 373–5.

[43] London, Dr. Williams's Library, MS 12.8; Lewis, *Complete History*, 46, 365–72; Manchester, John Rylands University Library, MS 49.

[44] Lewis, *Complete History*, iii–xvii; Bodley, MS Gough Kent 14, fol. 117r; John Lewis, *The*

The histories of John Lewis thus built on more than fifty years of English Protestant scholarship and polemic about the vernacular Scriptures. They developed the insights of a new generation of collectors of printed books and collators of manuscripts and provided an account of heroic exemplars for modern printers and their readers. In the process, they helped to face down the detractors of the Authorized Version. But above all, they gave new life to the claim that the essentials of English Protestantism had been known in England well before the Reformation, and countered the arguments of those who were, in Lewis's words, 'paving the way for Popery, by alienating the minds and affections of the English from the Reformation'.[45]

Peterhouse, Cambridge and All Souls College, Oxford

Life of the Learned and Right Reverend Reynold Pecock (1744). See also LPL, MS 942, no. 47 (Wharton to Tenison, 20 Jan. 1692); Jeremy Gregory, *Restoration, Reformation and Reform, 1660–1828* (Oxford, 2000), 91–2; John Shirley, 'John Lewis of Margate', *Archaeologia Cantiana*, 64 (1951), 39–56.
[45] Bodley, MS Eng.Hist.c.273, fol. 8r.

MEMORIES OF FAITH: THE 'CHRISTIAN SUTRAS' OF EIGHTEENTH-CENTURY CHINA

by LARS PETER LAAMANN

D RAWING on official documents filed at the First Historical Archives[1] in Beijing, and on missionary correspondence located at the Archivio storico 'de Propaganda Fide' in Rome,[2] this paper will focus on printed manifestations of popular Christianity during the mid-Qing period. It will argue that, following the exclusion of foreign missionaries after the imperial edict of 1724, tendencies towards inculturation accelerated.[3] Early nineteenth-century sources reveal that the Christian villagers were well aware of the fact that they had preserved but a fraction of what the foreign priests had introduced several generations earlier, yet the sheer memory of their ancestors' faith was sufficient to provide the religious and social cohesion which characterized Christian life during the eighteenth century. While developing into a syncretic expression of a belief originally introduced by European missionaries, popular Chinese Christianity absorbed elements of other religious systems, mainly popular Daoism and Buddhist millenarianism, as well as 'Confucian' patterns of social morality. The spiritual writings memorized and passed from generation to generation in semi-literate rural communities played an important part in the formation of a new, Christian expression of popular religiosity. Increasingly relying on the (oral) recollections of ancestors and community elders, generations of

---

[1] Hereafter FHA. These are the 'China Number One Historical Archives', the former Imperial Archives. Most material consists of memorials sent by provincial governors to the imperial administration, as well as imperial edicts. The documents presented in this article exclusively pertain to the 'Grand State Council Records for Palace Memorials'. For a systematic overview, see *Zhongguo diyi lishi dang'anguan guancang dang'an gaishu* [*An Outline of the Collections of the First Historical Archives*] (Beijing, 1985).

[2] Hereafter APF. For a complete overview see Josef Metzler, *Inventario dell'archivio storico della Sacra Congregazione per l'Evangelizzazione dei Popoli o 'De Propaganda Fide'* (Rome, 1983).

[3] For a brief introduction to the currently used terminology, see R. Costa, *One Faith, Many Cultures: Inculturation, Indigenization and Contextualization* (Maryknoll, NY, 1988). It should also be borne in mind that Roman Catholicism remained the sole representative of Christianity in China until the early nineteenth century, when Protestant missionaries of North European origin began to proselytize. Chinese Nestorianism had already become extinct prior to the Mongolian invasion in the thirteenth century.

Chinese Christians used Christian tracts in order to boost their sense of Christian identity. Before proceeding to analyse the nature and impact of such printed 'memories' of the Christian faith, it is necessary to survey the development of Chinese Christianity during the eighteenth century in general.[4]

* * *

In the aftermath of the subjugation of the Ming empire (1368–1644) by Manchurian forces, the new Qing dynasty (1644–1911) had to deal with the threat of violent insurrection within its borders and therefore perceived any unauthorized gatherings as subversion against the state. The European missionaries employed by the imperial administration had been welcomed since the 1590s, their Christian religion – known as the Teachings of the Lord of Heaven (*tianzhujiao*) – being protected by imperial decree and its propagation tolerated. The harmonious relationship between the Jesuits at the imperial court and the Kangxi Emperor (1662–1723) began to suffer when the Vatican refused to tolerate the accommodating policy of the Jesuits towards the perform-ance of the traditional rites for deceased ancestors.[5] Irritated by the papal interference into the affairs of his own empire – including the lives of his trusted Jesuit servants – the Kangxi Emperor enforced a licence system in December 1706, followed by a ban on proselytiza-tion, and on the construction of new churches in May 1717. China's Christian communities now began to feel the consequences of the state's growing suspicion. The atmosphere deteriorated further after the accession to the throne of the Yongzheng Emperor (1723–36). Claiming that foreigners created disorder in the empire by propagating a deity superior to Heaven (*tian*) – the basis of legitimacy for any ruling dynasty – the governor for Fujian, Zhang Boxing (1652–1725), submitted a petition requesting that all foreign missionaries be expelled, the Christian communities dispersed and their churches

---

[4] This article will not primarily deal with the issue of inculturation, though it developed out of my recently completed Ph.D. thesis, 'The inculturation of Christianity in late imperial China' (University of London, 2001).

[5] For more insight into the so-called Rites Controversy, see George Minamiki, *The Chinese Rites Controversy: from its Beginnings to Modern Times* (Chicago, 1985), as well as David E. Mungello, ed., *The Chinese Rites Controversy: its History and Meaning* (Nettetal, 1994). An important archival source is BL, Eur. MSS 867.g.13.(3): Pope Alexander VII, 'Préjugez légitimes en faveur du decret de N.S. Père le Pape Alexandre VII. (le 23 Mars 1656) et de la pratique des Jésuites, au sujet des honneurs que les Jésuites rendent à Confucius et à leurs ancestres' (Paris, *c.*1700).

converted into educational institutions.[6] The governor was anything but a friend of Christianity – and of the foreigners who spread the creed in his province. His rationale was simple: punitive measures were necessary to 'rectify the minds of the people, confused and dumbfounded by foreign teachings'. Uncontrollable elements had infiltrated his province, taken advantage of the ignorance and innocence of his subjects, and spread beyond control.[7]

Following the ascent of anti-missionary officials in Yongzheng's entourage and the arrest of leading pro-Jesuits in the first months of 1723, Manchurian noblemen and leading state officials requested the prohibition of Christianity in China and the expulsion of all foreign missionaries, except from Beijing 'where they could be useful'. Such memorials provided the basis for the so-called Yongzheng Edict of 10 January 1724, which prohibited all missionary activity outside Beijing and Macau – though stopping short of outlawing Christianity altogether. Nevertheless, between 1725 and 1732 three general persecutions against Christianity in the empire were authorized. The petition owed as much to the fratricidal politics of the late Kangxi court as to the tensions between the Jesuits and their enemies in Europe. Some historians have reduced his decision to the new Emperor's personal wrath against the Christian Sunu clan.[8] The rapid fall from grace of the Manchurian nobleman Sunu and the members of his influential family is well documented, both through surviving court records and in the relations of the court missionaries. Sunu (1648–1725) and the heir-pretenders Acina (Yinsi, 1681–1726) and Seshe (Yintang, 1683–1726) were members of the imperial clan who had embraced Christianity during the Kangxi period.[9] As a general background to this

---

[6] For a detailed account of the Christian missions during two first decades of the eighteenth century, see Antonio Sisto Rosso, *Apostolic Legations to China of the Eighteenth Century* (South Pasadena, CA, 1948).

[7] Zhang Boxing's reasonings are presented in a letter by Domenico Perroni of 1723, Cf. APF, SOCP 'Indie Orientali' XXXI (1723–1725), fol. 147. The letter itself refers to the martyrium of Francisco Buccheretti and Giovanni Batista Messari, among other missionary novices.

[8] An edict from the early years of the Yongzheng Emperor's rule, reprinted in Wang Zhichun, ed. Zhao Chunchen, *Qingchao rou yuan ji* [*Records of Hospitality towards Strangers in the Qing Dynasty*] (Beijing, 1989), 64–6, reveals his discerning religious spirit.

[9] See the unpublished paper by Eugenio Menegón, 'Surniama Tragoedia: religion and political martyrdom in the Yongzheng Period', presented at the Symposium on the History of Christianity in China, Hong Kong, 2–4 Oct. 1996. The legal proceedings against the members of the Sunu clan can be inspected in *Wenxian congbian*, as the 'Case against Yinsi and Yintang' [*Yinsi yintang an*].

turmoil we should recall that the Qing empire was still struggling to quell rebellions threatening the legitimacy of the Manchurian overlords as such.[10] The very same year saw the promulgation of laws aimed at countering the spread of 'heretical teachings' (xiejiao) other than Christianity, mainly originating from millenarian Buddhist movements. These adverse conditions help explain why throughout the brief but eventful Yongzheng period, Christianity had been publicly marked as a subversive, 'heretical' creed, aiming to undermine the stability of the empire through involvement in court affairs.[11]

To the remaining missionaries the new policy was an impediment: provincial churches had to be abandoned for the safety of the capital, buildings belonging to missionaries were confiscated, and the remaining foreign pastors had to propagate their faith under cover of the night.[12] To local Christian communities the consequences were often disastrous, forcing their leaders underground in times of official investigation. The mere rumour of belonging to a 'heretical sect' was sufficient to incur punishment. Village elders and members of the rural elite were urged to report on 'suspicious' communities wherever they could be detected. Religious proselytization had thus become politicized, missionaries branded as rebel leaders.[13] The persecutions of the late Kangxi and Yongzheng eras were concentrated in those provinces, in particular south-eastern Fujian, where magistrates and circuit officials had already been criticizing the presence of missionaries.[14] Nevertheless, many Christians continued to maintain

---

[10] For a more detailed picture of the insurrections during the early Qing period, see Zhou Yumin and Shao Yong, Zhongguo huibang shi [History of China's Brotherhoods and Societies] (Shanghai, 1993), ch. 1. The importance the Qing attached to a merciless policy towards rebels of all persuasions is vividly illustrated in J.J.M. de Groot, Sectarianism and Religious Persecution: A Page in the History of Religions (Leiden, 1901), 340–9.

[11] Ibid., 273–4.

[12] The observations are based on the diary of the Roman missionary Carolus a Castorano, for the years 1698–1724: BAV, MS Lat. Vat. 12849, 'Brevis narratio itineris ex Italia usq. ad Chinam'. It contains (alongside a detailed baptismal record of Chinese Christians) an account of individual persecutions against Christian villagers and missionaries during this period, in particular the campaign of 1714 in Shandong province.

[13] As in the case of the Chinese missionary Cai Zu, arrested in Fujian province in 1733. 'Traitor' (jianmin) Cai was found in the company of two Portuguese nationals and of several books, including a volume depicting 'Christian paintings and statues' (tianzhujiao tuxiang). See Wang Zhichun, Qingchao rou yuan ji, 86.

[14] The Yongzheng memorial sent shockwaves through the missionary community, and was hastily translated for relay to Europe. See, for instance, the letter of 1724 by Domenico Perroni to the Propaganda offices in Rome: APF, SOCP 'Indie Orientali' (1723–5) XXXI, fols 40–2, 125–31.

healthy links with local officials in several important urban centres. Despite the imperial edict, the magistrates of certain districts even connived at the presence of European – as well as Chinese – missionaries.[15] But to the detriment of the China mission, frictions between the missionary orders weakened the position of the missionaries immensely – and in particular that of the Jesuit order. The despair felt by many was eloquently expressed by Johannes Müllener, immediately after the Yongzheng edict had been issued:

> Since the edict has come into force – the missionaries arrested and the churches occupied and desecrated by the public militias – the Christians and neophytes have been chased out of the city perimeters, with few earthly possessions. The Certificate [of toleration] . . . has been torn up. And with it, the arrogance and the vanity, which made us seem so great in China. It's all over and vanished with the wind.[16]

The first decades of the Qianlong period (1736–96) are best described as an 'unexpected opportunity' for the empire's struggling Christian communities. Following the harshness of the Yongzheng rule, China's Christians pinned their hopes on the incumbent Qianlong Emperor. Despite having grown up under the tutelage of the Yongzheng Emperor, the young Emperor did not share the latter's personal aversion to the influence of the foreign men residing at court. His initial leniency towards Christianity has been explained by the new Emperor's fascination with Western technology and art.[17] Senior state

---

[15] Emphasised in a letter by Antoine Gaubil sent to Paris, 6 Nov. 1726: Antoine Gaubil, *Correspondance de Pékin 1722–1759* (Geneva, 1970), 128–9.

[16] Free translation of the original: 'Perciò si è messo in essecuzione il sudetto decreto, e li Missonarii sono scacciati, le chiese restano occupate, e profanate per il publico servizio: li christiani e neophiti, benche perseguitati in altri luoghi, con puochi danari, se tirano fuora de tra vagli. Il Diploma, ò patente imperiale va . . . per esser abbruggiato, e cosi l'arroganza e la vanità questi noi . . . fui cioè grandi di Cina, è finita, e svanita col fumo.' AFP, SOCP 'Indie Orientali' XXXI (1723–5), fols 188–9.

[17] The role of the painter Giuseppe Castiglione, SJ (Chinese name, Lang Shining) – whose work included depictions of the victorious Qing troops, European landscapes and the construction of the Yuanmingyuan summer palace – has been widely speculated on. The fact that Castiglione never mastered the Chinese language makes the Emperor's favourite court missionary even more enigmatic. His quiet yet persistent interventions on behalf of China's Christians, however, certainly left an impression on the Emperor. It has even been argued that the paintings and robot toys produced for the Emperor did more for the advancement of Christianity in the empire than any theological discourse. See the unpublished conference paper by Alabiso Alida, 'Castiglione and the introduction of European painting and architecture in China', for the international symposium 'China and the World in the Eighteenth Century', Beijing, June 1995.

officials, however, were alarmed by increasing sectarian activity in the empire and were furthermore still influenced by the repressive Yongzheng years. The uprising of the Muslim population of Shaanxi in the years following his accession to the throne exacerbated the determination of certain anti-Christian elements within the elite to deal with the Christians effectively before they too became a problem. Bowing to their pressure, the Emperor not only refused to alter his father's edict, but reinforced legislation aimed at punishing Manchurian bannermen who entertained contact with Christian missionaries. Sporadic government action followed suit, for instance when in the winter of 1737 officials seized a Chinese Christian about to baptize a dying infant in a street in Beijing. Absolving street orphans before their imminent death was also one of the routine rites performed by the foreign missionaries, giving rise to allegations of perversion and superstitious practices. The incident thus gave state officials a first opportunity to test the friendship between the young Emperor and the court missionaries. Though the suggested death penalty was converted to severe caning after earnest pleading by court Jesuits, the verdict and the ensuing confirmation of the Yongzheng edict proved that any initial optimism had been premature.[18] With progressing age, the Emperor announced policies of increasing severity. Owing to the personal intercession of court missionaries, however, persecutions were usually brief and rarely resulted in direct fatalities.[19] The early Qianlong edicts did, however, allow local magistrates to arrest Christians in their districts, though it is vital to understand that the persecutions against Christian communities were part of the wider campaign against 'heretical sects' which was unfolding at the same time.[20] The anti-Christian edicts of the years 1747–9, for instance, coincided with unrest in the predominantly Muslim western areas of the empire.[21] The same years were marked by a vigorous resurgence of

[18] The incident is reported in Zhang Ze, *Qingdai jinjiaoqi de tianzhujiao* [*Catholic Christianity during the Qing Prohibition*] (Taibei, 1992), 120–1.

[19] The executions of Bishop Sanz and four other European priests in 1746 can thus be regarded as exceptions.

[20] This also affected the Three-Teachings-in-One (*sanjiao heyi*), which combined Daoism, Buddhism, and Confucianism into a highly popular syncretic movement. Three-in-One temples were destroyed and often only survived under the guise of Confucian academies, where its founder Lin Zhaoen (1517–98) was displayed in the manner of the Confucian sages. See Kenneth Dean, *Lord of the Three in One: The Spread of a Cult in Southeast China* (Princeton, NJ, 1998), 17–18.

[21] Despite repeated reassertions from Chinese Christians and European missionaries that the two religions were not identical. See Ma Zhao, 'Shilun Qianlong shiqi (1736–1796)

millenarian Buddhism, which had proliferated in all parts of eastern China.[22] In its terminology and punitive action, the anti-heresy drive of the Qianlong years forced popular Christian and Buddhist movements into the same category of 'heretical cults' (*xiejiao*).

State action continued with the anti-Christian persecutions of 1753 in Hubei, 1754 and 1759 in Fujian, in the 1760s in Sichuan, 1767 in Guangdong, 1768 in Henan, and 1774 in Jiangxi province.[23] Foreign missionaries were expressly forbidden to go ashore, while traders had to limit their transactions to the port of Guangzhou. Nevertheless, a number of European missionaries ventured to penetrate the hinterland from the safe haven of Macau. Frequenting the country lanes connecting the Cantonese mainland with Macau, the missionaries obtained and distributed 'heretical scriptures' (*xieshu*). Moreover, the missionaries had established connections with local Christians who promised to print and distribute copies of such scriptures in other provinces. Afraid of the 'inflammatory' (*pian-huo*) effects of the unchecked proliferation of heterodox literature, the state officials decided to adopt a hostile stance against Christians who cooperated with foreign missionaries. The renewed anti-Christian action formed part of an anti-heresy drive, which in the 1780s culminated in a first major campaign against the (Buddhist) Eight Trigram movement, following an uprising in Shandong province. Shandong had already gained notoriety as the origin of the Wang Lun uprising of 1774, and exerted a magnetic attraction on similar heterodox movements.[24] The Qianlong persecutions intensified following the end of a military campaign against Muslim insurgents in Gansu province, triggered by the discovery in December 1784 of two foreign priests in the vicinity of Xi'an, a major city in central China. Though the initial impact was first felt by the Christians of the districts surrounding the capital, other provinces quickly followed suit. Interrogations produced evidence of thriving Christian communities throughout central and northern China.[25]

chajin tianzhujiao shijian' ['A preliminary study of events relating to the prohibition of Christianity during the Qianlong period, 1736–1796'] (MA dissertation, Research Centre for Qing History, Renmin University of China, Beijing, 1999), 30–2.

[22] See de Groot, *Sectarianism and Religious Persecution*, 280–7.

[23] See Ma Zhao, 'Shilun Qianlong shiqi', p. 19. For Sichuan province see Léonide Guiot, *La Mission du Su-tchuen au XVIIIme siècle: vie et apostolat de Mgr Pottier* (Paris, 1892), 149.

[24] See Susan Naquin, *Shantung Rebellion: The Wang Lun Uprising of 1774* (New Haven, CT, and London, 1981), xiii–xv, for a brief account of sectarian insurrection in the province.

[25] For the historical background of Christianity in the provinces of Shanxi and Shaanxi, see Fortunato Margiotti, *Il cattolicismo nello Shansi dalle origini al 1738* (Rome, 1958).

Meanwhile the situation was becoming more difficult even in the Chinese capital, which was technically excluded from the Yongzheng edict. The bishops of Beijing found it increasingly difficult to extend protection into the surrounding provinces, mainly due to a severe shortage in numbers: in 1785 seven Chinese priests shared their pastoral duties with the sixteen remaining foreigners.[26] It was nevertheless from the centres in Beijing that the Christian communities in the surrounding provinces gained their logistical and moral support during a period when the missionary presence in the rest of the empire was limited and transient.[27] A well-documented example of clandestine missionary existence in the provinces was the Austrian Father Laimbeckhoven, who spent most of his time as a missionary travelling under cover of the night on barges and along forsaken country lanes. Any home or hostel which granted him accommodation did so at its peril, as magistrates offered instant payment to any informer.[28] Chinese missionaries had the natural advantage of visually blending in with the local populations visited, although they suffered also from mistrust and isolation.[29]

All, however, was not lost. Foreign missionaries, when and where present, took special care of the young Chinese novices, on whom the whole mission would soon have to rely. Theological training was provided at seminaries in the capital and in Macau – the two areas excluded from the general prohibition of missionary activity. During the latter half of the century, the Missions Etrangères de Paris expanded from their earlier operations in Siam, establishing centres of theological training for novices from China. The priests of the

---

[26] Beijing's bishops during the period of prohibition were all Europeans: Bernardinus della Chiesa (d. Dec. 1721), Francisco da Rocha Froes (d. June 1733), Polycarpo Souza (d. May 1757), Damascenus Salutti (left office April 1780), Alexander de Gouvea (d. July 1807), and finally Joachim de Souza-Saraiva (in office until 1818, but not replaced by a residing bishop until 1826). See Zhao Qingyuan, *Zhongguo tianzhujiao jiaoqu huafen jiqi shouzhang jieti nianbiao* [*Annual Compendium of the Dioceses and their Leaders in Catholic China*] (Tainan, 1980), 27.

[27] It is estimated that some 40 missionaries, Chinese and European, were risking their lives for their cause. See Ma Zhao, 'Shilun Qianlong shiqi', 8.

[28] Gottfried-Xavier Laimbeckhoven, S.J. (Chinese name: Nan Huairen, 1707–87) is mentioned in conjunction with his successor as Bishop of Nanjing, Nathanael Bürger O.S.F. (d. 1780) in Joseph de Moidrey, *La Hiérarchie catholique en Chine, en Corée et au Japon (1307–1914)* (Shanghai, 1914), 28–30, 242–3. See also Joseph Krahl, *China Missions in Crisis: Bishop Laimbeckhoven and his Time 1738–1787* (Rome, 1964).

[29] See the moving letter by the Chinese priest Cassius Joseph Taj, sent to the Vatican on 25 Dec. 1779: APF, SC 'Indie Orientali' XXXVI (1779–81), fol. 236r.

Chinese College at Naples were soon to join their Parisian confrères in the erection of missionary colleges in China.[30] All in all, however, the foreign presence was merely of marginal importance, leaving most of the initiative to the flourishing Christian communities in the provinces.[31] It is also remarkable that the last persecutions of the Qianlong period lost momentum due to the resistance of local officials sympathetic to Christianity.[32] In a report for the Vatican, the Chinese convert Francesco Maria Zen summarized the situation for the Christians of Nanjing towards the end of the eighteenth century: though reduced in size, lacking an official clerical hierarchy and deprived of overt places of worship, Christian communities congregated regularly, though secretly, thus escaping the attention of officials and mischievous neighbours. Deprived of foreign leadership, Christian life was now firmly in the hands of the Chinese Christians.[33]

The attitude of the Jiaqing government (1796–1821) towards Christianity changed from a policy of benign neglect during its first decade to one of relentless persecution for the remaining fifteen years. The tolerance of the early Jiaqing may have had its roots in genuine ignorance, aided by the remaining court missionaries, who deliberately deflected from their continuing spiritual work. Another factor was the clandestine nature of all missionary activity: to the officials of the capital, rural Christianity was very nearly 'invisible'.[34] Furthermore, many of the areas with Christian communities were penurious, causing magistrates to conclude that not enough fiscal gain could be expected to warrant arduous investigations of remote villages. The year 1796 was a turning point for the Qing dynasty, which now saw itself confronted with unrest emanating from the sectarian movement throughout the entire empire.[35] Earlier uprisings, such as the Wang Lun rebellion of 1774 and the White Lotus rebellion of 1786, could be

---

[30] The correspondence of the Chinese novices of Naples is analysed in Francesco D'Arelli, *La Missione Cattolica in Cina tra i secoli XVII–XVIII* (Naples, 1995).

[31] The Monastery of the Nativity, in the vicinity of Chengdu, is a good example. The centre accommodated nearly 700 novices and formed the basis for missionary activity in and south of Sichuan. See Zhang Ze, *Qingdai jinjiaoqi de tianzhujiao*, 156–9.

[32] Such as De Pei, governor of the Hu-Guang double-province, a secret Christian who assisted the persecuted community throughout his official life (1688–1752). See Krahl, *China Missions in Crisis*, 3–4, 9–10.

[33] See APF, SC 'Indie Orientali' XXXVI (1779–81), fols 283–4, 266–9.

[34] This fact is underlined in numerous examples of missionary correspondence. See, e.g., APF, SC 'Indie Orientali' XXXVI (1779–81), fol. 117.

[35] See the excellent study by Barend ter Haar, *The White Lotus Teaching in Chinese Religious History* (Leiden, 1992).

quelled within a matter of months. The great uprising of 1796 took seven years to pacify, leaving the greater part of the White Lotus movement outside the area of suppression by and large intact. In an effort to regain the initiative, the Qing government promulgated a series of general persecutions against heterodox movements, which also targeted the Christian communities.

The new century began with a big calamity for China's Christians. Frater Adeodato de Santa Maria, OSA (Chinese name: De Tianci), an Italian Propaganda missionary, intended to inform his Augustinian confrères about the areas administered by missionaries of the Augustinian order. His map was discovered in 1805 by government officials due to 'a substantial lack of prudence displayed by the Europeans in Beijing, who transported many pages of letters interspersed among a great number of books in Chinese on matters of the Holy Faith'.[36] The officials suspected that the map was part of a European plot for an invasion of the Qing shores, igniting a persecution which would be felt throughout the century and which culminated in the general persecution of 1811. The decades of intense government action against Chinese Christianity were only brought to an end following the concessions to the 'Christian' powers which emerged victorious from the gunboat diplomacy of the nineteenth century.

*　*　*

During the long century of missionary prohibition and religious inculturation, the writings employed by Chinese Christians were central to the maintenance of the faith. As their Buddhist competitors had done for over fifteen centuries, the Catholic missionaries put great emphasis on the provision of written materials which could be employed for the propagation of their faith.[37] The Bible in its entirety would only become available once the Protestant missionaries of the

---

[36] 'Un' imprudenza non considerata dalla parte degli Europei Pekinesi, in rimettere molti plichi di lettere interessanti con gran copia de libri cinesi trattandi di materie della Santa Religione . . .'. This is the beginning of the account by Emmanuele Conforti on the persecution of 1805. Cf. APF, SC 'Cina and Regni Adiacenti' III (1806–11), fol. 398r.

[37] A comprehensive bibliography of Chinese translations of European writings can be found in Henri Bernard, 'Les Adaptions chinoises d'ouvrages européens: Bibliographie chronologique depuis la venue des portugais à Canton jusqu'à la mission française de Pékin, 1514–1688', *Monumenta Serica: Journal of Oriental Studies of the Catholic University of Peking*, 10 (1945), 1–57, 309–88. The contents of H. Verhaeren, *Catalogue de la Bibliothèque du Pé-t'ang* (Beijing, 1949), reflect the wealth of European sources the Jesuit translators could draw on.

early nineteenth century had entered the Chinese mission field.[38] To what extent, however, did the absence of a comprehensive Bible translation matter to the Chinese convert? It should firstly be remembered that the relative value of the Bible is less pronounced in the Catholic tradition than in the Reformed churches, which were after all created in order to 'return' to the scriptural origins of Christianity. Secondly, despite the fact that the Confucian tradition had enshrined its own classical writings (*jing*) into a fixed canon, there is no parallel in Chinese religious culture to the Christian concept of a divinely ordained 'Alpha to Omega' – of a permanently fixed scriptural edifice which cannot be altered through human intervention.[39] The heterodox movements of late imperial China, on the contrary, actively added an incessant flow of religious scriptures (also referred to as *jing*), either Daoist texts or Buddhist sutras, to the popular religious universe. The state examination system produced a highly literate elite, to whom the education of the general population was a moral imperative. Through gentry-funded initiatives and traditional village schools, pupils in rural China received their basic education trough the medium of the 'Three-Character Classic', *Sanzijing*, and therefore possessed a basic degree of familiarity with Confucian principles and with the style of canonical writings.[40] China's semi-literate villagers thus shared the same deep respect for the written word as the Confucian elite, and would therefore quite naturally allocate great importance to religious ideas codified in written form.

[38] M. Broomhall, *The Bible in China* (1934), published to commemorate the 120th anniversary of Robert Morrison's translation of the New Testament in 1814, contains a detailed account of the story of the Bible in China. The first full Bible translation – the *Shentian shengshu* [*The Sage Scripture of Divine Heaven*] by J.R. Morrison and W. Milne – was not complete until 1823, though an earlier version had been produced by J. Marshman (1815–22) in India. See Broomhall, *Bible in China*, 50–97, and (for the extraordinary background of the first Chinese Bible translation) W.W. Moseley, *The Origins of the First Protestant Mission to China* (1842). See also Jost O. Zetzsche, *The Bible in China: History of the 'Union Version' or The Culmination of Protestant Missionary Bible Translation in China* (Sankt Augustin, 1999).

[39] For a comparative analysis of the written word in Christendom and in China, see Xiaochao Wang, *Christianity and Imperial Culture: Chinese Christian Apologetics in the Seventeenth Century and their Latin Patristic Equivalent* (Leiden, 1998), 184–6.

[40] Though still far from any notion of 'universal', the educational system of late imperial China profited from the educationalism inherent in Confucianism. Many rural districts, in particular in the Jiangnan, had an ample supply of charity schools (*yixue*), community schools (*shexue*), and private academies (*shuyuan*). See Kung-Chuan Hsiao, *Rural China: Imperial Control in the Nineteenth Century* (Seattle, WA, 1960), 235–58. The *Sanzijing* owed its existence to the Confucian reformer Zhu Xi (1130–1200) and was used for primary education well into the twentieth century.

By the middle of the Qing period, the state institutions had become sufficiently aware of the threat emanating from sectarian movements to ban the distribution of their writings. This policy must be seen against the background of millennarian Buddhism, which from the 1430s proliferated as a direct consequence of popular religious writings, known as *baojuan*, literally 'precious scrolls'.[41] *Baojuan* formed the spiritual ammunition of more than a dozen major movements, in particular those in the tradition of the Luo sect.[42] Sectarian writings appealing to rural populations would often be concealed by orthodox titles and an official-looking 'coating': pages of officially approved religious commentaries concealing a heterodox textual core.[43] The state acted against sectarian movements by impounding as many *baojuan* as officials could find, and by sending the woodblock matrixes to the imperial capital, for inspection by the Grand Council and for ultimate destruction.[44] The incriminated persons fared little better: the standard punishment for the possession of subversive writings was 100 blows with the heavy cane.[45] Officials were employed in certain provinces with the sole task of producing Confucian counter-propaganda in the guise of such sectarian writings, in order to 'enlighten the commoners'. During the late imperial period, books were being printed for an ever-increasing audience in the metropoles of eastern China, percolating as second-hand items along the main waterways into the empire's vast interior. Their contents invariably reflected the mental preoccupations of the readership –

[41] See Richard Hon-Chun Shek, 'Religion and society in late Ming: sectarianism and popular thought in sixteenth and seventeenth century China' (University of California, Berkeley, Ph.D. thesis, 1980), 155–7. Not unlike the Communist literary propaganda of the 1940s and 1950s, *baojuan* often played on the theme of moral fortitude in adverse conditions.

[42] The use of *baojuan* by the founder of the Luo movement should be seen as a measure of its popularity, since its founder Luo Qing (1442–1527) disapproved of the 'empty recitation' of religious tracts. Cf. Zhou Yumin and Shao Yong, *Zhongguo huibang shi*, 27–8.

[43] See Daniel Overmyer, *Precious Volumes: An Introduction to Chinese Sectarian Scriptures from the 16th and 17th centuries* (Cambridge, MA, 1999).

[44] See Susan Naquin, 'Transmission of White Lotus sectarianism', in D. Johnson, A. Nathan, and E. Rawski, eds, *Popular Culture in Late Imperial China* (Berkeley, Los Angeles, and London, 1985), 265. Naquin estimates the number of destroyed White Lotus scriptures between the years 1720 and 1840 at *c*.2,000 books, equalling 400 titles.

[45] See L.C. Goodrich, *The Literary Inquisition of Ch'ien-lung* (Baltimore, MD, 1935), 275. Despite this clear legal position, the state usually took a rather more relaxed attitude towards prosecuting distributors of such 'seditious writings' – at least prior to the great millenarian uprisings of the latter half of the Qing period. See also Overmyer, *Precious Volumes*, 229–30.

whether this audience formed part of the elite or belonged to a more common background – and were easily affected by social change.[46] The writings of Christian missionaries followed this time-honoured literary tradition of religious expression, rejuvenating the vocabulary of popular religiosity with new names and concepts, yet remaining truthful to the style and argumentative structure of their Confucian and Buddhist competitors.[47]

The arrest of Father Adeodato in 1805 alerted the state to investigate the dealings of China's numerous Christian communities, as well as the continuing propagation of the faith by foreign and Chinese missionaries. The edict ordering Adeodato's exile explicitly mentioned the use of translated writings for Christian proselytization: 'The books . . . were originally all in Western script, making them inaccessible to the commoners of the interior. The results of the latest investigations have revealed that their newly printed writings are all in Chinese characters – the intention of this fact is self-evident.'[48] The ensuing condemnation emphasised the 'corrupting influence' of such materials on the minds of the Chinese and, even more importantly, on the members of the Manchurian aristocracy.[49] To Qing officials, such highly venerated religious 'sutras' were reminiscent of the feared White Lotus, an umbrella term for the millenarian Buddhist movements of the late imperial period. As with other printed examples of heresy, officials began to compile registers of Christian writings, impounding and destroying scriptures as well as printing blocks.[50] In the official terminology, Buddhist and Christian liturgical objects and writings merged into one large category of religious 'heresy'. Sacred

---

[46] For a summary of popular book printing, as well as the printing and distribution of books as a mass commodity, see Evelyn Sakakida Rawski, *Education and Popular Literacy in Ch'ing China* (Ann Arbor, MI, 1979), 111–23.

[47] The Protestant missionaries of the nineteenth century would quickly learn the same lesson. See Alice Henrietta Gregg, *China and Educational Autonomy: The Changing Role of the Protestant Educational Missionary in China, 1807–1937* (Syracuse, NY, 1946), 12–18.

[48] See FHA, document 493, section 3, catalogue 167, scroll 9258, nos 35, 36. The reporting officials are Cao Wenzhi, Wu Mingqiu, and Liu E.

[49] See the Propaganda document relating to the same event: APF, SOCP 'Indie Orientali' LXXIII (1817), fols 33–4.

[50] See Susan Naquin, *Millenarian Rebellion in China: The Eight Trigrams Uprising of 1813* (New Haven, CT, and London, 1976), 19–24. Also, for the concrete example of the Adeodato case, APF, SOCP 'Indie Orientali' LXXIII (1817), fol. 35. The *Po-xie xiang bian* [*Detailed Refutation of Heresy*] compiled by the nineteenth-century official Huang Yubian, magistrate of districts in Zhili from 1830 to 1842, contains reprints of 68 popular religious *baojuan*, accompanied by a condemnatory appeal to the public to adhere to the path of orthodoxy. See Shek, 'Religion and Society in Late Ming', 158–60.

scriptures, official investigators observed, were either 'chanted aloud' (*nian*) or read quietly for 'meditative fasting' (*chisu xiuxing*). In the popular expressions of Christianity and Buddhism alike, singing – that is, '*baojuan* recitation' (*xuan juan*) – often led to a state of trance, inviting spirits into the world of the living.[51]

What did the spiritual diet of the eighteenth-century Christians consist of? The most voluminous publications were missionary works originating from early missionary activity. A frequently copied item was the compilation of the conversations of Julio Aleni and his fellow missionaries by the convert Li Jiubiao, published between 1630 and 1640 as the *Kouduo richao* (*Daily Record of Oral Exhortations*).[52] By the close of the eighteenth century, this Confucio-Christian masterpiece had become one of the standard texts of Chinese Christianity, as well as a target of anti-heretical government action.[53] The same goes for the highly intellectual writings of Yang Tingyun, a 'Christo-Confucian' of the seventeenth century, who made history by introducing Christianity to his fellow scholar officials as a rival to (orthodox) Buddhism. Despite the hostility which subsequently arose, Yang Tingyun's *Tian-shi mingbian* - 'A discourse on the differences between Buddhism and Christianity' – was still frequently cited during the closing decades of the eighteenth century.[54] In fact, many similar titles had reached a broad popular readership, often outside the urban centres visited by the early missionaries and in spite of the exclusive nature of their original target audience. In addition to the copious works by Julio Aleni and Emmanuel Diaz – such as *Sanshan lunxueji* (*Recorded Sermons from the Three Mountains*), *Tianzhu shengjiao sizi jingwen* (*Four Character Hymnal on the Sacred Faith in the Lord of Heaven*), or *Tianzhu jiangsheng yanxing jilüe* (*Recorded Phenomena on the Words and Deeds of the Lord during his Descent to the World*) – the early writings of Matteo Ricci (mostly the *Tianzhu shiyi* - *True Account of the Lord of Heaven* and

[51] On the hymnals of the Taiping, see Rudolf G. Wagner, *Reenacting the Heavenly Vision: the Role of Religion in the Taiping Rebellion* (Berkeley, CA, 1982), 89; Shek, 'Religion and Society in Late Ming', 200–1.

[52] The *Kouduo richao* is the subject of Erik Zürcher, 'The Lord of Heaven and the Demons – strange stories from a late Ming Christian manuscript', in G. Naundorf, K.-H. Pohl, and H.-H. Schmidt, eds, *Religion und Philosophie in Ostasien: Festschrift für Hans Steiniger zum 65. Geburtstag* (Würzburg, 1985), 357–75.

[53] See Nicholas Standaert, 'Chinese Christian visits to the underworld', in Leonard Blussé and Harriet T. Zurndorfer, eds, *Conflict and Accommodation in Early Modern East Asia: Essays in Honour of Erik Zürcher* (Leiden, New York, and Cologne, 1993), 56.

[54] See Nicolas Standaert, *Yang Tingyun: Confucian and Christian in Late Ming China: His Life and Thought* (Leiden, 1988).

Tianzhu jiaoyao - Outline of the Christian Faith) helped Christians define the understanding of their faith. But it was in particular the shorter meditational writings which proved intellectually accessible to the majority of Chinese Christians, such as the *Tianzhu shengjiao rike* (*Daily Lessons in the Sacred Faith*) by Luigi Buglio and Emmanuel Diaz, or the *Yesu shengti daowen* (*Prayers Reflecting on the Sacred Body of Jesus*) by Aleni. In a memorial of the year 1814, for instance, two such 'heretical books' (*xieshu*), attributed to the Jesuits Joseph de Mailla and Aleni, are described in great detail.[55] The two volumes, *Shengnian guangyi quanbian* (*A Complete Almanac of Blessings*) and *Wanwu zhenyuan* (*The True Origin of All Things*), had survived the destruction of the Northern Cathedral (Beitang) – and thus symbolically the century of prohibition as such. Other survivors of the razed cathedral are dozens of pamphlets which shed light on the 'liturgical diet' supplied to the faithful of the capital region. The *Calendarium generale perpetuum diocesis Pekinensis* compiled by Bishop Gouvea in 1788, for instance, contains 170 pages of meditative texts, prayers and psalms for different occasions. Most of these were based on subjects familiar to Catholics all over the Christian world, but several must have been composed for the succour of the harassed community in Beijing, in particular the meditations for the martyrs of the missions to Japan, India, and China.[56]

The fate of the Beitang reflects the changing fortunes of the capital's Christian community.[57] Founded in 1693, the Beitang served a growing local community, harbouring an increasing amount of scriptural materials, mainly used for the proselytization of the capital's literati elite. Following the edict of 1724, it was decided to concentrate the holdings of all missionary libraries in the Library of the Holy Saviour.[58] The newly stocked library included the holdings of Beijing's four cathedrals, more than a dozen missionary book collections from private collections in Beijing and the provinces, as well as a

[55] See FHA, original document number 501, section 3, catalogue 167, scroll 9261, no. 15; reporting officials Ying He and He Ning.

[56] The *Calendarium generale* is part of the Beitang collection (shelf mark 2875), at present kept at the National Library (Peking Library) without access for the general public. Queries on the current state of the collections should be addressed to the Chinese section of the British Library, London.

[57] See Lars Peter Laamann, 'The Current State of the Beitang Library', *Bulletin of the European Association of Sinological Librarians* (Sept. 1996), 11–13.

[58] Churches were usually dedicated to Christ the Saviour, whereas chapels and prayer houses for female believers were devoted to Mary. The *Beitang* library hence had the official name *Bibliotheca Sancti Salvatoris*. See Margiotti, *Il cattolicismo nello Shansi*, 583 n.43.

considerable number of titles of unclear origin. Unlike the manuscript archives, the book collection has survived the disturbances of the two centuries following its erection without major damage.[59] Its arduous journeys included a temporary refuge in a Christian cemetery in Beijing, a sojourn in a small Lazarist parish in Inner Mongolia, followed by years of administration by the Russian Orthodox mission. It was only allowed to return to its original home once the mission had been re-established under the protection of the French state in the middle of the nineteenth century. The church building then had to be reconstructed, since the original building was destroyed by fire in 1827, during the final eruption of anti-Christian state action, which forced the local clergy as well as the most prominent members of Beijing's Christian life to seek refuge in the surrounding countryside.[60]

Eighteenth-century official sources abound in evidence of 'seditious scrolls' circulated by Christian communities. The state was fully aware of the edifying effect of printed materials, and was hence determined to tackle the problem at its root. In a report from the turn of the century, we thus read of a public tribunal in Guangzhou, culminating in the public immolation of more than a hundred Christian titles, lasting for three months.[61] During the 1805 persecution in Beijing, hostile bystanders hurled abuse and hard objects at the representatives of the Christian religion.[62] By the turn of the century, it became obvious that the churches in the capital were being used for printing, storing, and distributing printed materials. In a memorial by the State Council of 1810, the supreme ministers appealed to the Emperor to have officials enter the missionaries' premises, read through the entire material, calculated at 173 titles, and subsequently to destroy all Chinese language titles, lest they be distributed to Chinese

---

[59] Regrettably the manuscript collection fell victim to a fire in 1864. Rumours of the existence of a recently discovered cache of archival materials were ill-founded, as I witnessed myself in 1995. The papers were indubitably not examples of the expected missionary correspondence, but simply hand-written filing cards for a catalogue – probably Verhaeren's.

[60] The fate of the book collection – and that of the congregations of Beijing – is spelt out in a letter by Emanuele D. Goldino, attaché of the Portuguese ecclesiastic administration of Goa, sent to Rome from Macau in Oct. 1806: APF, SC 'Cina et Regni Adiacenti' III (1806–11), fol. 196r.

[61] Letter by Luigi da Signa, from Shanxi province to Rome, 7 March 1806: APF, SC, 'Cina and Regni Adiacenti' III (1806–11), fol. 106v.

[62] Ibid., fol. 107r.

commoners.[63] From an edict issued in 1811 we know that books and woodblock matrices stored in the houses of the Europeans were confiscated, and that the auspicious portal character columns were ordered to be erased. Books were to be handed over to the authorities and all written communication with Chinese Christians outlawed – even though the latter were likely to be illiterate. Fearful of the effect of letters sent by the European missionaries to the Christian communities of the provinces, a blanket ban was imposed on all missionary correspondence.[64]

What the ministers regarded as politically dangerous was the 'private' nature of the Christian communities, escaping the watchful eye of the fatherly state. An investigation into the Christian communities in Ba-xian, Sichuan, for instance, reveals that memorizing and reciting Christian writings at home – either in private or in the company of fellow believers – was common practice.[65] The oldest members of the congregation, in their seventies, had kept copies of writings composed and donated by European missionaries in the years preceding the Yongzheng edict of 1724. Once memorized, it was seen as the father's duty to ensure that his children learnt the holy words by heart.[66] Those who could read were given Christian tracts to recite in private, while the others had to learn the sutras 'from the lips of their teacher' (*kou-chuan*). When the Ba-xian Christians were questioned about the nature of the writings, the answer was emphatic: 'orthodox and beneficial, and by no means heretical'. They were recited as a sign of filial respect, in order to admonish each other to act as positive role models in daily life. 'Christian sutras' condemned treachery, theft, heresy, and lewdness, and were furthermore instrumental in preventing accidents and in prolonging one's life.[67] The teachers of the faith

---

[63] The edict of JQ 15 (1811) is reprinted in the 'Veritable Records of the Jiaqing Emperor', vol. 142, and cited in Zhang Ze, *Qingdai jinjiaoqi de tianzhujiao*, 165–70.

[64] Cf. APF, SC 'Cina & Regni Adiacenti' III (1806–11), fol. 400r. The source is a description of the Adeodato case.

[65] See the printed collection *Ba-xian dang'anguan* [*The Ba-xian Archives*], Ba-xian / Sichuan, Part 5, Section 13, 'Christianity and Heresy', 240–5: 'Cases resulting from an investigation into Christianity in Ba-xian, QL 47–48 [1782–1783]'.

[66] The Japanese parallel case is illustrated in Christal Whelan, 'Written and unwritten texts of the *Kakure Kirishitan*', in John Breen and Mark Williams, eds, *Japan and Christianity: Impacts and Responses* (Basingstoke, 1996), 122–37, esp. 126–33. A comparative presentation of written materials introduced to and printed in Japan by the Jesuits is provided in J.F. Moran, *The Japanese and the Jesuits: Alessandro Valignano in Sixteenth-Century Japan* (London and New York, 1993), 145–60.

[67] See 'Cases resulting from an investigation into Christianity in Ba-xian', 242. Explicitly

worked without demanding any payment, and instead of congregating crowds, the sutras were recited and taught in the circle of family and friends. Due to the popularity of the Catholic saints (and in particular of the Virgin Mary), *vitae* of such pillars of the Catholic faith were among the first European writings to be translated.[68]

Interestingly, the officials rarely elaborated on the contents of impounded books and pamphlets, though these would routinely be sent as incriminating material to the State Council.[69] All memorials were in unison, however, that towards the end of the eighteenth century hundreds of Christian titles were in circulation. This comes as no surprise since throughout the years of repression the court missionaries were busily printing and distributing religious materials. The Europeans who remained in Beijing made use of their presence by composing by now illegal materials for what remained of their China mission. During the 1730s, de Mailla's well-known *Shengshi churao* (*Nourishment for a Prosperous Age*), as well as a *vita* of the Christian saints entitled *Shengnian guangyi* (*Almanac of Blessings*) in twenty-four chapters, proved so popular that they had to be reprinted several times. The shorter sequel expounding sections of the Bible (*Shengjing guangyi*), printed and distributed in the early 1740s, introduced the main tenets of Christian doctrine – as well as the contributions of Ignatius Loyola – along the pattern of a daily almanac. *Ruijianlu* (*Records of Accurate Reflections*), a popularized version of the gospel, was written in the first year of the Qianlong period (1736) by Ignace Kögler, S.J. Within a few years it had spread to remote areas over the whole of northern and central China. In the eighth year of the Qianlong reign (1744), the Beijing Christian Yin Hongxu published *Zhujing tiwei* (*The Basic Meaning of the Lord's Scriptures*), a condensed catechism in eight chapters, and also wrote *Bo huijiao* (*Refutation of Islam*), which never reached the printing blocks.[70] Three years later the

mentioned titles are: *Tianzhu jiaoyao* [*Summary of the Religion of the Lord of Heaven*], by Matteo Ricci, S.J. (1605); the *Wanwu zhenyuan* [*True Origin of All Things*]; *Bi wang* [*Fleeing Evil*]; *Tianzhu jingshu* [*The Sutra of the Heavenly Lord*]; a *Zhaozao tian, di, renwu zhenzhu* [*True Lord of All Creation*]; and the *Jiaoyao xulun* [*Prolegomena to the Essential Aspects of the Faith*].

[68] Often cited *vitae* are the *Tianzhu shengjiao shengren xingshi* [*Lives of the Saints of the Catholic Church*] and the *Shengmu xingshi* [*Life of the Holy Mother*]. See Margiotti, *Il cattolecismo nello Shansi*, 279.

[69] See the memorial by Zhuang Yougong of QL 19 (1766): FHA, section 3, catalogue 167, scroll 9258, document no. 9.

[70] The *Bibliotheca Missionum* makes reference to some of the titles listed above. Unfortunately, information on many eighteenth-century publications remains scarce.

Chinese Christian Sun Zhang, who worked for the palace administration as a translator, published the tract *Xing-li zhenquan* (*True
Explanation of Nature and Principle*) expounding the tenets of Christianity along the argumentation of Song-Ming Confucian doctrine. In
1758, unperturbed by the threat of harsh penalties, he even translated a
synopsis into Manchurian, for use by bannermen. Shortly afterwards
the Chinese priest Shen Dongxing authored *Yijian daoyi* (*Simplified
Guide to the Art of Praying*), widely admired for its elegant style. The
year 1766 saw the publication of another booklet for prayer, the
Chongxiu jingyun (*Essential Compilation for Adoration and Meditation*) by
the court officials An Guoning and Lin Deyao – a condensed version of
an original from the Yongzheng period. The latter also wrote a
biography of Ignatius Loyola (*Sheng yinajue*), the *Sheng shaowulüe jiuri
jingli* (*Nine-Day Rite According to St Xavier*), in addition to *Zhaoyong
shenjing* (*Reflections of the Eternal Sacred Mirror*). Five years later, in 1771,
the court official Florian Bahr, S.J., wrote his *Shengyong xujie* (*Sequel to
the Holy Hymns*), plus a *vita* of St John Nepomuk (*Sheng ruowang
niebomu zhuan*), published prior to his death in the same year. Other
publications from the end of the Qianlong period include a synopsis of
the Old and New Testaments, *Gu-xin shengjing*, by Louis de Poirot, S.J.,
as well as titles which no longer survive but are nevertheless
mentioned in memorials, such as these three titles found in the private
collection of a Cantonese Christian in the year 1784: *Zhu sumi pian*
(*Illuminating coarse Superstitions*), *Chuhui dawen* (*A First Catechism –*
which may, however, refer to the *Chuhui wenda* by Pedro de la
Pinuela), and *Yi ping* (*Righteousness Comprehended*).[71] When the
numbers of Christian intellectuals and foreign priests began to
diminish towards the end of the century of prohibition, ordinary
Chinese Christians stepped in, by copying earlier writings and by
distributing these to the Christians of the surrounding countryside.
When, for instance, state interrogators extracted the confessions of a
rural Christian community in Henan province, the villagers revealed
that they had obtained 'Christian sutras' composed by missionaries in

[71] Most of the above writings are kept at the British Library and at the Peking Library.
As these titles only refer to the surviving examples, we have to assume that there was a far
more substantial body of publications printed in the imperial capital by foreigners and
Chinese Christians alike. Adrianus Dudink, 'The Zikawei Collection in the Jesuit
Theologate Library at Fujen University (Taiwan): background and draft catalogue', *Sino-
Western Cultural Relations Journal*, 18 (1996), 1–40, provides insight into the abundance of
translations and compositions by European missionaries, mostly originating from the
seventeenth and early eighteenth centuries.

the capital through the itinerant Christian Yuan Huzi – 'Bearded Yuan'. Ignorant of the prohibitions against Christianity proclaimed during the early Qianlong period, Yuan used a sojourn in Tongbo to admonish people to 'lead a virtuous life, and to spread happiness for the sake of the life to come'. The resulting interest in the teachings of the bearded disciple of the Lord of Heaven, and the Christian writings from the capital, produced eighteen converts.[72]

By the second decade of the nineteenth century, the links with the thriving Christian exclaves of Xiwanzi and Anjiazhuang preserved Beijing's embattled Christians as members of a wider religious movement, which had learnt to rely on the almost exclusive spiritual and practical guidance of half a dozen Chinese priests.[73] If the movement of people could not be controlled, the supervision of printed materials proved even less feasible. This was particularly true for writings other than printed volumes ('sutras'), including pictorial motifs, auspicious emblems, portal character columns, but most of all short religious tracts, passages from the Bible or meditative texts.[74] From the confessions of the Christian elder, Wang Xiangsheng, we learn that there was a custom in his village of passing cards with the names of Christian neighbours to other Christians, so that they could 'pray for their salvation while chanting the sutras'.[75] Otherwise, there was no need for any name registers, because the homes of Christians could quite easily be identified from the street: instead of the traditional protective scrolls adorning the door posts, a simple cross was affixed to the door. Furthermore, the Christians in the Suizhou area used 'piety lists' (*xiaodan*) during the recital of Christian scriptures.[76] Two unnamed 'sutras' (*jingjuan*) were discovered in the home of Wang

---

[72] See *Shiliao xunkan* [*Ten-Daily Publication of Historical Materials*], vol. 12 (series: 'Heaven'), 421. 'Bearded Yuan' is described as being actively involved in the Southern Cathedral of the capital, and being employed by the Board of Astronomy.

[73] In addition to Xie Madou and John-Chrysostom Kho (Chinese name unknown) there were four secular priests. These six priests were strengthened by successive visits by Mouly (1835–42), Joseph Gabet (1837–42), Evariste Huc (1841–2), Florent Daguin (1843), and Joseph Carayon (1843). See E.R. Huc, *Souvenirs of a Journey through Tartary, Tibet and China During the Years 1844, 1845 and 1846*, 2 vols (Beijing, 1931), 1:39.

[74] The Chinese priest Matthew Kou translated pamphlets on Purgatory and on the Ten Commandments into colloquial Chinese. See Guiot, *La Mission du Su-tchuen*, 232–3. FHA, document 501, section 3, catalogue 167, scroll 9258, nos 16, 17, refers to the discovery in 1747 of 'privately printed sutras and pictures, talismans and books' in the Christian village Sanggu in Wanping District, Shuntian Prefecture.

[75] Ibid.

[76] Perhaps illustrated spiritual instructions.

Xiangsheng. Both volumes, the memorial points out, were 'hand-written' (*moxie*), that is, not printed. Investigations in other households produced a variety of titles, including early missionary translations by Matteo Ricci and Michele Ruggieri, in addition to 'fasting manuals' and 'rosaries' (*zhaidan* and *suzhu*, respectively – both Buddhist terms), as well as ritual texts, such as the Ten Commandments. Several of the scriptures are commented on as being 'worn and incomplete' (*canque*), which indicates their age and use.[77]

One example of pamphlets composed by Christians from memory comes from the hamlet Longmentan, near Chongqing in Sichuan province.[78] The pamphlets mentioned are a *Tianzhu jing* (*Scripture of the Lord of Heaven*), *Shengmujing* (*Scripture of the Holy Mother*), *Xinjing* (*Scripture of Faith*), as well as a *Chuzao tiandi jiangben* (*Commentary on the Creation*). We owe knowledge of these titles to the apostate He Guoda, a seasonal worker employed as a cotton harvester by Christian landowners in Sichuan province. Having been initiated into the basic principles of their faith by local Christians, He Guoda declared that he had only learned the beginning of each of the Christian scriptures by heart and, being illiterate, that he merely knew of these writings what the Christians had disclosed by word of mouth. Of the *Tianzhujing* we learn that

> in an ode entitled 'Our Heaven', among others, it is mentioned that one will suddenly see the truth, one's true body-and-soul will be sanctified, one's wisdom will become like that of an emperor, able to behold the infinite cosmos. I am waiting for you [sinners] now to put your guilt on me, so that you will not have anything any more to be desired. I shall show my mercy and take away your bad luck, your nightmares.

The *Shengmujing* seems to be a translation of the Ave Maria:

> *Er-fu* Holy Ma-li-ya, fulfilled among the holy. The Lord has bestowed you with Righteousness, and has liberated you from your legion of grief. And despite having despatched you for only a brief time, you will soon be with the Lord of Heaven forever. Holy Ma-li-ya, when you ascend to Heaven, turn towards me. . . .

---

[77] See Margiotti, *Il cattolecismo nello Shansi*, 277–81.

[78] See FHA, category 3, catalogue 167, scroll 9258 [492], nos 19–20. The memorial is dated QL 39.4.12 (i.e. 21 May 1774).

The *Xinjing* is nothing less than the Creed. In the simplified version reproduced by He Guoda, it runs like this: 'I believe in the all-capable Lord of Heaven, who sent his extraordinary son down [to earth] with the sacred seal.' The brief account of the *Chuzao tiandi jiangben* seems like an abridged version of the introduction to Genesis: 'In the beginning of the creation of Heaven and earth, all human beings were made by the Lord of Heaven, and the same Lord of Heaven created the multitude of humanity.'

These printed fragments of the Christian faith were memorized by a manual labourer, with a self-professed interest in 'black magic'. Aided by apostates and Christians on the margins of their congregations, other religious movements also made use of such textual fragments – usually isolated and out of context – borrowing ideas, images, and terminology from their Christian rivals for their own incantations. Early nineteenth-century reports by missionary visitors confirm that this was indeed common practice.[79]

*   *   *

In eighteenth-century China Christianity, with its plethora of religious writings, seemed as puzzling to the investigating imperial officials as the other popular sects which made use of printed materials. The fact that most villagers had difficulties deciphering the characters of the title pages alone should not lead us to underestimate their value. Printed scriptures on the contrary added to the range of iconographic objects which made Christianity a truly popular religion at a rural level. During the eighteenth century the chanting of Christian scriptures took place in a religious territory which was largely in flux: either ignored or classified as 'heretical' by the guardians of Confucian orthodoxy, Christianity developed from a recognizably foreign implant to a genuine expression of popular religious life. The alien origins of Chinese Christianity, however, bestowed a mysterious aura exerting an exotic appeal on the rural audience. The state's increasingly condemnatory verdict on Christianity at the beginning of the nineteenth century can be explained by two developments. Firstly, the process of Christianity's inculturation had

[79] Cf. B. Willeke, 'The report of the Apostolic Visitation of D. Emmanuele Conforti on the Franciscan Missions in Shansi, Shensi and Kansu (1798)', *Archivum Franciscanum Historicum*, 84 (1991), 258. The relevant second chapter is entitled 'On abuses among the faithful and rites introduced to the people' ('De abusibus circa fidem et ritus inventis in populo').

rendered the religion highly accessible to the followers of other 'dangerous' religious movements, and secondly, the numbers of foreigners penetrating ever deeper into the empire increased drastically at the beginning of the century. Alarmed by the encroachment into southern Asia by Europe's colonial powers, the Qing administration now saw China's Christians as a potential threat to the state.

The history of Christianity in late imperial China is reflected in the development of Christian writings, which can be divided into three clearly discernible periods. The initial period, from the first contacts in the late sixteenth century to the end of the Rites Controversy, was characterized by the translation of European philosophical, (proto-) scientific, and religious concepts into the language used by the Confucian elite targeted by the Jesuit court officials. Akin to the traditions of the highly literate scholar-officials, the chosen medium consisted of printed, bound books – an expensive commodity which few subjects could afford first-hand. The first period of Christian writings was thus both Eurocentric and Confucianizing, elitist in the language and social position of its audience and therefore largely confined to the private academies and church libraries of the urban centres. During the second phase, the century of missionary prohibition (1724–1840), the face and essence of Christian writings underwent a radical transformation. Since the original target audience – scholar officials and members of the Manchurian aristocracy – was now actively discouraged from intellectual and spiritual contact with the remaining European missionaries, the latter began to concentrate on providing existing converts with spiritual nourishment, mainly prayer books and catechisms. The titles cited in this paper are characterized by their relative simplicity of style – a necessary prerequisite for reaching out to the farming communities of the provinces. The general ban on proselytization outside Macau and Beijing also necessitated a reduction in physical size, enabling the clandestine missionaries to travel with printed materials in their severely limited luggage allowance. Simultaneously, the Christian communities began to circulate their own religious writings – texts rather than complete scriptures – often recordings of oral tradition, and increasingly in the style of millenarian Buddhist writings. Such 'Christian sutras' were easily confused with 'heretical', hence illegal, millenarian sutras by the prosecuting officials, who often spent little time analysing the theological contents of impounded printed heresy. Following the proliferation of Western missionaries prior to the Opium Wars, and in particular in the wake of the mid-century treaties granting extraterritoriality to all foreign missionaries, clandestine missionary methods became obsolete and religious writings were once again produced and distributed by foreign clerics. Chinese Christianity began a new period of inculturation, which produced new types of religious writings. However, the impact of the renewed presence of foreign missionaries differed sharply from the first period of the China mission: rural communities were targeted through the use of pictures, vernacular style, and easily recognizable metaphors. Printed on modern printing presses with movable metal types, the quantity of printed materials could be increased whereas the price of printed items was brought down to more affordable levels. Both developments thus marked a clear end of the 'Christian sutras' which had come to characterize Chinese Christianity during the long century of missionary prohibition.

School of Oriental and African Studies, University of London

'I WILL TELL YOU A WORD OR TWO ABOUT CARDIGANSHIRE': WELSH CLERICS AND LITERATURE IN THE EIGHTEENTH CENTURY

by GERAINT H. JENKINS

IN the process often characterized by Welsh historians as 'the remaking of Wales in the eighteenth century',[1] the clergy played a central role in the literary and national revival. While the national and international contexts of these cultural movements are of paramount importance, particularities also count, and need to be integrated into the larger picture. An examination of the special flavour of the careers of several literary-minded clerics and other writers in the deeply rural county of Cardiganshire offers a means of throwing light on some of these broader themes, and of illustrating the importance of literacy, culture, and learning to relatively humble middling sorts within a particular community notorious for its isolation, poor communications, monoglottism, and slow-moving economy.

Although Wales became increasingly accessible as the eighteenth century unfolded, travellers from England who ventured by coach, chaise, carriage, on horseback, or on foot to what were widely considered in the metropolis to be 'barren', 'desolate', and 'dark' western corners of the Celtic fringe were often scathingly blunt about the wretched state of communications and the social isolation of communities in which the habitual daily language was Welsh. A pastoral county of upland plains, valleys, and coastal lowlands, Cardiganshire was characterized by poor communications. Samuel Horsley, Bishop of St David's, took five and a half hours to travel the twenty miles from Cardigan to Aberaeron in July 1790,[2] and, on finding himself far from the madding crowds in the fastnesses of the county, the traveller Benjamin H. Malkin observed in 1804 that the appearance of strangers was 'still an occurrence of some wonder. I know of no district so confined within itself.'[3]

---

[1] Trevor Herbert and Gareth Elwyn Jones, eds, *The Remaking of Wales in the Eighteenth Century* (Cardiff, 1988).

[2] Aberystwyth, National Library of Wales [hereafter NLW], MS 6203E, fol. 34.

[3] Benjamin H. Malkin, *The Scenery, Antiquities, and Biography, of South Wales* (1804), 321.

Like beauty, however, perceptions of distance lie in the eye of the beholder, and many Cardiganshire people made light of the long and arduous journey to London. Four of the five men who will figure prominently in this paper thought nothing of tramping or riding to the metropolis and back. Lewis Morris, the cultural patriot and Rabelaisian satirist, regularly travelled to London to joust with Grub Street writers, tumble with kitchen maids and whores, and disconcert government officials who dubbed him 'the proud hot Welshman'.[4] Although he affected to yearn for rural life and the fresh air of Wales, Morris thrived in the hurly-burly of London's glamorous thoroughfares and seedy byways. When the Methodist evangelist Daniel Rowland was ordained deacon in March 1734 he walked every step from Llangeitho to London for the ceremony.[5] The stocky legs of Evan Thomas Rhys, a shoemaker-cum-poet, carried him regularly from Llannarth to London: 'He hath travelled', wrote Lewis Morris of him, 'he hath seen St. Paul's and Westminster Abbey, and hath sung to the King, (God stand with his Grace) (Duw safo gyda'i Ras), tho he never saw him.'[6] Evan Evans (Ieuan Fardd/Ieuan the Poet), who flitted to and from eighteen different curacies during his chequered career, including the livings of Apple-dore in Kent and Newick in Sussex, was no stranger to London. In desperation, this embittered cleric, who regularly swallowed lethal doses of alcohol, joined the 34th Regiment of Foot, only to be discharged within four days for allegedly being 'disordered in his mind'.[7] The pull of London and the south-east was therefore strong, and the people of Cardiganshire, including merchants, drovers, and garden girls, certainly did not balk at the prospect of a five-hundred-mile round journey. So perceptions of distance are important.

It would also be a mistake to believe that eighteenth-century Cardiganshire, with its population of at most forty thousand people, most of whom were monoglot Welsh speakers, was some kind of provincial backwater. 'I will tell you a word or two about Cardi-ganshire',[8] was the opening line in one of Lewis Morris's letters, and he,

---

[4] J.H. Davies, ed., *The Letters of Lewis, Richard, William and John Morris, of Anglesey (Morrisiaid Môn) 1728–1765*, 2 vols (Aberystwyth, 1907–9) [hereafter *ML*], 1:246.

[5] Eifion Evans, *Daniel Rowland and the Great Evangelical Awakening in Wales* (Edinburgh, 1985), 30.

[6] Hugh Owen, ed., *The Letters of the Morrises of Anglesey (1735–1786)*, Parts 1–2 (1947–9) [hereafter *ALM*], 2:532.

[7] Aneirin Lewis, ed., *The Correspondence of Thomas Percy and Evans Evans* (Baton Rouge, LA, 1957), xxvii.

[8] *ALM*, 1:113.

like several of his predecessors in the mining industry, glowed with pride as he celebrated the rich deposits of lead in this 'Cambrian Peru'.[9] It is striking how prominently Cardiganshire men figured among those cultural patriots and religious reformers who were determined to transform age-old ways of life by establishing printing presses, grammar schools, academies and circulating schools, literary societies, book clubs, and subscription ventures. The Vale of Teifi, which sported a strong indigenous literary tradition dating back to the days of the *penceirddiaid* (chief poets), was also highly regarded by contemporaries for the vigour of its spiritual life. An impressive band of religious reformers, including Anglicans and Dissenters, literary scholars, bards, and antiquarians, all of whom were fired by a burning zeal for saving souls and a proper pride in their literary heritage, helped to galvanize the religious, cultural, and educational revivals of the eighteenth century.[10] The first official printing press to be set up on Welsh soil was established by Isaac Carter in the south of the county, at Trerhedyn or Atpar, near Newcastle Emlyn, in 1718. The principal epicentre of Welsh Calvinistic Methodism was Llangeitho in the Aeron valley, and the mother church of Welsh Arminianism and Unitarianism was established at Llwynrhydowen in 1733. Nor should we forget that the first College in Wales was opened at Lampeter in 1827. These achievements are all the more remarkable given that eighteenth-century Wales, let alone Cardiganshire, had no institutions of statehood, no centres of learning, museums, and scientific academies, and no populous capital city.[11]

The third point which requires emphasis is that the reputation of the county's inhabitants for hard drinking was not necessarily an impediment to literary endeavour. It is true that, as a result of energetic and prolonged bingeing, many of the gentry drank themselves into oblivion and an early grave, and that clerics who hobnobbed with them were prone to drink themselves under the table. Alcohol

[9] W.J. Lewis, 'Lead mining in Cardiganshire', in Geraint H. Jenkins and Ieuan Gwynedd Jones, eds, *Cardiganshire County History*. Volume 3. *Cardiganshire in Modern Times* (Cardiff, 1998), 160–81; Emyr Gwynne Jones, 'Llythyrau Lewis Morris at William Vaughan, Corsygedol', *Llên Cymru*, 10 (1968), 29.

[10] Geraint Bowen, 'Traddodiad Llenyddol Deau Ceredigion 1600–1850' (University of Wales, M.A. thesis, 1943); Geraint H. Jenkins, 'Bywiogrwydd Crefyddol a Llenyddol Dyffryn Teifi, 1689–1740', *Ceredigion*, 8 (1979), 439–72; idem, *Literature, Religion and Society in Wales 1660–1730* (Cardiff, 1978).

[11] Geraint H. Jenkins, *The Foundations of Modern Wales: Wales 1642–1780* (Oxford, 1987), ch. 6, 10.

evidently soothed the pain of illness and frustrated ambitions, and it anaesthetized them from the tedium of pastoral life. But drink was part and parcel of daily life. People did not simply drink in alehouses, taverns, and inns; they drank at home in the convivial company of friends and visitors. Alcohol was a staple fare and many clerics, especially penurious curates, ignored Bishop William Lloyd's injunction to 'dabble a little, but not be drowned',[12] and also resisted the efforts of Methodist reformers to bring them to their senses. Four of the five men who figure in this paper were inordinately fond of liquor and some of them placed an intolerable strain on their kidneys and liver. Lewis Morris, a remarkable polymath, was a lumbering barrel-bodied man who enjoyed convivial company. This stranger to weight-watchers was known, at least in private, as 'the Fat man of Cardiganshire'.[13] The restlessly misanthropic cleric Evan Evans was described by Samuel Johnson as 'incorrigibly addicted to strong drink',[14] and one London Welshman ostracized him because 'when he came to see him, if he sipt even a little small Beer it used to make him look wild which rather frighten'd his wife'.[15] Even Daniel Rowland, a pillar of the Calvinistic Methodist cause, was rebuked by his straitlaced and unlikeable colleague Howel Harris for 'licentiousness in eating, drinking, Laughing'.[16] Welsh Calvinistic Methodism has never been overburdened with a sense of humour: Harris's idea of fun was to be on his knees in prayer at 4 a.m. and his classic diary entry, 'Had a temptation to laughter today', has entered the annals of Welsh folklore. Like most Welsh poets, Evan Thomas Rhys was fond of the bottle, especially the traditional glutinous and soporiferous Welsh ale, and his bardic companions, rightly or wrongly, believed that excessive drinking betokened manliness, stamina, and a lively muse. This was an age when drunkards were joyfully satirized and we should bear in mind that hard drinking was a stimulus as well as an anaesthetic.

At this point we can turn to the individuals selected as representative of eighteenth-century Cardiganshire writers, and of the cultural changes which were sweeping across Wales at that time. The first of

---

[12] NLW, MS 11303D, fol. 86v.

[13] *ALM*, 1:370, 2:535.

[14] Gerald Morgan, *Ieuan Fardd* (Caernarfon, 1988), 7.

[15] Aneirin Lewis, 'Llythyrau Evan Evans (Ieuan Fardd) at Ddafydd Jones o Drefriw', *Llên Cymru*, 1 (1950–1), 245.

[16] Tom Beynon, 'Howell Harris and Daniel Rowland', *Cylchgrawn Cymdeithas Hanes Eglwys Methodistiaid Calfinaidd Cymru*, 31 (1946), 91–2.

them reflected the revival of interest in 'British' or 'Cambro-British' history. Born at Penywenallt, a farmhouse in the parish of Llandygwydd, in 1693, Theophilus Evans spent most of his clerical career in Breconshire, but, as the old saying goes, once a Cardiganshire man always a Cardiganshire man.[17] Evans sported dual, even triple, identities. He prided himself on being a Cambro-Briton, a fervent High Churchman, and an ardent Tory. His great grandfather, Griffith ap Ieuan Jenkin, lived to be 100, and his grandfather Evan Griffith – 'Captain Tory' as the Puritans called him – was as strong as an ox, and reputedly capable of resting a cart fully laden with hay on his back, or throwing a six-pound plummet a distance of a hundred yards. Whilst locked up in Cardigan castle during the Commonwealth, his wife Matilda gave birth to a child. When informed of the glad tidings, and without pausing to confirm the gender of the child, 'Captain Tory' cried, 'By God, the child shall be christened Charles.'[18] This child was Charles Evans, father of Theophilus, and there is little doubt that Theophilus Evans inherited the physical and intellectual robustness of his grandfather.

Theophilus Evans is a figure of national importance because, at the tender age of twenty-three, he published a marvellous epic entitled *Drych y Prif Oesoedd* (*A Mirror of the First Ages*) in 1716. He did so at a time when the Welsh, like many 'non-historic peoples' in Europe, were in severe danger, in the words of the almanacer Thomas Jones, of being 'blotted . . . out of the Books of Records'.[19] Whereas the Irish were haunted by their history, the Welsh at that time seemed destined to be consigned to the dustbin of history forever.[20] The tiny group of Leviathans who dominated landed properties showed little enthusiasm for the literary heritage of the 'clownish' Welsh, and precious historical manuscripts in their private libraries were wantonly exposed to the ravages of rain, mildew, and mice. Edward Lhuyd, the father of Welsh and Celtic studies, had died prematurely at the age of forty-nine in 1709 and there was hardly anyone to take up his torch. It is extraordinary, therefore, that this precocious young man in his early

---

[17] Geraint H. Jenkins, *Theophilus Evans (1693–1767): Y Dyn, ei Deulu, a'i Oes* (Aberystwyth, 1993).

[18] Theophilus Jones, *A History of the County of Brecknock*, 2 vols (Brecknock, 1805–9), 2:274.

[19] Thomas Jones, *The British Language in its Lustre* (1688), sig. A3r.

[20] Geraint H. Jenkins, 'Historical writing in the eighteenth century', in Branwen Jarvis, ed., *A Guide to Welsh Literature c.1700–1800* (Cardiff, 2000), ch.2.

twenties, who had never darkened the door of a university, should have published a wonderful epic tale designed to rescue the national history of Wales from the enormous neglect and condescension of English historians. Most historians are in their prime when they embark on this kind of magnum opus. Robert John Pryse or Gweirydd ap Rhys was sixty-three when he published his *Hanes y Brytaniaid a'r Cymry* (*History of the Britons and the Welsh*) in 1872. The matchless J.E. Lloyd was fifty when he published his celebrated *History of Wales to the Edwardian Conquest* in 1911, and in more recent times John Davies was fifty-two when his single-volume Welsh-language history of Wales saw the light of day in 1990.

Drych y Prif Oesoedd is hardly an objective piece of work by a dispassionate scribe. Far from it. But it struck all the right chords among a people who yearned for a vigorous, entertaining, Cymricized interpretation of their native history. Evans's epic soap-opera was a massive fillip for the so-called 'British history' associated with the name of Geoffrey of Monmouth. By the late Stuart period Geoffrey's captivating tale had become something of a joke among stuffy academics in England, but Theophilus Evans was in no mood to abandon the glorious origins of the Welsh. In a racy narrative, replete with battles and conquests, epic victories and bitter defeats, he rehabilitated the notion that the Welsh were the first and rightful owners of these islands and he restored legendary heroes – Brutus, Beli and Brân, and especially Arthur – in the affections of the Welsh. Secondly, he seized on the theories of the Breton monk Paul-Yves Pezron, author of *L'Antiquité de la nation et de la langue des Celtes* (1703), and rejoiced in the glorious, even sacred, origins of the ancient Celtae who were descended from Gomer, grandson of Noah, and who had spread from Asia Minor to all parts of Europe. In one presumably winsome flight of rhetoric, he claimed that no people could trace their native tongue to an earlier period than could the Welsh:

> And who do you think spoke the Welsh language at that time, but GOMER, the eldest son of Japheth, son of Noah, son of Lamech, son of Methuselah, son of Enoch, son of Jared, son of Mahalaleel, son of Cainan, son of Enos, son of Seth, son of Adam, son of God?[21]

---

[21] Theophilus Evans, *Drych y Prif Oesoedd* (Amwythig, 1740), 7. The English translation is taken from George Roberts, *A View of the Primitive Ages* (Ebensburg, PA, 1834), 17.

Evans was enthralled by the bravery and sacrifices of the old Britons and he contrasted their valour sharply with the cowardice and perfidy of the Irish, the Picts, and the Saxons. The nineteenth-century essayist Emrys ap Iwan (Robert Ambrose Jones) reckoned he would have made a fine war correspondent, and this epic tale certainly stood the test of time.[22] An emended version, some ten thousand words longer than the first edition, appeared in 1740, and by the twilight of the Victorian age twenty-one editions had been published. Even the Welsh-Americans arranged the publication of an English translation in Ebensburg, Pennsylvania, in 1834 in order to sustain the historical memory of those who had emigrated to 'this Land of Equal Rights'.[23] For the best part of two hundred years, Theophilus Evans was the most popular remembrancer in Welsh-speaking Wales. As Lewis Morris rightly observed, *Drych y Prif Oesoedd* helped to rescue 'our national history from the dirt that is thrown upon it'[24] and to enable Welsh readers, for the first time, to read and enjoy a bold, rollicking version of their past in their own tongue.

The second luminary who merits attention was of very different colour. A representative of Augustan and neoclassicist values, Lewis Morris was the Welsh counterpart of Swift, or Pope, or Gay. Morris set himself the daunting task of reviving Welsh letters by establishing the first legal printing press in north Wales, publishing periodicals and books, chivvying like-minded scholars and savants, and setting up the celebrated London-based Society of Cymmrodorion. Although born in Anglesey, he spent the prime of his life (from 1742 to 1765) living in mid-Cardiganshire, where he became thoroughly familiar with the topography and mores of his adopted country. *A Short History of the Crown Manor of Creuthyn in the County of Cardigan* (1756) revealed not only his skills as a surveyor and a steward but also his intimate knowledge of what amateur historians liked to call 'natural curiosities'. Morris earned the undying wrath of local squires for jealously guarding Crown interests over the highly lucrative lead mines. Among those who despised Morris was the unscrupulous 'Vulture Knight', Sir Herbert Lloyd of Peterwell, who incarcerated him in

---

[22] David Thomas, 'Drych y Prif Oesoedd', *Y Traethodydd*, 19 (1951), 125; Prys Morgan,'Y Ddau Theophilus: Sylwadau ar Hanesyddiaeth', *Taliesin*, 19 (1969), 36–45; Glanmor Williams, 'Romantic and realist: Theophilus Evans and Theophilus Jones', *Archaeologia Cambrensis*, 140 (1991), 17–27.
[23] Roberts, *View of the Primitive Ages*, x.
[24] *ALM*, 2:447.

Cardigan gaol in 1753 following a bitter dispute over the exploitation of lead ores.[25] But Llewelyn Ddu ('Black Llewelyn'), as Morris was often called, was not an easy man to silence. His letters, around four hundred of which have survived (perhaps as little as a tenth of his total correspondence), are peppered with literary gems, puns, doggerel, intimacies, gossip, jokes, and invective. They are also a vivid portrait of an irremediable hypochondriac, for Morris was tormented, inter alia, by piles, itches, rheums, vomits, sweats, ulcers, gout, rheumatism, nose bleeds, palsies, and a host of other erratic and sometimes excruciating bodily ailments, only some of which were relieved by taking copious supplies of the waters at Llandrindod Wells. In the twentieth century, the prim Nonconformist editors of his correspondence often had recourse to the dreaded abbreviation u.f.p. (unfit for publication), for this convivial, lecherous Welshman liked to use 'foul' language (as did Pope and Swift) in his letters, and he was also capable of fits of towering rage. He was the most knowledgeable Welshman of the mid-eighteenth century and also the most compelling writer. In modern parlance, he belonged to the 'can-do men' and the range of his attainments was staggering. He could fashion a harp and play it, build a boat and sail it, compose a *cywydd* and sing it to the accompaniment of the harp.[26] He was an antiquary, a philologist, an etymologist, a hydrographer, a mineralogist, a cartographer, a poet, and a Celticist. Often he would append the word 'Philomath' to his name in order to remind lesser beings of his many-sidedness, especially his interest in mathematics and 'natural philosophy'.[27] To Morris, life was a great learning experience and he accumulated knowledge voraciously. He rightly believed that no Welsh contemporary could match him for knowledge, and his correspondence is littered with the phrase 'Nid pawb a ŵyr hyn' ('Not many people know this').[28] Like many of the upwardly mobile middling sorts in Hanoverian Wales, he enjoyed parading his Olympian knowledge before the unlearned and the boneheaded. When he travelled through parishes in Cardiganshire in 1761 he affected an air of superiority and claimed that the clergy

---

[25] D. Lleufer Thomas, 'Lewis Morris in Cardiganshire', *Y Cymmrodor*, 15 (1901), 1–87; Tegwyn Jones, *Y Llew a'i Deulu* (Talybont, 1982).

[26] Bedwyr Lewis Jones, 'Lewis Morris (1701–1765)', in idem, ed., *Gwŷr Môn* (Caernarfon, 1979), 60.

[27] *ALM*, 1:1; Branwen Jarvis, 'Lewis Morris, y "Philomath" Ymarferol', in Geraint H. Jenkins, ed., *Cof Cenedl X: Ysgrifau ar Hanes Cymru* (Llandysul, 1995), 61–90.

[28] *ML*, 2:5. See Alun R. Jones, '"Ymrwbio yn ein Gilydd mal Ceffylau": Llythyrau Lewis Morris', *Llên Cymru*, 22 (1999), 80–92.

'looked on me as an oracle'.[29] Like many gifted self-made men (he was a cooper's son), he assiduously courted patrons and often gave the impression in his letters that life was a daily battle against fools, blockheads, and knaves. Morris published little in his lifetime (his major work, 'Celtic Remains', a dictionary of place-names and personal names, remained unpublished until 1878), but his letters are at least the equal of those of Pope and Swift. Here is his description of the bibulous Welsh poet Goronwy Owen:

> What beggar, tinker, or sowgelder ever groped more in the dirt? A tomturd man is a gentleman to him. The juice of tobbacco in two streams runs out of his mouth. He drinks gin or beer till he cannot see his way home and has not half the sense of an ass, rowls in ye mire like a pig, runs through the streets with a pot in his hand to look out for beer; looks wild like a mountain cat, and yet when he is sober his good angel returns and he writes verses sweeter than honey and stronger than wine.[30]

He once described a bishop of Bangor as a 'filthy, smelly, useless man' ('dyn bawaidd drewllyd di-ddaioni'),[31] and English-speaking placemen and favourites as 'fit for the Business, as an Elephant to breed Goslings'.[32] In 1748 he informed William Vaughan of Corsygedol that 'any body that hath Eyes may see that their business [that is, bishops and clergymen] is F . . . ing ye poor Laity out of the money'.[33] Morris was also a highly gifted writer of satirical, comic, and smutty prose and poetry,[34] and he reckoned that the 'drudgery' of translating devotional books into Welsh for the benefit of the lower orders was best left 'to some heavy brother of the Church, that is fit for nothing else. No ship-builder puts his best caulker to pitch oakum'.[35] He was more anxious to create an elite middle-class culture and to satisfy its tastes. His best work – Welsh adaptations or translations of essays and satires by Brown, Gay, and Swift – were deliberately designed to provoke, tickle, and offend. Essays, squibs, prefaces, anecdotes, literary

---

[29] *ML*, 2:392–5.

[30] Ibid., 1:489.

[31] Ibid., 1:346.

[32] *ALM*, 1:185.

[33] Bangor, University of Wales (Bangor), MS Bangor (Mostyn) 7606.

[34] Jenkins, *Foundations of Modern Wales*, 392–3, 404–5; Alun R. Jones, 'Traethiadau Lewis Morris', *Taliesin*, 108 (2000), 64–83.

[35] *ALM*, 2:422.

puns, and admonitions flowed from his pen with extraordinary fluency and they deserve to be better known. Physicians, lawyers, and especially clergymen were judged to be fair game, and what purported to be the last speech of the Revd Thomas Ellis of Holyhead provides a good illustration of the kind of burlesque he enjoyed:

> O ye Gods & Demigods, Fauns, Sylphs Dryades & Hemidryades, Fa la la mi fa. Hold my head, give me either Patience or power enough to punish mankind that disobey my Commands; O I faint, I die! Some Lukewarm Fire! My eyes dart columns of water I'll burn you all to snow, stand off. Elixir salutis, Pancakes & Pudding, St Jerom & Augustine and all the Fathers of ye Church, and some pills of Hiora cum Agarick for heavens sake, o blister me Bleed me, some warm water, o give me a Clyster [36]

Morris was besotted by words and I strongly suspect he was a supremely good conversationalist as well as an enthralling writer. Until his death in 1765 he was reckoned to be the leading authority on Welsh letters, and although he did not publish much he exercised an enormous influence on his protégés. Like Samuel Johnson, he prided himself on his ability to 'move freely from one task to another',[37] to master different genres and accomplishments, and to open up new fields of inquiry. By comparison, in these days of Research Assessment Exercises and narrow specialisms, how blinkered and inadequate we appear to be alongside this Renaissance man.

One of those whom Morris took under his wing is our third gifted native of Cardiganshire. No portrait exists of Evan Evans or Ieuan the Poet of Cynhawdre, near Ystradmeurig, but he was an easily recognized figure in his day. Often dubbed Longshanks or Longobardus or Ieuan Brydydd Hir (Ieuan the Tall Poet), this lifelong bachelor curate was an unusually tall man. Penurious, ill at ease, and restless, he was a manic depressive, and a long scar on his neck signified a botched suicide attempt. Educated at Edward Richard's celebrated school at Ystradmeurig, three miles from his home, he spent four years at Merton College, Oxford, but left without a degree – partly, one suspects, because he had succumbed to heavy drinking. For much of his life as a wandering curate he was awash with alcohol. Unlike his

---

[36] BL, MS Add. 14928, fol. 33. See also Hugh Owen, *The Life and Works of Lewis Morris (Llewelyn Ddu o Fôn) 1701–1765* (Llangefni, 1951).

[37] Pat Rogers, *Johnson* (Oxford, 1993), 2.

mentor Lewis Morris (who knew how and when to bow and scrape), Evans was a forthright critic of the Church establishment and of spurious Celticists, and he seems to represent the decline of neo-classicism and the emergence of a more influential Romantic sensibility. It is easy to imagine him as the personification of Gray's celebrated 'Bard', poised above the river Conwy's foaming flood:

> Robed in the sable garb of woe
> With haggard eyes the Poet stood;
> (Loose his beard and hoary hair
> Steam'd, like a meteor to the troubled air) . . .[38]

Evans coined the popular epithet 'Esgyb Eingl' ('Anglo Bishops') to describe the indifferent, lazy, or venal bishops who were appointed to the see of St David's and the other Welsh dioceses in the Hanoverian period. Not a single Welsh speaker was appointed to St David's, the largest of the Welsh dioceses, in the eighteenth century. The average tenure of these birds of passage was five years. Their absenteeism was compounded by their penchant for rewarding English-speaking favourites with lucrative livings, ignoring the claims of well-qualified, Welsh-speaking candidates, and permitting the degraded lower clergy to eke out wretched lives on inadequate salaries.[39] As Paul Langford has recently noted, it was a commonplace among the English that those who were not English (and more especially if they were Celtic-speaking peoples) were lesser beings to be pitied or derided.[40] The inept mumbling (in what was presumably Welsh) by prelates during visitations and confirmations caused mystification and resentment, and their denial of preferments to gifted and ambitious Welsh clergymen became a major bone of contention. No Welsh writer was more scathing on this topic than Evan Evans.[41] Not without justification, he believed that English-speaking bishops ascribed superior status to the

---

[38] Quoted in R. Paul Evans, 'Mythology and tradition', in Herbert and Jones, ed., *The Remaking of Wales*, 164.
[39] Geraint H. Jenkins, 'Yr Eglwys "Wiwlwys Olau" a'i Beirniaid', *Ceredigion*, 10 (1985), 131–46; idem, 'The Established Church and Dissent in eighteenth-century Cardiganshire', in Jenkins and Jones, eds, *Cardiganshire County History*, 3:453–77.
[40] Paul Langford, *Englishmen Identified: Manners and Character 1650–1850* (Oxford, 2000), 314.
[41] NLW, MS 2009B; Gerald Morgan, 'Ieuan Fardd (1731–1788): Traethawd ar yr Esgyb Eingl', *Ceredigion*, 11 (1990), 135–46; Geraint H. Jenkins, '"Horrid unintelligible jargon": the case of Dr. Thomas Bowles', *Welsh History Review*, 15 (1991), 494–523.

English tongue and were determined to foist it upon the monoglot Welsh, thereby consigning them to 'Ignorance, Irreligion and Slavery'.[42] 'O bishops, O princes', wrote Lewis Morris of Evans in July 1760, 'O ye fat men of the land, why suffer ye that man to starve?'[43] Evans was convinced that bishops looked upon him 'with an evil eye',[44] and in published and unpublished works he railed against the 'predatory wolves' who were turning his beloved church into 'a den of thieves'.[45] He despaired of ever receiving a decent preferment and his unrelenting attacks on the ecclesiastical establishment, his devotion to drink, and his anglophobia, meant that his ambitions were constantly thwarted. Not surprisingly, Evans preferred the company of like-minded poets – sextons like Dafydd Jones of Trefriw, John Powell of Llansannan, and Robert Thomas of Llanfair Talhaiarn – who appreciated fine ale and lively conversation and who found solace and inspiration in the Welsh cultural past.[46]

The best way to understand Evan Evans is to recognize that he believed that the Welsh language was not only the oldest and most copious tongue in Europe but also the vehicle of some of the most memorable poetry ever written. It was a matter of great joy to him that ancient British verse was vastly superior to 'the wretched rhymes of the English'.[47] He was never happier than when 'his nose [was stuffed] in some vellum Ms',[48] and when he discovered the Gododdin of Aneirin his shrieks of delight were redolent of Cortes discovering the New World.[49] Over a long period he spent his leisure hours copying old Welsh manuscripts in order to preserve the extraordinary bardic tradition for posterity. His *Specimens of the Antient Poetry of the Welsh Bards* (1764) was not only a powerful riposte to James Macpherson's spurious Ossianic poems – he believed Macpherson was 'a downright cheat'[50] – but also a celebration of the finest early Welsh poetry from the days of Aneirin to the Poets of the Princes. The *Specimens* is second

---

[42] D. Silvan Evans, ed., *Gwaith y Parchedig Evan Evans (Ieuan Brydydd Hir)* (Caernarfon, 1876), 41.

[43] *ALM*, 2:471.

[44] Ibid., 2:620.

[45] NLW, MS 2009B, passim; Evan Evans, *Casgliad o Bregethau*, 2 vols (Mwythig, 1776), 1, sig. b4b.

[46] Lewis, 'Llythyrau Evans Evans', 239–58.

[47] Evans, *Gwaith y Parchedig Evan Evans*, 131–2.

[48] *ALM*, 2:492.

[49] Ibid., 1:349.

[50] Lewis, *Correspondence of Percy and Evans*, 100.

only to Lhuyd's *Archaeologia Britannica* in the roll of honour of seminal books on Welsh literature in the eighteenth century. It inspired, among others, Thomas Gray, and it also helped to stimulate the Celtic Revival in England.[51] Evans, too, was no mean poet: he penned *awdlau* (odes) and *cywyddau*, and his most celebrated *englynion* (stanzas) – to 'Llys Ifor Hael' – were composed in 1779 during a visit, in the company of the incomparable Iolo Morganwg, to the ruins of the court of Ifor ap Llywelyn at Gwernyclepa, near Bassaleg, in Monmouthshire. In these stanzas he memorably depicted brambles covering the ruins of ancient splendour, owls screeching in halls of song, and bounteous patrons who were no more. Appalled by the 'glaring enormities' of Saxon bishops and landowners, and the 'blind prejudice' of English historians, in his other poems Evans sang the praises of valorous Welsh heroes – 'brave Caradoc', 'the valiant Rhys', 'the brave Llywelyn' – who had 'stain'd their lances red with hostile blood'.[52] His publication *The Love of our Country* (1772) is another pioneering work, not least because he portrayed Owain Glyndŵr not as an uncouth rebellious bandit but as a valiant warrior for the national cause:

> When under heavier pressures still they lay,
> And bold usurping Henry bore the sway,
> The great Glyndwr no longer could contain,
> But, like a furious lion, burst the chain,
> None could resist his force: like timorous deer
> The coward English fled, aghast with fear.[53]

For all his faults, this flawed genius, who died in 1788 in the lonely farmhouse near Tregaron where he had been born, was one of those organic intellectuals who emphasised the cultural distinctiveness of Wales and encouraged his fellow countrymen to delight in the glories of their literary and historical past.[54] He deserves a better fate than to be patronized by Samuel Johnson as 'Poor Evan Evans'.[55]

---

[51] E.D. Snyder, *The Celtic Revival in English Literature 1760–1800* (Cambridge, MA, 1923); Ffion Llywelyn Jenkins, 'Celticism and pre-Romanticism: Evan Evans', in Jarvis, *Guide to Welsh Literature*, 104–25.

[52] Evans, *Gwaith y Parchedig Evan Evans*, 136.

[53] Ibid., 142.

[54] Gwyn A. Williams, 'Romanticism in Wales', in Roy Porter and Mikuláš Teich, eds, *Romanticism in National Context* (Cambridge, 1988), 24. For the background, see Prys Morgan, *The Eighteenth Century Renaissance* (Llandybïe, 1981).

[55] Morgan, *Ieuan Fardd*, 7.

Alongside Evan Evans, the fourth luminary to be considered here seems to have been (and probably was) a model of propriety. Within Britain he was certainly the best known, and within Cardiganshire he is the only one of the five whose memory is enshrined (at Llangeitho) in a full-scale memorial statue. The work, by Edward Griffith, the Liverpool-born sculptor, commemorates Daniel Rowland of Llangeitho, the most powerful and influential Methodist preacher in eighteenth-century Wales. It was unveiled in September 1883. During the ceremony 'a great & lusty cheer from the crowd time after time made the Hills ring out in the distance'.[56] Outside Wales a more familiar icon is the image of the aged Rowland, commissioned by the Countess of Huntingdon and engraved by Robert Bowyer shortly before Rowland's death in 1790. This is the Rowland whom Thomas Charles remembered as 'the old grey-headed Elijah'[57] – the venerable saint with flowing white hair, bushy eyebrows, a long ample nose, and pursed lips. However, we should seek to divest ourselves of this image and recall that when he threw himself into the Methodist cause in 1735 he was a mere stripling of twenty-four and even at the time of the powerful Llangeitho revival of 1762 he was still only fifty-one.[58] 'We are a heap of Boys O pity us',[59] cried his colleague Howel Harris as they rode through Cardiganshire and embarked on careers as powerful and eye-catching preachers. More than any other of the five Cardiganshire men dealt with in this paper, Rowland depended on the spoken word to convey his convictions. Neither able to, nor interested in, providing vigorous intellectual leadership, Rowland's principal aim was to capture the hearts of humble craftsmen, artisans, farmers, and their wives by means of itinerant evangelical activity, powerful preaching, pastoral oversight in *seiadau* (societies), love-feasts, and hymn-singing festivals.

Initially, Rowland acquired a reputation for strident, intimidating sermons characterized by dreadful flashes and thunder, the terror of the law, and the condemnation of sinners. He was known as 'yr offeiriad crac'[60] (the angry priest). The unregenerate were described by

---

[56] Dafydd Ifans, 'Edward Griffith a Cherflun Llangeitho', *Cylchgrawn Cymdeithas Hanes y Methodistiaid Calfinaidd*, nos 9–10 (1985–6), 73.

[57] John Owen, *A Memoir of the Rev. Daniel Rowlands* (1840), 90.

[58] Derec Llwyd Morgan, *The Great Awakening in Wales* (1988), 69.

[59] Tom Beynon, 'Howell Harris's visits to Cardiganshire', *Cylchgrawn Cymdeithas Hanes y Methodistiaid Calfinaidd*, 30 (1945), 50.

[60] John Owen, *Cofhad am y Parch. Daniel Rowlands* (Caerlleon, 1839), 17.

this Welsh Boanerges as vile, polluted worms, 'lumps of deformity',[61]
and some time elapsed before he tempered these bloodcurdling
threats with the balm of God's grace. 'Dewch trosodd i Langeitho'
('Come over to Llangeitho') is one of William Williams Pantycelyn's
celebrated lines, and if one were to do so nowadays one would find a
village Anglicized by an invasion of drop-outs, hippies, and second-
home owners. But in the eighteenth century Rowland's ministry was
of necessity thoroughly Welsh-speaking. Like many Johnny-come-
latelys in the eighteenth century, Howel Harris was filled with a
pathetic desire to please genteel sorts in London and Wales, but
Rowland worked feverishly in his native patch and in his native
tongue among the young and often unlettered enthusiasts who
peopled the society meetings.[62] According to one nineteenth-century
commentator, Llangeitho was his 'grand sphere of action'[63] and, as the
principal Mecca of the Calvinistic Methodist cause, it deserves to be
better known. There is only one reference to Llangeitho in W.R.
Ward's *The Protestant Evangelical Awakening* (1992) even though, in an
international context, it counts as much as Halle, Herrnhut, and
Northampton in Massachusetts. Rowland's name was synonymous
with Llangeitho, and Iolo Morganwg, who was no friend of the
Methodists, described it in 1802 as 'that Mecca of Wales that was
devotedly visited by the Welsh Methodists annually as the tomb of
Mahomet is by the Turks'.[64] Pilgrims travelled on foot, on horseback,
and by boat from all parts of Wales to hear Rowland preach and to
attend monthly communions, and this extraordinary epicentre of
Welsh enthusiasm buzzed with excitement as worshippers praised the
Lord, leapt with joy, shed tears, and cried 'Glory', 'Amen', and
'Hallelujah'. Deeply envious of Rowland's success as a preacher,
Howel Harris wrote: 'Surely there is no such ministry in Wales. I
never heard the like.'[65] Rowland was so busy ministering to his flocks
that he had no time to write books, though he did permit Thomas
Davies of Haverfordwest to edit his sermons and, alas, to 'dress

---

[61] Daniel Rowland, *Eight Sermons upon Practical Subjects* ([1774]), 22.

[62] Eryn M. White, *Praidd Bach y Bugail Mawr: Seiadau Methodistaidd De-Orllewin Cymru* (Llandysul, 1995); eadem, '"The World, the Flesh and the Devil" and early Methodist societies of South West Wales', *Transactions of the Honourable Society of Cymmrodorion*, ns 3 (1997), 45–61.

[63] Edward Morgan, *Ministerial Records; or Brief Accounts of the Great Progress of Religion* (1840), 159.

[64] Mari Ellis, 'Ysgafnhau'r Baich', *Taliesin*, 109 (2000), 56.

[65] Evans, *Daniel Rowland and the Great Awakening*, 73.

Rowlands in fine clothes' by inserting in his sermons gratuitous classical phrases and English words.[66]

By the time of Rowland's death in 1790 Welsh Methodism had been transformed within two generations from a spontaneous, inchoate, and informal group of enthusiasts into a robust national movement of twice-born Christians. The enthusiasm associated with Llangeitho was an integral part of that process and it is high time we recognized Daniel Rowland as a truly international figure. His success is all the more impressive in view of the fact that Calvinistic Methodism was widely detested, not least by the four other figures mentioned in this paper. Anti-Methodist propaganda poured from the presses and it evidently aroused the same fears and antagonisms as Jacobitism. Theophilus Evans deeply shocked one of his hearers at Llanwrtyd Wells by thundering loudly against the young evangelists: 'I never heard such a sermon in my Life, ye Devil made him as bold as a Lion calling ye ministers of Jesus Christ false Prophets, hotheaded fools and such Like Expressions.'[67] Evans mustered 417 subscribers to support his venomous *History of Modern Enthusiasm*, published in 1752, in which he parodied the preaching techniques of the likes of Daniel Rowland: '*he sees* Hell-Flames *flashing in their Faces*, and they are *now! now! now! dropping into Hell! into the Bottom of Hell! the bottom of Hell!*'[68] Living close to Llangeitho set Evan Evans's teeth on edge and he blamed corrupt absentee Saxon bishops for creating the climate in which 'the most arrant rogues under the sun'[69] were able to peddle their hotheaded enthusiasm. In Lewis Morris's eyes, Methodists were 'vermin',[70] and in a coruscating mock sermon he claimed that the likes of Daniel Rowland were amoral hypocrites who enticed nubile young women to society meetings and encouraged them to perform lewd deeds in dark corners.[71] While listening to Daniel Rowland fulminating against his hero, Dafydd Llwyd of Llwynrhydowen, Evan Thomas Rhys composed

---

[66] Owen, *Memoir of Daniel Rowlands*, 179; Daniel Rowland, *Tair Pregeth* (Caerfyrddin, 1775); idem, *Three Sermons upon Practical Subjects* (1778); idem, *Deuddeg o Bregethau ar wahanol Destynau* (Llanbedr, 1865). See also Gomer M. Roberts, 'Tanysgrifwyr Pregethau Cymraeg Daniel Rowland', *Cylchgrawn Cymdeithas Hanes y Methodistiaid Calfinaidd*, 45 (1960), 35–45.

[67] Gomer M. Roberts, 'The Trefecka letters (nos. 427–459)', *Cylchgrawn Cymdeithas Hanes y Methodistiaid Calfinaidd*, 46 (1961), 178.

[68] Theophilus Evans, *The History of Modern Enthusiasm* (1752), 79.

[69] *ALM*, 2:688.

[70] Alun R. Jones, '"Vermin [who] creep into all corners through the least crevices": Lewis Morris and the Methodists', *Transactions of the Honourable Society of Cymmrodorion*, ns 4 (1998), 24–35.

[71] NLW, MS 67A, fols 57–68.

an extempore verse mocking Rowland for his presumption in casting all 'heretical' anti-Calvinists into the eternal bottomless pit.[72] We need to be reminded from time to time that Calvinistic Methodism was not universally popular either in Cardiganshire or in Wales in the eighteenth century, and it is to Rowland's credit that he continued to blow the gospel trumpet loudly until his death in 1790.

The final representative treated here is little known within Wales, let alone beyond. Evan Thomas Rhys, a humble shoemaker, cobbler, and poet from Llannarth, can be found under two different entries in the *Dictionary of Welsh Biography*, one of the few examples known to me of the august editors of that splendid volume tying themselves into knots. One entry is under Evan Thomas and the other, by a different contributor, under Ifan Thomas Rhys. Perhaps that inadvertent error is appropriate since he was, according to Lewis Morris, a 'piece of curiosity'. This is Morris's description of him in 1761:

> I met at Llannarth, a thing in the shape of a man designed for a poet, and contained very good stuff, if he had fallen into good hands to be remodelled. . . . When I shewed him some incorrectness in the stile and some faults in orthography, he immediately swallowed it by wholesale. . . . He is not above 50 years of age, and his intellect's very strong, therefore may be licked up into the form of a poet with a little trouble, he is known by the name of Evan Thomas y Crydd a Phrydydd.[73]

By all accounts, he had unusually long arms and was able to untie the buttons of his breeches without bending; when composing poetry a large blue vein would swell above his eye like a 'large leech'.[74] Highly prized for his wisdom and common sense, he penned lively, convivial, free-metre verse in local taverns.[75] His original ambition had been to enter the Anglican ministry and, according to Lewis Morris, he had the theological works of John Stackhouse and John Tillotson 'at his fingers' ends'.[76] He regularly borrowed books from the splendid library of the Revd John Pugh of Motygido, Llannarth, whose mastery of languages

---

[72] Evan Thomas Rhys, *Diliau'r Awen; sef, Crynodeb o Waith Awenyddol y Diweddar Ardderchog Brydydd Evan Thomas Rhys*, ed. W.H. Griffiths (Aberystwyth, 1842), 27–8.

[73] *ALM*, 2:532–3.

[74] Rhys, *Diliau'r Awen*, viii.

[75] John Howell, ed., *Blodau Dyfed* (Caerfyrddin, 1824), 274–5, 276–7, 405–10; D.J. Davies, *Hanes Hynafiaethau ac Achyddiaeth Llanarth, Henfynyw, Llanllwchaiarn a Llandysilio-Gogo* (Caerfyrddin, 1930), 84.

[76] *ALM*, 2:532.

and fame as a schoolmaster was such that even in the late nineteenth century local schoolchildren used to chant:

Jupiter in recto facit, Jovis in genitivo
So says Pugh of Motygido.[77]

Craftsmen like Evan Thomas Rhys were prominent among subscribers to Dissenting books, and one of Edward Lhuyd's correspondents was deeply impressed by the number of blacksmiths, joiners, glovers, weavers, and shoemakers in the south of the county who were able to give a 'very good account of their faith'.[78]

Evan Thomas Rhys might not have been more than an interstitial figure, but he represented a new generation of prickly young Arminians, Arians, and Unitarians who inhabited a fiefdom demonized by the Methodists as 'The Black Spot' ('Y Smotyn Du'). Rhys was a member of Llwynrhydowen, the first Arminian chapel in Wales and the epicentre of the Black Spot. His mentor was Jenkin Jones, a blacksmith's son who had founded Llwynrhydowen and six other Arminian churches by the time of his death in 1742. His successor, the polyglot David Lloyd of Brynllefrith, was described by Dr Andrew Kippis as the best-read man he had ever met, and Evan Thomas Rhys fell under the spell of 'the great giant of Rhydowen' ('cawr mawr Rhydowen'), as one poet dubbed him.[79] As the century wore on, growing numbers of Calvinists defected to Arminian, Arian, and Unitarian causes, partly because they loathed the 'strange fire' which Methodism emitted but also because they were genuinely interested in rational inquiry and the cause of political and religious liberty. Several Dissenting academies, notably those at Carmarthen and Llan-non, positively encouraged unorthodox theology and intellectual discourse, and some of those who liked to style themselves 'friends to liberty' deployed their arguments with such vigour that leading Methodists deliberately avoided engaging with them in public disputes. Evan Thomas Rhys is therefore a good example of the rugged, populist, anticlerical, and anti-Calvinist tradition which gained ground in south

---

[77] S.C. Passmore, 'The Revd. John Pugh, Motygido, Llannarth (1690–1763) and his school', *Ceredigion*, 12 (1996), 43–4, 46.

[78] Edward Lhuyd, 'Parochialia', Supplement to *Archaeologia Cambrensis*, Part 3 (1909–11), 68; David Jenkins, 'The part played by craftsmen in the religious history of modern Wales', *The Welsh Anvil*, 6 (1954), 90–7; Jenkins, *Literature, Religion and Society*, 289–90, 296–7.

[79] D. Elwyn Davies, *'They Thought for Themselves'* (Llandysul, 1982), 26–9.

Cardiganshire and which later spread to the industrial communities of
Glamorgan. The mutual suspicion and hostility between the demons of
the Black Spot and the holy rollers of Llangeitho was long-lasting, and
the likes of Evan Thomas Rhys were much more receptive to liberal
principles and to the ideals of liberty and toleration. Had he lived to
witness the French Revolution he would almost certainly have become
a revolutionary sympathizer and a political activist. His verse, too,
which was included in anthologies by leading Welsh Jacobins,[80] would
have resembled Iolo Morganwg's rants against 'the Lord's elect':

> With mad fanatic jumping,
> With folly bawl'd aloud,
> Wild rant & pulpit thumping,
> We charm the silly crowd,
> When a jumping we do go.[81]

Cardiganshire, then, was the mother church of the Unitarian cause,
and by the early nineteenth century a fortress of 'heretical' churches
had been established in defiance of Anglicanism and Calvinistic
Methodism.

While each of these five men was in his own way very different
from the others, they all cherished books and manuscripts, and were
voracious readers. Printing presses in Wales were busy in the eighteenth century: over the course of the century more than two and a half
thousand Welsh books were published, many more than had been the
case in the Tudor and Stuart period.[82] Thanks largely to the
extraordinary success of Griffith Jones's circulating schools, it is
reasonable to suppose that around half the population of Wales had
learnt to read by the 1770s.[83] All sections of society were acquiring the
reading habit and developing a taste for books. Indeed, the poet
Goronwy Owen once claimed that he would sooner part with his wife
than with his books, and one suspects that others would have echoed
his sentiments privately. Lewis Morris's extraordinary library included
books on astronomy, geography, mathematics, navigation, and law, as

---

[80] NLW, MS 6238A.

[81] Ibid., fol. 395.

[82] Geraint H. Jenkins, 'The eighteenth century', in Philip Henry Jones and Eiluned Rees,
eds, *A Nation and its Books: A History of the Book in Wales* (Aberystwyth, 1998), 112.

[83] Idem, '"An old and much honoured soldier": Griffith Jones, Llanddowror', *Welsh
History Review*, 11 (1983), 449–68.

well as works by Dryden, Hobbes, Locke, Milton, Foxe, Pope, Swift, and Stillingfleet.[84] As a young man, Theophilus Evans gazed in wonder at the splendid array of manuscripts and printed volumes in the library of William Lewes at Llwynderw, and in his mature years he often quoted Seneca: 'Otium sine literis Mors est, et hominis viri Sepultura.'[85] His grandson, who adored him, said of him: 'of the value of money he knew little, books were his only treasures'.[86] Evan Evans loved books even more than a stiff drink, and two men with horses were required to carry his books from Llanfair Talhaiarn in Denbighshire to his birthplace in Cardiganshire in 1767.[87] Evans readily admitted that reading scholarly books was his 'chief delight and entertainment', and it was he who coined the much-used epithet 'A Lleufer dyn yw llyfr da' ('A good book is a man's Lantern').[88] Daniel Rowland's modest library was stocked with the tomes of Anglican and Puritan divines, and his son Nathaniel claimed that he knew almost the whole of the Welsh Bible by heart.[89] When Rowland ventured to Bristol to buy books William Romaine, the English evangelist, twitted him: 'I thought you had the Spirit of God to study his word, and to compose your sermons?'[90] But the truth is that Rowland was an avid reader, and his colleague Howel Harris, who deplored 'head knowledge', resented the fact that Rowland gave as much time as possible to reading. Books of a liberal and even seditious nature were meat and drink to the humble shoemaker Evan Thomas Rhys, and their contents were often read aloud in his workshop and in local taverns.

Although other notable scholars and writers like James Davies (Iaco ab Dewi), William Gambold, Alban Thomas, and Moses Williams also merit inclusion in this survey, it could not be argued that Cardiganshire produced a great constellation of talent in the eighteenth century. Indeed, in one of his surly moments, Lewis Morris declared that there were fewer clever people in Cardiganshire than anywhere else in Wales.[91] But this unfashionable county clearly did produce some

---

[84] NLW, MS 604D, fol. 104; *ALM*, 2:794–807.

[85] Evans, *History of Modern Enthusiasm*, sig. A2r.

[86] Jones, *History of the County of Brecknock*, 1:276.

[87] Aneirin Lewis, 'Ieuan Fardd a'r Gwaith o Gyhoeddi Hen Lenyddiaeth Cymru', *Journal of the Welsh Bibliographical Society*, 8 (1956), 131–2.

[88] Evans, *Gwaith y Parchedig Evan Evans*, 110. For a catalogue of Evans's books, see NLW, MS 2039D.

[89] Owen, *Memoir of the Rev. Daniel Rowlands*, 142–3.

[90] Morgan, *Ministerial Records*, 90–1.

[91] *ALM*, 1:113.

outstandingly gifted individuals who made a rich and lasting contribution to the cause of religion and learning both at local and
national levels. All of them, to a greater or lesser degree, were blessed
with the 'itch for Scribbling',[92] and it is a tragedy that their gifts were
not properly recognized in their day. We can only guess what they
might have achieved had governments, landowners, and bishops been
disposed to reward their talents properly. Lewis Morris, 'the Fat man of
Cardiganshire', was used to having the last word and the following
truism epitomizes the theme of this paper:

> there are some of these [ye mass of mankind] that are very
> uncommon spirits and of ye superior kind, though they have
> not the right opportunity of enquiring into ye nature of things.[93]

University of Wales Centre for Advanced Welsh and Celtic Studies

---

[92] *ML*, 1:342.
[93] Ibid., 1:238.

SOME ARCHITECTURAL ASPECTS OF THE ROLE OF MANUALS IN CHANGES TO ANGLICAN LITURGICAL PRACTICE IN THE NINETEENTH CENTURY

by JAMES BETTLEY

THE evangelical Francis Close, rector of Cheltenham and Dean of Carlisle, pithily observed in 1844 that 'Romanism is taught *Analytically* at Oxford [and] *Artistically* at Cambridge . . . it is inculcated theoretically, in tracts, at one University, and it is *sculptured*, *painted*, and *graven* at the other'.[1] The two forces to which he was referring – the Oxford Movement and the Cambridge Camden Society – emerged within a few years of each other, in 1833 and 1839 respectively. Although they were very different in the ways in which they achieved their ends, they were essentially products of the same *Zeitgeist*, and their influence combined to bring about radical changes to the conduct of church services and church affairs generally within the Church of England. The most significant and fundamental change was the reinstatement of the celebration of Holy Communion as the central act of Christian worship. Like the crucial doctrine of apostolic succession, which was the keystone of Tractarian philosophy, this sacrament provided a direct link with Christ, being a re-enactment of the ceremony which he instituted at the Last Supper. For the service was not simply, as it was for Protestants, a commemoration of that event; it was a renewal of Christ's sacrifice and was accompanied by a belief in the Real Presence. This is reflected in the terminology used. The Book of Common Prayer calls the service 'Holy Communion', which emphasises that part of the service where the people take part and share 'the Lord's Supper'. High Churchmen invariably referred to 'the Holy Eucharist', 'Eucharist' meaning 'thanksgiving', thus stressing the sacrificial aspect of the service which might be, in the more advanced ritualist churches, celebrated without the active participation of the congregation, as it had been before the Reformation. Further evidence of this attitude is the use of the word 'altar', with its sacrificial overtones, rather than the more domestic 'Lord's table'. It is also

---

[1] Quoted in James F. White, *The Cambridge Movement: the Ecclesiologists and the Gothic Revival* (Cambridge, 1962), 142.

significant that the so-called 'six points', adopted by the English Church Union in 1875 and thus formalizing a consensus on the points of ceremony worth fighting for in the ritual battles with the (Protestant) Church Association, all concerned aspects of the Holy Eucharist: eucharistic vestments, the eastward position, altar lights, the mixed chalice, wafer bread, and incense.[2]

The growth of ritualism within the Church of England was in large part a result of the revival of the celebration of the Holy Eucharist as the central act of Christian worship. For three hundred years, from the Reformation to the Oxford Movement, emphasis had been placed upon the services of Morning and Evening Prayer, with Holy Communion being celebrated perhaps only four times a year. Now that the focus of attention was shifting back from the pulpit to the altar, the consequences for the architecture and internal arrangement of church buildings were enormous.

An act as important as the celebration of the Holy Eucharist required an appropriate ceremonial, or liturgy, and an appropriate setting. The difficulty facing Anglican clergy was that these things had to be, in effect, reinvented. The Book of Common Prayer prescribed the necessary words, but said very little else about what was to be done when, or what equipment was needed, beyond the so-called Ornaments Rubric, 'That such Ornaments of the Church, and of the Ministers thereof at all times of their Ministration, shall be retained, and be in use, as were in this Church of England by the authority of Parliament, in the second year of the reign of King Edward VI.' This apparently simple statement gave rise to endless debate, first about what precise period was covered by 'the second year of the reign', and then about what 'ornaments' were at that time authorized for use. The rubric was widely taken to provide authority for referring back to the First Prayer Book of Edward VI (1549), which was compiled during the second year of his reign, although it did not come into effect until the third year; and any lack of explicit instructions contained in that book was ascribed to the common-sense notion that priests at that time, who had been fully instructed in pre-Reformation liturgy, did not need to be told what to do and simply continued to act in the old tradition. Such thinking placed a burden on the willing shoulders of antiquarians

[2] W.J. Sparrow Simpson, 'The Revival from 1845–1933', in N.P. Williams and Charles Harris, eds, *Northern Catholicism* (1933), 58; J.S. Reed, *Glorious Battle: the Cultural Politics of Victorian Anglo-Catholicism* (Nashville, TN, 1996), 69.

and theologians who set to the task of establishing what pre-Reformation practice had been. This gave rise to such massive and influential works as the Cambridge Camden Society's *Hierurgia anglicana* (1848), which was intended to be both archaeological and practical:

> Let us endeavour to restore everywhere amongst us the Daily Prayers, and (at the least) weekly Communion; the proper Eucharistic vestments, lighted and vested altars, the ancient tones of Prayer and Praise, frequent Offertories, the meet celebration of Fasts and Festivals (all of which and much more of a kindred nature is required by ecclesiastical statutes).[3]

Such works were not, however, for day-to-day use. There was clearly a need for manuals, both for the clergy who had to conduct the services and for the laity who attended them: both might be deterred by their lack of familiarity with the liturgy. *Steps to the Altar; a Manual of Devotions for the Blessed Eucharist*, compiled by 'a parish priest' and published in 1846, was aimed at the layman and was based upon the works of such seventeenth-century Anglican divines as Bishops Andrewes, Cosin, and Ken, and was thus reassuring. Most of the manuals available at this time, however, were Roman Catholic. An example is Frederick Charles Husenbeth's *Missal for the Use of the Laity* (1837), interesting because it was illustrated by the architect and Roman Catholic convert A.W.N. Pugin. Pugin's depiction of an ideal high altar is very similar to one of the illustrations in his book of *Designs for Gold and Silversmiths* (1836), one of a series of highly influential works which provided inspiration for those seeking examples of authentic medieval work to imitate. The link between liturgy and architecture is clearly indicated by the part which Pugin and other architects played, through devotional works such as these, in creating the image of the ideal setting for celebration of the Holy Eucharist.

Other Roman Catholic works included two by J.D.H. Dale: *Ceremonial according to the Roman Rite translated from the Italian of Joseph Baldeschi Master of Ceremonies of the Basilica of St Peter at Rome*, first published in 1853, and *The Sacristan's Manual*, first published in

---

[3] Quoted in (inter al.) A. Symondson, 'Theology, worship and the late Victorian church', in Chris Brooks and Andrew Saint, eds, *The Victorian Church: Architecture and Society* (Manchester, 1995), 195.

1854. The former went into at least eleven editions, and from the first included a frontispiece which illustrated the correct manner of censing the altar and oblations and which was included, with only minor modifications, in a number of other publications.[4] It is significant that for the second edition of 1859, the altar was no longer of the Roman type, but had been anglicized. *The Sacristan's Manual; or, Hand Book of Church Furniture, Ornament, &c. Harmonized with the most Approved Commentaries on the Roman Ceremonial and the Latest Decrees of the Sacred Congregation of Rites* also went into a number of editions, the third being published in 1874, and according to P.F. Anson 'found its way into many ritualistic rectories, where the directions given to Roman priests and sacristans were diligently followed by their Anglican opposite numbers'.[5] Some of these works were more obviously concerned with architecture than with liturgy: *St Charles Borromeo's Instructions on Ecclesiastical Building*, translated by the architect G.J. Wigley and illustrated by his partner S.J. Nicholl,[6] was published in 1857. Although it was essentially a Roman Catholic manual it was welcomed by the *Ecclesiologist*,[7] and enjoyed a great vogue among High Anglicans.[8]

Before long, however, there was no need for ritualist Anglicans to resort to Roman Catholic manuals, although doubtless many of them continued to do so. The Ecclesiological (late Cambridge Camden) Society had provided an Anglican answer to Pugin's books of designs, publishing two series of model designs for furnishings and fittings by the Society's favourite architect, William Butterfield, in 1847 and 1856 under the title *Instrumenta ecclesiastica*; and in 1858 came an acceptably Anglican version of such works as Husenbeth's *Missal. The Directorium anglicanum; being a Manual of Directions for the Right Celebration of the Holy Communion, for the Saying of Matins and Evensong, and for the Performance of Other Rites and Ceremonies of the Church, according to the Ancient Use of the Church of England*, was compiled by the Revd John Purchas (a leading ritualist who was to become notorious following the judgement given against him for illegal practices in 1870)[9] with the

---

[4] For example, *Ritual Notes*, 8th edn (1935).

[5] P.F. Anson, *Fashions in Church Furnishings* (1965), 176.

[6] Illustrations exhibited at the Architectural Exhibition, London, 1857–8.

[7] *Ecclesiologist*, 19 (1858), 101–2.

[8] Anson, *Fashions*, 176.

[9] Indeed, the *Ecclesiologist* thought it unwise of Purchas to have revealed so much of ritualistic practice to 'a scoffing and irreligious public' (quoted in Anson, *Fashions*, 178).

assistance of a number of other well-known experts in the field, such as the Revds Thomas Chamberlain, F.G. Lee, J.M. Neale, and T.W. Perry. There was an appendix on music, contributed by Thomas Helmore, and another on floral decorations by John Oakley (who, however, had his name removed from later editions). For the first time, a work of this sort was fully illustrated, by J.W. Hallam of Oxford, a draughtsman who worked for a number of ecclesiastical architects,[10] and who also made designs for the church furnishers Cox & Sons[11] and Jones & Willis.[12]

The aim of the *Directorium anglicanum* was to put 'the Priest of the nineteenth century on a par with the Priest of the sixteenth as to ritual knowledge',[13] and to achieve this it provided detailed instructions, with authorities cited, for conducting services in a manner which would have been recognized by a priest in the second year of Edward VI's reign, including a list of the necessary ornaments of the church and of the ministers. These were helpfully amplified by the illustrations. The frontispiece showed the priest and his assistants approaching the altar at the beginning of the service; the remaining illustrations, more diagrammatic, provided details of vestments, layout of the chancel, an example of a fully vested altar, and a diagram of the altar to clarify the difference between the north *side* and the north *end* – a distinction which was crucial, as the Book of Common Prayer stipulated that the celebrant should stand at the north *side* of the altar, whereas ritualists adopted the so-called eastward position, with their backs to the congregation, and justified this (to their own satisfaction, if not that of their opponents) by standing just to the north of the middle of the front of the altar.

The second edition of the *Directorium* appeared in 1865, being edited by Frederick George Lee, a clergyman who designed his own church, St Mary's, Aberdeen.[14] Lee also partly illustrated his later *Glossary of Liturgical and Ecclesiastical Terms* (1877). Most of the other

[10] Including William White, William Wilkinson, J.P. St Aubyn, Charles Buckeridge, J.W. Hugall, and S.J. Nicholl (who was also associated with Cox & Sons). See *Builder*, 24 (1866), 905; 25 (1867), 390; 26 (1868), 589, 842–3; 27 (1869), 666–7; 28 (1870), 106–7, 166–7, 786–7; 29 (1871), 586–7, 886–7; 38 (1880), 387; 40 (1881), 44; 41 (1881), 330–2.

[11] Cox & Sons, *Illustrated Catalogue of Gothic and Other Artistic Domestic Furniture, Fittings, Decorations, Upholstery and Metal Work* (1872).

[12] *An Illustrated Catalogue of some of the Articles in Church Furniture manufactured by Jones and Willis (Willis Brothers)* (Birmingham, 1880).

[13] Preface to 1st edn, quoted from 3rd edn (1866), viii.

[14] *Ecclesiologist*, 23 (1862), 239.

illustrations in the *Glossary* were by Orlando Jewitt after Pugin, but one was contributed by the architect Edmund Sedding.[15] It was Sedding whom Lee chose as the illustrator of his edition of the *Directorium.* Hallam was a competent draughtsman of the 1860s Gothic Revival, but Sedding was altogether a more interesting choice, and in the preface to the new edition Lee praises 'Mr Sedding's able drawings, so full of Catholic feeling and a correct taste for the best form of Christian art.'[16] Edmund Sedding was the elder brother of John Dando Sedding, and at this time they were in partnership in Penzance. They had both been pupils of George Edmund Street and moved in advanced ritualist circles;[17] Edmund was as well known for his interest in ancient church music as for his architecture.[18] Sedding's illustrations (Figs 1–2) show very clearly just what was required in a fashionable ritualist church: furniture, fittings, vestments, and decoration are all shown, which must have given an enormous impetus to those whose livelihoods depended upon designing, manufacturing, and supplying the articles in question. The *Directorium* was published in a third, cheaper edition in 1866, and a fourth in 1879; it formed the basis for two further works by Lee, *Notitia liturgica* (1866) and the *Manuale clericorum* (1874).

The other widely used and cited work was *The Eucharistic Manual*, by the Revd George Rundle Prynne, vicar of St Peter's Plymouth, first client of G.E. Street (for Par church, Cornwall, in 1848), and father of the architects G.H.F. and E.A.F. Prynne. Originally published in 1864, it was intended primarily for the laity and explained the use of such unfamiliar features as vestments, altar lights, and incense. As with many other books of this type, part of it later appeared in a different guise as *Plain Instructions on the Blessed Sacrament* (1872).

One of the most prolific authors of the 1860s and 1870s was the Revd Orby Shipley, whose career as an Anglican clergyman was cut short when he seceded to Rome in 1878. He was best known for editing three annual volumes of 'essays on questions of the day', *The Church and the World* (1866–8), which included contributions by

---

[15] 'Pastoral staff designed by the late Mr. Edmund Sedding': *A Glossary of Liturgical and Ecclesiastical Terms* (1877), 273.
[16] Quoted from 3rd edn (1866), xliii.
[17] Symondson, 'Theology, worship', 197.
[18] *DNB.* He was the father of the architect Edmund Harold Sedding (d. 1921).

Fig. 1   John Purchas, *Directorium anglicanum*, 2nd edn, revised F.G. Lee
(London, 1865): 'The Holy Eucharist' (frontispiece) by Edmund Sedding.
British Library Shelf-mark 3475.E.17. By permission of the British Library.

Fig. 2   John Purchas, *Directorium anglicanum*, 2nd edn, revised F.G. Lee (London, 1865): 'Bird's-eye view of a chancel', by Edmund Sedding. British Library Shelf-mark 3475.E.17. By permission of the British Library.

Street[19] and William Burges.[20] In 1863 Shipley published *The Divine Liturgy: a Manual of Devotions for the Sacrament of the Altar*, aimed at those preparing to take communion, 'the highest Act of Christian Worship, as well as the most important and efficacious public service of Almighty GOD, which the Church sanctions.'[21] His greatest achievement was his *Ritual of the Altar*, first published in 1870, which he came to regard as his final gift to the Church of England. Unlike Purchas and Lee, who were at pains to stress that their work was derived from English sources, Shipley was quite open about the fact that he incorporated material from the Roman Mass, on the justified grounds that the English office had originally been taken from the Latin rite: 'the English rite has been supplied with devotions and directions taken from the rock whence the stone of the Office originally was hewn.'[22] There were advantages in bringing English services more into line with other branches of the Catholic Church:

> this will be of much service, especially to laymen who travel, as well as to the bulk of our home-stopping congregations. The latter will see the Holy Office celebrated with more of ritual pomp and circumstance, absolutely; and by comparison with what they see abroad, the former will not be so much repelled by the cold and perfunctory manner in which Mass is so often said amongst ourselves.[23]

Apart from reprinting the Prayer Book service intact, Shipley added rubrical directions (with considerable detail as to preparations, vestments, and so forth, as well as the manual acts), private prayers (in Latin and English), and some plainsong. As for the legality of his proposals, 'if we cannot obtain the judgement of the Church of the present day upon the matter of Ritual, we must go back to the judgement of the Church of earlier times.'[24] His manual was 'not intended to be in accordance with the judge-made law of the land, but

---

[19] 'The study of foreign Gothic architecture, and its influence on English art', *The Church and the World* (1866), 397–411.
[20] 'Art and religion', *The Church and the World* (1868), 574–98, which includes a memorable attack on what he calls 'the Original and Ugly School' of modern church architecture.
[21] *Ritual of the Altar* (1870), vi.
[22] Ibid., xx.
[23] Ibid., xxxiv.
[24] Ibid., lii.

[is] declared to be in harmony with the Use of the Catholic Church in England, as imposed by legitimate authority'.[25]

The second edition of Shipley's *Ritual* appeared in 1878, the year in which he left the Church of England. The position he adopted was extreme and unapologetic:

> The form of the English Office can only be allowed to be, liturgically speaking, the minimum of a valid offering of the highest act of Christian worship. . . . The right has been claimed and exercised of supplementing such Order from the ancient Rituals of the Church. [Anything not explicitly disallowed by the Prayer Book] is still the legitimate inheritance of the Anglican Communion . . . The RITUAL OF THE ALTAR contains the maximum of ceremonial desiderated by English Catholics.[26]

Notable differences between this and the first edition are the inclusion of a full list of ornaments, taken from a *Kalendar of the English Church* (1877), and

> The Illustrations (as well as the design for the cover) [which] are, with a few exceptions, from the pencil of the Rev. ERNEST GELDART, who was good enough to draw them himself upon the wood. The idea of representing the Manual Acts was borrowed from an Edition of the Dominican Missal published in the last century at Rome.

The result was a highly original work. *Notes on Ceremonial*, an anonymous manual first published in 1876 that gave 'ritual directions', had included, as well as a diagram showing the 'mode of censing the altar [and] oblations',[27] a series of plans of the sanctuary showing the positions of the officiating clergy at various points in the service. *The Ritual of the Altar* went very much further than this, with forty-seven illustrations 'of the positions of the celebrant and sacred ministers at high mass', and a further twenty-five diagrams or details 'of manual acts, common forms, and usages of divine service'. (Figs 3–4). The cartoon-like drawings provided guidance to clergy apparently unprecedented and unsurpassed. It is impossible to say how widely the book was used; it was lavishly produced, and unlike the *Directorium*

---

[25] Ibid., xliv.

[26] Unnumbered pages.

[27] Similar to the diagram included in Dale's *Ceremonial*, but four fewer swings of the censer because of the absence of monstrances.

General Rubrics.

sustaining with his right hand either the foot of the Chalice, or the right arm of the Celebrant, placing the left hand upon his breast, says with him : *We offer unto Thee*, covers the Chalice with the pall, placed upon the Altar as above (sec. 5.), and the Paten with the corner of the Corporal (see H.). The Deacon remains at the right of the Celebrant (16.) till the

(16.)

Alms are presented, and the Sub-deacon stands on his own step behind the Priest.
(If the Priest's Host be laid upon the Corporal, then, the Sub-deacon, standing at the Epistle-corner (having been vested
• in the Humeral Veil by the acolyte), receives from the Deacon, into his right hand, the Paten, which he covers with the extremity of the veil hanging from his shoulder. He then goes behind the Celebrant, before the midst of the Altar, and there stands holding it, elevated as high as his breast, to the end of the Pater Noster. But at Mass for the Dead, the Paten is not so held by the Sub-deacon.)
9. *Come, O Thou* (see 17.), having been said, the Celebrant, while the Deacon ministers the incense-boat, and says : *Bless, reverend Father*, puts Incense into the censer, saying : *At the intercession.* Then the Celebrant, receiving the censer at the hand of the Deacon, making no previous reverence to the Cross, censes
viii. 9.

the Oblations (I.) forming over the Host and Chalice three signs of the Cross with the censer (the Deacon in the meanwhile holding the foot of the Chalice with his right hand), saying : at the 1st, *Let this Incense ;* at the 2nd, *which Thou hast blessed ;* at the 3rd, *ascend unto Thee, O Lord ;* at the 4th, describing three circles round the Chalice and Host, the 1st and 2nd by swinging the Censer from right to left, and the 3rd from left to right,

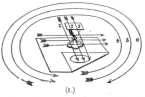

(I.)

and let Thy loving-mercy ; at the 5th and 6th, *descend upon us.* Having thus censed the Oblations, he censes the Cross and Altar, in the manner directed above (v. 3.), the Deacon assisting him, holding up the border of the chasuble. When he censes the Cross, the Deacon removes the Chalice but not off the Corporal, towards the Epistle-side, and replaces it when the Cross has been censed.

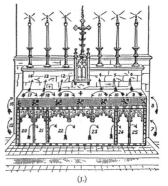

(J.)

At each swing of the Censer, the Celebrant says the following words : 1. *Let my*
viii. 9.

Fig. 3   Orby Shipley, *The Ritual of the Altar*, 2nd edn (London, 1878): sample page illustrated by Ernest Geldart. British Library Shelf-mark 3475.D.6. By permission of the British Library.

General Rubrics.

della (41.), when the Priest turns round to give the Blessing. They continue kneeling, till he has made the genuflection after the Blessing, and then all rise together.

XIV. Of the Ablutions and the Gospel according to S. John.

HAVING carefully wiped every Fragment of the Hosts off the Paten and out of the Ciborium or vessel with the thumb and forefinger of the right hand, and also from his fingers, into the Chalice, the Celebrant, with his thumbs and forefingers joined, takes the Chalice with his right hand below the knob of the cup, and reverently consumes the Sacrament with every Particle. Which done, he says: *Grant, O Lord;* at the same time holding out the Chalice over the Altar to the server on the Epistle-side, wine being poured into it, he cleanses the Chalice and drinks the Ablution ; then, he receives wine and water on the thumb and forefinger of each hand (S.) into the Chalice (xviii. 8.),

(S.)

wipes them with the purificator, saying in the meanwhile : *Let Thy Body,* and takes the Ablution. Then, if necessary, he holds out the Paten or Ciborium, that is, when there is difficulty in cleansing it of the Fragments, for an Ablution of water, which he pours into the Chalice, and consumes. Which done, he wipes his mouth, the Paten or Ciborium, and the bowl and lip of the Chalice. Then he places the purificator over the Chalice ; then the Paten ; over the Paten the pall ; having folded the Corporal, he places it in the burse ; he covers the Chalice with the

xiv. 1.

veil, upon which he puts the burse ; and lastly places them in the middle of the Altar, as at the beginning of Mass.

At Low Mass, the Ciborium may be left upon the Altar, and will be afterwards removed by the Priest : but at High Mass the Sub-deacon will take it and place it upon the credence with the sacred vessels (T.), unless it be the custom to keep

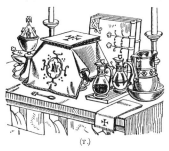

(T.)

it in the Tabernacle or Aumbry or Sacrament House.

2. Which done, the Celebrant standing before the midst of the Altar with hands joined upon it, and head bowed, says : *Let this my bounden duty.* With hands extended and placed upon it, he kisses the Altar, and then goes to the Gospel-corner of the Altar, where having said : *The Lord be with you,* and R. *And with thy spirit,* with the right thumb first signing the Altar, if he be reading from the Altarcard, or the book at the beginning of the Gospel, then his forehead, mouth and breast, he says : *The beginning of the Gospel according to S. John,* or : *The beginning, or The sequence of the Gospel according to S.——,* and R. *Glory be to Thee, O Lord.* Then, with hands joined, he reads the Gospel : *In the beginning,* or some other as is proper. When he says, *And the Word was made Flesh,* he genuflects towards the Gospel-side, and rising continues to the end ; which ended, the server standing on the Epistle-side, answers : *Thanks be to God.*

At Mass for the Dead, when the Priest has said, *Let this my bounden duty,* as above, and kissed the Altar, he goes to

xiv. 2.

Fig. 4   Orby Shipley, *The Ritual of the Altar*, 2nd edn (London, 1878): sample page illustrated by Ernest Geldart. British Library Shelf-mark 3475.D.6. By permission of the British Library.

anglicanum never appeared in a cheap edition (presumably because of Shipley's secession, but perhaps also because of its more advanced character).

One church where it definitely was used was Little Braxted in Essex. There Ernest Geldart, the illustrator, was rector. He had trained as an architect before taking holy orders and successfully combined the two careers. Geldart's other contribution to the genre of liturgical manuals was *A Short Explanation of the Ceremonies of the Holy Eucharist* (1876), 'Translated from the Latin of J.H. Hazé, and adapted to the liturgy of the Church of England. By a priest of that Church.' In the preface he states that he is 'following the Ritual of the Altar by the Rev. Orby Shipley, as being the most conscientiously complete work the English Church has yet seen upon the Celebration of the Holy Eucharist'. The only illustration is a frontispiece (Fig. 5), which appears to be modelled on Sedding's frontispiece to the second edition of the *Directorium anglicanum*.[28]

During the 1860s and 1870s these manuals proliferated and, although some placed more emphasis than others upon particular usages (such as fasting communion or incense), all agreed upon the general principles and requirements: the use of vestments, vested altars, candlesticks, flower vases, credence table, piscina, and sedilia; that services should be sung or said (that is, fully choral or, more controversially, 'either recited on a single note (intoned), or with the use of certain simple inflections, which constitute "Plain Song"');[29] and processions. Such elaborate ritual required large numbers of participants. For a High Celebration, the *Directorium anglicanum* called for a priest, deacon and sub-deacon (gospeller and epistoler), assistant priest, 'ceremoniarius' or director of the ceremonies, four acolytes,[30] and unspecified numbers of 'thurifers, with incense boat-bearer', not forgetting a surpliced choir and choirmaster-organist.

The consequences of all this do not form part of this paper, but they can be briefly indicated. The 'Ornaments of the Church, and of the Ministers thereof' had to be designed, manufactured, and supplied, and a whole industry sprang up to meet the demand – only to wither again

---

[28] There is also little to choose between Geldart's altar and the one illustrated in *The Reformation and the Deformation*, published by Mowbray in 1868 (reproduced in Anson, *Fashions*, pl. 3).

[29] F.G. Lee, *Notitia liturgica* (1866), 20.

[30] For whom separate manuals (e.g. Charles Walker's *Server's Handbook* of 1871) were available.

Fig. 5   Ernest Geldart, *Short Explanation of the Ceremonies of the Holy Eucharist* (London, 1876): frontispiece. British Library Shelf-mark 3475.C.56(10). By permission of the British Library.

in the twentieth century. Churches had to be altered to accommodate the new ritual and its accompanying impedimenta: vestries were needed for robing, with special cupboards for the storage of vestments, plate, and other equipment. The sanctuary needed to be properly laid out, with an altar of sufficient size; the number and dimensions of the steps on which the altar stood were carefully described in such works as J.T. Micklethwaite's *Modern Parish Churches* (1874), not just to draw attention to the focal point in the church but to ensure that it was possible for the officiants to gather and move around the sanctuary during the ceremony. The choir and its accompanying organ needed to be accommodated in the chancel rather than in a gallery at the west end, thus bringing them firmly under the control of the priest and integrating them into the service. Consideration was also given to circulation, for communicants and for processions.

The role of the Cambridge Camden Society in the development of ecclesiastical architecture in the nineteenth century was enormous and has been much discussed, but a large part of the impetus for the changes which they promoted was aesthetic, antiquarian, and Romantic, and placed most emphasis upon medieval precedent and architectural style. The influences to which this paper has drawn attention had very little to do with style, but were almost entirely driven by the need to respond to practical considerations, and in this they were often assisted by architects working in the best tradition of their profession, and in a surprisingly modern way, to provide an architectural solution to the particular needs of their clients.

COMMUNICATIONS BETWEEN CULTURES: DIFFICULTIES IN THE DESIGN AND DISTRIBUTION OF CHRISTIAN LITERATURE IN NINETEENTH-CENTURY INDIA

by GRAHAM W. SHAW

THE nineteenth century saw the heyday of Protestant missionary activity in the Indian subcontinent. South Asia – even then with one fifth of the world's population – was such a magnet for Christian missionaries that it was estimated that one-third of all such 'labourers in foreign lands' were operating there. This was despite the deliberate policy of the East India Company to discourage missionary activity in India (used throughout this paper in the old sense of 'undivided India') as liable to foment unrest and therefore upset the *economic* health of the country which from the Company's perspective was of paramount importance, not its *spiritual* well-being.[1] This antipathy was the reason, for instance, why William Carey and colleagues founded their famous pioneering mission in 1798 not in Calcutta in the Company's territory but further up the Hooghly river in the tiny settlement of Serampore then under Danish rule.[2]

But the East India Company could not hold out against the rising tide of evangelicalism in Great Britain, and many of its own employees were themselves committed Christians. It even on occasion found itself under direct attack in Christian tracts published at home, for instance when it was discovered that the Company took a percentage of the pilgrim tax levied on Hindus visiting the temple of Jagannath at Puri in Orissa, regarded as 'the Sebastopol of Hindu idolatry' and notorious for the supposed self-sacrifices of people under the wheels of the temple-car.[3]

As British rule extended to more and more territory throughout the first half of the nineteenth century, so in its wake Christian missionaries gradually fanned out across the subcontinent, though

---

[1] See Julius Richter, *A History of Missions in India* (Edinburgh and London, 1908), 128–9.

[2] See E.D. Potts, *British Baptist Missionaries in India, 1793–1837: the History of Serampore and its Missions* (Cambridge, 1967).

[3] See Graham W. Shaw, 'The Cuttack Mission Press and early Oriya printing', *British Library Journal*, 3 (1977), 31.

always dwarfed by the sheer geographical scale of their chosen field and by the enormous populations they found there. In 1861, there were just 541 foreign missionaries in India (mostly British, but with a large American contingent, plus some Germans, French, and so on), potentially ministering to a population of almost one hundred and eighty million – that is, approximately one missionary to 330,000 of the population of India at that time (see Table 1).[4]

By the mid-century, however, there was growing recognition on the part of the missionaries that all their activity, and not least the enormous efforts put into publishing, had not been matched by any great results in conversion. Again by 1861, as Table I shows, there were estimated to be some 213,000 Christians in South Asia and Burma. If we exclude the figures for Burma and Ceylon where special factors applied, that figure comes down to 138,500 on the subcontinent proper. Of those, nearly eighty per cent were concentrated in South India, where conversion dated back to the Portuguese period and the efforts of St Francis Xavier in the 1540s (he was said to have converted up to fifty thousand at that time alone). The number of conversions that can be taken as a direct result of fifty years or so of effort in the nineteenth century can probably therefore be put at no more than eighty thousand. Or if we say that widespread efforts at conversion only started in the 1830s, that is about 2,700 converts per year of mission activity, or five conversions achieved per missionary year. A meagre harvest of souls, particularly given the initial vaunting ambition and boundless confidence of the first generation of evangelical missionaries in India, Carey and his ilk!

Missionaries began to ponder possible reasons for this failure. Clearly there were a number of factors at play, and this paper will not consider in detail those that do not pertain to publishing directly. But one or two may be briefly mentioned. First and foremost, there was great innate resistance to conversion by the various communities. For Hindus, conversion to Christianity presented a very real practical difficulty. It was literally a life-changing decision, and not just in the spiritual sense. Loss of the Hindu religion meant loss of a recognized place in society – loss of caste – and most importantly, loss of occupation and livelihood. Muslims were reckoned to provide the hardest challenge for missionaries as,

---

[4] Table taken from Joseph Mullens, *A Brief Review of Ten Years' Missionary Labour in India Between 1852 and 1861* (1863), 175.

Table 1. *Missionary Activity in India, 1861*

Province	Population	Foreign Missionaries	Native Christians
Bengal, Bihar, Orissa & Assam	40,850,000	113	20,774
North-West Provinces	28,045,000	60	3,638
Oudh	6,000,000	9	225
Rajputana, Scindia & Holkar's territories, etc.	18,000,000	5	–
Punjab, Delhi, etc.	14,776,000	42	1,226
Punjab Native States	7,154,000	–	–
Bombay	11,845,000	38	1,916
Bombay Native States	3,438,000	2	315
Central Provinces	6,500,000	3	212
Hyderabad State	10,600,000	–	–
Madras Presidency & Native States	28,650,000	210	110,237
Ceylon	1,846,000	37	15,273
Burma	1,436,000	22	59,366
TOTALS	179,140,000	541	213,182

sharing so much with Christianity, it was not an easy task to get across the differences. Sikhs were felt to be a better prospect than Hindus, having at least renounced the evil of caste. There was also the bewildering linguistic complexity of India that confronted any missionary, with at least twenty major languages and many hundreds of minor languages and dialects written in a wide variety of scripts – an enormous linguistic hurdle to get over before one could get into one's 'converting stride', particularly when so few grammars and dictionaries of those languages had yet been written, at least for consumption by Westerners.[5]

But debate also centred specifically upon the kind of Christian literature which was being prepared and circulated. There was of course the vexed technical question of how to convey certain Christian concepts such as the Trinity into Indian and therefore essentially Hindu or Islamic languages. There was also the impression that too much Christian literature had been very aggressive in tone, targeting

[5] On the efforts of British pioneer linguists in India see, for instance, D. Kopf, *British Orientalism and the Bengal Renaissance: the Dynamics of Indian Modernization, 1773–1835* (Calcutta, 1969).

indigenous religions 'head on'. As one missionary, the Revd T.V. French, put it: 'Almost the whole range of our religious literature, with the exception of a few hymns and commentaries, [is] dwarfed and shrunken into polemical discussion.'[6] The very first Christian tract to be printed in India, by the Tranquebar missionaries on the Malabar coast in 1713, had been entitled in Tamil *Akkiyanam*, literally 'Ignorance' or, as the German missionaries more colourfully translated it, 'The Abomination of Paganism'. This overtly polemical tradition continued and intensified until it reached a climax perhaps in the works against Islam produced by the German Pietist, the Revd Carl Gottlieb Pfander. In the 1840s and 1850s he confronted Muslim clerics in open debate at Agra, but was ultimately defeated by a 'technical knock-out' as the Muslim scholars countered with charges that the Christian tradition itself was corrupt.[7]

Discussion also centred on how far Christian literature in India was ineffective because the printed book itself was failing as a physical, visual, and cultural artefact. In other words, was the Christian message not getting across not only because of the alien linguistic garb in which it was dressed but also because of the physical form through which it was being conveyed? The enormous amount of missionary literature being published in India by the mid-century is shown in Table 2 for the decade 1852–63 alone.[8] These figures represent a staggering average of no fewer than 860,000 books and tracts per year coming off the various mission presses in the subcontinent. To this figure must be added an annual issue of 160,000 volumes of Scripture, as a total of 1,634,940 copies of biblical parts translated into over twenty languages were published during the same decade.[9]

With regard to the problem of books specifically as *printed* books, we should remember that in the first half of the nineteenth century 'indigenous India' was still very much in the era of the manuscript. There were whole castes of professional scribes – the Hindu *kayasths* – and their Muslim equivalents – the *katibs* – whose very livelihood was the mass duplication of the written word, whether for governmental, religious, literary, scientific, or leisure purposes.

---

[6] *Conference on Urdu and Hindi Christian Literature, held at Allahabad, 24th and 25th February, 1875* (Madras, 1875), 7.

[7] See Avril A. Powell, *Muslims and Missionaries in Pre-Mutiny India*, London Studies on South Asia, 7 (Richmond, 1993), ch. V–VI.

[8] Mullens, *Brief Review*, 163.

[9] Ibid., 153.

Table 2. *Missionary Publication in India, 1852–63*

Issuing Society or Press	Languages of publication	Number of books/tracts issued
Calcutta Tract Society	Bengali, Hindi, Urdu, etc	1,267,892
Orissa Mission Press	Oriya	372,300
Assam Mission Press	Assamese	?
Tirhoot Mission Press	Hindi-Kaithi	330,000
North Indian Tract Society	Hindi, Urdu, etc.	c. 300,000
Ludhiana Mission Press	Panjabi, Persian, etc.	112,800
Bombay Tract Society	Marathi, Gujarati, etc.	542,264
Surat Mission Press	Gujarati	170,000
Madras Tract Society	Tamil, Telugu, Kannada, etc.	1,301,253
Bangalore Mission Press	Kannada	275,564
Vizagapatam Society	Telugu	171,000
Mangalore Mission Press	Kannada, etc.	143,000
Tellicherry Mission Press	Malayalam, etc.	63,600
Cottayam Mission Press	Malayalam	?
Nagercoil Mission Press	Tamil	397,196
Palamcottah Mission Press	Tamil	328,425
Tranquebar Mission Press	Tamil	?
South India School Book Soc.	English	276,586
Church Vernacular Educ. Soc.	English	805,653
Jaffna Mission Press	Tamil	623,500
Singhalese Tract Society	Sinhalese	295,500
Burma Mission Presses	Burmese, Karen, Sgau, etc.	827,500
TOTAL		8,604,033

With some few exceptions, fine calligraphy was not the hallmark of Indian manuscript production. The printed typefaces which the missionaries used (and in many cases designed and cast for the first time, for instance at the famous Serampore type-foundry) presented real problems in terms of legibility and acceptability to the reader's eye. The standardization of orthography which type-design imposed tended to distance the script from the reader, especially when that standardization was imposed by foreign missionaries working from a European perspective. This was a problem which had continually beset missionaries printing in India and had led many, beginning with the Tranquebar Lutherans in the early eighteenth century, to circulate Christian texts incised on palm-leaves, using Tamil scribes to copy them out using a traditional stylus. This practice was still continuing over a century later, with the Baptists at Cuttack in Orissa, for instance, as reported by the Revd Amos Sutton in the 1830s: 'We have had some thousand copies of an excellent tract called "The Jewel Mine of Salvation" written out on the tall [= talipat palm] leaf and distributed. This method has the advantage of being easily understood; for the natives are not used to a printed character.'[10]

By the 1820s, however, a new printing technique had been introduced into India which could avoid the problems associated with typography. This was lithography, literally 'writing or drawing on stone', in which the text to be printed was first written by hand on special paper and then transferred on to a limestone slab using a greasy lithographic ink. The surface of the stone was next treated with dilute nitric acid which ate away the non-inked areas leaving the inked text in relief; the slab was then washed with water and printing ink applied over the stone; finally a sheet of paper was placed on the stone to be passed through a press or simply rubbed over with a brass cylinder to obtain an impression. To a society still so wedded to the manuscript as India was, lithography provided a link between printing and that hand-written, scribal tradition. It combined the cultural attributes of the manuscript with the technical advantages of rapid duplication. Lithography made the printed book no longer an alien cultural artefact but something visually more familiar and therefore culturally more acceptable. The mass-produced manuscript was, through lithography, a paradox realized.

Overall, surprisingly, the missionaries did not make as much use of lithography (which posed none of the script-related problems of letter-press) as might have been expected. Some did use it very extensively indeed for printing tracts, such as the American Presbyterians at Ludhiana and Allahabad or the Basel Mission at Mangalore, but they hardly used lithography at all for printing the Bible or portions of it. Perhaps the missionaries considered, as was said in Europe, that a lithographed book lacked the visual authority of the letter-press printed page, and that therefore the Bible's impact as text might be diminished, devalued, or even undermined by the use of lithography. Compared to letter-press, lithography might give an air of imper-manence, of the everyday, which was totally inappropriate for a message of eternal truth. In India the reverse was true. It was the

---

[10] Amos Sutton, *A Narrative of the Mission to Orissa* (Boston, 1833), 282.

letter-press printed page which lacked visual authority, being totally alien to traditional Indian book-production. It was still the manuscript which was vested with visual and cultural authority, and this was the key to lithography's rapid acceptance and lasting appeal, particularly though not exclusively among the Muslim communities in India, with their emphasis upon the hand-written word in its highest artistic expression, calligraphy.[11]

Before turning to the physical characteristics of the Christian book in India, the criticisms of its intellectual design may be briefly examined. These were detailed by John Murdoch, whom we might dub the 'architect of Christian missions in India' in the nineteenth century. He begins by considering the title:

> A missionary offered a heathen a tract on the death of Christ. The man refused it saying, 'Do you wish to cause my death?' The native titles of works often give no idea of the contents. 'The Necklace of Jewels', 'The Rose Garden', 'Cup of Nectar', are specimens. . . . The chief design . . . is to give the tracts as native a look as possible, and prevent the people seeing at a glance that they are Christian publications.[12]

Murdoch then considers how the tract should be sequenced and styled to achieve maximum impact:

> Some English narrative tracts commence with moralizing or platitudes. This is to be avoided. Attention should be secured by beginning at once with the narrative. The moral can be drawn at the conclusion. . . . I very much like the plan of introducing pertinent quotations from their own books and shastras into addresses. Some of them are very striking; and my impression is that the people will generally understand your subject, as these references serve as a key. . . . The daily occupations of the people may be turned to account. . . . As the bulk of the people are engaged in agriculture, such subjects as 'Sowing and Reaping', 'The Barren Tree', 'Prayer for Rain', etc. will be specially interesting.[13]

---

[11] See Francis Robinson, 'Islam and the impact of print in South Asia', in N. Cook, ed., *The Transmission of Knowledge in South Asia* (Delhi, 1996), 66–9.

[12] John Murdoch, *Hints on the Management of Tract Societies in India* (1870), 14.

[13] Ibid., 15–16.

Pursuing this more subtle approach further, Murdoch advocates an almost complete Hindu 'disguise' for Christian tracts:

> Hinduism may be the means of securing attention . . . much Christian truth may be interwoven in a tract commencing with some Hindu god or shrine. The most popular native books have similar subjects, and Christian publications starting with them, will sell more readily than any others. . . . It seems to me that tracts drawn up in the style of Tamil tales, for which . . . the Old and New Testaments would furnish ample material, . . . would be more likely to be read and sought after than most of our present tracts.[14]

Murdoch finally shrewdly notes that illiteracy as such is not the nub of the problem in getting tracts actually *read* rather than merely taken and discarded (one literate person after all may read aloud to many illiterates); it is creating Christian literature that is in tune with popular Indian taste and sentiment:

> It is not merely the scarcity of readers that is so serious a hindrance to the tract distributor, but even more, the absence in the native heathen mind of all love of reading anything, except that it has the rhythm and sing-song of native poetry . . . the bulk of the native literature is in verse, and most of the people are still in the ballad stage. Strenuous efforts should be made to secure effective tracts in poetry.[15]

Many of the aesthetic concerns of the book as a physical object surfaced during the Punjab Missionary Conference at Lahore in the early 1860s. Initially many missionaries had been deceived by the apparent eagerness with which Indians seized their printed books: 'With the exception of now and then a proud, self-important Brahmun, they are ready to tear us in pieces in order to get them.'[16] This eagerness was often not so much thirst for the Word of God as curiosity towards the printed book as an alien cultural object or, more mundanely, the tempting prospect of a free gift of paper, for pleasure as well as business purposes. For instance, 'An experienced missionary . . . was at first surprised with what avidity a large sheet containing the Ten

---

[14] Ibid., 16–17.
[15] Ibid., 17–18.
[16] Sutton, *Narrative*, 273.

Commandments was sought for by boys. Nothing that he had was in such demand. He soon found out that the object was to make kites!'[17] As an example of the printed scriptures put to business use, we may quote the Revd J.G. Driberg:

> As Mr Marriott [another missionary] and myself were one day passing through the native town, we observed a shopkeeper busily employed in arranging and laying out for sale, several little articles on pieces of paper which he tore out of a book. It immediately struck me that the volume he was thus destroying was most probably a copy of the Holy Scriptures . . . and on examining the book I found my suspicion was too true. I asked the man how he came in possession of the book, and why he was thus destroying it: he replied, that one has only to apply to the Padre Saheb . . . and could obtain as many as he wished, and his object in asking for them was to have paper to wrap up his wares.[18]

Paper was, and still is, commonly used in India for wrapping up spices and medicines. Sometimes it was the binding rather than the paper which attracted interest, as at a certain Sivaratri festival where the missionaries took care 'to save our books from destruction, by certain classes of natives, who take them for the bindings',[19] presumably to re-use for Hindu texts.

In contrast to this eagerness, other missionaries had reported extreme reluctance, particularly on the part of the priestly Brahmin caste. It was not the book itself which was offensive, but the giver or, more precisely, contact with the giver. Close physical contact with a European missionary or a low-caste convert, regarded as equally impure by a Brahmin, would result in pollution. Sometimes this could be avoided, as the Tranquebar missionaries reported, by the tract being placed on the ground or on to a cloth held out by a Brahmin. In Bombay Presidency it seems the book itself was often regarded as impure by Brahmins because the ink with which it was printed was thought to contain animal grease, which would again be a source of pollution.[20]

---

[17] Murdoch, *Hints*, 53–4.

[18] J.G. Driberg, *Report on the Nurbudda Mission* (Calcutta, 1847), xli–xlii.

[19] Mullens, *Brief Review*, 156.

[20] Gérald Duverdier, 'L'Imprimerie protestante en Inde (1712–1850)', *Revue française d'histoire du livre*, 43 (1984), 367.

At the Lahore conference some missionaries such as the Revd J.H. Budden of the London Missionary Society at Almora argued that 'European printing, and European wood-cuts and engravings, are unobjectionable, and even desirable',[21] presumably for their edifying qualities. Other, more experienced, voices, however, such as that of the Revd John Newton from the American Presbyterian Mission, Lahore, realized that the missionaries must reconsider their whole approach to printing and publishing if they were to reach their audience effectively, particularly the Muslims. A more sophisticated, subversive tactic was called for. The holy text needed to be presented in a physical form to which the Indians would be more receptive, and this meant borrowing from and copying the oriental or Islamic book.[22]

The reaction of an Indian reader to a Christian book was vividly summarized by the Revd C.W. Forman, also of the American Presbyterian Mission, Lahore:

> On receiving an Urdu book, one of the first things which strikes the recipient, is the European style of binding; the next, is the name on the back in Roman letters. He opens the book, and finds in the *back part* of it an English title-page. It has been printed with Arabic or Persian *type* - which he can with difficulty read; whilst diacritical marks, which he does not at all understand, are scattered over its pages. Moreover, the title of the work is repeated at the head of each page – which every native reads as a part of the text, – thus obscuring its meaning. If our object had been to deter the people from reading our books, we could scarcely have devised means more likely to succeed ... I would have our books made so much more attractive; and besides, some who are now ashamed to be seen with a Christian book in their hands, (because every passer-by can see at a glance what *is* a Christian book), would then read them, without fear of being called Christians.[23]

Others such as the Revd H.E. Perkins of the Church Missionary Society put it more patronizingly, but reached the same conclusion:

> Instead of the flowery title-page, the limp cover, and the running oblique gloss, of a genuine native work, we have had the stiffly

---

[21] *Report of the Punjab Missionary Conference held at Lahore in December and January, 1862–63* (Lodiana, 1863), 269.

[22] Ibid., 283.

[23] Ibid., 285.

formal, straight lines, the rigid binding, and the cut-and-dried appearance which a severe Anglo-Saxon taste has conventionally taught us to deem beautiful. It may be said, that this is but a very small matter; and so it is: but if we are to catch with guile the unconverted, and allure from mischievous idleness our Native converts, we must stoop to their notion of things, and not force them up to our own.[24]

On the use of lithography specifically, some were reluctant to accept it as tantamount to pandering to oriental standards, but nevertheless saw it as a necessary temporary expedient until such time as the Indians could be weaned entirely from their own 'inferior' writing systems and were 'civilized' enough to adopt the Roman alphabet. Thus the Revd J.S. Woodise of the American Presbyterian Mission, Kapurthala:

> The vernacular characters are not adapted to the progressive spirit of the age. As the native mind begins to rise to the level of western civilization, it will demand a literature co-extensive with its new wants. This can never be furnished in any of the barbarous characters now in use. We have been told . . . that no type can be formed which will enable them to *print* books in the Persian character. They must all be *lithographed*. This fact of itself demonstrates, that the Persian character could never meet the wants of an enlightened people . . . It is impossible that such a cumbersome, impracticable, and illegible character should ever find acceptance, where another, so superior as the Roman, was available.[25]

Newton, by contrast, appreciated that lithography provided the cultural link with the manuscript tradition which Christianity could adopt for its own purposes: 'It would be wise to take the costly and highly-esteemed manuscripts as models for imitation. The illumination so much admired in these can be easily and cheaply imitated by the lithographic process.'[26] Newton's thinking was clearly in tune with the newer generation of missionaries in India who did not follow their predecessors in focusing only on the perceived 'evils' to be found in non-Christian religions, but were prepared to adopt a more conciliatory tone and to avoid outright condemnation.

[24] Ibid., 277.
[25] Ibid., 289.
[26] Ibid., 283.

The question of the circulation of Christian literature must now be addressed. That distribution was as important as preparation was widely recognized. As John Murdoch put it: 'As much energy must be devoted to securing a circulation for books in India as is expended in their preparation, or they will lie as lumber on the shelves.'[27] But innate resistance to receiving books was frequently encountered. 'The object in distributing them [Scriptures] is now generally known, and as a consequence the leading Hindus and Mohammedans prevent as much as possible their sale by interfering at the stands'[28] – this at Lucknow, a great centre of Shia Muslim faith and culture. The mere act of reading was thought to present dangers:

> Cases of conversion to Christianity from reading our publications make many of the natives think that it is dangerous to be brought into contact with them. . . . Mussulmans are found warning Hindus, Hindus are found warning Mussulmans, friend warns friend, and parents warn their children against the danger incurred in reading Christian publications.[29]

At the lowest level this evoked the superstitious reaction that the books themselves had magical properties which could bring about automatic conversion:

> The books are meant to contain charms or enchantments by which those reading or even handling them may be made Christians against their will. In some instances villagers have brought back books purchased, and thrown them down in apparent alarm at the danger supposed to have been incurred in taking them.[30]

Originally the missionaries had simply distributed their Scriptures and tracts free of charge to all and sundry on the regular tours of their mission's territory. To take one example from a report of the Dacca mission for 1854: 'In a large place near the Fanny river, about twelve Brahmins and others ran after the Dawk for two miles, and standing near my palki almost out of breath begged most importunately for a

---

[27] John Murdoch, *The Indian Missionary Manual: or, Hints to Young Missionaries in India*, 2nd edn revised (1870), 462.
[28] *Report on Colportage in the Methodist Episcopal Church Mission, U.S.A., in India, for the Year 1866* (Lucknow, 1867), 13.
[29] Ibid., 24.
[30] Ibid., 23–4.

tract or a Gospel.'[31] But this 'scatter-gun' approach was ineffective and very wasteful of the resources put into producing the literature. It was this which prompted a change in policy from free distribution to charging for publications. Some very small tracts and single-sheet handbills containing essential truths of the Christian religion continued to be issued gratis, but most publications were charged, based on the argument that Indians would have more respect for something for which they paid rather than something given away free. Some tract societies feared that distribution figures would plummet as a result, but once it was found on its first widespread adoption in 1848 by the Bombay Tract Society that this did not happen, pricing for Christian publications became the norm.

Pricing made finding suitable outlets for publications even more essential. At some of the larger mission stations a book-shop was opened. The recommendation was that:

> It should be in an eligible part of the bazar, and need not be kept open all day. It can be made the business of some one of the native helpers or Christians to keep it open at certain times in the day, or the shop can be made a preaching place, and books offered for sale at preaching times.[32]

Such bookshops did not have to be permanent; they could be temporary or seasonal. For instance, at Budaon 'for three months during the barsat [= monsoon], a book shop was kept up with good success in the Budaon bazar. When the rains closed, the work of regular canvassing was resumed throughout the district.'[33] Given that the amount of time they could devote to distributing tracts and books was limited, the missionaries were also recommended to use native booksellers to circulate Christian literature, but obviously on a strictly commercial basis: 'Frequently native shop keepers and booksellers are glad to take for sale on commission some of our publications, and sometimes they are willing to buy a good quantity of books at low prices.'[34] This was felt to be a very worthwhile channel for distribution as 'books from their hand may find an unsuspected reception where they would not otherwise go' and as 'the relative

---

[31] *Annual Report of the Dacca Mission, for the Year MDCCCLIV* (Dacca, 1855), 14.
[32] *Report on Colportage*, 28. See also John Murdoch, *Mission Book-Shops, in Connection with Bazar Preaching* (Calcutta, 1864).
[33] *Report on Colportage*, 11.
[34] Ibid., 28.

proportions of Christian and native book-shops and book-hawkers are probably about as one to thirty. The inequality is becoming greater every year.'[35]

The attempt was also made to graft the circulation of Christian literature on to existing religious networks and routes. This was seen most clearly in the missionaries' targeting of fairs and festivals, large and small. For instance, again at Budaon: 'During the Ganges mela in November, all the native helpers worked faithfully in the distribution of the Scriptures with tracts and books, for several days. A large distribution entirely by sale was made in this way.'[36] John Murdoch even went so far as to publish for missionaries a detailed guide to Hindu and Muslim festivals in the preface to which he wrote: 'Besides being used as starting points for Christian addresses, it is desirable to have cheap tracts on the principal festivals, which might be offered for sale when they are about to be celebrated.'[37] That is, tracts specifically relating to the festivals themselves should be prepared in the hope that they would be readily bought by Hindu or Muslim pilgrims, not suspecting that the title might be misleading. For instance, in 1838 the very first tract printed by the Baptist missionaries on their newly arrived press at Cuttack in Orissa was *Sri Sri Gundica yatrar mahascarya phal* (*The Wonderful Advantages of the Procession to Gundicha*) aimed at Hindu pilgrims to the notorious car-festival of Jagannath at Puri every June: 'There are myriads of pilgrims continually passing and repassing who, furnished with the Scriptures here in Bengalee, Hindoosthanee, Napaulese, etc., may carry them to the very confines of India.'[38]

But for distribution to be made as wide as possible, a network of colporteurs, paid book agents preferably from among the Indian converts, needed to be put in place, to cope with the sheer geographical vastness and large but rurally scattered population. For instance, the American Methodist Episcopal Church Mission in India concentrated on the area of Kumaon, Garhwal, Rohilkhand, and Avadh (modern north-west Uttar Pradesh) with a population of over fourteen million: 'The only missionary agency that can rapidly and generally reach all this vast population is a system of colportage. The missionaries with their native preachers, by their ordinary mode of working, could not

[35] Ibid., and Murdoch, *Indian Missionary Manual*, 463.

[36] *Report on Colportage*, 11.

[37] John Murdoch, *Hindu and Muhammadan Festivals* (1904), [iii].

[38] Sutton, *Narrative*, 41.

generally reach this population in the next twenty years.'[39] In 1866, for instance, just fourteen colporteurs visited no fewer than 907 towns and villages in three districts of Uttar Pradesh (Bareilly, Lucknow, and Moradabad) and distributed a total of 11,879 Old and New Testaments, single Gospels and Scripture portions, and miscellaneous Christian books and tracts – 7,442 were sold, 4,437 given away free.[40]

Although great strides were made with this tactic, the resistance to *accepting* tracts on the part of the unconverted seems to have been matched by a resistance to *selling* tracts on the part of native converts: 'Something should be done to remove the impression found among native helpers that it is beneath their position and importance to engage in selling books.' Even if this resistance could be overcome, it was frequently felt that it was very difficult to find people with enough commitment to make the colportage system truly effective, and various means were recommended to ensure maximum benefit – only paying by commission on sales, asking for regular reports of sales to be submitted, auditing stock, and so on.[41] But to take one successful use of book-agents, the Bareilly station of the American Methodist Episcopal Church Mission reported that: 'We have an agent employed, whose special business is to attend all great gatherings such as bazars, melas, &c., for the purpose of selling books; also to visit the schools, shops and other places where he may find persons willing to buy.'[42] Schools were seen as a particular target. In Budaon district the American missionaries 'proposed to revisit every village school in the district, numbering upward of 140, and place a copy of Barth's Scripture History in the hands of every teacher for the use of the school, and at the same time make sales of Scriptures to all who might wish to buy.'[43] Even here, however, resistance could be found: 'Often where a school is visited, the teacher by a word or look will effectually check the sale or even gift of a single tract.'[44]

Schools were the source of another bugbear for the Christian missionaries. In 1854 Sir Charles Wood, President of the Board of Control of the East India Company, had issued the famous dispatch which committed the British government in India for the first time to

---

[39] *Report on Colportage*, 5–6.
[40] Ibid., 19.
[41] Ibid., 22.
[42] Ibid., 9.
[43] Ibid., 11.
[44] Ibid., 24.

providing a widespread system of education for Indians from primary school to university.[45] Initially the missionaries had thought they would be well-placed to take advantage of this – by making their educational books (with very heavy Christian messages attached) the staple of text-book use in the new government schools as well as in the schools which the missions themselves ran. However, the British government in India stressed that the scheme of instruction was to be secular, with the declared principle of 'perfect religious neutrality'.[46] Therefore, for instance, Christian ministers could not be employed as government professors. John Murdoch claimed that this principle of religious neutrality was not being maintained. It had indeed been used systematically to ensure that no *Christian* content entered into school text-books. For instance, Mr Howard, one-time Director of Public Instruction in Bombay Presidency, had proposed that 'a complete series of English school books should be produced expressly for the use of Indian boys, from which every Christian allusion might be effectually weeded.'[47] But Murdoch did not see this neutrality being applied with equal force to other religions. For instance, in the *Tamil Minor Poets* published by the Madras Director of Public Instruction there were six invocations to the Hindu god Ganesha. This was regarded as particularly pernicious in promoting the Hindu belief that if Ganesha is duly worshipped with offerings he will grant success in study: 'Books are put into their hands by the British Government in which they are told to worship Ganesa to make progress in their studies.'[48] The Madras Government school books were also castigated by Murdoch for being full of fatalistic teachings associated with transmigration, such as that those who in a previous life 'delighted themselves by eating crabs, breaking off their claws, shall in this life wander about as miserable lepers, their hands being deprived of their shell-like fingers',[49] and they also contained *Panchatantra* stories that extolled the virtues of suttee, widow-burning. The *Panchatantra*, a text much favoured by schools because of its simple written style, was particularly condemned by

[45] See Sir H. Verney Lovett, 'Education and missions to 1858', in H.H. Dodwell, ed., *The Indian Empire, 1858–1918, with Chapters on the Development of Administration, 1818–1858, The Cambridge History of India*, 6 (Delhi, 1964), 117–20.

[46] John Murdoch, *The Idolatrous and Immoral Teaching of Some Government and University Text-Books in India* (Madras, 1872), 4.

[47] Ibid., 5.

[48] Ibid., 7.

[49] Ibid., 11.

Murdoch for encouraging trickery and deceit, teaching boys how to create enmity between friends, and how to conquer an enemy by pretended friendship. This, regrets Murdoch, 'is the text-book of morals which the Madras Educational System offers instead of the New Testament'.[50] Other books were condemned for their sheer indecency as Murdoch saw it, such as the Hindi *Prem sagar* (literally *The Ocean of Love*) containing tales of Krishna, or *Tirikatukam (The Three Spices)*, a Tamil didactic work prescribed for the Madras matriculation examination in 1871, which included advice such as 'the night that has rolled away without the embrace of gracefully adorned women ... [is among] sources of grief to the sensible'.[51] On Islam, Murdoch noted that the prefaces to the Punjab Government editions of the Persian poet Sa'di's *Gulistan* and *Bostan* both include praise of the Prophet Muhammad as 'the intercessor of people, ... the guiding teacher',[52] and so on. The *Gulistan*, noted Murdoch, contained two especially objectionable chapters on youth and love, and on imbecility and old age (with tales of old men bedding beautiful young virgins, and suchlike), but the Punjab Director printed the entire work unexpurgated and the Madras University prescribed it for the First Examination in Arts 1872.[53]

Yet just as the Christian missionaries were becoming more 'subversive' and savvy in regard to the production of their literature and more organized and controlled in its circulation, they began to feel the heat of competition. Other faiths were responding to the Christian challenge by establishing their own presses, not simply to produce anti-Christian material but positively to promote and promulgate their own faiths. To take a few examples, the Hindu Dharma Sabha in Bengal began issuing numerous tracts; likewise the Vibhuti Sangam in Tinnevelly in the far south in Tamil Nadu.[54] So too with the Brahmo Samaj which 'has a press at work from which a considerable number of books and tracts have been issued, while several newspapers are printed in its interests. . . . The leaders of the Brahmo Samaj appreciate the power of the press, and hence are laboring to prepare and circulate a literature in India inculcating their belief.'[55] The supreme irony was

[50] Ibid., 16.
[51] Ibid., 19.
[52] Ibid., 9.
[53] Ibid., 24.
[54] Duverdier, 'L'Imprimerie protestante', 368.
[55] *Report on Colportage*, 7.

that in not a few cases it was men whom the missionaries had themselves trained up in the ways of the press who were taking the lead in establishing non-Christian presses, such as a former helper of the Wesleyan missionaries in Ceylon who in 1842 founded the Saivaprakasa Sabha and published no less than twenty-five tracts in defence of Hinduism.[56]

Muslims too were increasingly mobilizing themselves in pamphleteering counter-offensives. Joseph Mullens of the London Missionary Society was surprised, when preaching at Sabulgarh near Gwalior, to be told by a pundit that 'there was a rival of mine in the place, a Mohammedan, who had come with a large bundle of Mohammedan pamphlets and tracts to sell.' These were, just as he feared,

> the cheap, popular, attractive treatises, which are issuing from the Cawnpore and other Mussulman presses, urging to a reformed Mohammedanism . . . in which the spirituality of Christianity, and the pseudo-spiritualism of Soofeeism, are imposingly and artfully combined, written with all that advantage of style and phraseology which natives of this country, writing from their own peculiar standing-point, and with the resources of the language perfectly at their command, must possess.[57]

In other words, excellent examples of what Christian literature in India aspired to be but so seldom achieved.

The British Library, Asia, Pacific, and Africa Collections

---

[56] Ibid.
[57] Mullens, *Brief Review*, 168–9.

DEALING WITH DEVELOPMENT:
THE PROTESTANT REVIEWS OF JOHN HENRY
NEWMAN'S *AN ESSAY ON THE DEVELOPMENT OF*
CHRISTIAN DOCTRINE, 1845-7

by ERIK SIDENVALL

THE greatness of John Henry Newman's *Essay on the Development of Christian Doctrine* has been acknowledged many times since it was first published in 1845. Its international repute was secured by the beginning of the twentieth century; for example, the future Archbishop of Uppsala, Nathan Söderblom, writing on the modernist movement, described it and its author in 1910 as 'the most significant theological work, written by England's foremost theologian, and together with Leo XIII, the most important man in the Roman Catholic Church during the last century'.[1] This estimation is confirmed by the impact Newman's book has had on twentieth-century theology.[2] One recent observer has judged that it is 'significant, less for its positive arguments . . . [than] for its method of approach to the whole problem of Christian doctrine in its relation to the New Testament'.[3] In other words, Newman's book touches on a central topic of modern theology.

If the numerous studies of Newman's *Essay* published during the last hundred and fifty years have generally emphasised the creative aspects of Newman's approach to history, its reputation among nineteenth-century Protestants was in many cases quite the opposite.[4] The object of this paper is to examine the many replies

---

[1] Nathan Söderblom, *Religionsproblemet inom Katolicismen* (Stockholm, 1910), 35: 'den teologiskt viktigaste alstringen av Englands förnämste teolog och katolicismens, åtminstone jämte Leo XIII, mest betydande personlighet under det gångna seklet'.

[2] See for example Aidan Nichols, *From Newman to Congar: The Idea of Doctrinal Development from the Victorians to the Second Vatican Council* (Edinburgh, 1990).

[3] Bernard M.G. Reardon, *From Coleridge to Gore: A Century of Religious Thought in Britain* (1971), 146.

[4] See C.L. Brown, 'Newman's minor critics', *Downside Review*, 89 (1971), 13–21; Owen Chadwick, *From Bossuet to Newman: the Idea of Doctrinal Development* (Cambridge, 1957), 164–84, 236n; Maurice Nédoncelle, 'Le Développement de la doctrine chrétienne: J.B. Mozley, critique anglican de Newman', *Oecumenica* (1971–2), 156–74; David Nicholls, 'Newman's Anglican critics', *Anglican Theological Review*, 47 (1965), 377–95.

Newman's book generated between 1845 and 1847, in order to understand why, and in what ways, it was described as a challenge to customary Protestant interpretations of Christianity.

Newman emerged as one of the leaders of a group of young High Churchmen at Oxford University, the Tractarians, during the early 1830s. His sermons and various publications soon earned him a certain reputation as an able theologian in the eyes of the educated classes. However, with the publication of Richard Hurrell Froude's *Remains* in 1838–9, rumours of 'Romanizing' tendencies at Oxford seemed to be confirmed. Newman became one of the principal targets of Evangelical hostility. His reputation did not exactly improve when *Tract 90*, in which Newman tried to demonstrate that the Thirty-Nine Articles were not incompatible with the Tridentine creed, attracted the attention of British readers a few years later. After this incident, Newman became for a couple of years the centre of attention in Protestant English society. Even though he tried to retire to his semi-monastic settlement at Littlemore, his every move was monitored by the public eye. In the wake of the turmoil surrounding the Oxford Convocation of 1845, during which W.G. Ward's *Ideal of a Christian Church* was condemned and Newman's last tract was saved by the intervention of the Proctors, rumours of his imminent departure from the Anglican Church started to appear in the press.[5] Nevertheless, Protestants had to wait until October that year for their suspicions to be confirmed. A flow of hostile publications followed the reports of Newman's secession to Rome.[6] In this situation Newman's *Essay* appeared, and rapidly sold out. For various reasons, many men and women were eager to see how the former vicar of St Mary's justified his 'perversion' to Catholicism.[7]

Newman's *Essay*, however, was not a volume filled with revelations of a private character. It was a philosophical treatise in which Newman tried to demonstrate that the traditional Protestant objections to Roman Catholicism – that it disregarded the Bible, and misinterpreted the Fathers – were invalid. Newman argued that what had been considered corruptions in Protestant polemics were just proper

---

[5] H.P. Liddon, *The Life of Edward Bouverie Pusey*, 4 vols (London, 1894–8), 2:444. See also the Wesleyan *Watchman* (2 July 1845).

[6] I have treated these reactions in Erik Sidenvall, 'Meanings in John Henry Newman's conversion: a study of the Church of England press, 1845–1846' (University of Lund, Licentiate's thesis, 1999).

[7] See for example the *Standard* (13 Oct. 1845).

evolutions of the original 'idea' of Christianity. His conclusion was that the post-Tridentine Roman Catholic Church was the only true development of the apostolic Church.

It therefore comes as no surprise that the *Essay* first of all was seen as a challenge to Protestantism in every form. R.A. Willmott declared in a review published in *Fraser's Magazine* that

> perhaps, of all the subjects which the author endeavours to demolish, not one engages so much of his attention as that religious designation which is known as *Protestant*. Almost from the very first page of the book, the attack upon Protestantism begins. Whatever be historical Christianity, we are assured that it is not the religion of Protestants.[8]

Most Protestant reviewers endorsed this interpretation. However, they described the challenge of Newman's book in slightly different ways.

Those who supported a rather 'high' interpretation of the Anglican tradition maintained that Newman's *Essay* was nothing but an attack on the authority of Christian antiquity. To William Barter 'its principle is calculated, if it were possible, to shake the authority of the Primitive Church of Christ.'[9] A reviewer in the *English Review* described what was at stake at some length:

> [W]ith the present theory, historical tradition is gone; truth in the earliest ages was but in its infancy, – weak, undefined, undeveloped; the age of primitive Christianity was an age of darkness compared with the present light of Rome; the Fathers may be set aside as men in the mere pupilage of theology. And even if their testimony to the then received doctrine can be extracted, it is as useless to indicate the real extent and comprehension of present revealed truth, as an egg is to unveil the future form and prowess of the eagle. Antiquity is gone.[10]

In other words, these reviewers described Newman's treatment of the

---

[8] *Fraser's Magazine for Town and Country*, 33 (March 1846), 256.
[9] Willam Barter, *A Postscript to the English Church not in Schism: Containing a Few Words on Mr. Newman's Essay on Development* (1846), 13.
[10] *English Review*, 4 (Dec. 1845), 399. Even the 'moderate Evangelical' George Stanley Faber argued in a similar way; see his letters in the *Christian's Monthly Magazine, and Church of England Review*, 5 (1846) 233-48, 353-75.

history of the Church as a radical contradiction of the very foundation of High Church theology.[11]

Furthermore, to advanced High Churchmen supporting Tractarian views, Newman's book was seen not only as a challenge to patristic authority, but was related to a more practical problem: the threat of further apostasies from the Church of England. The arguments of the former leader could tempt the ardent but hesitant disciple to take the final step. As one reviewer explained: '[t]o those, indeed, who are looking about for excuses for secession, the slightest arguments will appear convincing; and to them, therefore, Mr. Newman's book may be satisfactory'.[12]

On the other hand, to those of a more decidedly Protestant inclination, Newman's *Essay* seemed to be an attack on the status of the Bible, or indeed upon revelation itself. The liberal Anglican, H.H. Milman, asked his readers:

> According to this theory, what is the New Testament? It is no Revelation; it is but the obscure and prophetic harbinger of a Revelation. It is no great harmonious system of truths; it has but the rude outlines, the suggestive elements of those truths; it is no code of law, but a rudimental first conception of a law. Its morality is no establishment of great principles, to be applied by the conscience of the individual man, but a collection of vague and ambiguous maxims. Of the way of salvation it utters but dark and oracular hints; it has brought life and immortality but into a faint and hazy twilight; the Sun of Righteousness rose not to his full meridian till the Council of Trent.[13]

Another liberal Anglican, Baden Powell, described the challenge of Newman's theory in an article published in the *Edinburgh Review*:

> It reduces all questions of difference to a mere question of *degree*; and regards both as but consecutive parts in *one* work and design. It thus breaks down the boundary between inspiration and opinion, between Divine and human doctrine, between the

---

[11] For the importance of patristic authority in the High Church tradition, see Peter Benedict Nockles, *The Oxford Movement in Context: Anglican High Churchmanship, 1760–1857*, pbk edn (Cambridge, 1997), 104–45.

[12] *English Churchman* (4 Dec. 1845). See also the *Surplice* (6 Dec. 1845).

[13] *Quarterly Review*, 77 (1846), 415. See also *Christian's Monthly Magazine, and Church of England Review*, 5 (1846), 17–37, 272–85; *Edinburgh Review*, 84 (1846), 219–21 (article written by Baden Powell); ibid., 86 (1847), 397.

voice of revelation and the conclusions of reason, or the suggestions of mere feeling or imagination; and in thus effacing the
landmarks of the Christian's spiritual inheritance, it cannot but
hazard the secure enjoyment of it.[14]

Evangelical reviewers, both churchmen and Dissenters, pointed in a
similar direction. Newman's *Essay* was but a malignant defence of
unscriptural uses and beliefs.[15] Nevertheless, since it seemed to be an
attempt to facilitate Tractarian secession to the Church of Rome, the
anonymous reviewer in the *Churchman's Monthly Review* could see a
positive value in Newman's volume:

> If we rightly apprehend the object of this publication, – and we are
> by no means sure that we do so, notwithstanding that we have
> perused it very attentively, – we heartily wish it success. That
> object we assume to be to demonstrate to the author's associates in
> doctrinal opinion, who still remain in communion with the
> Church of England, – the peril, yea, the impossibility, of
> continuing in their present position.[16]

Depending on their own theological preferences, the vast majority
of Protestant reviewers saw Newman's *Essay* as a challenge towards
either patristic or biblical authority. In other words, it seemed to
threaten the very foundation of Christian theology. It was therefore
easy to see Newman's theory of development as an offspring of an even
more serious threat towards Christianity. In the words of H.H. Milman
once again: '[i]t is the preliminary hazard to the great desperate stake
which is to be played by the whole book, and, as he [Newman] himself
knows, has already been tried with serious consequences not only to
the Church of Rome, but to Christianity itself.'[17] R.A. Willmott used
rather more imaginative language: '[i]t is German infidelity commun-
icated in the music and perfume of St. Peter's; – it is Strauss in the
garment and rope of the Franciscan.'[18] In other words, Newman's book

---

[14] Ibid., 221.
[15] *Churchman's Monthly Review* (Jan. 1846), 68–83; *Baptist Magazine*, 48 (1846), 153–7,
224–31.
[16] *Churchman's Monthly Review* (Jan. 1846), 70.
[17] *Quarterly Review*, 77 (1846), 406.
[18] *Fraser's Magazine for Town and Country*, 33 (1846), 256. David Friedrich Strauss (1808–
74), German theologian and disciple of Hegel, provoked fury all over Europe with his *Das
Leben Jesu* (2 vols, Tübingen, 1836). In these volumes Strauss treated the biblical narrative of
Jesus as a 'myth', an embodiment of the 'idea of humanity'. To orthodox English Protestants,
Strauss became the epitome of German rationalistic theology.

displayed a 'rationalistic' tendency;[19] his Romantic theology was judged to be a dangerous path, leading away from Christianity.[20] This interpretation probably seemed to be confirmed by the favourable reviews Newman's book received in the Unitarian *Christian Reformer*.[21] These reviewers found in Newman's theory a confirmation of the Unitarian position. Since Newman had been 'compelled by the force of evidence to acknowledge that the so-called orthodoxy of the present day is not to be found in the primitive ages', his *Essay* was seen as yet another concession of the Trinitarians.[22]

Thus, orthodox Protestant observers saw in Newman's *Essay* not just an apology for the Roman Catholic Church, but a threat to the very foundations of English Protestantism. This book was a dangerous publication. It raised questions that threatened to undermine the faith of its readers, its arguments could lead them either into the Roman Catholic Church, or into unbelief. However, it can be argued that, by indicating the dangerous tendencies inherent in Newman's arguments, these reviewers sought to diminish the influence of the *Essay*. By placing Newman's publication in an established pattern, and by appealing to the Protestant sentiment of their readers, they tried to render Newman's *Essay* less attractive.

Newman was the first person publicly to advance a theory of development in England. Moreover, he used it to justify the claims of the Roman Catholic Church. To some it seemed as if 'new light has been suddenly thrown upon the distinctive doctrines of that [C]hurch'.[23] Therefore, by revealing how Newman's theories stood in opposition to the theological foundation of English Protestantism, these reviewers placed this new line of argumentation in an ancient scheme. Long before Newman's *Essay* was published, Roman Catholic theologians had been accused by High Church theologians of under-

---

[19] The most eloquent exposition of this view is found in William Palmer [of Worcester], *The Doctrine of Development and Conscience Considered in Relation to the Evidences of Christianity and of the Catholic System* (1846), 88–9, 128–33. See also, for example, Charles James Blomfield, *A Charge Delivered to the Clergy of the Diocese of London, at the Visitation in October MDCCCXLVI* (1846); Samuel Wilberforce, *A Charge, Delivered to the Candidates for Ordination; and a Sermon, Preached at the General Ordination, in the Cathedral Church of Christ, Oxford, December 21, 1845* (Oxford, 1845).

[20] See Sheridan Gilley, 'The Church of England in the nineteenth century', in Sheridan Gilley and W.J. Sheils, eds, *A History of Religion in Britain: Practice and Belief from the Pre-Roman Times to the Present* (Oxford, 1994), 302.

[21] *Christian Reformer*, 2 (1846), 357–9 (signed H.P.), 462–72 (signed H.H.P.).

[22] Ibid., 359.

[23] *Oxford and Cambridge Review*, 2 (Feb. 1846), 135.

mining the authority of the Fathers:[24] the fact that the Church of Rome disregarded the authority of the Bible was a commonplace in anti-Catholic agitation;[25] and already in the wake of the French Revolution conservative thinkers had maintained that there was a connection between 'infidelity' and the papal church.[26] Newman's theories may have been new to English readers, but they exhibited just the same kind of Romanism, a theology which the Anglican tradition had encountered for centuries.[27]

Furthermore, to point out that Newman's theories displayed rationalistic tendencies, that they shunned biblical and patristic authority, could in fact be an easy way to dismiss Newman and his new book. For example, note how the anonymous writer of a short pamphlet addressed Newman:

> We will know only of '*one* Sacrifice,' one Justification *by Faith only*; *one* High Priest; one Mediator; only of two sacraments ordained by Christ himself, as pledges and means of His grace; He is the Author and Finisher of our faith, His written Word the sun and centre of our system. You may look for development in the gradually increasing moon, but how can you hope to add anything to the noon-day light of the sun? You may develope [*sic*] truth out of mist, but you cannot improve upon what is perfect already. Such then, Sir, is the truth which seems to me to strike at the root of your theory; for if indeed *all needful Christian* truth was declared eighteen hundred years ago, there is no place left for development of Christian doctrine now. The contents of the Sacred Volume are either completely true or completely false.[28]

This course of action naturally presupposes that those who engaged in this sort of polemic could rely on a firm Protestant identity among their readership; that a certain ideology was taken for granted by both

---

[24] Nockles, *Oxford Movement in Context*, 104–9.

[25] John Wolffe, *The Protestant Crusade in Great Britain 1829–1860* (Oxford, 1991), 109–10.

[26] W.H. Oliver, *Prophets and Millennialists: the Use of Biblical Prophecy in England from the 1790s to the 1840s* (Auckland, 1978), 58; James J. Sack, *From Jacobite to Conservative: Reaction and Orthodoxy in Britain, c.1760–1832* (Cambridge, 1993), 244–5.

[27] See also Christopher Wordsworth, *Letters to M. Gondon* (1847), 9–10.

[28] An Anglican Priest, *A Few Words Addressed to the Author of 'An Essay on the Development of Christian Doctrine'* (1846), 8–9. This example shows that the 'either – or' argument was already used in the reception of Newman's *Essay*. Compare Josef L. Altholz, 'The mind of Victorian orthodoxy: Anglican responses to *Essays and Reviews*, 1860–1864', *Church History*, 57 (1982), 196.

readers and writers. Most reviewers addressed a readership supporting a firm orthodox theology. As events were to prove only a few years later, anti-Catholic prejudice was one of the central features in the frame of mind of men and women living in the mid-nineteenth century.[29] Therefore, at least in some respects, a successful way of dealing with Newman's theory of development was probably just to appeal to the theological attachments of the groups of men and women addressed in these publications. When the former Tractarian was exposed as a man whose theories challenged the very foundations of Christianity, this undermined his own claim to authoritative status.

In conclusion, the Protestant reviewers of Newman's *Essay* tried to establish a connection between the Church and the book. They formulated their opinion of this volume with the needs and beliefs of their readers in mind. In other words, their interpretations influenced the Church, but their interpretations were also influenced by the Church. This places the discussion of the Anglican or Protestant responses to Newman's *Essay* in a different light. When modern historians examine the philosophical and theological force, or lack of force, in the objections brought against Newman's theories, those who read these various responses for the first time may have been more interested in seeing the former Tractarian exposed as a Rationalist, as a man who questioned biblical and patristic authority. Our preoccupations and interests are not always the same as those of the historical actors whom we are studying.

Lund University

---

[29] Hugh McLeod, *Secularisation in Western Europe, 1848–1914* (2000), ch.6.

THE TEXT AS SACRAMENT:
VICTORIAN BROAD CHURCH PHILOLOGY

by JEREMY MORRIS

THE description 'Broad Church' popularized by W.J. Conybeare in his famous article on 'Church Parties' in 1853, whilst claiming as distinctive the watchwords 'Charity and Toleration' and 'the desire of comprehension', made no specific reference to philology.[1] Yet philology was not a minor fad for the Broad Church. Though its connections with theology are not obvious today, it provided a vital tool for those theologians who were seeking to defend the authority and integrity of the Bible in a context in which, as they saw it, the emergence of critical historical and scientific approaches to the natural world had the potential to undermine the sacred canon, and to relegate it to a position of relative importance only in the human story of religion. Their study of philology therefore merits renewed attention by historians, as a contribution to the reception of the Bible as book in the Victorian Church.

The Broad Church expounded an approach to textual reading which assumed that philology was a kindred discipline to theology. Through their attitude to books, literary classics, and 'high' culture, its participants tended to dissolve the distinction between the 'Book' of Christianity, the Bible, and other books. Their aim was not to downgrade scriptural inspiration, as some have supposed, but to see literature itself as a sacred and inspired work, with the Bible as its apex.[2] Their study of language assumed an inherent sacramentality in words. Reading was a devotional activity. Attention will be paid to four representatives of the school, with a description of philology as practised by J.C. Hare, F.W. Farrar, and R.C. Trench, and then a closer examination of F.D. Maurice on its theological and philosophical presuppositions. Finally there will be brief consideration of the sources of all four

---

[1] W.J. Conybeare, 'Church parties', in S. Taylor, ed., *From Cranmer to Davidson. A Church of England Miscellany* (Woodbridge, 1999), 340.

[2] Compare Gladstone's conviction that Homer was a parallel, if inferior, 'revelation' to the Bible: H.C.G. Matthew, *Gladstone 1809–1874* (Oxford, 1986), 153.

theologians' understanding of language and text, and of the formation of the Philological Society of London.

* * *

This was a diverse group of men, none of whom would willingly have owned the term 'Broad Church'. Yet they were bound together by ties of friendship, teaching, and family, and they were members, albeit perhaps minor ones, of that closely-knit Victorian intellectual elite traced so famously by Noel Annan.[3] Maurice studied under Hare at Trinity College, Cambridge, and later married Hare's half-sister.[4] Trench also studied under Hare at Trinity, and remained a lifelong friend.[5] Farrar studied under Maurice at King's College, London, remained a friend, and later became an undergraduate and even later a Fellow at Trinity.[6]

Friendship alone did not signify an identity of views. Nevertheless, there was sufficient agreement between them on the study of language to justify the term 'school'. In their hands, philology was both a technical historical discipline and a means for accessing the divine wisdom embedded in human culture. The language of the Bible subserved its religious purpose. Biblical criticism assumed, not an independent power of rationality by which the text could be measured and (if necessary) 'corrected', but an intrinsic commitment of faith in the truth of the inspired word.

Philology emerged out of the common nineteenth-century regard for the ancient world.[7] Julius Hare praised Greek literature for its 'serene transparent brightness', and claimed that this was actually 'the characteristic of the Christian mind'.[8] Trench held up 'a few Greek and Latin books' as exemplary of 'the shaping moulding power' of books in human history.[9] Hare, with Connop Thirlwall, devoted much of the *Philological Museum*, a short-lived journal founded by both men in

[3] N.G. Annan, 'The intellectual aristocracy', in J.H. Plumb, ed., *Studies in Social History* (1955), 241–87.

[4] F. Maurice, *Life and Letters of F.D. Maurice*, 2 vols (1884) is the standard biography; but see also F.M. McClain, *Maurice, Man and Moralist* (1972); on Hare, see N.M. Distad, *Guessing at Truth. The Life of Julius Charles Hare (1795–1855)* (Shepherdstown, WV, 1979).

[5] J. Bromley, *The Man of Ten Talents. A Portrait of Richard Chenevix Trench* (1959), leans heavily on M. Trench, *Letters and Memorials of Richard Chenevix Trench, Archbishop* (1888).

[6] See R. Farrar, *The Life of Frederic William Farrar* (1904).

[7] See R. Jenkyns, *Dignity and Decadence: Victorian Art and the Classical Inheritance* (1991).

[8] J.C. Hare, in J.C. Hare and A.W. Hare, *Guesses at Truth*, new edn (1866), 68.

[9] R.C. Trench, *The Fitness of Holy Scripture for Unfolding the Spiritual Life of Men* (Cambridge, 1845), 13.

1831, to classical material.[10] This reverence for the ancient world led to a disparagement of much 'modern' literature at first glance surprising in writers who rated so highly the poetry of Wordsworth and Coleridge. But they perceived the spirit of the past to be lacking in many of the moderns. Bentham and Hobbes, declared Hare, were the two masters of the 'selfish school', scorning the wisdom of the past.[11] Those who valued it were rare indeed. They included, Hare continued, Burke and Coleridge, who were 'third-thoughted men', valuing dormant truths and delighting in reviving them.[12] In the *Philological Museum*, philology signified the study of the *logos* in history, the embedding of the divine wisdom in the culture and literature of civilization.[13] 'Philology', as Hare said, 'ought to be only another name for Philosophy. Its aim should be to seek after wisdom in the whole series of its historical manifestations.'[14]

It is perhaps no wonder that Hare, who spent part of his childhood in Weimar and further encountered German thought at the feet of Coleridge himself, should imbibe so completely the spirit of *Altertumswissenschaft*, the German Romantic movement's search for the spirit of ancient civilization.[15] But it was a spirit shared equally by his circle, and even by associates from an altogether different stream of 'Broad Church' thought, the Oriel 'Noetic' school of Edwards, Hawkins, and Arnold.[16] It was marked by a fascination with the accumulation of etymological detail, and with the empirical study of languages. Farrar, for example, published two significant and widely-read contributions to the subject, his *Essay on the Origin of Language* (1860), and a sequel, *Chapters on Language* (1865). In 1851 Trench published a hugely popular introduction to philology, *On the Study of Words* (reprinted at least fourteen times before 1900), and helped to plan what eventually became *The Oxford English Dictionary*.[17] Even Hare, a less systematic thinker, was fascinated by philological detail.

---

[10] R. Brent, *Liberal Anglican Politics* (Oxford, 1987), 165–6.

[11] J.C. Hare, in Hare and Hare, *Guesses at Truth*, 149.

[12] Ibid., 160.

[13] Distad, *Guessing at Truth*, 79. To this must be added Duncan Forbes's account of the theories of history shared by the Broad Church, in his *The Liberal Anglican Idea of History* (Cambridge, 1952).

[14] J.C. Hare, in Hare and Hare, *Guesses at Truth*, 525.

[15] Distad, *Guessing at Truth*, 79.

[16] For a comparison of these two 'schools', see Brent, *Liberal Anglican Politics*, 144–83. Brent's account of 'Liberal Anglicans' ultimately leans much more heavily on the 'Noetics' than it does on the 'Trinity' circle.

[17] H. Aarsleff, *The Study of Language: England* (1983), 223–43.

The *Philological Museum* consisted almost entirely of detailed philological enquiries, and he spent over forty pages of his *Guesses at Truth* (1827) examining the etymology of the words 'I' and 'Thou'.[18] Perhaps Maurice in turn was guided by this to base his study of *The Conscience* (1868) on the implications of the word 'I'.[19]

Broad Church philology also encouraged speculation on the origin of language. Though with varying emphases, all of these writers sought to steer a third course between two popular but extreme conceptions – the materialist notion that language was an artificial product, and the 'pre-Adamic' notion that language itself was revealed by God. Farrar, for example, asserted that the ability to construct language was God-given, but God did not himself construct language for human beings; instead it was a 'discovery' of human history.[20] Speech was a correlative of human understanding, and so developments in language matched those in human thought and culture: 'The impulse to self-development, and the capacity for it, are indeed innate in the higher races of men; but to assert that the results of this impulse were revealed, is to contradict both History and the order of nature.'[21] 'Higher races' is telling, because Farrar considered some racial origins definitely superior to others.[22] His views were perhaps unusual in this respect; but his argument about language as a revealed capacity was certainly not. Trench also defended the divine institution of language through 'the power of naming', rather than the revelation of an actual vocabulary.[23] Language, he concluded, was 'a witness for great moral truths', since God himself had imprinted the seal of truth on it, so that men 'are continually uttering deeper things than they know'.[24]

Biblically conservative, and arguably 'High' rather than 'Broad', Trench placed more emphasis on the divine creation of language according to Genesis than did the rest of the group.[25] But there is a

---

[18] Hare and Hare, *Guesses at Truth*, 97–149.

[19] F.D. Maurice, *The Conscience. Lectures on Casuistry* (1868), esp. ch. 1, 'On the word "I"', 1–23.

[20] F.W. Farrar, *Chapters on Language* (1865), 3.

[21] Ibid., 7.

[22] See especially F.W. Farrar, *Essay on the Origin of Language* (1860), ch. 1, 'The Origin of Language'. Farrar, who knew Darwin and preached his funeral sermon, may have been influenced by the application of evolutionary theory to human development. See also idem, *Families of Speech* (1874).

[23] R.C. Trench, *On the Study of Words*, 6th edn (1855), 17.

[24] Ibid., 10.

[25] Ibid., 16–17.

parallel between these authors' account of the origin of language, and their view of the language of the Bible. Just as they discounted both materialist and word-creationist accounts of linguistic origins, so too they rejected both rationalist accounts of Scripture and theories of verbal or literal inspiration. In effect, they defended a theory of inspiration which acknowledged the absolute truth of the text, but also accounted for its production as human literature. Farrar asserted that revelation was itself continuous throughout the text, but that many parts of the text were delivered in a manner 'relative to the immediate needs of the ages in which they were uttered'.[26] Trench, in defence of the idea that the Bible was like other books, called the written word a 'necessary condition of historic life and progress', and traced evidence for Scripture's unique authority in its internal coherence, unity, and spiritual force.[27] The historical, literary, and linguistic analysis of the Bible provided a hermeneutic principle for these theologians which made sense simultaneously of creation, of providence, of the history and truth of the biblical text, and of human history itself. As Farrar argued, 'a great part of the Bible is history, and all History, rightly understood, is also a Bible. Its lessons are God's divine method of slowly exposing error and of guiding into truth.'[28]

Philology was an accessory study to support the highest possible estimate of the Bible. The human study of the Bible was necessary because it was, from one side, a human book. Enlisting the support of the Fathers and the Reformers, Farrar asserted:

> [From] such a formula fairly apprehended there is no need to shrink. The Bible indeed is not a common book. It is a book supreme and unique, which will ever be reckoned among the divinest gifts. . . . But yet, being a book . . . it can only be interpreted as what it is. The ordinary methods of modern criticism . . . afford to us the best means of discovering . . . both the original meaning of the sacred writers and whatever admissible indications of other and larger meanings may be involved in what they taught.[29]

---

[26] F.W. Farrar, *The Inspiration of Holy Scripture. An Exercise for the Degree of B.D.* (printed in London, nd; deposited with Cambridge University Library), 29.

[27] Trench, *Fitness of Holy Scripture*, 15.

[28] F.W. Farrar, *The History of Interpretation* (1886), xiii.

[29] Ibid., xix–xx.

Modern critical techniques, then, had a vital role in the religious reading of Scripture. Correlatively, read critically but with the eye of faith, the Bible possessed a mystical significance, as a supreme means by which the believer passed through language into possession of eternal truth, and so into the presence of God himself. As Trench proclaimed in his Hulsean lectures for 1845, the Bible was:

[The] organ and instrument of all the gifts, powers, and tendencies, by which the individual is privileged to rise above himself, to leave behind and lose his dividual [sic] phantom self, in order to find his true self in that distinctness where no division can be, – in the Eternal I AM, the ever-living Word.[30]

* * *

In F.D. Maurice there is a more sustained and systematic presentation of the philosophical and theological framework to which Trench was alluding. John Coulson placed Maurice firmly in a tradition of 'fiduciary' language, contrasted with the 'analytical' mode pioneered by Bacon.[31] Maurice, like Hare, Trench, and Farrar, took his lead from Coleridge's insistence that poetical language better represented reality, especially through metaphor, than could the constricted analytical language of Bentham.[32] The language of devotion, in acts of worship, signified 'the entrance into a Mystery, into the presence of that Absolute and Eternal Truth, which words may speak of but cannot embody'.[33] Maurice was not interested in the purely analytical presentation of different layers of meaning *per se*. He traced the penetration of the created world by God himself, through meaning, the ordering of the world, patterns of relationship, and the ebb and flow of history, and through these things the human capacity to enter a real relationship with God. This implied a quality of human relatedness to God – an understanding of 'communion' – which closely

---

[30] Trench, *Fitness of Holy Scripture*, 22.

[31] J. Coulson, *Newman and the Common Tradition* (Oxford, 1970). Ironically Maurice himself did not so regard Bacon, seeing him instead as much a Platonist as a forerunner of empiricism: see F.D. Maurice, *Moral and Metaphysical Philosophy*, 2 vols, new edn (1873), 2:215. As H. Aarsleff has pointed out, the identification of Bacon as an empiricist is essentially a late nineteenth-century view: *From Locke to Saussure* (1982), 126.

[32] Coulson, *Newman*, 9. More recently 'analytical' or 'scientific' language has been recognized as itself metaphorical; see especially J.M. Soskice, *Metaphor and Religious Language* (Oxford, 1985).

[33] F.D. Maurice, *Thoughts on the Rule of Conscientious Subscription* (Oxford, 1845), 12–13; see also I.T. Ramsey, *On Being Sure in Religion* (1963), 48–90 (quotation at 67).

paralleled the inner Trinitarian relations themselves.[34] True reading required a pattern of *exitus* and *reditus*, according to which the possibility of spiritual growth towards God is implied in the very process of 'placing' the meaning of particular words in their true context.

In Maurice's early lecture 'On Words', delivered around 1838, he denied that words were 'arbitrary signs of ideas'.[35] This was an attack on Locke, who, rejecting innate ideas, had argued that words were signs of ideas by 'voluntary imposition'.[36] But this individualistic view implied a social compact to fix the meaning of words for which there was no historical evidence and no logical plausibility.[37] Both Johnson's 'lexicographical' method of establishing meaning (by the compilation of different meanings) and Horne Tooke's 'etymological' method (tracing a single root) made the connection of words with absolute value impossible.[38] Words, Maurice argued, 'do indeed bear witness to man's connection with that which is earthly and material . . . but . . . they are also found to testify, and that not weakly or obscurely, of man as a spiritual being'.[39] What was needed was an approach which took into account 'the living, germinating power of words'.[40]

Close analysis of the word 'right' uncovered a hierarchy of verbal meaning, in which there is an implicit ordering of the world, enabling ascent from lower to higher ontological levels. First, the 'lowest' use of 'right', as opposed to 'left', indicated an ordering, a 'rightness', in the world. Then, in 'right' as in legal entitlement, was a deeper sense of ordering, 'some rule made for me'. Finally 'right', as opposed to 'wrong', implied a 'fixed, immutable standard', by which 'I declare

---

[34] See J.N. Morris, 'A social doctrine of the Trinity? A reappraisal of F.D. Maurice on eternal life', *Anglican and Episcopal History*, 69 (2000), 73–100.

[35] F.D. Maurice, *The Friendship of Books* (1893), 25–7.

[36] John Locke, *Essay on Human Understanding*, 3.2.1, quoted in R. Harris and T.J. Taylor, *Landmarks in Linguistic Thought. 1. The Western Tradition from Socrates to Saussure*, 2nd edn (1997), 126. The title of Maurice's lecture may have been a deliberate echo of the title of the third book of Locke's *Essay*, 'Of Words'.

[37] Maurice, *Friendship*, 26. Maurice almost certainly misunderstood Locke, failing to take account of his defence of innate capacities; see N. Wolterstorff, *John Locke and the Ethics of Belief* (Cambridge, 1996), and A.P.F. Sell, *John Locke and the Eighteenth-Century Divines* (Cardiff, 1997).

[38] Tooke, in his *Epea pteroenta, or, The diversions of Purley* (1786, 1798; modern edn, 1993) was widely assumed to have developed Locke's ideas about language into a compact system of theoretical linguistics; see C. Bewley and D. Bewley, *Gentleman Radical: a Life of John Horne Tooke, 1736–1812* (1998).

[39] Maurice, *Friendship*, 39.

[40] Ibid., 40.

myself in subjection to a law which I am bound to obey'.[41] It led on to a 'perfect Teacher, Reprover, Guide' who delights to 'absolve His creatures that He may bring them into that service which is the only freedom'.[42] The word 'word' itself reached the highest application of human language in its use as 'Word' at the beginning of John's Gospel.[43] The very structure of language was an imprint of God's ordering of the world. The human capacity to rise in spiritual orientation to God was implicit in the very nature and use of words.[44]

Returning late in life to this typically Platonic theme of illumination and ascent, Maurice said language could not be 'acquired', like a lifeless object; but, studying it, '[a] light flashes out of a word sometimes which frightens one'.[45] Ordinary language was sanctified by repeated use: common words were 'truly sacred'.[46] Maurice's reading of Scripture in a spirit of devotional if critical awareness tended to reinforce the integrity of its books.[47] He could declare that the Scriptures were a 'living unity'.[48] But he could also assert that the Bible and Church interpreted each other as 'facts'.[49] Biblical inspiration was an ongoing, hermeneutic fact, as well as a historical one: the faithful interpreter, in reading the text, was shaped by it.[50] Read this way, the text itself was a sacramental power, conjoining metaphysical truth with verbal form: 'I fancied the Scripture language, instead of shrinking into a little corner of its own, and declining all comparison with any other, was capable of being tested by the metaphysical inquiries and beliefs of all peoples and ages.'[51] Conversely, the sacraments were 'the transcendent language,

[41] Ibid., 42–4.

[42] Ibid., 44–5.

[43] Ibid., 45.

[44] Modern applications of the Platonic idea of a scale of ascent include Austin Farrer's 'doctrine of the cone' in *The Glass of Vision* (Glasgow, 1948), 19–30, though Maurice would not have accepted Farrer's implicit sharp contrast between nature and supernature.

[45] Maurice, *Friendship*, 265.

[46] Maurice, *Conscience*, 14.

[47] For John Wolf, Maurice saw revelation as 'self-authenticating': W.J. Wolf, 'Frederick Denison Maurice', in W.J. Wolf, J.E. Booty, and O.C. Thomas, *The Spirit of Anglicanism: Hooker, Maurice and Temple* (Edinburgh, 1982), 78.

[48] F.D. Maurice, *The Patriarchs and Lawgivers of the Old Testament* (2nd edn, 1855), 333.

[49] F.D. Maurice, *The Kingdom of Christ, or Hints to a Quaker respecting the Principles, Constitution and Ordinances of the Catholic Church*, 2 vols (4th edn, 1891), 2:178.

[50] '[When] our pride is taken down . . . then once again may He speak to us out of the Book, and make us understand that He is the centre of that unity to us which all our schemes and theories about the Bible have been seeking to dissolve': F.D. Maurice, *The Acts of the Apostles* (1894), 280.

[51] F.D. Maurice, *Sequel to the Inquiry, What is Revelation?* (1860), 15.

bringing out truths full orbed of which in our [ideas?] & systems we can but exhibit one side'.[52]

*   *   *

What were the sources of this understanding of philology? Briefly, two points may be made. The first is that Broad Church philology was part of a general reaction against the materialism of the dominant linguistic tradition of Locke and Horne Tooke.[53] Maurice alleged that Locke had rejected everything which could not be demonstrated by reason, and so had 'succeeded in persuading those who believed very little, not to pretend more than they did', reducing the divine power of religious language to material reference.[54] A case in point was the word 'eternal', reduced to a sense defined by material rewards and punishments.[55] In concert with the 'New Philology' pioneered by Sir William Jones, Broad Church philology rejected Tooke's linguistic speculations, and his conclusion that 'all words can be reduced to names of sensation'.[56] Though their motivation was ultimately religious, at the same time they too sought in linguistic study 'only facts, evidence and demonstration'.[57] Thus, whilst using philology for the committed if critical study of the Bible, they also spurred on the development of linguistics as a specialized discipline.

Second, none of this would have been possible for the Broad Church without Coleridge, whose seminal influence on Broad Church Anglicanism is well known.[58] No philologist himself, he nevertheless countered the materialism and rationalism of the philosophical radicals. In addition to his role as conduit for continental thought, he helped to rehabilitate the metaphysical tradition of English theology, supplying in the process (particularly in his development of the distinction between Reason and Understanding) a philosophical framework through which critical study could be seen to facilitate the

---

[52] London, King's College Archive, Box 5037-M4-R: F.D. Maurice to Sara Coleridge, 1 March 1844.

[53] See Aarsleff, *Study of Language: England*.

[54] F.D. Maurice, *Theological Essays*, 3rd edn (1881), 396.

[55] The pertinent text, in addition to the *Theological Essays*, is F.D. Maurice, *The Word 'Eternal' and the Punishment of the Wicked* (Cambridge, 1853). See also Morris, 'A social doctrine', 80–1.

[56] Aarsleff, *Study of Language: England*, 73.

[57] Ibid., 127.

[58] See C.R. Sanders, *Coleridge and the Broad Church Movement* (Durham, NC, 1942) and A.R. Vidler, *F.D. Maurice and Company. Nineteenth-Century Studies* (1966).

perception of religious truth. The *Confessions of an Enquiring Spirit* (1840) specifically encouraged the view that reading the Bible like any other book led to its full evaluation as inspired literature. Significantly, Farrar's *History of Interpretation*, written in 1885, concluded not with German hermeneutics but with Coleridge, who first showed his contemporaries 'to acquire their estimate of Scripture from the contents and from the claims of Scripture itself, [and] not from the theories and inventions of men respecting it'.[59]

The influence of Broad Church philology took institutional form in 1842, with the formation of the Philological Society of London to investigate 'the Structure, the Affinities and the History of Languages; and the Philological Illustration of the Classical Writers of Greece and Rome'.[60] Over half of the founding members were clergy, and the Broad Church were strongly represented, including Hare, Maurice, Arnold, Stanley, Connop Thirlwall, Derwent Coleridge, R.D. Hampden, Henry Hart Milman, Archibald Tait, and William Whewell, amongst others.[61] Prominent High and Low clergy were largely absent. Thirlwall became the first President. Published papers were technical exercises in the history and analysis of language, and explicit theological discussion was rare. The Philological Society, then, illustrated the emergence of a technical, specialized approach to linguistic study, but it also fired the imagination and interest of theologians who sought in philology yet one more key to unlocking the secrets of the Book of Life.

Trinity Hall, Cambridge

---

[59] Farrar, *History of Interpretation*, 422.
[60] *Proceedings of the Philological Society*, 1 (1844), i.
[61] Ibid., 1–5.

A JOURNAL. *LA CIVILTÀ CATTOLICA*
FROM PIUS IX TO PIUS XII (1850–1958)[1]

by OLIVER LOGAN

THE explosion of the periodical press in mid-nineteenth-century Italy provoked a substantially new form of literary engagement on the part of clergy and lay militants. Following the 1848 revolutions, which in Italy had brought about the temporary collapse of the papal monarchy, Italian clericals identified the periodical press as a dangerous and even 'nefarious' force and as the most powerful instrument of their liberal opponents. The remedy, so the founders of the Jesuit opinion-journal *La Civiltà Cattolica*, among others, asserted, was to combat the liberals with their own weapons: to counter the 'bad press' with the 'good press'.[2] An extensive but mainly local and, in

---

[1] *La Civiltà Cattolica* (Naples, April–Sept. 1850; Rome, 1850–70; Florence, 1871–86; Rome 1887 to present) [hereafter *CC*]. The journal has been published roughly fortnightly, in 4 volumes a year, in 18 series up to 1903, but designated simply by year thereafter. Up to 1933, articles were anonymous. For the period to 1903, authorship is identifiable from G. Del Chiara, *Indice generale della "Civiltà Cattolica" (aprile 1550 – diciembre 1903)* (Rome, 1904). This was not accessible to the present writer. Authorship of anonymous articles (indicated in brackets) has here been identified in some instances from the works containing extracts indicated below and from secondary sources; editorials have been attributed to the then editor. Series of articles on specific themes and serial novels were often subsequently published as books under the name of their authors and advertised in the end-papers of the periodical. On *CC* generally, see Gabriele De Rosa, 'Le origini della *Civiltà Cattolica*', in De Rosa, ed., *Civiltà Cattolica 1850–1945. Antologia*, 4 vols (Florence, 1971–3), 1:9–101; Giandomenico Mucci, *Carlo Maria Curci. Il fondatore della "Civiltà Cattolica"* (Rome, 1988); Francesco Dante, *Storia della "Civiltà Cattolica" (1850–1891). Il laboratorio del Papa* (Rome, 1990), all of which contain extracts. See also Gaetano Greco, '*La Civiltà Cattolica* nel decennio 1850–1859', *Annali della Scuola Normale di Pisa. Classi di lettere e filosofia*, ser. 3, 6 (1976), 1051–95; Ruggero Taradel and Barbara Raggi, *La segregazione amichevole. "La Civiltà Cattolica" e la questione ebraica 1850–1945* (Rome, 2000). Roberto Sani, 'Un laboratorio politico e culturale: *La Civiltà Cattolica*', in Andrea Riccardi, ed., *Pio XII* (Roma and Bari, 1984), 409–36, and idem, *De De Gasperi a Fanfani. "La Civiltà Cattolica" e il mondo cattolico italiano nel secondo dopoguerra (1945–62)* (Brescia, 1986) are primarily concerned with the review's political stance after World War II. For biographical details, reference is here made to *Dizionario biografico degli Italiani* (Rome, 1960-) [hereafter *DBI*] and Giorgio Campanini and Francesco Traniello, eds, *Dizionario storico del movimento cattolico in Italia 1860–1980*, 3 vols in 5 (Turin, 1981–4) [hereafter *DSMCI*].

[2] [C.M.Curci], 'Il giornalismo moderno e il nostro programma', *CC*, ser. 1, 1 (1850), 5–24; [idem], 'Nuovo prospetto per l'anno 1851', *CC*, ser. 1, 4 (1851), 1–7; [idem], 'Le nostre speranze', *CC*, ser. 1, 5 (1851), 12–13; [idem], 'Il regno dell'opininione', *CC*, ser. 2, 1 (1853), 5–20. For other periodicals see Bianca Montale, 'Lineamenti generali per una storia

many instances, ephemeral Catholic periodical press did in fact develop in Italy from the mid-nineteenth century, asserting Catholic and essentially conservative values against secular ones. In united Italy much of this press was clericalist and 'intransigentist', demanding the restoration of the papacy's temporal power and resisting compromise with the new order, although part of it was liberalizing and 'conciliatorist', seeking to reconcile Catholics to the new order.[3] The two great survivors from this proliferation of Catholic periodicals, both intransigentist, were *La Civiltà Cattolica* (1850+), and the Vatican newspaper *L'Osservatore Romano* (1861+). The former was unusual in aiming at a national circulation and was a pioneer in the development of commercial distribution networks.[4] Over the decades, its editorial team or 'college' of Jesuits, subject to a collective discipline, sought to combine lively polemic with information, erudition, and entertainment in an attractive and readily marketable product. This college, alongside the faculty of the Collegio Romano (*alias* Gregorian University), has constituted the main intellectual force of the Jesuits in Italy; indeed, it has substantially been the intellectual vanguard of hard-line clericalist Catholicism there. It has generally enjoyed a privileged relationship with the Vatican, and has contributed to the papacy's teaching. The concern with social and political order which marked the periodical from its inception was a characteristic feature at least up to the pontificate of Pius XII (1939–58), after which the papacy became more detached from political matters.

The opening editorial of 1850 declared: 'we are led to write by the desire to contribute towards healing the wounds of our unhappy Italy and in the persuasion that the damage caused by journalism can in some measure be tempered by good writings'. Civilization, it asserted, was a European phenomenon and was the creation of Catholic Christianity. This civilization had been undermined in turn by Protestantism, Jansenism, and Enlightenment Philosophism. Now Socialism raised its hydra-head and Europe stood on the brink of social dissolution. A restoration of the idea of authority was only

---

dell'*Armonia* dal 1848 al 1857', *Rassegna storica del Risorgimento*, 43 (1952), 476; Franco Malgeri, *La stampa cattolica a Roma dal 1870 al 1915* (Brescia, 1965), 28–9; Antonio Cestaro, *La stampa cattolica a Napoli dal 1860 al 1904* (Rome, 1965), 65.

[3] For a brief introduction, Franco Malgeri, 'La stampa quotidiana e periodica e l'editoria', *DSMCI*, 1/i:273–95.

[4] De Rosa, 'Le origini', 23–33; Dante, *Storia*, 66–7. In 1853 the journal had a print-run of 13,000 copies and 11,000 subscribers: Greco, '*La Civiltà Cattolica*', 1055.

possible on the bases of Catholic ideology.[5] Certain of the periodical's founders had aspired to establish an opinion journal even before 1848, but it was the painful experiences of revolution that precipitated the foundation of *La Civiltà Cattolica*.[6] The annexation of the bulk of the Papal States to the new Italy in 1860–1, and that of Rome and the Legations in 1870, confirmed the animus of the Jesuit journal and fired its polemic yet further.

The most significant members of the founding team were Fathers Carlo Curci (1826–91, its first editor), Luigi Taparelli d'Azeglio (1793–1862), Matteo Liberatore (1810–92), and Antonio Bresciani (1798–1862). Curci was the organizing genius who established a peninsula-wide, and indeed world-wide, distribution network. An independent spirit, he was removed from the editorship in 1854, subsequently becoming a harsh critic of the papacy's defence of the temporal power and leaving the Jesuit Order in 1877.[7] Taparelli is regarded as the founder of the neo-scholastic Jesuit school of political thought in modern Italy.[8] Liberatore is perhaps best known as a neo-scholastic political and social thinker and was to be involved in the drafting of Leo XIII's encyclicals *Aeterni patris* (1879) on the study of St Thomas Aquinas, *Immortale Dei* (1885) on the Christian constitution of states, and, pre-eminently, *Rerum novarum* (1891).[9] Bresciani, primarily a litterateur and antiquarian, achieved a late fame as a writer of novels.[10] The periodical's early numbers, alongside a news-chronicle covering the Italian States, Europe, and the USA, mainly featured polemical articles attacking the ideology underlying 'the Revolution', and asserting that Catholicism was the essential support for social and political order. There was also the so-called *parte amena* (entertainment section), primarily comprising a serial novel, beginning with Bresciani's *L'Ebreo di Verona* (*The Jew of Verona*), a polemical and fantastic depiction of the 1848 revolutions. Rapidly the periodical engaged in two new ideological campaigns. The first related to *educazione*, that is

---

[5] [Curci], 'Il giornalismo moderno', 11–21. Cf. [idem], 'Le nostre speranze'; [idem], 'Il teologizzare della *Civiltà Cattolica*', *CC*, ser. 1, 10 (1852), 5–18; [idem], 'Il fatto e il da farsi della *Civiltà Cattolica*', *CC*, ser. 1, 11 (1852), 5–20, 129–42.

[6] De Rosa, 'Le origini', 9–22; Dante, *Storia*, 57–86.

[7] G. Martina, 'Curci, Carlo Maria', *DBI*, 31:417–22; Mucci, *Curci*.

[8] Marcello Craveri, 'Padre Luigi Taparelli D'Azeglio', *Nuova Rivista Storica*, 52 (1968), 631–60; Dante, *Storia*, 11–56.

[9] D. Ambra, 'Liberatore, Matteo', *DSMCI*, 3/i:470–1; Dante, *Storia*, 87–120.

[10] A. Coviello Leuzzi, 'Bresciani Borsa, Antonio', *DBI*, 14:179–84. Alessandra Di Ricco, 'Padre Bresciani: populismo e reazione', *Studi storici*, 22 (1981), 832–60.

upbringing from the earliest years in the family and at school: the problem of *educazione* was seen as the fundamental one at the base of the disturbed social order; youth had been corrupted by the inheritance of the Enlightenment, Rousseauist pedagogy not least.[11] The second was for the 'restoration' of Thomist philosophy as opposed to the eclecticism that had hitherto dominated Italian theological faculties and seminaries. The Italian Jesuits were central to the campaign which culminated in Leo XIII's encyclical *Aeterni patris* giving Thomism pride of place in Catholic theological teaching.[12] Increasingly, the review sought to keep its readers informed in a range of areas, notably Church history, archaeology, ethnography, and natural sciences.[13]

What was the journal's intended readership? Its style was suited to readers of a middling level of culture.[14] An 1851 editorial stated that it was addressed above all to the younger generation: ordinands in seminaries and in the *studia* of religious orders and also lay youth, which was plagued by curiosity.[15] In due course, almost certainly, the intended public came to include the activists of the developing lay Catholic movement. The original component of this was constituted by the adult cadres of *Gioventù Cattolica* (Catholic Youth), founded in 1868 under Jesuit inspiration, which organized pupils of Catholic schools as the Church's errand-boys in the work of Catholic re-conquest.[16] Subsequently, sundry lay organizations engaged in 'social' activities were brought together under the umbrella organization of the Opera dei Congressi, founded in 1874. A Jesuit, Fr Bartolomeo Sandri, was the *éminence grise* of Giovanni Paganuzzi, who was the dominant figure in the organization in its first decades.[17] An organization of devout lay militants, largely drawn from the elites, did indeed correspond to an ideal nurtured by the Jesuits almost from the

---

[11] Already highlighted in [Curci], 'Il fatto', 140.

[12] De Rosa, 'Le origini', 51; Dante, *Storia*, 73, 78–86; also Roger Aubert, 'Aspects divers du Néo-Thomisme sous le pontificat de Léon XIII', in Giuseppe Rossini, ed., *Aspetti della cultura cattolica nell'età di Leone XIII* (Rome, 1961), 133–227.

[13] For a summary table of areas covered, see 'La quarta serie della *Civiltà Cattolica*', *CC*, ser. 3, 12 (1858), appendix, 11–15.

[14] Di Ricco, 'Padre Bresciani', 842.

[15] [Curci], 'Nuovo prospetto', 5.

[16] Lorenzo Bedeschi, *Le origini della Gioventù Cattolica* (Bologna, 1959); Gabriele De Rosa, *Il movimento Cattolico in Italia. Dalla Restaurazione all'età giolittiana* (5th edn, Rome and Bari, 1959), 50–4.

[17] Angelo Gambasin, *Il movimento sociale nell'opera dei Congressi* (Rome, 1958), passim; De Rosa, *Il movimento*, passim.

time of their foundation. Their organ gave supportive coverage to the activities of the Opera. Here it must be emphasised that *La Civiltà Cattolica* encouraged 'social action', but not political activism.[18] The Opera included a women's organization dedicated to what was regarded as the peculiarly feminine province of the defence of moral values, operating as a pressure group organizing petitions. The contents of the Jesuit journal, and in particular the serial novels, leave little doubt that it was trying to develop the consciousness of ladies, not only wives and mothers but also militants.

La Civiltà Cattolica has always been a highly polemical organ, alternating between invective, abstract philosophical discussion, and antiquarian erudition. In its ideological commitment up to 1958, a dominant role was played by polemic against secularist ideologies, notably liberalism, democratic radicalism, socialism, and (in due course) 'bolshevism', which were endlessly portrayed as forming a monstrous line of descent, stemming ultimately from the Reformation and the Enlightenment. There was polemic, too, against 'false brethren' such as 'liberal Catholics', a contradiction in terms, so our Jesuit journalists asserted.[19] In the first decade of the twentieth century, *La Civiltà Cattolica*, most notably with the articles of the redoubtable Enrico Rosa (1870–1938), played a leading role in the campaign against 'Modernism' and, indeed, in the very definition of the concept of a 'Modernist' deviation.[20]

A notable contribution of the journal lay in the area of social and political thought, branching out from Thomism. Here the key founding figures were Taparelli and Liberatore. Major theorists between the 1930s and the 1960s were Angelo Brucculeri (1879–1969) and Antonio Messineo (1897–1978).[21] Taparelli's interests were primarily in institutional forms. Perhaps his most important

---

[18] Cf. Giorgio Fedalto, 'La Civiltà Cattolica e il laicato cattolico 1868–1901', in Luciano Osbat and Francesco Piva, eds, *La Gioventù Cattolica dopo l'Unità, 1868–1901* (Rome, 1972), 513–29.

[19] 'Un liberale cattolico?', *CC*, ser. 1, 1 (1850), 537–43; 'I cattolici liberali in Italia', *CC*, ser. 6, 6 (1866), 24–37; 'La nuova appellazione di Cattolici liberali', *CC*, ser. 6, 11 (1867), 17–30, 144–53; 'Ripugnanza del concetto di Cattolico liberale', *CC*, ser. 7, 8 (1869), 5–19.

[20] *CC*, 1906(1)–1910(4), passim. The relevant encyclicals of Pius X were: *Pieni l'animo*, 27 July 1906 (*CC*, 1906(3), 385–93), and *Pascendi*, 8 Sept. 1907 (*CC*, 1907(3), 709–53). On Italian Jesuit attitudes to 'Modernism' and the role of Enrico Rosa in particular, see Annibale Zambarbieri, *Il Cattolicesimo tra crisi e rinnovamento. Ernesto Buonaiuti ed Enrico Rosa nella prima fase della polemica modernista* (Brescia, 1979).

[21] Giorgio Campanini, 'Brucculeri, Antonio', *DSMCI*, 3/i:134–5; idem, 'Messineo, Antonio', ibid., 2:371–4; Sani, 'De De Gasperi a Fanfani', 12–22 and passim.

contribution to the tradition of *La Civiltà Cattolica* was as the developer of an organicist social theory. According to this the family, under the direction of the *paterfamilias*, was the primary cell of society, 'corporations' such as guilds and then municipalities being higher-level organisms.[22] Taparelli's organicist theory has been portrayed as a development of Thomist thought, but perhaps misleadingly; rather, what it most strongly recalls is the thought of Althusius, an early seventeenth-century Calvinist of Dutch origin![23] Taparelli's intellectual inheritance, among the Jesuits of our college and in the Catholic world more generally, can be seen especially in the conception of the family as the basis of society and in corporatist theory. Liberatore's later articles from 1887 onwards reflected the concerns manifest in the European Catholic social movement with issues of 'political economy' and 'the social question', that is with the social disruption caused by industrialization. It was the development of this movement that occasioned the encyclical *Rerum novarum*, written in consultation with the universal Catholic episcopate but substantially drafted by Liberatore. He, in his writings, was a harsh critic of liberal *laissez faire* and called for state intervention to moderate it; he looked to workers' associations which he saw as the successors of the guilds of old.[24] An impetus to the amplification of corporatist theory by the Jesuits was to be given by Pius XI's encyclical *Quadragesimo anno* (1931), celebrating the fortieth anniversary of *Rerum novarum* while extending its thinking, and the first papal document to give authoritative status to a corporatist theory that held up 'mixed unions' of employers and workers as a social ideal (a thesis that had, in fact, been deleted from Liberatore's draft of *Rerum novarum*).[25] In the 1930s, Brucculeri applauded in generic terms the principle of the 'corporate state' which the Fascist regime had proclaimed, but insisted on a Catholic reading of the term, in line

[22] See especially 'Lo Stato e la patria', *CC*, ser. 1, 7 (1852), 36–45, 149–64, subsequently published in L. Taparelli, *Esame critico degli ordini rappresentativi*, 2 vols (Rome, 1854), 2:221–46; cf. Oliver Logan, 'Italian identity: Catholic responses to secularist definitions c.1910–48', *Modern Italy*, 2 (1997), 55; for a bibliography of Taparelli's writings, see Dante, *Storia*, 264–71.

[23] Johannes Althusius, *Politica methodice digesta* (Herborn, 1603): Eng. edn, *The Politics of Johannes Althusius*, tr. and abridged by F.S. Carney, preface by C.J. Friedrich (1964).

[24] Dante, *Storia*, 87–125 and, for a list of Liberatore's works, 272–83. Of these, especially relevant here are: the series under the general title 'Dell'economia politica', *CC*, ser. 13, 5 (1887) – ser. 14, 4 (1889), passim, and the article 'Le associazioni operaie', *CC*, ser. 14, 4 (1889), 513–28. On the drafting of *Rerum novarum* see Sandor Agocs, *The Troubled Origins of the Italian Catholic Labor Movement* (Detroit, 1988), 68–70.

[25] Reproduced in *CC*, 1931(2), 385–416, 481–500.

with *Quadragesimo anno*, asserting that the family was the true basis of society and warning against such 'statist' readings of the concept, together with ideas of nationalization of the economy ('integral corporatism'), as were current within Fascism.[26] Messineo's reputation is tarnished by a series of articles, at the time of the Ethiopian war, ultimately justifying the principle of a populous nation seizing living space.[27] More creditably, he engaged, from the mid 1930s, in a critique of totalitarianism on grounds of natural law: he developed the concept of the 'human person', a being possessed of rights which in part related to his supernatural end, as the entity whose interests the state should serve. Further, he counterposed an organicist conception of the nation as a natural entity to theories identifying the state as the constituent and formative element of the nation, here engaging with Italian Fascist theorists.[28] The concept of the 'human person' was later prominent in the thought of Pius XII, who esteemed Messineo highly. With the concept of the human person, among others, Messineo might seem to have been a conduit of the ideas of Jacques Maritain;[29] ironically, it fell to him to deliver a public attack on Maritain's *Humanisme intégrale* in 1956.[30]

Exposition of papal encyclicals has been a major engagement of the Jesuit journal. The 'line' of encyclicals was often discernible in its pages

[26] See A. Brucculeri's articles: 'L'economia corporativa', *CC*, 1933(4), 560–71; 'Dal corporativismo cristiano-sociale al corporativismo integrale fascista', *CC*, 1934(1), 225–37, 449–60; 'L'aspetto religioso delle corporazioni', *CC*, 1934(2), 345–6; 'L'aspetto etico delle corporazioni', ibid., 462–75; 'Corporatismo e Tomismo', *CC*, 1934(4), 574–83.

[27] See A. Messineo's articles, 'L'annessione territoriale nella tradizione cattolica', *CC*, 1936(1), 190–201; 'Necessità economica ed espansione coloniale', ibid., 378–94; 'Propaganda della civiltà ed espansione sociale', *CC*, 1936(2), 99–110, 290–303, 374–86; 'La vita dello Stato e il caso di necessità', *CC*, 1936(3), 123–34, 197–208; 'Necessità di vita e diritto di espansione', *CC*, 1936(4), 363–73, 451–60; 'Estensione e limiti del diritto di espansione vitale', ibid., 363–75, 455–69; 'Emigrazione e diritto di espansione vitale', *CC*, 1937(1), 304–18, 410–21, 524–32.

[28] See Messineo's articles, 'Autonomia e autolimitazione nella filosofia dello Stato', *CC*, 1933(1), 324–36; 'Le garanzie dell'idividuo e dello stato', *CC*, 1933(3), 326–38; 'Il problema della nazione', *CC*, 1938(3), 97–110; 'Gli elementi costituivi della nazione e della razza', ibid., 209–23; 'Natura ed essenza della nazione', ibid., 304–17; 'Nazione e stato', *CC*, 1938(4), 102–15; 'Nazione e stato nella gerarchia degli enti sociali', ibid., 289–303; 'La nazione come realtà assoluta e assoluto valore', *CC*, 1939(1), 302–16, 509–23; 'La nazione valore essenzialmente relativa', *CC*, 1939(3), 203–14, 302–12; 'La persona umana nella società nazionale', ibid., 481–95. Cf. A. Brucculeri, 'Il concetto cristiano dello Stato', *CC*, 1938(3), 19–31, 1938(4), 385–98, criticizing Nazi totalitarianism. On Messineo's significance see Campanini, 'Messineo'.

[29] Sani, 'Un laboratorio', 412.

[30] A. Messineo, 'Umanesimo integrale', *CC*, 1956(3), 449–63.

some time before their publication, suggesting that members of the college were normally, at the very least, *au courant* with the drafting process; some, certainly, were actively involved.[31]

During its first century *La Civiltà Cattolica* was strongly ultramontane and infallibilist. Furthermore, it constantly celebrated the historic role of the papacy and its contribution to 'civilization'. Along with other intransigentist journals, it promoted 'devotion to the pope' and the personality cults attaching to individual popes, above all Pius IX, Pius X, and Pius XII.[32] Following the tradition of the Jesuit Order as a whole, the journal also ardently promoted devotion to the Sacred Heart of Jesus and Marian cult. In the nineteenth century, devotion to the Sacred Heart and to Mary Immaculate marked out ultramontane clerical militants. With our Jesuits, the theme of the Sacred Heart was linked to that of a restoration of the Christian and ultimately the social order: devotion to the Sacred Heart, including solemn acts of reparation for the offences to it perpetrated by the profane modern world, was the most appropriate response on the part of the devout in answer to the rebellion against God that had brought society to the brink of dissolution.[33] The cult of the Virgin Mary was also seen as a prophylactic against the evils of the age and her intercession as warding off the punishment that these evils provoked.[34]

Educazione, in its full range of connotations, was always a major concern of the review, being seen as the key to the character of society, for good or ill. With this topic the Jesuit team built upon a tradition of Italian Catholic thinking on upbringing going back to the sixteenth

---

[31] The case of Liberatore has been noted. Fathers Brandi, De Santi, and Pavissich were involved in the drafting of Pius X's encyclical *Il fermo proposito* (1905), which laid the basis for the reorganization of the lay Catholic movement: S. Tramontin, 'Pavissich, Antonio', *DSMCI*, 3/ii:634–5.

[32] On the 'devotion' generally, Annibale Zambarbieri, 'La devozione al Papa', in Elio Guerriero and Annibale Zambarbieri, eds, *Storia della Chiesa: XXII, La Chiesa e la società industriale 1878–1922*, 2 pts (Milan, 1990), 2:9–81; Oliver Logan, 'Pius XII: *romanità*, prophesy and charisma', *Modern Italy*, 3 (1998), 237–48.

[33] See especially 'Il culto al cuore dell'Uomo-Dio', *CC*, ser. 9, 6 (1875), 513–27. On the devotion generally, see: Annibale Zambarbieri, 'Per la devozione al Sacro Cuore in Italia tra '800 e '900', *Rivista di storia della Chiesa in Italia*, 41 (1987), 361–431; Fulvio De Giorgi, 'Forme spirituali e forme politiche. La devozione al Sacro Cuore', ibid., 48 (1994), 365–469; Daniele Menozzi, 'Una devozione politica tra '800 e '900. L'intronazione del s. Cuore nelle famiglie', *Rivista di storia e letteratura religiosa*, 33 (1997), 29–65.

[34] See esp. [Giuseppe Calvetti], 'Congruenze sociali di una definizione dogmatica sull'immacolato concepimento della B.V. Maria', *CC*, ser. 1, 8 (1852), 377–96; 'Il domma e la civiltà' *CC*, ser. 2, 8 (1854), 481–504; cf. Logan, 'Pius XII', 244.

century.[35] Good *educazione* started in the family; it was continued through religious instruction and, where feasible, through teaching by dedicated clergy or nuns. In liberal Italy, the review conducted major campaigns defending the interests of Catholic schools. Here its publicists commonly deployed organicist theory, asserting that parents, as heads of the primary cell of society (the family), had a right to have their children educated as they wished. They used the same organicist argument when urging on the campaign for obligatory retention of religious instruction in municipal primary schools, asserting that it was essential to the moral health and indeed the very fibre of the nation.

The serial novels published in the journal (first developed by Fr Bresciani, a veteran castigator of the Romantic school in literature who in fact, in his own way, wrote Romantic novels) were highly didactic. The declared objective of the first, *L'Ebreo di Verona*, portraying the 1848 revolutions (primarily that at Rome), was to expose the machinations of the secret societies. The young Jew Aser, a noble and heroic figure, begins as an arch-conspirator but sees the evil of the 'sect' of Young Italy and denounces it. Illuminated by the love of a conventionally pious Catholic girl, he is converted to Catholicism, before being killed off by his creator. The major theme of the work is the corruption of youth by the forces of the 'Revolution'. The dramatic problem is that the nationalist movement, as led by Mazzini and Garibaldi, has appealed to noble sentiments but has betrayed them. The Italians, for all their civilization, are not ready for unity and will not be so until they have acquired the severe primitive virtue, grounded in the faith, of the much-maligned Croats (exemplified by the warrior-damsel Olga) or the Catholic mountain-folk of Switzerland who have defended their liberties in the war of the Sonderbund.[36] The theme of *educazione* is explored in the sequel *Lionello*, which describes the protagonist's fall from grace and entry into the secret societies.[37] In *Ubaldo ed Irene*, the effects of *educazione* conducted according to the principles of Voltaire and Rousseau are contrasted with those of a Christian upbringing.[38] The delineation of character by Bresciani and succeeding authors of serial novels seems to derive from traditional Jesuit analysis of differing temperaments among penitents.

---

[35] Oliver Logan, 'Counter-Reformatory theories of upbringing in Italy', *SCH*, 31 (1994), 275–84.

[36] 'L'Ebreo di Verona', *CC*, ser. 1, 1–7 (1850–1) passim.

[37] 'Lionello', *CC*, ser. 1, 8–10 (1852), passim.

[38] 'Ubaldo ed Irene', *CC*, ser. 2, 2–12 (1853–5) passim.

Character-formation and the role of the family are central concerns. If anything, it is the female characters who are the most closely studied and in these novels we can perceive the working out of the central paradox in Italian Catholic attitudes towards the family and towards gender roles manifest from the late sixteenth century: while the official position was moderately patriarchalist, women were recognized as the 'devout sex' *par excellence*. A wise woman, we are led to realize, is not overtly self-assertive, but knows how to get her way. A variety of acceptable female personality-types and roles are indicated. Women may be 'angels' or they may be strong personalities with wills of supple steel; with the twentieth century a new female role model is delineated: the female Catholic Action activist, self-reliant and full of initiative. However, when women depart from their 'natural' roles by engaging in revolutionary activities, political agitation, or the activities of militant secularist feminism, they are liable to become monstrous.[39]

The motif of 'civilization' and its quintessential identification with Catholicism was a constant and integrating theme of *La Civiltà Cattolica* from its inception, civilization being understood first and foremost in ethical terms and only secondarily in cultural ones.[40] The theme was taken up in Leo XIII's first encyclical, *Inscrutabili dei consilio* (1878), and yet further developed in the Jesuit journal.[41] While our Jesuits asserted that man was defined by his supernatural end, their focus was on the *bonum vivere* (the good life) in this world. There was a messianic, regenerationist thrust in the journal, regeneration being conceived of essentially in social terms. The connotations of the term 'Catholic civilization' were, furthermore, integralist: Christianity was identified with Christendom, with the confessional society; ideological pluralism was rejected. For the first century of its existence, *La Civiltà Cattolica* was the voice of an embattled Italian Church. After the revolutions of 1848 and in the liberal era it played a significant role in the formation of an intransigentist clerical mentality in Italy; in the years of Catholic political abstention between the 1860s and the first decade of the twentieth century, it sought to shape committed

---

[39] See esp. 'Donna antica e donna nuova', *CC*, 1906(2)–1908(1), passim. NB also 'Emma, prima e dopo', *CC*, ser. 16, 8–17 (1896–7), passim.

[40] Cf. Oliver Logan, 'Christian civilization and Italic civilization: Italian Catholic theses from Gioberti to Pius XII', *SCH*, 33 (1997), 475–86.

[41] *Inscrutabili dei consilio*, 21 April 1878, reproduced in *CC*, ser. 10, 6 (1878), 385–402, at 388–94.

Catholics as a people apart, like the Israelites in the desert. Following the two World Wars it raised the spectre of the 'bolshevik peril' in Italy with apocalyptic rhetoric. *La Civiltà Cattolica*, however, for all its privileged relationship with the papacy, only represented a section of Italian Catholics. For the first half-century of its existence, it could be seen as merely the vanguard of a clericalist sect within the Italian Catholic community. In the twentieth century, there was a substantial lack of rapport between the journal and Catholic political activists, whether the first Christian Democrats at the turn of the century, the Popolari after World War I, or the Christian Democrats after World War II. The latter, indeed, tended to have a very different religious and political culture from that purveyed by the Jesuit organ and they accepted the pluralist world that it had so long rejected.[42]

University of East Anglia

---

[42] On the cultural formation of the latter, see Renato Moro, *La formazione della classe dirigente cattolica 1929–1937* (Bologna, 1979). Moro particularly focuses on the formative role of *Azione fucina*, the organ of the Catholic university students' federation and of *Studium*, the review of the Catholic graduate association.